LEGAL ETHICS AND THE ATTORNEY GENERAL

A Canadian Analysis

Legal Ethics and the Attorney General

A Canadian Analysis

ANDREW FLAVELLE MARTIN

UNIVERSITY OF TORONTO PRESS
Toronto Buffalo London

ISBN 978-1-4875-5473-6 (cloth)   ISBN 978-1-4875-5477-4 (EPUB)
                                   ISBN 978-1-4875-5476-7 (PDF)

Library and Archives Canada Cataloguing in Publication

Title: Legal ethics and the Attorney General : a Canadian analysis /
    Andrew Flavelle Martin.
Names: Martin, Andrew Flavelle, 1983– author.
Description: Includes bibliographical references and index.
Identifiers: Canadiana (print) 20240413393 | Canadiana (ebook)
    20240413431 | ISBN 9781487554736 (cloth) | ISBN 9781487554774 (EPUB) |
    ISBN 9781487554767 (PDF)
Subjects: LCSH: Attorneys general – Canada. | LCSH: Legal ethics – Canada.
Classification: LCC KE4752 .M37 2025 | DDC 345.71/01–dc23

Cover design: Susan Zucker
Cover image: iStock.com/pixhook

We wish to acknowledge the land on which the University of Toronto
Press operates. This land is the traditional territory of the Wendat, the
Anishnaabeg, the Haudenosaunee, the Métis, and the Mississaugas of the
Credit First Nation.

University of Toronto Press acknowledges the financial support of the
Government of Canada, the Canada Council for the Arts, and the Ontario
Arts Council, an agency of the Government of Ontario, for its publishing
activities.

For my wonderful mother, Josephine Elizabeth Flavelle, and for her wonderful father, Sir Joseph David Flavelle, Bart.

Contents

Acknowledgments

This book and the research underlying it would not have happened without the support of many folks. First, I am grateful to Allan Rock and Michael J. Bryant for contributing their very gracious forewords. Elizabeth Matheson has been an absolutely invaluable research assistant. Rebecca Parker and Lisa Sillito have also provided wonderful staff support. My sincere thanks to Daniel Quinlan and the University of Toronto Press team, Sathya Shree Kumar at Apex, and Virginia Ling for the indexing.

This book draws on a decade of research. I have been lucky to have excellent research assistants on these projects and others, including Brenna Reimer, Nicole Arski, David Barry, Michelle Bérubé, Michael Cormier, Natascha Joncas, Morris Odeh, and Olivia Pearson.

I am grateful for the generous support that the underlying previously published research has received from many sources, including the Ontario Bar Association Foundation and the Social Sciences and Humanities Research Council of Canada. I am particularly grateful to the Schulich Foundation, which has funded much of my research at Dalhousie and without which this book simply would not have been possible. I would also like to thank the *Manitoba Law Journal* for graciously allowing me to incorporate into this book material that was first published there.

My thanks also go to the many law librarians who have improved my research and my day-to-day life, particularly those of the Great Library of the Law Society of Ontario, the Bora Laskin Law Library at the University of Toronto, the UBC Law Library, and the Sir James Dunn Law Library at Dalhousie University.

An academic career is a perilous undertaking. I would not be where I am today without my many mentors – most of all Kent Roach, the Honourable Robert J. Sharpe, Adam Dodek, and John Gregory. Likewise,

Canada's incredibly supportive legal ethics community, including members of the Canadian Association for Legal Ethics/Association canadienne pour l'ethique juridique. Special thanks to Senator Brent Cotter, Richard Devlin, Amy Salyzyn, Alain Roussy, Stephen Pitel, Pooja Parmar, Basil Alexander, and the Honourable Justice Alice Woolley. These people are both brilliant and wonderful.

I recognize the many educators that have had a positive impact on my life, including John Fautley and Scott Baker; Brian McCue, W. Graydon Robson, Tony Myrans, David Galajda, Aubrey Foy, Robert Arril, and Peter Jamieson; Les Casson, Douglas Caldwell, P. Ken Rose, and Harriet Feilotter; Hamish Stewart, Carol Rogerson, Jim Phillips, Bruce Chapman, the Honourable Justice Michael Code, and the Honourable Justice Lorne Sossin; and Lawrence O. Gostin and Michael Frisch. And I will always have a special place in my memory for Catherine Dauvergne, who gave me my first academic appointment and, in so doing, changed my life.

And of course my dear friends – including Elaine Wong, John Papadopoulos, Candice Telfer, Graham Boswell, Jared Wilcox, Leslie Walden, Nikos Harris, Regine Tremblay, Brandon and Katrina Trask, Ian Stedman, Deanne Sowter, Rob Currie, Archie Kaiser, Cynthia Chewter, and the Honourable Harry LaForme, IPC, OC, KC.

Most importantly, I thank my family, especially my wonderful mother Elizabeth Flavelle and her wonderful husband David Windeyer.

Author's Note

On 15 October 2024, shortly before this book went to press, a Hearing Committee of the Law Society of Alberta released its decision in *Law Society of Alberta v Madu*, 2024 ABLS 20. Kelechi Madu, KC, while Minister of Justice and Solicitor General of Alberta, had directly contacted the Edmonton Chief of Police in response to being pulled over and ticketed by a member of the Edmonton Police Service. The panel held that this was conduct deserving of sanction. Subject to any appeal to the Benchers and any further appeal to the Alberta Court of Appeal, this would be only the third time that a law society had attempted to discipline a lawyer for their conduct while Attorney General – and the first time that such an attempt was successful.

The panel emphasized the duty to encourage respect for the administration of justice and the high profile of the Minister. See especially paragraphs 158, 161, 165, and 167:

> At the time of the events in question, Mr. Madu was one of the highest profile lawyers in Alberta, if not also Canada. As Alberta's Minister of Justice and Solicitor General, he was required to ensure that public affairs are administered according to law and to superintend all matters relating to the administration of justice in Alberta that are within the powers or jurisdiction of the Legislature or the Government. ...
>
> At all material times, Mr. Madu was therefore in a unique position of power and authority—relative to [the Police Chief], other lawyers and to members of the public, generally. If anything, his conduct should have set an example. ...
>
> In short, Mr. Madu's conduct, regardless of his intent, created the appearance of impropriety: that the Minister of Justice and Solicitor General could sidestep the processes available to members of the public faced with the same situation and potentially avail himself of a result

through that process. It is inconsistent *Law Society of Alberta v Madu* with Mr. Madu's commitment to equal justice for all within an open, ordered and impartial system. A hallmark of that system is transparency – not private dealing. Far from encouraging public respect for the administration of justice, Mr. Madu's conduct is reasonably perceived as sidestepping the process entirely and thus eroding public confidence in the administration of justice and in the legal profession. It was irresponsible and failed to meet the high standard required to retain the trust, respect and confidence of other members of the profession and members of the public. ...

The present case is thus a prime example of the heightened risk contemplated in the Commentary to Rule 7.4-1: that the legal profession may more readily brought into disrepute where the lawyer in issue is also a high-profile politician. That risk is particularly germane here, where the lawyer is the Chief Law Enforcement Officer of the province.

The panel also emphasized that, in accordance with rule 7.4-1 (the rule on lawyers in public office), it was holding Madu to the same standard as all practicing lawyers (see para 166). The panel specifically rejected Madu's submission "that this is an 'unusual or remarkable prosecution' that should have never gone this far" (para 141), i.e., that the law society should not have attempted to discipline Madu.

In these respects, the reasons of the panel are generally consistent with my analysis in chapter 2 – particularly as to the duty to encourage respect for the administration of justice and the high profile of the Attorney General – as well as my emphasis on the importance of accountability.

Subject to any appeals, *Madu* is thus a very important precedent for law society discipline of an Attorney General, as well as a reassuring indication that law societies may indeed be willing and able to pursue such discipline.

Foreword

ALLAN ROCK[1]

Much has been written about the nature and scope of the office of Attorney General. It is not difficult to find books, articles, and commentary devoted to discussions about the responsibilities of the person who occupies this complex and storied post. They range from the academic to the political and deal with everything from the exercise of prosecutorial discretion to the impact on the portfolio of the *Canadian Charter of Rights and Freedoms*, and the ways in which the Attorney General's role differs from that of Cabinet colleagues. Some of the best writing on the subject has been produced by those who have held the office, including such giants as Ian Scott and Roy McMurtry of Ontario.

But there is one subject on which both academics and practitioners have been relatively silent to date. It arises from the fact that in discharging many of their duties, Attorneys General are practising law and are therefore subject to that profession's rules of professional conduct. How are those rules applied to the conduct of Attorneys General? And if occupants of that office fail to comply with those rules, how are they best held to account? In this volume, Andrew Flavelle Martin, Assistant Professor at the Schulich School of Law at Dalhousie University, addresses those complex questions in the Canadian context and examines the issues that arise when decisions and actions of "the chief law officer of the Crown" are evaluated from the point of view of legal ethics.

Martin makes an unanswerable case for holding Attorneys General to the standards of professional conduct prescribed in the rules adopted by the law societies. After all, as he persuasively argues, citizens have expectations of Attorneys General, both legal and political, that are higher than those of other elected politicians. We expect the Attorney General to embody the principles and observe the norms established by the profession's codes – even, because of the nature of the office itself, when the Attorney General is not a lawyer. He quotes the words of former Ontario Chief Justice James McRuer, who made clear his lofty perspective: "[t]he office [of the Attorney General] should be restored to its traditional authority, responsibility, and dignity. Its occupant should rank in precedence next to the Prime Minister."

Among the principal and most obvious of the Attorney General's professional responsibilities is to encourage respect for the administration of justice, not to interfere with judicial proceedings and to refrain from public statements that might prejudice an ongoing proceeding. But lawyers' ethical standards extend farther than that, to include the duties of loyalty, integrity, and the avoidance of conflicts of interest. Simply stated, Attorneys General are bound by "the laws of lawyering," despite the fact that they can sometimes be (to use Martin's words) "politically inconvenient."

It is one thing to insist that the rules apply: but what are the consequences for an Attorney General if they are not followed? Martin points out that provincial law societies have traditionally been reluctant to enforce their rules by initiating professional discipline proceedings against Attorneys General. In some cases, the protection afforded by parliamentary privilege can narrow their jurisdiction to do so. (In my own experience as a past Chair of the Discipline Committee and subsequently Treasurer [CEO] of the Law Society of Ontario, I cannot recall a circumstance in which we considered applying the discipline lens of the licensing body to a critical examination of the words or deeds of an Attorney General.)

It is here that Martin distinguishes between *enforcement* of the rules, which seems unlikely given the attitude of the law societies, and the *accountability* of Attorneys General for falling below ethical standards of the profession. That accountability – which Martin argues is essential – can take many forms. Drawing from my own experience as Attorney General of Canada, I was keenly aware that I was at all times accountable for my stewardship of that portfolio not only to the Prime Minister but also to the House of Commons. There was, of course, a daily reckoning in Question Period, an exercise related more directly to political theatre than professional responsibility. But I was mindful too of the possibility, should major transgressions be alleged, of more serious forms of accountability in the House, and Martin deals with them in his text: measures imposed by the Speaker, censure by the House, and ultimately, resignation – indignities I am relieved to report that I was spared.

Martin's deep research and insightful analysis have therefore filled a major gap in the literature involving the office of Attorney General.

He has produced a thorough and thoughtful handbook to inform and guide not only Attorneys General but also the officials, staffers, and colleagues of those who occupy that office. He reminds us of the importance of Attorneys General reflecting in their every official act the norms and standards of the legal profession and argues compellingly for a true accountability that will make compliance with those standards more likely. We can only hope that the policies and practices he recommends are adopted, and we are indebted to Martin for both the quality of his scholarship and the force of his advocacy.

Foreword

MICHAEL BRYANT[1]

There are grand responsibilities and ancient perks that come with being an Attorney General. My experience in other Cabinet portfolios was different. The expectations can be high for any Cabinet Minister, but I felt more like a cog in the First Minister's machine, than when I served as Attorney, who sometimes, donning the quasi-judicial mantle, stands aside from Cabinet. That Chief Legal Officer independence bleeds over into judicial reform policies too – typically not part of an election platform or Throne Speech. Some Attorneys choose to be "team players" who work closely with the First Minister. Others, like Ontario's McMurtry and Scott, ran "an alternative government," as Premier Bill Davis joked of his famously activist Attorney General of ten years.[2]

I took the same approach to the job of Attorney General – a posture of recalcitrance, in the eyes of some. But I just decided that this was the job, necessitating an independence that would fulfil its constitutional promise, even though it limited my Cabinet career trajectory. It was my personality, especially given my relative youth, and naïveté. I was pure Gatsby, with his "extraordinary gift for hope,"[3] extraordinarily deluded. Serving for over four years as the 35th Attorney General of Ontario would be the pinnacle of my career, but I could not know that as the youngest ever to hold that office.

I raise this to make the point that an Attorney General is a fallible human being serving in an office of high constitutional ideals, which history has treated unkindly. When serving as Attorney General that person is operating on a pedestal untethered to reality. And "a pedestal may be a very unreal thing,"[4] to quote Oscar Wilde, for observer and participant alike. Is one to be a realist, bowing to political expediency, under the illusion that it's better to fight another day, or an idealist, risking removal from that pedestal, if not today than at the next Cabinet shuffle? Or, as my legislative seatmate and Solicitor General Rick

Bartolucci liked to ask me, sotto voice: "do you want to be a hero or a martyr?"

Of this central fact, in this book, the author struggles with scholarly might. Professor Andrew Flavelle Martin wishes to test his own high standards for Canadian federal, provincial, and territorial Attorneys General, based on his thorough research and reasoning. He seeks herein to test these high standards against the low conduct of some Attorneys, of the self-regulating legal profession, and competing constitutional doctrine. To take the high road is what Martin wants for Attorneys like and unlike myself, but he goes further than simply lamenting our propensity for taking the low road, and for the bar to lower the bar. The author drills down into history and constitutional law in order to find the best path for this important constitutional player.

Along the way, Martin revisits, in essence, Robert Bork's dilemma:[5] to risk the perception of self-interested expediency, in the name of institutional order, versus the martyrdom of political upheaval, in the name of constitutional purity. Bork chose the former. His justification? Bork was "saving justice," to borrow his memoir's title, "for the good of the Justice Department," he said at the time.[6] Dismiss not Bork's dilemma as puerile "politics," if only because Bork himself was an accomplished constitutional scholar and jurist. Better yet, in this book Professor Martin breaks down the nature of these competing interests of political order, individual expediency, institutional stability, and constitutional doctrine. One would think that Bork's dilemma would have a rich library of doctrinal analysis in the United States. Surprisingly, it does not. Nor do we have anything like this book in Canada. Accordingly, Andrew Flavelle Martin has done us all a great service in writing this book. He rightly points out that the scholarship on this subject is sparse. The consequence of this sparsity is that most Attorneys, within a day or so of being sworn in, find themselves staring at binders of materials printed up by the Ministry, all amounting to an annotated instruction manual for the Attorney General in question. While valuable, those binders cannot match the work distilled into this book. If nothing else, then, Martin has written a book that will be read by every provincial, federal, and territorial Attorney for many years to come. Not many authors can say that.

Martin's publisher is hoping for a market larger than that elite group, which I trust will be met. In fact, besides the student of constitutional law, this book should assist commentators, journalists, regulators, scholars, courts, and legislators as they all hold Attorneys to account.

Martin is wistful in his hopes that some of his conclusions are hardly worth mentioning. It turns out the obvious is too often neglected, he demonstrates, when it comes to Attorneys General. For instance, Martin must be right to say, in effect, that lawyers subject to the law of lawyering should find no immunity in their appointment as Attorney General, just as he is, in my view, correct that this point is observed in the breach. In fact, this book is touching on the failure of both lawyers and their regulators to put paid this very principle, no matter the profession.

One lawyer shared with me an early experience in high university office, when they were asked to sign documents for which they had no knowledge of the underlying information or undertaking to be validated. I've had the same experience in executive jobs where the CEO was expected to authorize a matter about which I had zero knowledge. The lawyer's pithy response to the administrative request for her signature was on point: "maybe my predecessors authorized in oblivion, but I have duties as a member of the bar that I can't avoid just because I have this non-legal job."

A great irony is revealed herein by Professor Martin: that an Attorney General, of all people, would imagine this lawyer's reasoning applied not to an Attorney General. I would like to think that I complied with my lawyerly obligations, but that is for Martin and his peers to decide. I had no choice but to revere Attorneys McMurtry and Scott, whose namesakes I branded on our Ministry headquarters, back in the day. McMurtry was the Chief Justice during my tenure, and a frequent sounding board throughout. Scott was alive and spritely, post-stroke, and I'd learned directly from Ian prior to his stroke, as a student in his seminar co-taught by Hon. Patrick Monahan. Was my discipleship to McMurtry and Scott relevant to Premier Dalton McGuinty's Cabinet making? He said so, when I got the call. I may have had my moments, behind closed doors, when I was able to utter those powerful words borrowed from Ian Scott: "I must *stand aside* from Cabinet and advise you as your Chief Legal Officer that ..." That "standing aside" sums up the "two hats" of both political and quasi-judicial roles of the office. One does not cancel out the other. Rather, Attorney Scott articulated the pivot necessary to fulfil both roles, bolstering Bagehot's portrayal of our colonial constitutional origins as "dignified" and "efficient."[7]

Which brings me to the author's oft-repeated self-assessment that he is overly optimistic and idealistic. This is an illustration of Martin's highly accessible scholarly and writing style. Rigorously researched and evinced, to be sure, but without jargon and inflated language. As an alleged "romantic," Martin sets himself off against contrary views which could be characterized as realism and *real politick*. Professor Martin understandably does not accuse those falling short of his high standards as ignorant, without the evidence to prove it. He is more apt to lament the imbalance as between the constitution's rare dignity and frequent efficiency.

But I will speculate that ignorance, not realism, may be the greatest obstacle to high standards of ethics for an Attorney General, for those other than the Attorney themselves. We Attorneys General know very well the expectations because our Deputy Minister, among others, hammers this point home, at least as much as the Official Opposition will point it out, not to mention media coverage of scholars like Martin and his oft-cited colleague, Professor Adam Dodek.

I knew Adam Dodek before he was Adam Dodek. When I was the cherubic Attorney, Dodek was my Policy Director and then Chief of Staff. His respectful reminders and cautions as to my unique constitutional duties as a quasi-judicial official and Chief Legal Officer were underscored by his insistence on calling me "Minister" or "Mr. Attorney," whenever others were present, despite our friendship and familiarity. This was unique, but so is Dodek, and everyone I had the honour of working with at the Ontario Ministry of the Attorney General. The "integrity" of the office itself, as Martin describes, was well fulfilled under its Ontario Ministry leaders of the day, in my time there. The integrity of the office simply demands more of those who serve in that office. Hence, Dodek's insistence on formality at all times, lest we together forgot the breadth of our responsibilities.

I do believe that ignorance is more the culprit than political expediency. Ignorance by parliamentarians themselves, who decreasingly belong to the legal profession, notwithstanding the uninformed presumption to the contrary, especially in provincial legislatures. Ignorance by the regulators, whose benchers too quickly dismiss Attorneys behaving badly as trivial politics, rather than daring to sharpen their constitutional legal quivers, aiming them at the quasi-judicial officers, without fear of social consequences. Ignorance or wilful blindness by public servants and their Deputy Ministers, all of whom ought to be familiar with the special role that agents of the Attorney General play within a government, along with the person in the role.

Therefore, if Martin is crestfallen by the modern Canadian Attorney, the same opprobrium is deserved for those charged with the powers of accountability. How many lawyers have filed complaints with their regulator against their Attorney of the day for conduct unbecoming of the office? How many law society benchers have spoken truth to power on this front? How many provincial governments have undertaken projects to better educate civil servants, and in turn their Ministerial leaders, about what it means to have quasi-judicial duties?[8] All these themes are thoroughly addressed in this treatise.

Martin's discussion of an Attorney resignation, so dramatically wielded in the United States during Watergate, is particularly important and too often forgotten as a politically nuclear tool at our disposal. I did almost[9] resign as Attorney, in 2003, when the Premier's office came close to "ordering" me to appeal a trial judgment that we felt had no arguable grounds for appeal. I demurred, permitting the appeal deadline to pass. However, there were no negative repercussions for me, for exercising my quasi-judicial role, to the credit of Premier of the day. But when I found myself defending my position to the Premier, and Dodek was doing the same with his counterparts, there was no Canadian book devoted to the subject, to wield as a shield and a sword against those who might, inadvertently, undermine our Constitution. Thanks to Andrew Flavelle Martin, that is no longer true.

LEGAL ETHICS AND THE ATTORNEY GENERAL

1 Introduction: The Attorney General and the Practice of Law

The Attorney General plays a complex and unique role in the federal, provincial, and territorial governments. Nonetheless, there is not only relatively little academic legal literature on the Attorney General in the Canadian context, but also relatively little knowledge and understanding of the role and professional responsibilities of the Attorney General among the public, the media, policymakers, and politicians – including at least some Attorneys General themselves – particularly regarding their status as a lawyer and the duties that flow from that status.

Consider the following three illustrative scenarios:

- May 2014: Minister of Justice and Attorney General for Canada, Peter MacKay, reinforces false and misleading allegations of misconduct against the Chief Justice of Canada that had been made by the Prime Minister.[1] In doing so, MacKay flagrantly breaches his professional duty as a lawyer to encourage respect for the administration of justice. Despite this breach and at least one formal complaint, MacKay faces no disciplinary action by his licensing body, the Nova Scotia Barristers' Society.[2] Nor does he suffer any apparent political consequences.
- February 2019: In the face of allegations that the Prime Minister improperly attempted to interfere with the decision-making of Jody Wilson-Raybould as Minister of Justice and Attorney General for Canada, Wilson-Raybould adamantly asserts that solicitor-client privilege and her professional duty of confidentiality as a lawyer preclude her from discussing the saga.[3] After Wilson-Raybould is granted a waiver by the Governor General in council,[4] her testimony makes it clear that powerful politicians and bureaucrats – including the Prime Minister and the Clerk of the Privy Council – were ignorant or contemptuous of the constitutional principle of

prosecutorial independence. At the same time, she defends her recording of a key conversation, despite such a surreptitious recording being contrary to the rules of professional conduct.[5]

- October 2019: Nova Scotia Minister of Justice (and Attorney General) Mark Furey tells reporters that striking members of the provincial Public Prosecution Service are greedy: "I'm troubled by the fact that our prosecutors are looking out for their personal financial best interests over the needs of victims."[6] Such remarks would arguably breach the professional duty of civility if made by a lawyer. Furey, however, is a non-lawyer and, thus, the Nova Scotia Barristers' Society has no regulatory or disciplinary jurisdiction over him. Though Furey's remarks are criticized in the legislative assembly and elsewhere,[7] he faces no apparent consequences.

The purpose of this book is to demonstrate that the Attorney General is – and should be – accountable for their conduct under the same law of lawyering that is applicable to all lawyers. The Attorney General is unique among elected politicians because they necessarily practice law in the course of their official duties. The Attorney General is accountable in all the ways that other elected politicians are accountable, plus one other way: as a lawyer. The legal and political expectations of the Attorney General are, therefore, higher than – and should be higher than – the expectations of other elected politicians.

Any explicit or implicit misconceptions that the Attorney General is not *really* a lawyer, that conduct wrongful for lawyers is not wrongful for the Attorney General, or that the forms of accountability appropriate for lawyers are not appropriate for the Attorney General, are understandable. They are also incorrect and deeply problematic as a matter of both law and policy. It is true that Canadian law societies, as regulators of the legal profession, almost never discipline the Attorney General. However, that does not mean that they should not or cannot do so. Indeed, the ability of law societies to do so and the real possibility of them doing so are both essential to the rule of law.

While I cheerfully admit to being romantic and idealistic,[8] there is nothing romantic or idealistic about the accountability of the Attorney General for violations of the law of lawyering.

If one had asked one of the great Attorneys General of modern Canadian history – for example, the late Ian Scott – I expect that they would consider it obvious and intuitive that the Attorney General is a lawyer, should meet the same standards as other lawyers, and should face some form of accountability for shortcomings.[9] The recent conduct of some Attorneys General, and the absence of any discernable political fallout for that conduct, both suggest that this understanding has been ignored, if not forgotten entirely. This fundamental concept – that the Attorney General is a lawyer and is subject to the same professional standards as other lawyers – is not novel but does seem to have been ignored or forgotten, at least in the Canadian context. Indeed, John Ll. J. Edwards, the leading authority on the office of the Attorney General in the United Kingdom and in the broader Commonwealth, was quite clear in his classic 1964 work *The Law Officers of the Crown*, and as recently as 1995 in a Canadian essay, that outside their prosecutorial decision-making, the Attorney General was and should be liable to professional discipline in the same way as any other lawyer.[10] Even Edwards, however, focused little on this professional accountability of the Attorney General as a lawyer.[11]

In this book, I explore how the rules of professional conduct for lawyers and the broader law of lawyering apply to the Attorney General. My goal is certainly not to identify and analyse every legal ethics issue that could arise for the Attorney General. Instead, I focus on the issues that are, in my view, most important and most illustrative in demonstrating the complexity of legal ethics for the Attorney General. I then consider the most important aspects of, and prospects for, accountability for the Attorney General. I then bring together these twin themes of complexity and accountability to draw out key lessons. The underlying and unifying current is that the Attorney General is a lawyer and should be understood by others, and by themselves, as being bound by the rules and norms of legal ethics. Indeed, this is true even in those rare and problematic instances where the Attorney General is not a lawyer, by which I mean that they are not a licensed member of a provincial or territorial law society.

A legal ethics model is thus a meaningful and unavoidable framework to understand the role of the Attorney General – most of all for the Attorney General themselves and for those around them – including their responsibilities and accountabilities. Conversely, any account or self-image of the Attorney General that ignores or minimizes their functional identity as a lawyer and the impact of legal ethics is necessarily a misleadingly simplistic one. Legal ethics also provides normative guidance to Attorneys General as they attempt to balance the inherent tensions in their role. This important role for legal ethics remains true even if and when the law society does not adequately enforce the law of lawyering, whether generally or specifically with regard to the Attorney General.

Indeed, throughout this book I consciously refer to accountability instead of enforcement. While the potential for professional discipline by the corresponding law society is important, it is not determinative. Indeed, law society discipline is not the sole accountability mechanism for many lawyers. Insofar as the Attorney General is legally or practically immune from law society discipline, the rules and norms of legal ethics nonetheless remain an established, clearly articulated, and appropriate framework for assessment and accountability. Such accountability may take multiple forms other than professional discipline. These forms could include political or parliamentary accountability – aided, prompted, or even instigated by the media and public pressure.

This book is necessary because little of the existing Canadian legal literature on the Attorney General explicitly addresses legal ethics and their application to the Attorney General. Most of that literature can be organized into two waves of scholarship, a concept I adopt from the work of Adam Dodek on the history of legal ethics literature in Canada.[12] The first wave focused on the prosecution function, including the relationship of Crown prosecutors to the Attorney General, the meaning and scope of prosecutorial discretion and prosecutorial independence, and the benefits of an independent Public Prosecution Service.[13] This wave most recently considered the independence of the Attorney General in the context of the SNC-Lavalin controversy.[14] The second wave, beginning in the 1980s, examined the broader role of the Attorney General, particularly given the impact of the *Canadian Charter of Rights and Freedoms*.[15] With few exceptions, both waves overlooked the implications of legal ethics for the Attorney General. This omission is not particularly surprising, given the limited academic and legal attention to Canadian legal ethics more generally throughout this time.[16] The only book-length elements of these two waves tended to be biographical or autobiographical.[17]

A third wave, lean and emerging only in the last decade, focuses on legal ethics and the Attorney General. This wave primarily comprises my own work,[18] which I synthesize and add to in this book. To date, this wave is primarily doctrinal. My hope is that this book will serve as a foundation not only for further doctrinal work, but also for other approaches to legal ethics scholarship, including empirical, critical, and comparative approaches, as well as approaches grounded in economics and literature.

Context

In this introductory chapter, I begin by explaining and exploring the practice of law by the Attorney General. First, I set out the duties of the Attorney General to establish that the Attorney General practises law.

Second, I discuss which rules of legal ethics are most relevant and applicable to the Attorney General. Third, I identify the client or clients of the Attorney General and explain the legal ethics implications. Fourth, I situate the Attorney General among other lawyers for the Crown, including the Deputy Attorney General and other government lawyers. Fifth, I identify the multiple roles of the Attorney General and explain the tensions among those roles. In subsequent chapters, I explore the key themes of complexity and accountability.

To begin, however, I need to address some terminology around legal ethics and the Attorney General. As I will explain later in this chapter, in the Canadian model a single legislator is both Attorney General and Minister of Justice. Provincial and territorial legislation tends to use one term or the other when discussing this officeholder and the part of the civil service that reports to them. In federal legislation the two roles are distinct, even though they are explicitly required by statute to be held by a single person. To the extent that these two roles are separable, the Attorney General is essentially the chief lawyer for the government, whereas the Minister of Justice is the member of Cabinet with ministerial responsibility for the administration of justice. The Attorney General practises law while the Minister of Justice does not.[19] I use the term "Attorney General" to refer to the person who holds both roles, primarily because the Attorney General role is what is special as compared to all other members of Cabinet.[20]

The term "legal ethics" also requires some explanation. Legal ethics does not have a concise consensus definition.[21] It is, however, a narrower concept than ethics or "law and ethics." Legal ethics generally refers to the branch of philosophy concerning ethics for lawyers, including but not limited to what is often referred to as "the law of lawyering."[22] While legal ethics includes lawyers' legal duties under legislation, rules of professional conduct, and case law, it also encompasses broader questions of morality and the role of lawyers in society.[23] As Dodek puts it, "Legal ethics is the applied philosophy of lawyering; it goes to the heart of what it means to be a lawyer and how to attempt to mediate between the conflicting duties that members of the profession owe."[24] There are many areas of ethics that are important that nonetheless do not come within legal ethics.

In this book, I focus primarily on the law of lawyering and how that body of law does – and should – apply to the Attorney General. I also address questions of what the Attorney General should do when the law of lawyering does not give a clear answer. I follow Dodek's imperative that "Canadian legal ethics must also attempt to situate ethical issues within a distinctly *Canadian* context."[25] Thus my choice of title,

Legal Ethics and the Attorney General: A Canadian Analysis, is conscious and deliberate. As I will return to later in this chapter, the modern role of the Attorney General in Canada is unavoidably intertwined with the historical role of the Attorney General in England. However, as the position of Attorney General across Canada is different in some important respects from its parallel in England, and even more so from its parallel in the United States,[26] my focus here is on the role of the Attorney General in Canadian jurisdictions.

1. *The Attorney General and the Practice of Law*

Legal ethics, including the law of lawyering, is only relevant to the Attorney General insofar as they are a lawyer or practise law, or both. In this part, I set out the duties of the Attorney General to establish that the Attorney General practises law – whether or not they are licensed as a lawyer by their corresponding provincial or territorial law society.

The duties of the Attorney General clearly include the practice of law. These duties are set out in statute and are largely consistent across Canadian jurisdictions and over time. For example, the Ontario *Ministry of the Attorney General Act* provides as follows:

The Attorney General,

(a) is the Law Officer of the Executive Council;

(b) shall see that the administration of public affairs is in accordance with the law;

(c) shall superintend all matters connected with the administration of justice in Ontario;

(d) shall perform the duties and have the powers that belong to the Attorney General and Solicitor General of England by law or usage, so far as those duties and powers are applicable to Ontario, and also shall perform the duties and have the powers that, until the *Constitution Act, 1867* came into effect, belonged to the offices of the Attorney General and Solicitor General in the provinces of Canada and Upper Canada and which, under the provisions of that Act, are within the scope of the powers of the Legislature;

(e) shall advise the Government upon all matters of law connected with legislative enactments and upon all matters of law referred to him or her by the Government;

(f) shall advise the Government upon all matters of a legislative nature and superintend all Government measures of a legislative nature;

(g) shall advise the heads of the ministries and agencies of Government upon all matters of law connected with such ministries and agencies;

(h) shall conduct and regulate all litigation for and against the Crown or any ministry or agency of Government in respect of any subject within the authority or jurisdiction of the Legislature;

(i) shall superintend all matters connected with judicial offices;

(j) shall perform such other functions as are assigned to him or her by the Legislature or by the Lieutenant Governor in Council.[27]

It is clear from this list that the Attorney General necessarily practises law, insofar as they serve as the Law Officer for Cabinet, provide legal advice to the Crown and the heads of ministries and agencies, and conduct all litigation for the Crown. Indeed, in his *Inquiry into Civil Rights*, Commissioner James McRuer (as he then was), after canvassing the equivalent provisions that existed at that time on the role of the Attorney General in Ontario and other provinces, recommended a statutory requirement that the Attorney General be a lawyer.[28] This role as "Chief Law Officer of the Crown" has also long been recognized in the case law.[29]

While the practice of law has both a formalistic meaning and a functional meaning, for the purposes of this book I apply a functional one. A formalistic meaning would be that the practice of law is what is done by persons who are licensed by a law society, whereas a functional meaning would be the particular tasks that constitute the practice of law. For example, the Nova Scotia *Legal Profession Act* provides that "the practice of law is the application of legal principles and judgement with regard to the circumstances or objectives of a person that requires the knowledge and skill of a person trained in the law."[30] The statutory functions of the Attorney General, as laid out above, constitute the "practice of law" under this characterization and, thus, it is appropriate to conclude that the Attorney General necessarily practices law in carrying out their mandate.[31]

While the statutory language quoted above states that the Attorney General "shall conduct and regulate all litigation for and against the Crown,"[32] there is disagreement in the legal literature as to whether, and when, the Attorney General should personally appear in court, especially in criminal proceedings. Brian Smith, while Attorney General for British Columbia, argued that regularly appearing in court was appropriate, because such a personal appearance "emphasizes the importance of the matter to the province, and subjects all aspects of the case to intense public scrutiny."[33] In contrast, Justice Marc Rosenberg, writing extrajudicially, cautioned that while such appearances "in important constitutional cases is proper and welcomed[, he] would be concerned, however, if the Attorney General appeared in more mundane cases, and especially in any criminal case."[34] In particular, Justice Rosenberg thought such appearances in criminal proceedings would create a public apprehension of "a personal or political agenda" and resulting unfairness to the accused.[35] Smith and Rosenberg did seem to agree that only Attorneys General who were competent litigators should make such appearances, though they did not frame the issue as one of competence – with Smith referring to Attorneys General who were "qualified and experienced" and Rosenberg using the example of "great counsel" (giving Ian Scott of Ontario as an example).[36] Similarly, for John Ll. J. Edwards, the appointment of Ian Scott as Attorney General for Ontario marked a sea change, as "[u]ntil very recently, the appearance of an Attorney General in person to argue a constitutional (or any other) case was calculated to reveal the incumbent's lack of forensic skills and experience."[37]

Although it is usually the Attorney General, acting through their lawyer delegates, who defends legislation against constitutional challenges, in some circumstances the Attorney General will direct their lawyers to concede that a law is unconstitutional or even actively argue against its constitutionality.[38] These positions in constitutional litigation became the subject of much debate after the adoption of the *Canadian Charter of Rights and Freedoms*.[39]

Oddly, despite these statutory duties that clearly constitute the practice of law, the Attorney General is not required to be a lawyer, that is, a member of the corresponding law society.[40] However, as I will argue further in chapter 6, such a non-lawyer Attorney General likewise necessarily practises law.

2. *The Attorney General and Legal Ethics*

Legal ethics is applicable and relevant for the Attorney General because the Attorney General practises law. While it is clear that the Attorney General practises law, that does not mean that, in reality, all parts of the law of lawyering are relevant to them.[41] For example, as it is rare for even the great Attorneys General to personally appear in court (or before a tribunal),[42] the duties of the lawyer when litigating would seldom be engaged.[43] Moreover, those duties, if and when engaged, would not raise issues specific to the Attorney General.

Given the role of the Attorney General as both a lawyer and a politician, the most relevant and important duties within the law of lawyering are readily identifiable. Like all lawyers, the core duties of loyalty (including confidentiality, candour, conflicts, and "commitment to the client's cause"),[44] integrity,[45] and competence are essential.[46] The duty of candour may mean giving "firm" and unwelcome advice.[47] Given the breadth of the scope of practice of the Attorney General – purportedly all legal matters involving the Crown – it would seem impossible for any Attorney General to personally meet their duty of competence. However, like all lawyers, the Attorney General can fulfil their duty of competence by "obtain[ing] the client's instructions to retain, consult or collaborate with a lawyer who is competent for that task" or by otherwise "becom[ing] competent."[48] Given the existence of a ministry or department of justice, consent would be implicit, at least for lawyers who are members of the public service if not for outside counsel. However, insofar as the Attorney General relies on departmental lawyers, the Attorney General has a keen professional self-interest in the competence of those lawyers. If the Attorney General did choose to appear in court, the duty of competence (as well as the duties of a litigator)[49] would be engaged.

Other duties relevant to all lawyers are those around withdrawal. In particular, withdrawal is mandatory "if ... a client persists in instructing the lawyer to act contrary to professional ethics."[50] While the circumstances in which a lawyer may withdraw are limited, one of those circumstances is where there is "a serious loss of confidence between the lawyer and the client" – including where "a lawyer is deceived by his client" or "the client refuses to accept and act upon the lawyer's advice on a significant point."[51] Any withdrawal, however, must be "for good cause and on reasonable notice to the client."[52] Where a lawyer is an officer or employee, withdrawal does not necessarily require resignation. Nonetheless, it is difficult to imagine circumstances where the Premier or Prime Minister does not remove the Attorney General from their role entirely where the Attorney General has purported to withdraw merely from a specific matter. Particularly important for the Attorney General, as I will discuss further in chapter 4, is that the law of lawyering does not allow for a lawyer to publicly disclose their reasons for withdrawal, unless one or more of the limited exceptions to confidentiality and solicitor-client privilege – such as future harm – are engaged.[53] While there is a cogent argument that the special role of the Attorney General should anchor an additional "public interest" exception to confidentiality, which would allow them to reveal their reasons for resignation where the conduct that prompted the resignation was egregious, in my view such an argument is most compelling where that reveal is made within the House or legislative assembly and thus protected by parliamentary privilege.[54]

Given the high visibility of the Attorney General and their obligations and opportunities to speak publicly, particularly important are the duty not to interfere with fair trial rights,[55] the duty to encourage respect for the administration of justice,[56] and the duty of civility.[57] In particular, the duty to encourage respect for the administration of justice requires that criticism of courts and tribunals not be "petty, intemperate or unsupported by a bona fide belief in its real merit" and explicitly recognizes that "if a lawyer has been involved in the proceedings, there is the risk that any criticism may be, or may appear to be, partisan rather than objective."[58] Moreover, the duty also encourages lawyers to defend "a tribunal [that] is the object of unjust criticism."[59] Indeed, at least in times past, this was particularly expected of the Attorney General. As noted by Craig Jones, "it was the traditional and honourable role of the attorney general to speak in defence of the courts when they were criticized, because by constitutional convention judges do not speak except through their judgments."[60]

To the extent that the Attorney General is ultimately responsible for criminal proceedings, the duties of the prosecutor are integral to that role.[61] While this role and its implications may be considered a matter of both public law and of legal ethics, the Attorney General must also uphold their own prosecutorial independence, that is, "[the] constitutional principle that the Attorneys General of this country must act independently of partisan concerns when exercising their delegated sovereign authority to initiate, continue or terminate prosecutions."[62] As I will return to in chapter 5, the Attorney General, like the Crown prosecutors who are their delegates, is immune from law society discipline for actions within the scope of prosecutorial discretion, absent bad faith.

Other rules of professional conduct, though perhaps politically inconvenient, are also applicable to the Attorney General. Consider here the absolute prohibition against surreptitiously recording conversations with lawyers or clients.[63] Although there may be times when secret recordings are expedient, whether for political purposes or to document wrongdoing,[64] such recording violates the law of lawyering regardless of any compelling reason for doing so.

Given that their political staffers often wield the power of the Attorney General, also relevant is the professional duty of lawyers to adequately supervise their non-lawyer staff and take complete professional responsibility for their actions.[65] As I will discuss below,[66] the law in most provinces is unclear as to whether a lawyer is responsible for other lawyers acting under their direction and authority. There is potentially some convergence here with the antiquated notion of ministerial responsibility. However, while ministerial responsibility may no longer be expected or enforced as a political matter, whether for the Attorney General or for other ministers, the responsibility of a lawyer for their staff may well be enforced by the law society.

As the Attorney General is perhaps the archetype for lawyers in public office, I also emphasize here the rule that "[a] lawyer who holds public office must, in the discharge of official duties, adhere to standards of conduct as high as those required of a lawyer engaged in the practice of law."[67] I note, however, that this rule has been applied unevenly to politicians, including the Attorney General, such that the duties of lawyers are often balanced against the roles and responsibilities of politicians.[68]

Likewise, as the Attorney General is both a lawyer and a politician, I emphasize that the rules of professional conduct explicitly require that any concurrent or outside interests or pursuits not interfere with a lawyer's professional duties: "A lawyer who engages in another profession, business or occupation concurrently with the practice of law must not allow such outside interest to jeopardize the lawyer's professional integrity, independence or competence. ... A lawyer must not allow involvement in an outside interest to impair the exercise of the lawyer's independent judgment on behalf of a client."[69] For my analysis, I assume that the Attorney General does not engage in the part-time private practice of law, as such outside practice of a profession is typically prohibited for members of Cabinet.[70]

It is worth emphasizing that many of these duties persist after the lawyer-client relationship has ended. Perhaps the most important such persisting duty for the Attorney General is the duty of confidentiality to the Crown as the client. In particular, that duty requires that "[a] lawyer must not use or disclose a client's or former client's confidential information to the disadvantage of the client or former client, or for the benefit of the lawyer or a third person without the consent of the client or former client."[71] Thus, assuming no exceptions to the duty of confidentiality are engaged, a former Attorney General who continues in politics as an opposition or backbench legislator cannot reveal such confidential information privately or publicly for political gain or for any other purpose.[72] Consider here the insistence of Jody Wilson-Raybould that she could not reveal Cabinet confidences or information subject to solicitor-client privilege due to her duty of confidentiality as a lawyer, unless or until those were waived.[73] As I will return to in chapter 5 and chapter 7, parliamentary privilege means that any such disclosures that are made in the legislative assembly would be subject only to consequences imposed by the assembly, potentially acting through the Speaker.[74]

3. *The Attorney General and Legal Ethics: Who Is the Client?*

To understand how the law of lawyering applies to the Attorney General, it is important to identify the client or clients of the Attorney General. While the Attorney General's main and ultimate client is the Crown (in right of Canada or of the province or territory), as an organizational client, the Crown acts, gives instructions, and receives advice through individuals and, ultimately, the Governor (or Lieutenant Governor) in Council through the Prime Minister (or Premier) and Cabinet.[75] Importantly, the duty of the Attorney General as a lawyer remains to the organizational client (i.e., the Crown) and not to the persons from whom they receive instructions.[76] The Attorney General will also, at least in some circumstances, assign their government lawyer delegates to defend members of the judiciary when sued for actions in their official capacity.[77] However, there is surprisingly intense disagreement over whether the legislature is also a client of the Attorney General.

This role as legal advisor to the legislature is clear in statute (when properly interpreted) and in case law, as well as in the academic literature. Recall that the statutory duties of the Attorney General include those "that belong to the Attorney General and Solicitor General of England by law or usage, so far as those duties and powers are applicable to Ontario."[78] It is explicit in the work of John Ll. J. Edwards that the role of the Attorney General in England included providing legal advice to the legislature on bills.[79] As for case law, the Supreme Court of Canada in *Krieger v. Law Society of Alberta* stated, albeit in *obiter*, that "[a]s in England, [Attorneys General] serve as Law Officers to their respective legislatures."[80] Moreover, during the hearing in *Miron v. Trudel*, Lamer C.J. clearly indicated that he considered the Attorney General to be counsel to the House of Commons: "I for one question whether it is possible for an Attorney General to make a concession that the House violated the *Charter*. I would not want to be a member of that House and see my lawyer make that concession."[81] This role is also mentioned in passing in the legal literature by Grant Huscroft ("[t]he Attorney General is also the Legislature's lawyer") and by Roy McMurtry during his term as Attorney General for Ontario ("[t]his responsibility to give legal advice to the legislature remains part of my role in Ontario even today"),[82] as well as by Dodek in an important op-ed in the *Globe and Mail*.[83]

Nonetheless, former Senior Legal Counsel to the House of Commons Steven Chaplin has argued that "[t]here is no basis for this conclusion as it relates to Attorneys-General in Canada. ... [T]here is no circumstance under which an Attorney General should be considered the legal advisor to a legislature in this country."[84] Specifically, he argued that my previous conclusions, published elsewhere,[85] "are based on a romantic, misplaced and outdated understanding of the role of Attorney General in the United Kingdom, and a failure to appreciate the significantly different history and role of the Attorney General in Canada."[86] Despite Chaplin's adamance, as I have explained elsewhere, I find his argument ultimately unconvincing – particularly his quick and, respectfully, unsupported dismissal of the authorities I have mentioned here.[87] While Chaplin is certainly correct that the legislative assembly has its own legal advisors (in roles such as the one he occupied as Senior Legal Counsel to the House of Commons), it does not necessarily follow that the Attorney General is not *also* a legal advisor to the legislature – admittedly a role that is vestigial or at least atrophied in practice.[88]

If the Attorney General is a legal advisor to the legislature on bills before it, then they would appear to be in a joint retainer in which they are providing legal advice on the same matters to both the Cabinet and the Legislature.[89] This joint retainer should mean that there can be no confidentiality as between these two clients.[90] However, given the controversy over this role as legal advisor to the legislature, I will not address this issue further here.

*4. The Attorney General, the Deputy Attorney General,
and Government Lawyers*

My focus in this book is specifically on the Attorney General themselves. However, they should be situated in the context of other lawyers for the Crown, including the Deputy Attorney General. While the Attorney General is the Chief Law Officer of the Crown, government lawyers (lawyers in the public service for the federal or provincial Crown)[91] support and fulfil that role. It is generally accepted that all government lawyers, including those who advise other ministries, should ultimately report to the Attorney General.[92] The literature on legal ethics for government lawyers largely follows Adam Dodek's "rule of law triangle" model and Elizabeth Sanderson's "three layers" model, under which government lawyers are understood as simultaneously being members of the public service, lawyers, and delegates of the Attorney General.[93] Under this approach, the key and complex interaction for government lawyers is between their duties as lawyers and their duties as public servants – two sets of duties that are constructed separately and rarely with each other in mind.[94] In contrast, the Attorney General is not a member of the public service and is instead a legislator and a member of Cabinet.

The Deputy Attorney General, like other deputy ministers, acts when the Attorney General is unable and also serves as the interface between the Attorney General and the members of the public service.[95] Indeed, as Elizabeth Sanderson emphasizes, the neutrality of the public service – a constitutional convention – requires this interface.[96] While the Deputy Attorney General is a Cabinet appointee,[97] they are nonetheless a member of the public service.[98] Among other things, they not only have a personal duty of political neutrality but, indeed, often face even more stringent restrictions on their political activity than do other public servants.[99] For these reasons, in my view the Deputy Attorney General is better functionally understood as the senior government lawyer than as the stand-in or substitute for the Attorney General. Thus, I do not focus in this book on the role of the Deputy Attorney General or the application of legal ethics to the Deputy Attorney General.[100]

Instead, I focus on the meaning of legal ethics for the Attorney General themselves, as opposed to what might be understood as their vicarious or supervisory liability for government lawyers (or lawyers on their political staff). The law of lawyering is largely silent on the responsibility of a lawyer for those lawyers who report to them, as opposed to their explicit responsibility for non-lawyer staff and articled students.[101] The main exception is Quebec, where the *Code of Professional Conduct of Lawyers* provides that "[a] lawyer must take reasonable measures to ensure that every person who collaborates with him when he engages in his professional activities and, where applicable, every firm within which he engages in such activities, complies" with the legislation on lawyers and professionals more generally.[102] It also provides more explicitly that "[a] lawyer who exercises authority over another lawyer must ensure that the framework within which such other lawyer engages in his professional activities allows him to comply with his professional obligations."[103] (This does not mean that the Attorney General does not have a moral responsibility as the chief lawyer for the Crown, parallel to the responsibility that Sanderson articulates for the Deputy Attorney General, to make it clear to government lawyers "that they are bound by their provincial or territorial law society code of professional conduct."[104]) In this respect, the responsibilities of the Attorney General for the lawyers of their ministry under the law of lawyering are significantly narrower than their responsibilities under ministerial responsibility. At the same time, by communicating or approving advice to Cabinet from ministry lawyers, including the Deputy Attorney General, the Attorney General becomes responsible for that advice. The law of lawyering explicitly and reasonably recognizes that any lawyer may need to enlist other lawyers to fulfil their responsibilities.[105] Thus, I focus on the Attorney General themselves.

5. *The Multiple Roles of the Attorney General*

A meaningful account of legal ethics and the Attorney General must consider their multiple roles and the ramifications of those roles for their duties as a lawyer.

I begin with the "two hats" model of the Attorney General.[106] As mentioned above when I addressed terminology, the same person is both the Minister of Justice and the Attorney General. These roles are distinct in some jurisdictions – federally, for example – but not in others.[107] Even where these roles are distinct, however, they remain a single Cabinet portfolio.[108]

As Minister of Justice, this person is the member of Cabinet responsible for justice policy and the administration of justice – matters such as courthouse funding, legal aid, and judicial appointments.[109] Like other Cabinet portfolios, this is a legitimately political role in which the Minister is one of many Ministers in Cabinet.[110] Some, such as former Ontario Attorney General Ian Scott, have suggested that this policy advice is special: "[A]n independent attorney general should bring to policy-making in government a particular concern for principle, for constitutionalism, and for rights. ... [I]t is the function of an independent attorney general to bring the focus of justice to questions of politics."[111] Nonetheless, Cabinet may legitimately choose not to follow such policy advice.[112] Given the Canadian system of responsible government, the Minister is responsible to the legislative assembly and must account for matters within their portfolio.[113] As is often recognized, these duties of this Minister do not mean they need to be a lawyer, in the same way that the Minister of Health need not be a doctor or other health professional.[114]

As Attorney General, however, this person is the Chief Law Officer of the Crown and provides objective legal advice to the Crown.[115] This role, as discussed above, entails the practice of law and is traditionally held by a lawyer – although I will discuss in chapter 6 the problems that arise when the Attorney General is not a lawyer. This role is purportedly apolitical, particularly as it relates to criminal proceedings.[116] As mentioned above, "it is a constitutional principle that the Attorneys General of this country must act independently of partisan concerns when exercising their delegated sovereign authority to initiate, continue or terminate prosecutions."[117]

The "two hats" model is not necessarily contrary to the duties of the Attorney General as a lawyer. The rules of professional conduct explicitly recognize that a client may legitimately seek, and benefit from, the lawyer's non-legal advice, including policy advice.[118] However, those rules also caution that the lawyer "should clearly distinguish legal advice from other advice."[119] Some commentators have argued that the roles constitute an inherent conflict of interest and should be separated.[120] Others, such as the Honourable Anne McLellan, argue that "such a structural change would diminish the credibility of the Attorney General's legal advice and lead to the loss of the broad perspective the joined roles provide to the person holding them."[121] I do not dispute that this dual role presents an inherent conflict of interest – for example, the Attorney General provides services to the court while being the most common litigant before it.[122] However, that conflict and the related temptations facing the government and the Attorney General are, for the most part, accepted and tolerated and managed, whether for principled or pragmatic reasons, historical or otherwise.[123] One important tool to do so is Memorandums of Understanding between Attorneys General and the Chief Justices of the courts for which they are responsible.[124] While a breach of such a Memorandum may provoke media attention and public pressure to resign, it likely also constitutes a violation of the duty to encourage respect for the administration of justice. I will return to this duty in chapter 2.

From a legal ethics perspective, the "two hats" create a risk that political factors would pose a conflict of interest for the Attorney General, in which that person's personal and political interests could influence the legal advice given to the Crown as the client. While typical accounts of the "two hats" model do not explicitly prioritize one "hat" over the other, former Ontario Attorney General Ian Scott argued that the Attorney General role takes priority over the Minister of Justice role: "It is understood in our province that the attorney general is first and foremost the chief law officer of the Crown, and that the powers and duties of that office take precedence over any others that may derive from his additional role as minister of justice and member of Cabinet."[125] Indeed, McLellan, in her report on the Minister of Justice and Attorney General for Canada, not only endorsed Scott's view but recommended that it be codified in federal legislation.[126] As a matter of legal ethics, Scott's position is consistent with the rules of professional conduct insofar as those rules demand that any concurrent or outside interests or pursuits do not interfere with or reduce the lawyer's professional duties.[127]

Moreover, in the "two hats" model, the person who occupies the single position of both Minister of Justice and Attorney General is bound by Cabinet solidarity. Cabinet solidarity means that all ministers are expected to publicly criticize Cabinet decisions only if they resign from Cabinet.[128] However, as I will discuss in chapter 4, it is unclear whether resignation is sufficient to allow such criticism by the Attorney General, given their professional duties of confidentiality and their obligation to protect solicitor-client privilege.

Further complicating the "two hats" model, some Canadian jurisdictions have not spun off the traditional public safety functions of the Attorney General into a separate ministry or department.[129] In those jurisdictions, though the Attorney General is not technically cross-appointed, they hold what would in other jurisdictions be two portfolios. I will focus on the legal ethics issues for a cross-appointed Attorney General in chapter 3.

Like all members of Cabinet,[130] in the Canadian system of responsible government, the Attorney General is by convention also a legislator. Thus, they must navigate the same tensions that face all ministers between their role as minister and their role as legislator,[131] particularly with regard to advocating for their constituents.[132] They must also navigate the tensions between their role as Attorney General and their role as a legislator. For example, while constituent advocacy by legislators and their staff is often exempted from the prohibition against the unlicensed practice of law,[133] meaning that such advocacy is permissible by non-lawyers, the Attorney General involved in such advocacy would likely face a conflict of interest between their duties to the Crown as client and their duties to the constituent as pseudo-client.

In many provinces, legislation on the legal profession also makes the provincial Attorney General an *ex officio* bencher of the law society.[134] The tension between this role and the Minister of Justice role – the Minister responsible for the law society and its legislation – may create issues around the independence of the bar.[135] However, anecdotal evidence suggests that Attorneys General seldom actively use their role as benchers, even by attending meetings. Legislation on the legal profession sometimes has a parallel provision making the federal Attorney General an *ex officio* bencher if they are a member of that law society. Given that the regulation of the practice of law is within provincial jurisdiction,[136] this bencher role for the federal Attorney General does not raise the same tensions as it does for the provincial Attorney General. In Ontario, such legislation also makes the provincial Attorney General "the guardian of the public interest in all matters within the scope of this Act or having to do in any way with the practice of law in Ontario or the provision of legal services in Ontario."[137]

The Attorney General also has a unique role in exercising *parens patriae* powers and litigating in the public interest.[138] While the Attorney General has a role with regard to protecting and overseeing charities, that role is not especially relevant to my legal ethics analysis and so I do not address it further here.[139]

Some commentators argue that the Attorney General has a greater internal role within government as "the defender of the rule of law," particularly with regard to compliance with the *Canadian Charter of Rights and Freedoms*.[140] At minimum, the Attorney General has an explicit and affirmative statutory duty to "see that the administration of public affairs is in accordance with the law."[141] This duty is unique to the Attorney General,[142] although it could potentially be imposed as a matter of contract on any lawyer by any client. While all lawyers have a professional duty not to assist their client in unlawful conduct and to withdraw if the client persists in such conduct,[143] generally lawyers do not have an affirmative professional duty to see that their clients act lawfully. Elizabeth Sanderson characterizes this special duty of the Attorney General as "a duty of fundamental and unique importance" and emphasizes its connection to the role of "guardian of the rule of law."[144] Ian Scott argued that "[a]ny discussion of the Attorney General's responsibilities must keep this fundamental obligation in mind" and emphasized that "[i]n advising on questions of constitutionality, the Attorney General must give paramount consideration to the obligation to ensure that government action complies with the law, in this case the supreme law of Canada."[145]

While many of these roles do not constitute the practice of law, the status of the Attorney General as a practising lawyer is still meaningful and relevant in all their roles. One reason is that it is often unclear in which role the Attorney General is acting at any given time – unclear not only to the government but also to legislators, the media, and the public. Indeed, while it is possible to separate out these roles in the abstract, in practice they are often closely intertwined, particularly the "two hats."[146] Another reason is that, while there is some debate in the legal ethics literature over whether law societies should regulate lawyers' extra-professional conduct,[147] the importance and visibility of the Attorney General as Chief Law Officer of the Crown would likely widen the scope of conduct that is legitimately a matter of law society attention.[148] I acknowledge that the rules of professional conduct on lawyers in public office seem to limit this scope: "Generally, the Society is not concerned with the way in which a lawyer holding public office carries out official responsibilities, but conduct in office that reflects adversely upon the lawyer's integrity or professional competence may be the subject of disciplinary action."[149] However, as the only elected official who necessarily practises law in the course of their duties of office, the Attorney General should be the most scrutinized of all the lawyers in public office. Likewise, they should face heavy scrutiny as one of the most powerful and high-profile lawyers in the province or territory. I also emphasize that one of the duties I have identified as being of special importance to the Attorney General – the duty to encourage respect for the administration of justice – explicitly applies to lawyers both in and out of their professional lives and particularly to those lawyers with high public profiles:

> The obligation outlined in the rule is not restricted to the lawyer's professional activities but is a general responsibility resulting from the lawyer's position in the community. A lawyer's responsibilities are greater than those of a private citizen. A lawyer should take care not to weaken or destroy public confidence in legal institutions or authorities by irresponsible allegations. The lawyer in public life should be particularly careful in this regard because the mere fact of being a lawyer will lend weight and credibility to public statements.[150]

For all these reasons, it will be difficult for the Attorney General to argue that conduct in any of their public roles should not be subject to the law of lawyering. Indeed, the Attorney General should embrace this responsibility.

While the Premier can remove the Attorney General from Cabinet, for any reason or for no reason, the Premier cannot disbar the Attorney General or otherwise threaten their status as a lawyer. To this extent, their power over the Attorney General as a member of Cabinet is limited. This limit makes the independence of the bar meaningful for the Attorney General.

The Organization of This Book

This book is organized in seven chapters after this Introduction. Chapter 2, chapter 3, and chapter 4 develop the theme of complexity. Chapter 2 considers the professional duty to encourage respect for the administration of justice as it applies to the Attorney General. It analyses two cases in which law societies have attempted to discipline Attorneys General for breaching these duties – the only two public instances in which law societies have *ever* attempted to discipline Attorneys General –

as well as other notable instances in which the duty appears to have been breached but no public disciplinary proceedings have resulted. Chapter 3 uses the unique case study of Quebec Premier and Attorney General Maurice Duplessis to demonstrate and analyse the tensions that occur when the Attorney General is cross-appointed to another portfolio, particularly that of Premier. Chapter 4 considers the potential legal ethics issues around the resignation of the Attorney General, including confidentiality as well as returning to the duty to encourage respect for the administration of justice.

Chapter 5, chapter 6, and chapter 7 turn to the theme of accountability. Chapter 5 demonstrates that, although some commentators suggest otherwise, the Attorney General does not enjoy absolute immunity to law society discipline. I set out and analyse the limited and specific respects in which they are immune. Chapter 6 analyses the odd situation of the non-lawyer Attorney General. I explain that while such an appointment is permissible under current case law, it is legally questionable and creates many legal ethics problems – particularly the problem that a non-lawyer is not subject to law society regulation or discipline. I propose potential legislative solutions to those problems. While law society discipline of the Attorney General is possible, and law society discipline of the non-lawyer Attorney General could be made possible through legislative amendments, it remains highly unlikely that law societies will exercise that disciplinary jurisdiction. For this reason, I consider alternative accountability mechanisms in chapter 7, with a focus on parliamentary accountability. I argue that codes of conduct for legislators and members of Cabinet can be used – and should legitimately be used – to impose accountability for breaches of legal ethics by the Attorney General, as should the powers of the Speaker under the Standing Orders.

I conclude in chapter 8 by reflecting on my analysis throughout the book. First, I provide a synthesis of options for reform that would recognize and strengthen the application of legal ethics to the Attorney General. In particular, I recognize that separating the "two hats" of Attorney General and Minister of Justice into two separate positions held by two separate individuals would be beneficial from a legal ethics perspective, but not necessarily from a public law perspective. Although I would not recommend that change at this time, it remains an option for the future. Against the backdrop of these options for reform, I then emphasize that, with or without viable mechanisms for accountability, the conduct of the Attorney General – both as a lawyer and otherwise – must be guided by integrity and self-respect. I ultimately circle back to the wisdom of two great authorities. The first is John Ll. J. Edwards and his emphasis on personal integrity: "in the final analysis it is the strength of character, personal integrity and depth of commitment to the principles of independence and the impartial representation of the public interest, on the part of the holders of the office of Attorney General, which is of supreme importance."[151] The second is former Attorney General for Ontario Ian Scott and his exhortation that the Attorney General is a lawyer first and a politician second: "the attorney general is first and foremost the chief law officer of the Crown, and ... the powers and duties of that office take precedence over any others that may derive from his additional role as minister of justice and member of Cabinet."[152]

PART I

Complexity

2 Complexity: The Duty to Encourage Respect for the Administration of Justice[1]

Introduction

In this chapter, I illustrate the complexity of legal ethics for the Attorney General by focusing on the duty to encourage respect for the administration of justice.[2] As I suggested in chapter 1, this duty is particularly relevant for the Attorney General. Indeed, it is the focus of the only two publicly reported matters in which law societies have attempted to discipline an Attorney General.

As lawyers in public office, Attorneys General are ostensibly held to the same standards of conduct as other lawyers.[3] Moreover, most lawyers have little, if any, rational incentive to publicly criticize the judiciary. However, politicians have strong incentives to attack an independent and unelected judiciary, particularly when judicial decisions protect minority groups or interests or are otherwise unpopular. While the Attorney General shares some of these incentives, they purportedly have a unique responsibility among elected politicians to defend the judiciary. Indeed, they are sometimes described as the "interlocutor between government and judiciary" or the "defender" of the judiciary.[4] Elizabeth Sanderson has further asserted that "[c]learly informed commentators see the … duty to defend the institution of the judiciary as fundamental to Canada's constitutional arrangements."[5] But this role tends to be articulated only vaguely in the literature and is rarely invoked publicly – explicitly or implicitly – by Attorneys General. While this duty is sometimes contested in other commonwealth countries, particularly in Australia,[6] my focus here is on the Canadian context.

The duty of the Attorney General to defend the judiciary is one with a long history but an unclear foundation and contested modern relevance.[7] In particular, it is unclear whether it is a special public law duty of the Attorney General or an implication of the duty of the Attorney General as a lawyer to encourage respect for the administration of justice – or both. Here, I focus on the duty of the Attorney General as a lawyer. I do so to emphasize the importance and complexity of the professional obligations of Attorneys General as lawyers.

This chapter is organized in five parts after this Introduction. In parts 1 and 2, I consider the two instances in which law societies have attempted to discipline an Attorney General. These instances involve a speech given by Claude Wagner of Quebec in 1965 and remarks to the media by Roger Kimmerly of Yukon in 1986. Then in part 3, I examine the more recent – and most severe – misdeeds of Peter MacKay as federal Minister of Justice and Attorney General, misdeeds for which MacKay, puzzlingly, did not face law society discipline. In part 4, I consider instances of apparent inaction by Attorneys General Ken Rostad (Alberta), Ron Basford (Canada), and Rob Nicholson (Canada), and contrast these to situations involving Attorney Generals Doug Downey (Ontario) and Geoff Plant (British Columbia). Finally, in part 5, I conclude by exploring the implications for an informed understanding of the professional duty to encourage respect for the administration of justice as it applies to the Attorney General.

Several observations are important at the outset. The first, which I return to in the chapters on accountability (chapter 5, chapter 6, and chapter 7), is that this duty is meaningful and its breaches serious, even if no apparent accountability follows such breaches. Thus, with great respect, I disagree with some observations by Harry Arthurs. In the 1990s, Arthurs, in his theory of "ethical economy" in lawyer regulation, characterized the duty to encourage respect for the administration of justice not only as a key example of the "[m]any provisions of the Code [that] are seldom discussed and almost never enforced," but also one that was "meant not to control lawyers' behaviour but to offer symbolic reassurance to the public" and, thus, had merely "educational and inspirational value."[8] Arthurs further observed that this duty was one of the "professional norms [that] are violated with virtual impunity."[9] With great respect to Arthurs, even if the *intention* of the rule was to be "symbolic," the centrality of the duty means there should be some meaningful accountability for its breach.

Second, the duty to encourage respect for the administration of justice can only be properly understood in conjunction with two other regulatory concepts. The first is the general duty of civility.[10] The second is the rule on public statements, which specifically references a lawyer's obligations to the courts and to the administration of justice: "[p]rovided that there is no infringement of the lawyer's obligations to the client, the profession, the courts, or the administration of justice, a lawyer may communicate information to the media and may make public appearances and statements."[11] The commentary to this rule emphasizes that a lawyer's professional obligations apply to such statements: "[T]he mere fact that a lawyer's appearance is outside of a courtroom, a tribunal or the lawyer's office does not excuse conduct that would otherwise be considered improper."[12]

Third, it is helpful to set out the modern articulation of the duty to encourage respect for the administration of justice. This duty is currently set out in rule 5.6-1 of the *Model Code of Professional Conduct* of the Federation of Law Societies of Canada: "[a] lawyer must encourage public respect for and try to improve the administration of justice."[13] This rule, on its face, appears to have two component duties: one to *encourage public respect for* the administration of justice and one to *improve* the administration of justice. However, with respect to MacDonald J. in *Stewart v. Canadian Broadcasting Corp.*, it may be misleading to consider these to be "two separate directions."[14] These paired aspects are closely intertwined and, indeed, at least somewhat inseparable. Improving the administration of justice is clearly one way to encourage public respect for the administration of justice. Thus, though for ease I will refer primarily to the duty to encourage respect for the administration of justice, I include within that phrase the duty to improve it. While my focus in this chapter is on public criticism of judges, I also note that more subtle attacks on judicial independence, such as breaches of Memorandums of Understanding between Attorneys General and Chief Justices,[15] might violate this duty.

Several elements from the commentary to rule 5.6-1 are particularly relevant to my analysis. First, the duty to encourage respect for the administration of justice applies both in lawyers' professional conduct and their extraprofessional conduct: "[t]he obligation outlined in the rule is not restricted to the lawyer's professional activities but is a general responsibility resulting from the lawyer's position in the community."[16] Second, "lawyer[s] in public life" – which would include the Attorney General – are cautioned to "be particularly careful ... because the mere fact of being a lawyer will lend weight and credibility to public statements."[17] Third, the duty prohibits not all criticism, but specifically "irresponsible allegations" and "petty" or "intemperate" or dishonest criticism,[18] recognizing that criticism may be necessary and appropriate. Fourth, lawyers have a positive duty to *defend* judges against "unjust criticism," primarily because "judges ... are often prohibited by law or custom from defending themselves."[19] Indeed, the wording of the rule itself indicates that the overall duty is a positive or affirmative one: lawyers not only have a duty not to discourage respect for the administration of justice but, indeed, a duty to encourage such respect.

The equivalent provisions in the Quebec *Code of Professional Conduct of Lawyers* are found in article 111:

> A lawyer is a servant of justice and must support the authority of the courts. He must not act in a manner which is detrimental to the administration of justice.
>
> He must foster a relationship of trust between the public and the administration of justice.[20]

While worded differently, article 111 of the *Quebec Code*, as a whole, corresponds closely to rule 5.6-1 of the *FLSC Model Code*, though the elements of the *FLSC Model Code* commentary are absent from the text of article 111. Note again that the framing of the duty – in particular, to "support the authority of the courts" and to "foster a relationship of trust" – is a positive one and not merely a negative one.[21]

Fourth, it is helpful to examine the harm that the duty seeks to prevent. I emphasize here the observation of the hearing panel of the Law Society of Upper Canada in *Law Society of Upper Canada v. Ann Bruce*[22] that inappropriate criticism of judges is harmful because of its effect on public respect for the administration of justice:

> Although the justices are the complainants it is not the impact on them personally that was the hearing panel's concern. It was the undermining of the integrity and authority of the justice system through reckless challenges of bias and egregiously disrespectful behaviour towards the court. If left unaddressed such behavior could, over time, undermine the public's perception of cornerstone principles of the justice system: the presumption of the court's impartiality and independence.[23]

In other words, unsupported allegations against judges are problematic not because such comments are an affront to the dignity of those judges, but because of the damage to the public's respect for the justice system.

Fifth, this duty is unusual because it is simultaneously both a prohibition and a potential defence. Encouraging respect for the administration of justice will sometimes require criticism of the administration of justice.[24] In other words, a lawyer accused of violating this duty may argue that their remarks or conduct were, instead, necessary to *fulfil* the duty.

Sixth and finally, there is a limited role for freedom of expression under the *Canadian Charter of Rights and Freedoms* in the context of this duty.[25] It is clear that lawyers accept restrictions on their *Charter* rights that would be unacceptable and unjustifiable for non-lawyers, particularly in the context of civility.[26] Given the serious risk of harm posed by lawyers' noncompliance with the duty to encourage respect for the administration of justice – indeed, a risk likely even greater than the risk of harm due to incivility – and the high visibility of the Attorney General, the *Charter* will appropriately play a relatively minor role.

Thus, even if law societies may have a reasonable reluctance to further enforce lawyer civility in the aftermath of *Groia v. Law Society of Upper Canada*,[27] they should have no such reluctance to regulate the duty to encourage respect for the administration of justice – for lawyers generally and all the more so for the Attorney General.

1. Claude Wagner (Quebec)

Against this backdrop, I now turn to case studies involving Attorneys General. I begin with Claude Wagner of Quebec.

Scattered throughout the sparse Canadian legal literature on the Attorney General, one will occasionally find passing reference to Claude Wagner as Attorney General of Quebec. Such references are typically two-fold: first, Wagner was reprimanded by the Barreau for a 1965 speech that was critical of a judge; and second, the reprimand was quashed on the basis of ministerial immunity. The most detailed account comes in a 1995 chapter by John Ll. J. Edwards, then (and still) the leading commentator on the role of the Attorney General:

> [T]he flamboyant Minister of Justice and Attorney General of Quebec Claude Wagner found himself having to meet charges of unprofessional conduct arising out of a speech, made at a public meeting, in which Wagner had sought to awaken the conscience of the bar to the widespread erosion of public respect for the bench and bar. The complaint in this case was lodged by the judge whose conduct had been attacked during the minister's speech. An essential part of the attorney general's unsuccessful defence before the Montreal Bar Council was that his actions were outside the disciplinary jurisdiction of the professional body. There followed a series of convoluted appeal proceedings culminating in a very brief judgment by the Quebec Court of Appeal, in *Barreau de Montreal v Wagner* [1968], declaring that the disciplinary powers of the bar did not extend to the minister of justice when exercising the executive powers of the Crown.[28]

These accounts leave many questions unanswered. What was the criticism? Why was it inappropriate in the eyes of the Barreau? What was the relevance, if any, to the Barreau of Wagner's role as the Attorney General and Minister of Justice?

The Speech

As quoted in the reasons of the Barreau, the problematic passage of Wagner's speech was as follows:

> En juin dernier, dans une petite ville d'une région rurale de la province, deux individus coursaient. L'un d'eux, dans la course, tuait une passante alors que son compagnon en blessait grièvement une autre.
>
> Le premier individu attend présentement son procès aux Assises. L'autre a fui les lieux de l'accident pour être finalement repéré quelques jours plus tard, grâce au travail de la Sûreté Provinciale. À la suite de nombreuses remises de la cause, l'avocat produisait devant la Cour, en chambre, le 30 août, une confession de jugement hors la présence du porte-parole de la Couronne et le juge condamnait l'individu à $25 d'amende, à $39 de frais avec interdiction de conduire pendant trois mois.
>
> L'accusé trouvé coupable n'était même pas présent. Il n'a pas remis son permis de conduire au greffier et son avocat, qui avait seul pris connaissance du jugement dans la chambre du juge, s'est abstenu de lui conseiller de remettre ce permis conformément au jugement.
>
> Trois semaines plus tard, le même chauffard conduisait illégalement une automobile et était impliqué dans un accident qui causa la mort du père et de la mère de sept enfants en bas âge. Qu'en pensez-vous ? Comment voulez-vous que la justice soit respectée comme il se doit lorsque des membres de notre ordre agissent ainsi?[29]

> Last June, in a small town of a rural area of this province, two individuals were racing. One of them, in the race, killed a passerby while his companion seriously injured another.
>
> The first individual is currently awaiting trial in Assizes. The other fled the scene of the accident before he was apprehended a few days later, thanks to the work of the Provincial Police. Following numerous postponements of the case, the lawyer produced before a judge, in chambers, on August 30, a confession of judgment without the presence of the crown attorney, and the judge condemned the individual to $25 fine and $39 in costs, with a three-month driving ban.
>
> The accused was not even present. He did not hand over his driver's licence to the clerk, and his lawyer, who alone had seen the judgment in the judge's chambers, refrained from advising him to hand over the licence in accordance with the judgment.

Three weeks later, the same driver was driving an automobile illegally and was involved in an accident which caused the death of the father and mother of seven young children. What do you think? How do you expect justice to be respected as it should be when members of our Order act in this manner?

In short, the problematic claim was that an impaired driver, who had caused several deaths, failed to surrender their licence after a previous impaired driving conviction because the judge had pronounced the sentence in the absence of the driver and defence counsel failed to inform the driver that their licence had been suspended.

Four points are worth noting about the speech and its aftermath. First, in the days after the speech, both the judge and the defence counsel vehemently denied Wagner's account.[30] Second, although Wagner did not name the accused, the Crown prosecutor, defence counsel, or the judge, the Barreau held that "[l]'affaire à laquelle Me Wagner se référait était facilement identifiable par de nombreuses personnes" ("[t]he case to which Mr. Wagner referred to was easily identifiable by many").[31] Third, Wagner appeared to be primarily criticizing defence counsel, particularly in posing the question "Comment voulez-vous que la justice soit respectée comme il se doit lorsque *des membres de notre ordre* agissent ainsi?" ("How do you expect justice to be respected as it should be when *members of our Order* act in this manner?")[32] Nonetheless, it was the judge, not defence counsel, who made the complaint to the Barreau. Likewise, the impact on the judge, not on defence counsel, was the primary concern of the Barreau. Fourth, it seems clear that Wagner was attempting – at least in part – to improve the administration of justice by identifying a recent shortcoming and exhorting fellow lawyers to do better.

Surprisingly, the part of the speech for which the Barreau proposed disciplining Wagner was not widely reported in the media.[33] Instead, the coverage focused on Wagner's call for the Barreau to reform itself. In Wagner's words:

Jamais, dans l'histoire du Barreau, a-t-il été aussi nécessaire qu'au moment présent, de réviser nos attitudes, de renouveler nos cadres, de modifier nos règlements, de transformer nos mentalités qui s'accrochaient à la tradition au détriment du progrès, d'écarter l'immobilisme nuisible aux intérêts de la société. Si le Barreau réussit à comprendre qu'il est au service de la population, qu'il n'a pas été conçu pour se servir de la population, il n'aura pas de difficultés à adopter, avec fermeté des positions conformes à cet esprit.[34]

Never in the history of the Barreau has it been as necessary as at the present time to review our attitudes, renew our frameworks, modify our regulations, transform our mentalities which cling to tradition to the detriment of progress, and to combat legal rigidity harmful to the interests of society. If the Barreau succeeds in understanding that it is at the service of the population, that it was not conceived to take advantage of the population, it will have no difficulty in firmly adopting positions in keeping with this spirit.

Wagner was adamant that the failures of individual lawyers had damaged public confidence in the profession as a whole.[35] These parts of Wagner's speech were not, at least explicitly, relevant to the disciplinary action taken by the Barreau. However, there was at least some public suspicion that Wagner was being disciplined for criticizing the Barreau. For example, an editorial cartoon in the newspaper *L'Action* pictured Wagner, with a huge bump on the head from a bar or pipe labelled "Barreau," above which was written "$100.00," with the caption "Wagner: Ça va, je ne contredirai plus le barreau" ("Wagner: Okay, I will no longer challenge the Barreau anymore").[36]

The Barreau

What exactly was the breach? According to the Barreau, the speech constituted a breach not because Wagner had criticized a judge, but because several key factual assertions in the speech were incorrect and Wagner, in relying on a police report, had failed to take reasonable steps to confirm them. (Wagner immediately challenged the factual findings of the Barreau in a public statement).[37] The failure to take reasonable steps was *especially* problematic – not less problematic – because Wagner was the Minister of Justice.[38] Indeed, the Barreau rejected Wagner's assertion of ministerial immunity. In doing so, the Barreau made two key points. As a factual matter, it was clear from the text of the speech that Wagner was speaking both as a lawyer and as Minister of Justice. As a matter of law, all members of the Barreau are subject to its rules, whether or not they hold public office – although it recognized the Minister's "plus grande latitude de traiter de sujets d'intérêt public" ("greater latitude in addressing subjects of public interest").[39] The reasons of the Barreau strongly suggest that if the criticism had been factually accurate, it would not have breached the duty – though there is no explicit statement to that effect.

The Barreau held that Wagner had violated multiple rules. This included article 66, which would now fall under the duty to encourage respect for the administration of justice, and article 84, which would now be subsumed into the general duty of civility:

(66) L'avocat doit servir la justice et soutenir l'autorité des tribunaux. Jamais il ne doit compromettre l'Honneur et la dignité du Barreau. Il doit être fidèle à ses clients, loyal et courtois envers ses confrères. Il est donc tenu d'observer scrupuleusement les devoirs que lui imposent les règles, traditions et usages professionnels.

(84) L'avocat a le devoir de maintenir à l'égard des tribunaux une attitude respectueuse dans sa conduite et ses paroles.

(85) Il ne peut publier ou communiquer pour publication un rapport de procédures judiciaires faux ou injurieux pour l'honneur ou la dignité de la magistrature.[40]

(66) The lawyer must serve justice and uphold the authority of the courts. The lawyer must never compromise the honour and dignity of the Barreau. He must be faithful to clients, loyal and courteous to his colleagues. He is therefore required to scrupulously observe the duties imposed by the rules, traditions, and professional practices.

(84) The lawyer has a duty to maintain a respectful attitude towards the courts in his conduct and his words.

(85) He may not publish or communicate for publication a report of judicial proceedings that is false or offensive to the honour or dignity of the judiciary.

While article 85 does not have a clear modern equivalent, and might appear as written to encompass legitimate criticism, it too would appear to be subsumed under the duty to encourage respect for the administration of justice. Although articles 66, 84, and 85 do not clearly indicate a duty to *improve* the administration of justice, improvement is clearly one way to encourage public respect.

The Barreau ordered a reprimand, a fine of $100, and costs.

The Judicial Review and the Appeal

In the aftermath of the decision by the Barreau, Wagner not only said that ministers should be immune from regulation by the Barreau – and, indeed, from any consequences other than those imposed by the legislature[41] – but even proposed exempting all government lawyers from the jurisdiction of the Barreau.[42] An editorial in *Le Soleil* adopted these arguments for ministerial immunity: "[l]'existence du Barreau est indispensable: elle garantit ses membres contre la sujétion au pouvoir public et permet de protéger la population contre les 'brebis galeuses' du droit. Mais il n'est pas de son ressort de la protéger contre les ministres, ni celui de la Justice ni les autres" ("[t]he existence of the Barreau is vital: it guarantees its members against subjection to popular power and allows the population to be protected against the 'bad apples' of the law. But it is not its responsibility to protect against ministers, neither the one of Justice nor the others").[43] In his application for judicial review, Wagner emphasized the importance of this immunity, as a Minister, from discipline by the Barreau.[44]

With the exception of one reference to "toutes les informations qu[e] [Wagner] possède" ("all of the information at [Wagner's] disposal"), the application judge on judicial review did not address the alleged substantive breach but instead focused on the ministerial immunity issue in quashing the order of the Barreau.[45] The judge emphasized not only that any person may comment on procedure and sentence, but that "c'est le droit et le devoir du Ministre de la Justice de rechercher, signaler, rapporter et même dénoncer les cas où, d'après son jugement et avec l'aide de toutes les informations qu'il possède, il y aurait eu mauvaise administration de la justice" ("it is the right and duty of the Minister of Justice to seek out, flag, report, and even denounce cases where, according to his judgment and with the help of all the information at his disposal, there has been a maladministration of justice")[46] and that the case discussed in the speech was such a maladministration. The application judge also found that Wagner was speaking as the Minister of Justice and not as a lawyer. With respect, this finding seems dubious and unsupported (at least by the reasons of the Barreau).[47]

While the Court of Appeal upheld the quashing on the basis of Crown immunity, Tremblay C.J.Q. did note that he did not completely agree with the reasons of the application judge.[48] Instead, Tremblay C.J.Q. held that, insofar as the speech was given in Wagner's capacity as Minister of Justice, the application judge was correct to quash the decision of the Barreau.[49]

As I will return to in chapter 5, I note and emphasize here that blanket ministerial immunity for Attorneys General from law society discipline is inconsistent with case law superseding *Wagner*. Thus it is unclear, both as a factual and legal matter, whether the judicial review judge and the Court of Appeal were correct to quash the Barreau's actions on that basis.

The Lessons

While the disciplinary action was quashed, the substantive analysis by the Barreau, insofar as it was unquestioned by the courts on judicial review and on appeal, remains important. Two major lessons about the duty to encourage respect for the administration of justice as it applies to Attorneys General can be drawn from the Wagner speech and its fallout. The first is about the difficult, though necessary, balance required for compliance with the duty, and the second is about accuracy in criticism of the judiciary.

The first lesson is that the duty to encourage respect for the administration of justice requires lawyers, and especially the Attorney General, to engage in a difficult and delicate balance in their criticism and defence of courts and judges. Consider the comments by the judge on judicial review about the duty and responsibility of the Minister of Justice:

> CONSIDERANT que c'est le droit et le devoir du Ministre de la Justice de rechercher, signaler, rapporter et même dénoncer les cas où, d'après son jugement et avec l'aide de toutes les informations qu'il possède, il y aurait eu mauvaise administration de la justice;
>
> CONSIDERANT qu'une sentence excessive ou trop minime imposée à un individu convaincu de crime ou d'infraction de même qu'une procédure illégale, irrégulière ou insolite employés lors d'une conviction, constitue dans l'opinion de la Cour une mauvaise administration de la justice;
>
> CONSIDERANT que, sans s'immiscer dans les décisions des tribunaux chargés de redresser des sentences inadéquates, toute personne, et à plus forte raison le Ministre de la Justice, peut dire ce qu'il pense de la procédure qui a été suivie et du châtiment qui a été infligé dans telle ou telle instance.[50]

> CONSIDERING that it is the right and the duty of the Minister of Justice to investigate, flag, report, and even denounce cases where, according to his judgment and with the help of all the information at his disposal, there has been a maladministration of justice;
>
> CONSIDERING that an excessive or too minimum sentence imposed on an individual convicted of a crime or offence as well as any illegal, irregular, or unusual procedures employed during the conviction, constitutes in the opinion of the Court a maladministration of justice;
>
> CONSIDERING that, without interfering in the decisions of the courts responsible for redressing inadequate sentences, anyone, and even more so the Minister of Justice, may express his views on the procedure that was followed and the punishment that was levied in that instance.

The judge held that Wagner made these comments in his role as Minister and not as a lawyer. Nonetheless, the judge's references to "le droit et le devoir du Ministre de la Justice" ("the right and the duty of the

Minister of Justice") to denounce errors in the justice system and, moreover, the ability of "toute personne, et à plus forte raison le Ministre de la Justice" ("anyone, and even more so the Minister of Justice") to comment on those errors, would apply equally to the duty of lawyers to encourage respect for the administration of justice and to improve it. If defence counsel and the judge had indeed acted improperly, Wagner would seemingly have a duty to identify and explain those errors, even to publicize them, in the hope of improving the conduct of lawyers and judges – that is, the administration of justice – in the future. Thus, to comply with the duty without breaching it requires careful balancing. In turn, the difficulty of this balancing and the problems of hindsight suggest that law societies should allow a significant role for the reasonable judgment of the individual lawyer.

This brings me to the second lesson from *Wagner*, which partly explains how an Attorney General is to determine and maintain this balance: any lawyer who criticizes a judge, and presumably another lawyer, must take reasonable steps to confirm the factual information underlying the criticism.[51] Indeed, the Barreau held that this obligation to take reasonable steps applied particularly to the Minister of Justice. As I mentioned above, the application judge on judicial review did note that Wagner had made the speech based on the information within Wagner's control. In my view, this is at most a qualifier on the legal proposition identified by the Barreau. A "reasonable steps" requirement impedes – potentially among other things – unsupported criticism. I acknowledge that some may suggest that such a requirement will have a chilling effect on criticism of judges by Attorneys General. Even if it does, this requirement seems necessary and important, if not unavoidable. In this respect, the Wagner matter suggests that where the rules of professional conduct require a lawyer's criticism of judges to be supported by "a bona fide belief in its real merit,"[52] a *bona fide* belief should be understood as requiring a lawyer to take reasonable steps to confirm the factual basis of the criticism.

While there are some indications that the duty may have previously required deserved criticism to be made privately instead of publicly, on balance it seems that both private and public criticism are appropriate. In its 1920 *Canons of Legal Ethics*, the Canadian Bar Association stated that "[w]henever there is proper ground for serious complaint of a judicial officer, it is a right and duty of the lawyer to submit the grievance to the proper authorities."[53] However, the *Canons* did not explicitly state that the grievance must *only* be submitted to those authorities and cannot *also* be made public. Similarly, the 1917 by-laws of the Barreau (the predecessor to the current *Code of Professional Conduct for Lawyers*) prohibited lawyers from making not only *false* accounts of judicial proceedings, but also accounts injurious to the honour or dignity of the judiciary.[54] There is no indication from the duty itself, in any of its various forms at the time of the Wagner speech or later, that deserved criticism should be made privately instead of publicly. Indeed, subsequent case law suggests that private criticism can be as much a breach of this duty as public criticism.[55]

To the extent that the decision of the Hearing Panel of the Law Society of British Columbia in *Laarakker (Re)*[56] suggests otherwise, that decision appears to be incorrect. *Laarakker* was a decision about the duty of civility, not about the duty to encourage respect for the administration of justice. However, the comments of the panel suggest that criticism of another lawyer should be made solely to that lawyer's regulator.[57] Presumably, this admonition would apply also to allegations of judicial misconduct. With respect, it is quite possible, if not probable, that some conduct that discourages respect for the administration of justice will not lead to disciplinary sanctions or even disciplinary proceedings. If the duty of lawyers was merely to refer problematic conduct to law societies and judicial councils and then to repeat, echo, or publicize denunciations by those bodies, that duty would be an anemic – if not a hollow – one that recognizes little role for professional judgment and individual duty.

The caveat to this second lesson comes by analogy to *Groia v. Law Society of Upper Canada*, in which Moldaver J. held that incorrect allegations of misconduct against other lawyers goes to competence instead of civility.[58] From the facts of *Groia*, this holding by Moldaver J. was apparently about *legally* incorrect, not *factually* incorrect, allegations of misconduct. Nonetheless, as competence goes beyond legal knowledge, it could be that factually incorrect allegations of misconduct against judges likewise go to competence and not to the duty to encourage respect for the administration of justice. Insofar as allegations of misconduct that are incorrect – whether factually or legally – necessarily harm respect for the administration of justice, in my respectful view, they would squarely violate this duty, though they may also simultaneously violate the duty of competence.

2. Roger Kimmerly (Yukon)

One of the rare law society decisions concerning a serving Attorney General is *Law Society of Yukon v. Kimmerly*.[59] As the underlying incident and its fallout were the subject of an excellent article by the Honourable Ronald Veale and Andrea Bailey,[60] I provide here only a brief description of the key facts. *Kimmerly*, at its core, is about judicial independence, as emphasized by Veale and Bailey,[61] but it is also inseparably intertwined with the duty to encourage respect for the administration of justice.

At issue in *Kimmerly* were comments the Attorney General made in media interviews. Kimmerly's department had instructed that the territorial Coat of Arms be hung behind the bench in the courtrooms in a new courthouse.[62] A judge ordered the Coat of Arms removed as a perceived intrusion on the appearance of judicial independence, and in the interim the Coat of Arms was covered.[63] When asked about the incident in the interview, the Attorney General replied: "[i]t brings the repute of the courts and the judiciary into disrespect in the Yukon, and I'm extremely saddened by the whole thing. ... There's no independence issue here at all in my view."[64] The Attorney General was also quoted in a local newspaper saying not only that "the entire matter is silly" but also that "the cloaking over of the coat of arms is insulting to the public."[65]

After a complaint had been made, Kimmerly stated in a letter to the Law Society that "I am cognizant of my role with respect to the judiciary and my responsibilities in that regard," but emphasized his duty to "defend" the government and asserted that "my comments on this particular issue were, in my view, responsible to both of my aforesaid duties."[66]

The ultimate reasons in *Kimmerly* focus primarily on the interaction between the duty to encourage respect for the administration of justice and the rule of professional conduct on a lawyer in public office (providing that such a lawyer is held to the same standard as a lawyer in practice).[67] A decision of the Law Society executive, which was later quashed, concluded that "Mr. Kimmerly, during the interview in question, acted in his capacity as Minister of Justice and, while his remarks may have been impolite and impolitic, he could not be found to be deserving of censure or disciplinary action."[68] The subsequent Committee of Inquiry, in dismissing the complaint, explicitly balanced Kimmerly's duties as a lawyer with his duties as Minister of Justice, including "his freedom to make fair and reasonable comment in the exercise of his right to speak out."[69] The Committee did make the following key observations:

> One can argue now that softer phrases might have been chosen by the member, but the Committee is not unmindful of the realities of political life and the position of the member as Minister of Justice at the end of a telephone. ... [J]ustice is not a "cloistered virtue" and ... comments in

situations such as this cannot and should not be taken out of context or constrained unless they clearly amount to comments which any thinking person would conclude to have "brought the administration of justice into disrepute."[70]

Explicit here is the balancing between the competing duties of the Attorney General. Implicit is that the Attorney General necessarily has more leeway than lawyers generally, given their special role.

These comments in *Kimmerly* reinforce the lesson from the Wagner incident that, given the careful balancing required to comply with the duty to encourage respect for the administration of justice without breaching it, law societies should allow a significant margin for the reasonable judgment of the Attorney General. More specifically, this incident suggests that there is a high threshold for criticism of judges to violate the duty and that the inquiry is a contextual one. I emphasize that I have elsewhere criticized this explicit balancing approach to the rule on lawyers in public office as being contrary to the plain language of the provision.[71] While Kimmerly made his comments in 1986, and so the *Canadian Charter of Rights and Freedoms* was in force, there is no mention of the *Charter* in the reasons of the Law Society.[72] Nonetheless, the balancing exercise around the Attorney General speech in *Kimmerly* does seem to foreshadow *Charter* freedom-of-expression considerations, as more recently articulated in the civility cases of *Doré v. Barreau* (on a letter to a judge) and *The Law Society of Manitoba v. Histed* (on a letter to counsel criticizing judges).[73] The Court in *Histed* framed the issue as "the proper balance between the constitutional right to freedom of expression and the need to regulate the conduct of members of the legal profession."[74] Indeed, while *Histed* is often referred to as a civility case, the rule on the duty to encourage respect for the administration of justice was one of several rules that were engaged in *Histed* and challenged by the lawyer on *Charter* grounds.[75]

Whereas the decisions of the Barreau in *Wagner* and of the Law Society in *Kimmerly* appear to balance the lawyer's duty to encourage respect for the administration of justice with other duties, in my view the more analytically sound approach is to recognize that balancing *within* the analysis of the duty to encourage respect for the administration of justice. The duty necessarily involves a balancing of apparently competing imperatives. It requires lawyers, especially the Attorney General, to defend the judiciary, as well as to criticize it where appropriate. It is the balance between these two imperatives that comprises the duty. In its balancing and contextual approach, although it does not consider ministerial immunity, *Kimmerly* is nonetheless quite consistent with the reasons on the judicial review in *Wagner* insofar as both recognize public comment on the justice system as the appropriate and necessary role of the Attorney General.[76]

At the same time, the result of that balancing determination on the facts of *Kimmerly* might be different today. In my view, given the strict approach of the law societies regarding incivility towards judges in *Doré* and *Histed*, both of which were upheld on judicial review, *Kimmerly* now seems quite lenient – although leniency, at least in the context of civility, seems apparent from the more recent decision in *Groia*.[77]

3. Peter MacKay (Canada)

While Wagner and Kimmerly are the only Attorneys General that have been the subject of discipline proceedings by their law society, there are other important instances in which the duty to encourage respect for the administration of justice has been breached but no law society disciplinary proceedings followed. The most important and egregious such instance is the conduct of Peter MacKay as Minister of Justice and Attorney General for Canada in 2014.[78] In contrast to the Wagner and Kimmerly incidents, which suggest that compliance with the rule requires delicate balancing and that law societies should allow a significant role for the reasonable judgment of the individual lawyer, this incident reinforces that some conduct is so problematic that there remains no role for balancing. While MacKay was never disciplined for this conduct – for whatever reason – the scenario remains valuable as a case study.

In the *Reference re Supreme Court Act, ss 5 and 6*, the Supreme Court of Canada determined that judges of the Federal Court and Federal Court of Appeal were ineligible for the three seats on the Supreme Court of Canada that are allocated to Quebec, quashing the Prime Minister's elevation of Justice Marc Nadon.[79] Months after the release of the decision, the Prime Minister's Office made a statement implying that Chief Justice McLachlin had inappropriately attempted to contact the Prime Minister regarding the *Reference* and that MacKay advised the Prime Minister that such a call would be "inadvisable and inappropriate."[80] The Chief Justice made a statement the next day explaining that the call to the Minister of Justice and Attorney General of Canada, in which the Chief Justice requested to speak to the Prime Minister, occurred well before the *Reference* was made to the Court and was intended merely to inform the Minister and the Prime Minister that there may be a live issue as to the eligibility of judges of the Federal Court of Appeal generally.[81] On the same day, MacKay made the following comments in Halifax:

> Clearly there was an issue over a pending appointment and after having spoken to the chief justice, it was my considered opinion that that call shouldn't take place. ... It was ultimately his (Harper's) decision whether he spoke to her or not, but I just felt as justice minister that it was not an appropriate call.[82]

MacKay was later asked about the matter in the House: "can the Attorney General tell us whether he considers it part of his job to ensure that there are never any attempts to intimidate the courts?"[83] In response, MacKay reinforced the Prime Minister's original comments in explaining why he advised the Prime Minister to decline the call from the Chief Justice: "[m]y office was contacted by the office of the Chief Justice. After I spoke with her on that call I was of the considered opinion that the Prime Minister did not need to take her call. Neither the Prime Minister nor I would ever consider calling a judge where that matter is or could be before the court of competent jurisdiction."[84] Confusingly, while MacKay said that he "rejec[ted] the premise of that question," he went on to say that "of course the role of the minister of justice and attorney general of Canada is to uphold the integrity of the entire justice system."[85] As Elizabeth Sanderson notes in an account of this situation, MacKay's statements in the House "left legal observers puzzled and concerned."[86] While MacKay in his House statement seemed to choose his words more carefully than in his Halifax statement, the meaning of the House statement is readily discernable, though slightly less explicit, than the meaning of the Halifax statement.

MacKay's conduct has received little attention in the legal literature, perhaps because there is little uncertainty that it was phenomenally wrongful. Brent Cotter explains that MacKay, as a lawyer – indeed, the Chief Law Officer of the Crown – had a duty not to merely stay silent, but a positive duty to defend the Chief Justice.[87] Cotter characterizes MacKay's failure to do so not only as "a stain on the office of the Attorney General of Canada," but as a breach of the duty to encourage respect for the administration of justice.[88] While Cotter suggested that, as Attorney General, MacKay was immune to professional discipline for this misconduct,[89] with great respect that suggestion appears to be mistaken.[90] Nonetheless, as with *Wagner*, the immunity issue is peripheral to my analysis here. Similarly, Adam Dodek emphasized the solemn role of the Attorney General:

> I am surprised and disappointed by the conduct of the Minister of Justice because he should be defending the independence of the judiciary, not impugning the integrity of the Chief Justice and the Supreme Court of Canada, which has the potential to undermine the rule of law. ... We should expect the highest level of conduct from the Minister of Justice and Attorney General of Canada. He is no ordinary politician and no ordinary lawyer. He has a duty, as the chief legal officer of the Crown, to defend the administration of justice and the rule of law.[91]

Former Attorney General for Ontario Michael Bryant was more emphatic: "[t]he incident marks the complete breakdown of the constitutional relationship between the executive and judicial branches, threatening Canadians' confidence that their government has an effective judicial watchdog to protect them against political hubris and worse."[92]

The criticism of Chief Justice McLachlin, explicit in MacKay's Halifax statement and readily inferable from MacKay's House statement, was both factually and legally incorrect. As a factual matter, the Chief Justice was calling not to discuss specific potential litigation, but to inform the Minister and the Prime Minister of the potential for a legal challenge. As a legal matter, as indicated in the Chief Justice's statement, it is completely appropriate for a Chief Justice to discuss the needs of their Court with the Minister of Justice, and potentially the Prime Minister, when there is a vacancy. Indeed, the subsequently revised edition of *Ethical Principles for Judges* provides that "Chief Justices and other judges with administrative responsibilities will necessarily have contact and interaction with the executive branch of government, including attorneys general, deputy attorneys general and court services officials. These engagements are appropriate provided that the interactions are not partisan in nature."[93] Any Chief Justice would rightly be concerned that a particular class of appointments could be challenged, which would leave the court shorthanded until that challenge was resolved – even more so on a relatively small court like the Supreme Court of Canada, with its nine justices. That the Supreme Court of Canada might ultimately decide such a challenge does not change this reality.

While a complaint was reportedly made to the Nova Scotia Barristers' Society as MacKay's licensing body, specifically alleging that MacKay had violated the duty to encourage respect for the administration of justice, MacKay was never disciplined for that alleged breach.[94] However, a complaint was made to the International Commission of Jurists.[95]

In response, the Commission held that "the criticism [by Harper and MacKay] was not well-founded" and that "[s]uch public criticism could only have a negative impact on public confidence in the judicial system and in the moral authority and integrity of the judiciary, and thereby on the independence of the judiciary in Canada."[96]

If the Barristers' Society had pursued discipline against MacKay, and if ministerial immunity was not a bar to discipline, what arguments might MacKay have made in his defence? There would appear to be at least five such arguments, of which only the first would be successful – and only partially.

The first such argument would be parliamentary privilege. Parliamentary privilege, as I will discuss further in chapter 5, would preclude any law society discipline for MacKay's House statement. However, the positive nature of the duty to encourage respect for the administration of justice narrows the effective impact of parliamentary privilege. The positive duty would apply to MacKay at all times. While MacKay cannot be disciplined for making unfounded allegations against the Chief Justice while in the House, parliamentary privilege would *not* relieve MacKay of the positive duty to defend the Chief Justice against allegations made by others, at least while outside of the House. Moreover, MacKay's first – and more explicitly problematic – statement was made outside the House.

Second, MacKay might have argued that the only enforceable duty is a negative one and not a positive one, such that all lawyers, including MacKay, only have a duty not to actively *discourage* respect for the administration of justice. Under this argument, any positive duty contained in the rules of professional conduct is merely aspirational. The first problem with this argument is that it is contrary to the wording of the rule and its commentaries. The second problem with this argument is that, even if MacKay's interpretation of the rule was correct, MacKay did not remain silent.

Third, on the facts, MacKay may have argued that the precise wording of the House statement did not actually violate the duty and that the purported derogatory implications of that statement were drawn by the media and other listeners. If one breaks MacKay's comments into two parts, both parts are true and, in themselves, do not disparage the Chief Justice:

i. "[T]he Prime Minister did not need to take her call."
ii. "Neither the Prime Minister nor I would ever consider calling a judge where that matter is or could be before the court of competent jurisdiction."

There are many potential reasons why it might have been unnecessary for the Prime Minister to take the call – MacKay did not actually say in his House statement that it would have been *inappropriate* for the Prime Minister to do so. One would certainly hope that the second part was true, i.e., "[n]either the Prime Minister nor I would ever consider calling a judge where that matter is or could be before the court of competent jurisdiction." It is the juxtaposition of the two parts, in all the context, that inescapably encourages listeners to understand the conduct of the Chief Justice as wrongful and to doubt her integrity. That is, it seems inescapable that listeners could reasonably interpret the remarks as impugning the integrity of the Chief Justice and that the remarks were intended to be so interpreted – or at least remarkably reckless to the possibility, if not actually so intended. MacKay's Halifax statement leaves no doubt of this intention.

Fourth, MacKay may have argued that the duty to improve the administration of justice required him to call out judicial misconduct. However, given that MacKay knew or should have known that the allegations were unsupported and misleading, and that there was in fact no judicial misconduct to call out, this argument would be unsuccessful. Moreover, the appropriate mode for that criticism, if deserved, would have been a complaint to the Canadian Judicial Council. The fact that MacKay made such a complaint neither before nor after the statement from the Prime Minister's Office suggests that MacKay knew the accusation was illegitimate or at least that there was a serious possibility that the Council would reject the accusation as baseless – and that the purpose of the statements was not to encourage respect for, or to improve, the administration of justice, but to attack the Chief Justice in retaliation for ruling against the government of the day.

MacKay's strongest argument, aside from parliamentary privilege, would have been that the duty of loyalty to the client prevented MacKay from publicly criticizing the Prime Minister and might have even required supporting the Prime Minister's allegations. Although as Attorney General, MacKay's client was the Crown and not the Prime Minister,[97] it seems obvious that the Prime Minister made those remarks in his official role. Under this argument, the duty to encourage respect for the administration of justice applied in this specific context only to lawyers other than MacKay (and presumably subordinate government lawyers). The challenge with this argument is that the duty of loyalty to the client is never absolute and is often counterbalanced by other duties. Moreover, when faced with apparently conflicting duties to the administration of justice and to the client, a better reconciliation of those duties would be to publicly remain silent instead of publicly supporting the Prime Minister's allegations.

Assuming that a disciplinary panel would reject these arguments, it seems likely that it would go on to find that MacKay had breached the duty to encourage respect for the administration of justice by making such statements. But what about MacKay's positive duty to defend courts from criticism? This situation – where the client or a representative of the client has publicly expressed unsupported criticism of judges – is a special one where a lawyer may indeed attract discipline for a failure of the positive duty.

In this context, MacKay likely had a duty to caution the Prime Minister about the Office's statement and to advise the Prime Minister to retract or correct the statement.[98] If the Prime Minister refused to do so, MacKay would have had to correct the statement himself; if MacKay determined that it could not be done, there was at least the discretion, if not the duty, to withdraw and resign. If discretionary on its face, the duty to encourage respect for the administration of justice makes resignation necessary and unavoidable in the circumstances. If the Prime Minister had merely rejected MacKay's advice but gone no further, that rejection would constitute a sound basis for a "serious loss of confidence between the lawyer and the client" (specifically where "the client refuses to accept and act upon the lawyer's advice on a significant point") that would allow MacKay to withdraw and thus resign.[99] Again, while withdrawal on that basis is optional on the face of the rule itself, not mandatory, it would appear to be necessary and unavoidable to exercise that option of withdrawal to fulfil the duty to encourage respect for the administration of justice. If the Prime Minister had instead instructed MacKay to repeat or confirm the criticism of the Chief Justice, and had persisted in those instructions even after MacKay had explained that it would be unethical for MacKay to follow them, then MacKay would have been required to withdraw.[100] This is not a situation where MacKay as a lawyer could have fulfilled his obligations by withdrawing from a single matter. Moreover, the root matter (the purported appointment and the subsequent litigation) had long concluded. Even if the reprehensible attacks on the Chief Justice stemmed from that matter, the harm of those attacks was to the administration of justice generally. In other words, the attacks on the Chief Justice were so vicious and unfounded that there would have been no other alternative but resignation, especially given MacKay's personal participation in those attacks.

These duties are reinforced by the duty of the lawyer not to "assist or permit" any "dishonest or dishonourable" conduct by the client.[101]

Criticism that the lawyer knows, or should know, is factually or legally incorrect would be dishonourable, as would inappropriate criticism, particularly given that the judge cannot defend themselves against any criticism.[102]

However, if MacKay had resigned,[103] it could have plausibly been argued that there was no obligation, or even discretion, for MacKay to publicly announce the reasons for the resignation.[104] Thus, with much respect, I disagree in part with Cotter's observation that "MacKay was obliged to intervene privately and to dissent publicly from the views of the Prime Minister."[105] While I think MacKay would have been justified in dissenting publicly and should have done so, it is not clear that he had an *obligation* to do so.[106] I will return to this issue in chapter 4.

The MacKay scenario provides two important lessons about the duty to encourage respect for the administration of justice, particularly in its application to the Attorney General. First, building on the Wagner and Kimmerly incidents, the MacKay scenario does provide additional lessons about public criticism of judges. Recall that *Wagner* suggests that a lawyer must take reasonable steps to confirm that any criticism of judges is factually correct. Less clear, but presumably following from that holding, is that for that criticism to be *bona fide*,[107] a lawyer must also take reasonable steps to confirm that the criticism is legally correct. The MacKay scenario reinforces this duty to take reasonable steps to confirm that the criticism is legally correct – though MacKay clearly knew, or should have known, that his criticism was legally incorrect. The MacKay scenario more squarely suggests that a lawyer should avoid factually correct statements from which a reasonable person could infer factually or legally incorrect criticism. While *Kimmerly* suggests that the threshold for a breach should be high, at least for the Attorney General and possibly for all lawyers, the comments by MacKay and the reasonable, if not intended, interpretation of those comments are far from borderline.

The second lesson from the MacKay scenario is that a lawyer, including the Attorney General, must withdraw where a client refuses to retract, or persists in, factually or legally incorrect criticism of a judge, unless the lawyer is able to renounce such criticism themselves. This unusual situation is a rare one where the positive duty is no longer merely aspirational and, thus, a lawyer may face discipline for a breach of that positive duty. The duty to encourage respect for the administration of justice transforms what would otherwise be an optional withdrawal into a mandatory withdrawal. Where that lawyer is the Attorney General, withdrawal would appear to require resignation.

In other words, the rule on mandatory withdrawal is not exhaustive of the situations in which withdrawal is mandatory.[108] The combination of the rule on optional withdrawal and the duty to encourage respect for the administration of justice requires a lawyer to repudiate or withdraw.

4. Mere (Public) Inaction?

What about instances of apparent inaction by Attorneys General? These situations are not about merely refraining from attacking the judiciary but, instead, about what an Attorney General should (and must) do to defend the judiciary against attacks by others – particularly other members of the Cabinet. These circumstances potentially present a much more difficult situation for the Attorney General. When a Premier or another minister makes inappropriate criticisms of a specific judge or of judges generally, does the Attorney General have a duty to denounce that criticism publicly, or to merely take steps internally to persuade that person to apologize for (or at least "clarify") those remarks? What if the person nonetheless refuses to do so, despite the efforts of the Attorney General? The contrasting scenarios of Ken Rostad, Ron Basford, and Rob Nicholson reinforce and contour the lesson about resignation and denunciation from the MacKay scenario discussed in the previous Part. Similarly, the examples of Doug Downey and Geoff Plant demonstrate what an Attorney General should do when a Premier's comments implicitly or explicitly attack judges and threaten judicial independence and, in so doing, approach the boundaries of appropriate criticism.

Ken Rostad (Alberta)

Ken Rostad was Attorney General for Alberta in 1994 when Premier Ralph Klein made some controversial remarks about judges. The incident and its fallout became part of the basis of motions for stays of criminal charges in *R v. Campbell*, grounded in the *Charter* right to "an independent and impartial tribunal."[109] An Alberta provincial court judge had refused to sit after learning of proposed pay cuts for judges.[110] One might argue that such action warranted a respectful but firm response from the Attorney General.[111] However, that is not what followed. Instead, Alberta Premier Ralph Klein stated in an interview that "[w]hoever appoints should be able to un-appoint. ... It seems to me if we have the power to hire, then we ought to have the power to fire."[112]

When the issue arose in the legislative assembly of Alberta, Klein acknowledged that there was a process required to remove a provincial court judge:

> There is no doubt about it: we hire judges. There is no doubt about it: we hire Provincial Court judges. As a matter of fact, for the last two to be hired, I recall quite clearly signing the order-in-council along with the Lieutenant Governor. There is a process, yes. And I stand to be corrected. To fire a Provincial Court judge also involves an OC, but there is a procedure that involves, I believe, the Judicial Council and the chief judge, I will have the hon. Justice minister supplement as to what that procedure is.[113]

Rostad then clearly affirmed the importance of, and the government's respect for, judicial independence: "there's no doubt that the Constitution sets out that the judiciary is an independent body, and in fact our democracy is predicated on that. I can affirm that the government of Alberta thinks that the judicial independence concept is paramount."[114]

However, the further question asking Rostad to denounce Klein's original comments – "Mr. Speaker, will the Minister of Justice agree that the comments made by the Premier went way too far – way too far – because they became a threat, a threat to the judiciary that is completely improper?" – was rejected by the Speaker.[115] There is thus no way to know what Rostad's answer would have been. Immediately thereafter, Klein, upon being asked whether "he made a big mistake in threatening the court,"[116] emphasized "I want to make this quite clear: I would never interfere in the conduct of an officer of the court and the administration of justice, and no one in this caucus would," but again repeated that where a judge refused to work, "I think that there is something fundamentally wrong with that."[117] The next day, after a similar question was posed to the Deputy Premier, Rostad emphasized that "[w]e have made it emphatically clear that this government thinks the paramount thing is judicial independence, and we stand behind that. ... [T]he Premier's comments of yesterday were very clear and were not in error."[118]

While Klein refused to apologize,[119] he did subsequently send the Chief Justice of the Provincial Court a letter of "clarification" claiming that his comments had been "misinterpreted":

> Dear Chief Judge Wachowich:
> I am writing this to you as the Chief Judge of the Province of Alberta
> in response to your request to clarify my Government's position on the
> issue of the independence of the judiciary. I have always respected and
> will continue to respect that independence. It is unfortunate that certain

comments I made concerning a Judge have been misinterpreted to suggest otherwise.

More particularly, I am well aware of the Provincial Court Judges Act and the process set out in it for issues involving judicial conduct. I have no intention or desire to interfere with that process. I accept that it properly provides for judicial independence including security of tenure which keeps Judges secure against interference by the executive in any manner other than as set out in the Act.

Let me assure you that nothing I said was intended to in any way impinge on the judicial independence of the Provincial Court. I have great respect for the Judges of the Provincial Court. I have no doubt that everyone attending before the Provincial Court will receive a full and fair hearing by it as an independent and impartial tribunal.

I hope this letter will set this matter straight and end any controversy.[120]

Klein refused to make the letter public, however.[121] This refusal represented a lost opportunity to mitigate the damage done to the public's respect for the administration of justice.

While the reasons in *Campbell* make no mention of Rostad other than quoting his remarks in the legislative assembly, Lamer C.J. in the *PEI Judges Reference* did mention Klein's statements:

I have decided not to comment on the remarks made by Premier Klein in the time period following the implementation of the salary reduction in Alberta, except to say that they were unfortunate and reflect a misunderstanding of the theory and practice of judicial independence in Canada. ... I note, and am comforted by the fact, that Premier Klein effectively distanced himself from those remarks later on in a letter he sent to Chief Judge Wachowich of the Alberta Provincial Court, in which he stated that he was "well aware" of the process established to deal with judicial conduct, and that he had "no intention or desire to interfere with that process."[122]

However, Lamer C.J. made no reference to Rostad and his responsibility as Minister of Justice.

It seems obvious that one or more lawyers cautioned Klein privately about the impact of the impugned remarks, planned or advised on the form and content of the Premier's response to the question in the legislative assembly, and drafted or advised on the form and content of the clarification letter. Indeed, the letter shows at least some movement from Klein's comments in the legislative assembly. Presumably, this lawyer was Rostad, perhaps in collaboration with other lawyers from the Department of Justice. But did Rostad have a duty to go further, to denounce Klein's comments or to resign? Given Klein's written and oral "clarifications," and Rostad's own remarks, the situation was, in my view, adequately resolved. Rostad's presumable private exhortations, and his own public remarks, had had some effect and thus Rostad had fulfilled his duty to encourage respect for the administration of justice – if not emphatically, then adequately. Klein's comments appear to be the minimum necessary. Indeed, the "clarification" letter should have been made public. However, it would seem foolhardy to realistically expect anything more from Klein. A denunciation by Rostad would have been gratuitous and would have likely violated the duty of loyalty to the client. There would seem to be little, if any, reason for Rostad to resign. But what about if the Premier had refused to clarify the remarks or even persisted in similar remarks tending to threaten judicial independence? This brings me to Ron Basford.

Ron Basford (Canada)

Ron Basford was federal Minister of Justice and Attorney General in late 1975 when André Ouellet, federal Minister of Consumer and Corporate Affairs, made the following statement after the acquittal of sugar companies for anti-competitive behaviour: "I will ask Ron Basford [the Attorney General] to launch an appeal. I find this judgment completely unacceptable. I think it is a silly decision. I just cannot understand how a judge who is sane could give such a verdict. It is a complete shock and I find it a complete disgrace."[123] In response to a question in the House of Commons about this statement, the Minister further commented, "I want to say that I have full confidence in Canadian justice. It was an extremely important case. I think we had an excellent case. Perhaps we did not have a good judge, but that does not prevent me from having excellent reasons to see to justice."[124] Basford, pressed in the House of Commons to adopt or repudiate Ouellet's statement, said: "[t]he judge in question was obviously acting in accordance with his duties and authority as a judge, and in accordance with the law as he saw it. We are considering the judgment in the case very carefully to determine whether an appeal should be made or not, and a decision will be taken on the best advice we can receive."[125] After this answer, in response to the repeated question, Basford maintained the position: "I have just said the judge was acting in accordance with what he perceived the law to be and I intend to go no further."[126]

Even though Ouellet's original remarks would lead to a contempt conviction that was upheld on appeal,[127] he demonstrated little remorse.

Later, the same day as his "good judge" remarks, Ouellet gave a weak apology:

> I must say, Mr. Speaker, that I did not mean to attack a Superior Court justice personally and that I did not do so. If I have given that impression, I am sorry and I apologize. I resent the fact that the hon. member ... is trying to give to my remarks an interpretation which was not intended. I did say and I repeat that the judgment which was passed yesterday in the case of sugar surprises me, disappoints me and even dismays me. I fully trust the judiciary, as I said in answer to the hon. member's question. ... He should have paid attention to my reply. At no time did I try to cast aspersion on the judiciary.[128]

Indeed, although the Court of Appeal quashed the portion of the contempt sentence requiring an apology, one of the judges on the appeal criticized Ouellet's "half-apologies."[129] Ouellet later resigned from Cabinet while the appeal from his contempt conviction was before the courts. However, there was no explicit, or even implicit, penance in Ouellet's resignation. Instead, Ouellet expressed concern about his own rights.[130]

There is of course no way to know whether Basford cautioned Ouellet privately, although, if he did, those efforts would appear to have been largely unsuccessful. Could – and should – Basford have clearly and emphatically denounced Ouellet's attack? Given Ouellet's apparent intransigence, should Basford have resigned? What steps, short of resignation, would have been sufficient to encourage respect for the administration of justice by defending the judiciary against Ouellet's criticism?

In my view, Basford's duty as a lawyer likely required him to convince Ouellet – or, ideally, the Prime Minister – to fully apologize and reinforce support and respect for the independent judiciary, or to do so personally, as had Rostad in Alberta. Thus, the Rostad context is distinguishable. If Basford indeed made such efforts, Ouellet and the Prime Minister evidently refused to do so in a meaningful way. If Basford was unwilling or unable to do so himself, whether because of the duty of loyalty or other considerations, then resignation was necessary. Recall that in the face of Ouellet's second statement, Basford offered a very weak defence of the judge. Ouellet's conduct, and the refusal of the Prime Minister to impose any public consequence on Ouellet, would constitute a sound basis for optional withdrawal, as in the MacKay scenario.[131] Likewise, the duty to encourage respect for the administration of justice would require this otherwise optional withdrawal. Like MacKay, if Basford had resigned, he may have credibly argued that his duty of loyalty to the client precluded publicly disclosing the reasons for the resignation. However, it may be that the statements of a Minister, as opposed to those of a Prime Minister or Premier, are less likely to represent the official position of the Crown as the client of the Attorney General; the interests of such a mere Minister are less likely to be contiguous with the interests of the Crown as client than those of the Prime Minister.[132] Thus, Basford might have considered a public repudiation of Ouellet's statement to be more consistent with the duty of loyalty to the Crown as a client than MacKay might have considered a public repudiation of the Prime Minister's statement.

Would it be possible for an Attorney General to do less than Basford or for a Minister to do less than Ouellet? Unfortunately, yes. This brings me to Rob Nicholson.

Rob Nicholson (Canada)

In February 2011, then-federal Minister of Citizenship, Immigration and Multiculturalism, Jason Kenney, gave an unprecedented speech. Kenney harshly criticized the Federal Court and the Federal Court of Appeal for interference in immigration matters, which criticism Kenney bizarrely framed as being "in the spirit of constructive dialogue between the legislative branch and the judiciary":

> [I]t strikes me as a good time to take a deeper look at a recurring challenge to any attempt to reform Canada's immigration system, which is how the Federal Court interprets the laws that Parliament has passed. And this is where I have some real concerns. … [E]ven the best efforts to reform our immigration system are not sufficient if they are not supported by the courts. … [P]roblems like this are too frequently created by judges who indulge in intrusive and heavy-handed review of decision making by the designated quasi-judicial decision makers in our system. … Cases in which, seemingly on a whim, or perhaps in a fit of misguided magnanimity, a judge overturns the careful decisions of multiple levels of diligent, highly trained public servants, tribunals, and even other judges. I believe most Canadians share my concern about such decisions. And I fear that such decisions do serious harm to the overall immigration system and prevent it from doing more good for deserving immigrants. And they undermine public confidence in the government's ability to enforce our laws as passed by Parliament, and therefore in the entire system.[133]

While the focus of the remarks was the Federal Court and the Federal Court of Appeal, Kenney also criticized sentencing decisions in criminal cases in his speech.

A few days later, the federal Minister of Justice was called upon in the House of Commons to defend the judiciary against Kenney's criticism – with specific reference to the duty of the Minister of Justice "to preserve the integrity of our legal system."[134] Instead of the Minister of Justice or a parliamentary assistant answering the question, Kenney responded by accusing the opposition Liberals of not wanting to deport "foreign criminals."[135]

Kenney's speech was widely criticized, though the criticism focused on Kenney and not on Nicholson.[136] However, when asked about the criticism of the speech by the Canadian Bar Association – "[y]our public criticism of judges who follow the law but not the government's political agenda is an affront to our democracy and freedoms" – Kenney's office remained unrepentant: "[i]n fact, [Kenney] looks forward to giving more such speeches in the months ahead."[137] Indeed, given that Kenney's spokesperson would later comment that "the minister does not have less speech rights than someone else,"[138] it seems quite clear that Kenney had resisted any cautions Nicholson might have expressed.

As with Basford and Ouellet, there is of course no way to know whether Nicholson cautioned Kenney privately, although if so, those efforts would also appear to have been unsuccessful. And as with Basford and Ouellet, Nicholson's duty as a lawyer likely required convincing Kenney – or, ideally, the Prime Minister – to affirm the government's confidence in the judiciary and its commitment to judicial independence, to do so personally, or to resign. Whereas Ouellet gave a weak apology, Kenney gave none at all, making the obligations on Nicholson clearer than those on Basford and, thus, making Nicholson's failure even more serious than that of Basford.

A Counterpoint? Adequacy: Doug Downey (Ontario)

What about the more recent events in Ontario, where Premier Doug Ford openly (and, indeed, adamantly) admitted his intent to appoint "like-minded judges" and justices of the peace who would be tough on crime?[139] Despite superficial similarities, this situation was fundamentally different from that of Rostad in Alberta or Nicholson federally. While Ford was clear about his goals in selecting judges, he – whether by luck or on the advice of Attorney General Doug Downey – did not cross a line by explicitly pressuring existing judges to rule in a certain way (as had Kenney) or appearing to question their security of tenure (as had Klein). Nonetheless, those comments could easily be interpreted as a criticism of serving judges for being soft on crime. To his credit, Downey himself did clearly and strongly emphasize that once judges are appointed, they are fully independent:

> There sure is a lot of finger-wagging about how the system works or should work, Mr. Speaker. But there's a fundamental misunderstanding of what judicial independence is. It's not appointing the judges. They are not to be appointing their own. We are democratically elected to select judges, and then they have their independence. …
>
> Now, the opposition and some in the bar are throwing around judicial independence – as if this has anything to do with judicial independence. …
>
> When you appoint a judge, it's very much like pulling back the arrow, and when you let go of the arrow you have no control anymore; it goes where it goes. When that judge puts on that sash, they have their independence. There is no kowtowing to a government of any stripe, and I can tell you that any lawyer who operates in the courts will verify that. If you think that a judge is kowtowing to any party – the one that appointed them that's not in power now or the one that is in power – that just does not happen. That is a fallacy.[140]

It would, of course, have been preferable if this recognition had come from Ford himself and in his original remarks or his many re-affirmations of those remarks. However, that seems beyond unlikely. Moreover, Downey may well have privately (but unsuccessfully) advised Ford to do so. This scenario, thus, demonstrates an acceptable response by the Attorney General to these kinds of circumstances. That is not to say that Downey's response was *ideal*, merely that it was adequate.

An Ideal Response: Geoff Plant (British Columbia)

In contrast, an example of an ideal response comes from Geoff Plant, who was Attorney General of British Columbia when Premier Gordon Campbell made inappropriate remarks about a judge's bail decision. Plant not only had a conversation with the Premier, but he also disclosed that conversation and his view of the remarks to the media with great candour: "His initial comments were certainly close to the line. … I can tell you that it gave me enough of a concern that I made sure we had a conversation."[141] Plant also emphasized the importance of respectful criticism of judges, both generally ("I think that reasonable people can disagree reasonably about judicial decisions. … The trick is to do it in a way that makes sure that you recognize that judges are entitled to be respected – and entitled to be respected whether they are right or wrong") and by the Premier ("Premiers are entitled to speak about public policy issues that are important, even when those issues arise in the context of judicial decisions. ... Generally speaking, premiers should not criticize judges or the decisions they make").[142]

Plant thus shows that the *ideal* response by an Attorney General – public repudiation, though gentle, of a Premier's comments – is not impossible, though it might be unlikely and unrealistic to the point of being dismissed as romantic. Idealism aside, adequacy is not necessarily mediocrity. Nonetheless, there should be a high standard and high public expectations of an Attorney General in such a situation.

5. Discussion and Conclusions

The duty to encourage respect for the administration of justice is a complex one, particularly in its application to the Attorney General. On the one hand, the duty is open-ended and potentially vast. On the other hand, the dual nature of the duty – both positive and negative – means that the duty may be both grounds for discipline and a defence against discipline. Unlikely though it seems that any lawyer, even the Attorney General, would be disciplined for a failure to meet the positive duty, that positive duty may provide a defence for a purported violation of the negative duty.

The case studies I have considered in this chapter provide important lessons about the duty to encourage respect for the administration of justice in its application to Attorneys General, even if those lessons are not particularly surprising. The lesson from *Wagner* is that a lawyer must take reasonable steps in the circumstances to confirm the factual accuracy of any criticism of the judiciary. Based on *Kimmerly*, I suggest that compliance with the duty requires careful calibration by the lawyer, given that the duty is a complex one that encourages appropriate criticism where warranted while, at the same time, prohibiting problematic criticism. As an analytical matter, the necessary balancing exercise should be internal to the duty itself, instead of balancing the duty against the other roles or responsibilities of the lawyer. Law societies should recognize the complexity of that determination by allowing reasonable latitude for public criticism of judges. I suggest that, even accepting such reasonable latitude, some conduct – such as that of Peter MacKay – is so problematic as to constitute a clear breach that balancing must not be allowed to permit.

Two lessons come from the MacKay scenario. I suggest that all lawyers, including Attorneys General, must take reasonable steps in the circumstances to confirm not only the factual accuracy of any criticism of the judiciary, but also its legal accuracy in order for that criticism to be *bona fide* as required by the rules of professional conduct.[143] Moreover, a lawyer's conduct should be judged purposively and by the reasonable interpretation of the public – a carefully worded statement that does not violate the duty on its face, but that is a breach by its clearly understood meaning, remains a breach.

Finally, the MacKay, Rostad, Basford, Nicholson, Downey, and Plant scenarios demonstrate the impact of the lawyer's duty to encourage respect for the administration of justice when a client inappropriately criticizes the judiciary. The lawyer must make good-faith efforts to urge the client to discontinue and apologize for such criticism. If those efforts are unsuccessful, the lawyer must repudiate that criticism themselves or, if they are unable to do so because of the duty of loyalty, withdraw. For an Attorney General, such withdrawal in turn likely leads to resignation.

As I will return to in chapter 8, I emphasize in closing that whether any specific lawyer – Attorney General or otherwise – faces professional discipline in any specific case is not necessarily an accurate measure or reflection of whether the conduct in question was wrongful. The mere fact that MacKay was not disciplined for his abhorrent attack on the Chief Justice does not mean that other lawyers, including but not limited to Attorneys General, cannot and should not learn from this wrongdoing and thus avoid such wrongdoing themselves. The same goes for Nicholson's sins of omission.

Neither should the conduct of Wagner or Kimmerly be emulated because they were not successfully disciplined. From a practical perspective, I have elsewhere criticized both ministerial immunity as applied in *Wagner* and the balancing approach to the rule on lawyers in public office as applied in *Kimmerly*.[144] From a principled perspective, there is nothing prudent or honourable about taking a risk or calling a law society's bluff. I would be mortified if any lawyer were to interpret the absence of any discernable professional consequences (or political consequences, for that matter) for MacKay's conduct, or even that of Wagner or Kimmerly, as permission to do the same, or worse, themselves. That would be a cynical and dangerous inference to draw, especially for Attorneys General. Indeed, this is yet another context in which the oft-repeated observation of John Ll. J. Edwards holds true: the most important bulwark against misconduct, like that by MacKay, is the "strength of character, personal integrity, and strength of commitment" of the Attorney General.[145] These duties are, at their root, a matter of honour, but one which the rules of professional conduct convert into a regulatory and legal imperative.[146]

This chapter demonstrates that the duty to encourage respect for the administration of justice is full of complexity in its application to the Attorney General. While this duty applies to the private and public conduct of all lawyers, the visibility of the Attorney General, and the resultingly powerful ability to encourage or discourage respect for the administration of justice, means that this duty is most important in its application to the Attorney General. In my view, the Attorney General, in respect of this duty – like all professional duties of lawyers – should be held to the same standard as all other lawyers. The suggestions by the courts in *Wagner* and the Law Society in *Kimmerly* that this professional duty must be balanced against the duties of office of the Attorney General, or even that this duty is trumped by the duties of that office, are problematic insofar as they create a lower standard for the Attorney General than for all other lawyers. Indeed, as per the Barreau in *Wagner*, the government resources available to the Attorney General may require them to make more efforts than other lawyers to confirm the basis of any criticism of the judiciary before that criticism is made.

While the duty of the Attorney General to defend the judiciary may have a constitutional basis, albeit an imprecise one,[147] the duty of the Attorney General as a lawyer to encourage respect for the administration of justice provides a supplemental and, indeed, independent basis for that duty, particularly given my questioning of the scope and power of ministerial immunity.[148] Thus, any change – deliberate or otherwise – to the underlying constitutional basis will not change the professional duty of the Attorney General as a lawyer. Although the case studies I have explored here illustrate the political and other challenges facing the Attorney General in fulfilling their duty to encourage respect for the administration of justice, they by no means suggest that the Attorney General should be exempt from that duty. Indeed, the Attorney General should set an example for the rest of the bar. These cases do, however, reveal that that duty is a nuanced one and that the Attorney General should be given some leeway in meeting that obligation.

The temptation or pressure for an Attorney General to breach their duty to encourage respect for the administration of justice with undue and inappropriate criticism of the judiciary is multiplied when the Attorney General is cross-appointed to another portfolio. The legal ethics issues caused by such a cross-appointment are the subject of chapter 3.

3 Complexity: The Cross-Appointed Attorney General[1]

Introduction

In this chapter, I analyse the unique case study of Quebec Premier and Attorney General Maurice Duplessis to demonstrate and analyse the tensions that occur when the Attorney General is cross-appointed to another portfolio, particularly that of Premier.

From time to time, a Premier or Prime Minister appoints themselves as Attorney General.[2] There is currently no legal impediment against such an appointment, given the undisplaced prerogative power to appoint the Cabinet.[3] I argue that this dual portfolio is inherently and incurably problematic from the perspective of legal ethics and professionalism and that it should be avoided and, indeed, prohibited. While the special and unique role of the Attorney General as Chief Law Officer of the Crown is duly recognized in the Canadian case law and legal literature,[4] this particular situation – Attorneys General with dual portfolios and specifically this dual portfolio – has not yet been squarely addressed. Issues similar in kind, though lesser in severity, will occur any time the Attorney General holds a second portfolio. I focus on the Attorney General who is also Premier because the issues are clearest, and the problems most intractable, in this context.[5]

While it is now rare for a Premier to serve simultaneously as Attorney General,[6] such a situation used to be more common – although it appears to have been uniquely Canadian.[7] For example, three of the four post-Confederation Premiers of Ontario did so.[8] Paul Romney characterizes this phenomenon as a "logical consequenc[e] of the province's political history and social structure."[9] More recently, during the constitutional negotiations of the early 1960s, the Premiers of New Brunswick and Alberta were also Attorneys General of their respective provinces.[10]

The springboard for my analysis is *Roncarelli v. Duplessis*,[11] by far the best-known case concerning the legality of the actions of such a Premier and Attorney General. *Roncarelli* is uniquely useful in the context of legal ethics and professionalism, as in the context of public law,[12] because Premier and Attorney General Maurice Duplessis was brazen in his actions and shockingly transparent about his motivations and considerations. The kinds of issues I raise in my analysis have almost certainly arisen for other Premiers who were also Attorneys General but remained hidden from public view and notoriety. It is the transparency in *Roncarelli* that not only makes the relevant issues concrete but brings them into stark relief.

The basic facts of *Roncarelli* are straightforward. Québec Premier and Attorney General Maurice Duplessis, in overt retaliation against Mr. Roncarelli for providing bail for many Jehovah's Witnesses – a group vilified by the Premier – ordered the Liquor Commission to revoke (or confirmed its decision to revoke) the liquor licence for Roncarelli's restaurant.[13] Roncarelli's action against Duplessis personally for damages was eventually successful.[14] What makes the case unusual is that it was unnecessary to speculate about Duplessis's purpose and motivation in revoking the liquor licence, as he was remarkably frank.[15]

At the outset, I acknowledge that Premier Duplessis likely would have taken the same actions even if he had not also been Attorney General. He could have chosen a pliant, or at least sympathetic, Attorney General, or one that agreed that his actions were appropriate. He could have rejected the advice of the Attorney General – if he even sought that advice before acting – or even chosen a new Attorney General who would give him legal cover. As Geneviève Cartier puts it, Duplessis's "concept of power was essentially based on the legitimacy of any action designed to preserve the culture and distinctiveness of the French Canadian nation, using audacious means at times, often bordering on disdain for public institutions."[16] Duplessis biographer Pierre Laporte was more dramatic: "Duplessis dominated his Ministers in every respect. ... That one party member instead of another should hold a portfolio had little import. For Duplessis was the beginning and the end of everything. On certain questions that came under his authority he did not even consult them."[17] In this context, a separate Attorney General would presumably have had little impact on Duplessis's decision-making. On the other hand, there is the romantic and idealistic possibility that a principled Attorney General would have advised against Duplessis's course of action, or even resigned in protest.[18]

I also recognize that, from both a political science and an administrative law perspective, Duplessis's dual role *per se* represented a concentration of power in one individual. While that important issue is essential context for my analysis, my argument is that it is, instead, the concentration of *functions* in one person that is problematic from the perspective of legal ethics and professionalism. The same person is both the legal advisor of the client and the ultimate decision-maker for the client.

This chapter is organized in four parts. In part 1, I canvass the reasons in *Roncarelli* and the treatment of the case in the legal literature, primarily to demonstrate that the judges of the Supreme Court, subsequent commentators, and even Duplessis himself appeared to view his roles as Premier and Attorney General as fused. In part 2, I examine the professional and statutory duties of the Attorney General and demonstrate how being Premier confounds those duties. Then, in part 3, I consider whether Duplessis's actions could – and should – have attracted professional discipline at the time, and whether similar actions might attract professional discipline today. Finally, in part 4, I illustrate other legal and practical consequences of being both Premier and Attorney General. I go on to reflect on the implications of my analysis, ultimately concluding that a lawyer cannot satisfy their professional obligations when acting as both Premier and Attorney General. These problems are similar in kind, but lesser in degree, when the Attorney General holds a second portfolio other than Premier.

Before continuing, I acknowledge that there may obviously be apparent benefits for the Premier to also be Attorney General. For example, a Premier may decide that the role of Attorney General is vital to fulfilling their policy agenda and absolute coordination between the two roles is desirable. A related potential benefit – at least to the Premier – and a rationale attributed to Duplessis by biographer Marguerite Paulin is to "consolidat[e] power."[19] Another reason applies if legal issues and inter-provincial negotiations loom, as during times of constitutional negotiations.[20] In such times, it may be strategically important for the Premier and Attorney General to indisputably speak with one voice. Another possibility, as when a Premier takes on *any* dual portfolio, is the desire to indicate to the public the importance of that other portfolio.[21]

These benefits, however, do not displace the harm: a Premier who is also Attorney General necessarily subordinates – and, indeed, sacrifices – their professional obligations as a lawyer and thus violates the law of lawyering. This is not to say that the possibility of regulatory and disciplinary consequences is the overriding reason, or even a main reason, that a lawyer should comply with their professional obligations. Neither is the ability of a lawyer to return to practice after concluding their life in politics. If nothing else, one might hope that the choice to knowingly violate the law could have political ramifications. Nonetheless, I maintain the idealistic hope that membership in a profession brings with it, at least sometimes, a commitment to meet the obligations that go along with that membership, in letter if not in spirit.[22]

Indeed, it is for this very reason – this temptation – that this cautionary tale remains relevant and necessary today, even though no Premier has succumbed to this temptation for decades. Disuse, whether because of deliberate forbearance or because of chance, does nothing to prevent it from happening tomorrow. For the next Premier who asks why they should not make themselves Attorney General and is not persuaded merely because the practice has been largely abandoned in recent years, this chapter provides a substantive and principled answer, even if not a definitive one.

One final note is necessary before I begin my analysis. It can be dangerous, if not unfair, to judge lawyers (and others) in hindsight by present standards. My twin goals in this chapter are, first, to demonstrate why the dual role of Premier and Attorney General was necessarily and incurably problematic at the time of the events in *Roncarelli* and, second, why it remains so today. While the standards of the legal profession are more explicit and detailed now than they were then, at a fundamental level, they remain largely the same. I will identify, where appropriate, not only the modern rules of professional conduct, as set out in the *Model Code* of the Federation of Law Societies of Canada and the Québec *Code of Professional Conduct of Lawyers*,[23] but also the rules applicable at the time of the events giving rise to the litigation in *Roncarelli*, as set out in the 1939 by-laws of the Barreau de Québec.[24] While limited, the behaviours prohibited by these by-laws are explicitly not exhaustive.[25] I will also refer to relevant canons from the 1920 *Canons of Legal Ethics* of the Canadian Bar Association.[26] One major point of contrast, however, is competence – a matter that was not regulated by Canadian law societies at the time of the events in *Roncarelli* but is ostensibly regulated now. As Amy Salyzyn explains, until the 1970s, it was unclear if competence was a basis for lawyer discipline.[27] Thus, my conclusions on Duplessis's competence should be read in this historical context.

1. *Roncarelli v. Duplessis*: Duplessis as Both Premier and Attorney General

The reasons in *Roncarelli*, including references to Duplessis's own public statements, reveal that Duplessis himself blurred or fused the two roles of Premier and Attorney General, as well as the sets of powers accompanying those two roles. In his testimony, Duplessis sometimes stated that he was acting in his role as Prime Minister and Attorney General, while at other times stating that he was acting in his role as Attorney General. For example, he said both that "je considère que c'est mon devoir comme Procureur Général et comme Premier Ministre en conscience dans l'exercice de mes fonctions officielles et pour remplir le mandat que le peuple m'avait confié et qu'il m'a renouvelé avec une immense majorité" ["I consider that it is my duty as both Premier and as the Attorney General in conscientiously carrying out my official functions and to fulfil the mandate given to me by the people, and which they renewed with a large majority"] and that he had given the order "moi-même, à titre de Procureur Général" ["myself, by virtue of my role as Attorney General"].[28]

Some of the judges also appeared to fuse the roles. For example, Rand J. wrote that "it appears that the action taken by the ... general manager and sole member of the [Liquor] Commission was dictated by Mr. Duplessis as Attorney-General and Prime Minister of the province."[29] In contrast, Taschereau J., writing in dissent, held that "c'est le Procurer Général, agissant dans l'exercice de ses fonctions, qui a été requis de donner ses directives à une branche gouvernementale dont il est l'aviseur" ["It is the Attorney General, carrying out his official functions, who is empowered to give directions to a branch of the government with respect to which he is an advisor"].[30]

The Supreme Court of Canada, in referring back to *Roncarelli*, sometimes recognizes Duplessis's dual role. For example, in the foundational case of *Nelles v. Ontario*, McIntyre J. noted that "Duplessis in the *Roncarelli* case purported to act not only as the Premier of Quebec but also as the Attorney General."[31] In other cases, perhaps revealingly, the Court refers only to his role as Attorney General, as did LeBel J. for the Court in *McCullock Finney c Barreau (Québec)*.[32]

The plentiful and rich literature on *Roncarelli* tends to blur, or at least de-emphasize, Duplessis's dual roles as Premier and Attorney General. For example, in his 1974 discussion of judicial review, Peter Hogg refers to Duplessis as merely the Premier and does not mention that he was also the Attorney General.[33] One of the few commentators who specifically and explicitly acknowledges the ways in which that dual role was problematic is Mary Liston.[34] Liston does so, albeit in passing, in the midst of an analysis of arbitrariness in the administrative law context:

> [T]he effects of his [Duplessis's] arbitrary actions were further exacerbated by the overlapping sources of power stemming from his two executive functions: the political role of prime minister and the advisory legal role of Attorney General. This blending of functions recalls Montesquieu's

most famous institutional remedy for the risks of arbitrariness: to separate and distribute power among several institutions and corresponding
persons so that no institution or official possesses an effective monopoly
or stranglehold.[35]

Liston also appears to be alone in explicitly noting that Duplessis's
actions, and the consequences of those actions, were "a disturbing
result from a man trained as a lawyer."[36]

2. Inherent Problems for the Professional and
Statutory Duties of the Attorney General

The dual role of Attorney General and Premier poses problems for
the professional duties of all lawyers and the statutory duty unique
to the Attorney General. As I will demonstrate, the core problem is
that the Attorney General must candidly advise themselves as Premier, advice which may well include dissuading themselves from an
unlawful course of action. They must also distinguish their actions
and decisions in both roles – not only to others but even in their own
mind – and possibly even resign as Attorney General because of their
own decisions as Premier. They must also resist the temptation to
prioritize their own personal and political interests as Premier, and
the instructions they as Premier give themselves as Attorney General,
over their duties to the Crown as the client.

To understand why the same person should not be both Attorney
General and Premier, recall from chapter 1 that the Attorney General
shares the professional duties of all lawyers but is also burdened with a
unique duty imposed by statute.

Like all lawyers, the Attorney General owes the client a duty of
loyalty, which includes component duties of candour, commitment,
confidentiality, and avoidance of conflicts,[37] as well as a duty of competence.[38] Recall that, under the rules of professional conduct, a lawyer in
public office is purportedly held to the same standards as a lawyer in
private practice.[39]

Alone among lawyers, the Attorney General has a positive duty to
see that their client – the government – acts lawfully.[40] This statutory
duty is far from a recent creation. Not only did this duty exist at the time
of the events in *Roncarelli*;[41] counsel for Duplessis indeed relied on this
duty, among others, to characterize his actions as being "justifiable as
having been done in good faith in the exercise of his official function as
Attorney-General and Prime Minister."[42] At the same time, the related
concept of the Attorney General as "Guardian of the Rule of Law"[43]

is a more recently articulated and recognized one to which, arguably, Duplessis should not be retroactively held.

An Attorney General who is also Premier will necessarily – and unavoidably – have difficulties fulfilling these professional duties and this statutory duty because they are one person performing both roles simultaneously. The six key professional duties are candour, independence from the client, protection of the interests of the organizational client, maintenance of the distinction between the lawyer role and the non-lawyer role, withdrawal, and competence. In the specific context of an Attorney General who is also Premier, many of these duties and the barriers to fulfilling them are closely intertwined. While it is critical to remember that the client is the Crown, not the Premier themselves,[44] the Premier nonetheless remains the person from whom the Attorney General ultimately takes instructions.

Among the professional duties of all lawyers, that most in peril when the Premier is their own Attorney General would seem to be the duty of candour – closely connected with the unique statutory duty to see that public affairs are conducted lawfully. Can a Premier truly be candid with themselves (as the ultimate representative of the client the Crown) that their proposed course of action is unlawful? Indeed, the rules of professional conduct emphasize that candour may require "firmness" that "will not please the client":

> Occasionally, a lawyer must be firm with a client. Firmness, without rudeness, is not a violation of the rule. In communicating with the client, the lawyer may disagree with the client's perspective, or may have concerns about the client's position on a matter, and may give advice that will not please the client. This may legitimately require firm and animated discussion with the client.[45]

It seems unlikely that an Attorney General as lawyer can be adequately firm and displeasing in "animated discussion" with themselves as Premier as required by this rule.[46] For example, if nothing else, can the Attorney General adequately caution themselves as Premier against making politically expedient, but legally problematic, public statements, such as those criticisms of judges discussed in chapter 2?[47] It seems unlikely.

A second professional duty that is imperilled is the duty to maintain independence from the client. It is worth emphasizing that an Attorney General and Premier may be particularly tempted to fulfil, and even exceed, their professional duties to the Crown as the organizational client at the expense of their duties to the administration of justice. The rules of professional conduct explicitly recognize that a lawyer who concurrently serves in a non-legal role must carefully protect their "integrity" and "independence."[48] Can an Attorney General avoid being the mouthpiece of the client when they share a single mouth with the Premier as the organizational client's non-legal mouthpiece?[49] Again, that seems unlikely – if not impossible. Indeed, the danger of client capture for in-house or government lawyers seems strongest here, in a similar way as if the CEO of an organization was also its chief legal counsel. Recall, however, that such a corporate officer is fundamentally different from a Premier who is Attorney General, given that the corporate officer lacks the Attorney General's unique positive duty to ensure lawfulness. It seems unlikely that the Premier can meaningfully restrain themselves from that course of action.

Similarly, a third professional duty that is necessarily problematic is the duty to act in the best interests of the organizational client, that is, the Crown. Recall that where a lawyer represents an organizational client, they must act in the best interests of the organization and not the person from whom they take instructions.[50] A Premier acting as Attorney General may be tempted to favour their own personal and political interests – both their personal political prospects and their vision for the province – over the legal interests of the government. Indeed, there is potential for a conflict of interest for a lawyer who holds both roles simultaneously.[51] While I recognize that lawyers can act despite a conflict of interest if the client gives "express," "informed," and "voluntary" consent,[52] given the Premier's unfettered (and undisplaced) prerogative discretion to choose their Cabinet, including the Attorney General,[53] it seems unrealistic that the Premier would seek such consent or that Cabinet would deny it if sought.

A related fourth concern is whether a person acting simultaneously as Premier and Attorney General can maintain the distinction between the two roles. As I mentioned in chapter 1, the rules of professional conduct also caution that "[a] lawyer must not carry on, manage or be involved in any outside interest in such a way that makes it difficult to distinguish in which capacity the lawyer is acting in a particular transaction."[54] Where the Premier is Attorney General, it may not be clear – for example, to members of their Cabinet or to bureaucrats – in which capacity they are instructing them. Are their statements policy advice (or direction) or legal advice? Ministers and others might reasonably assume that their instructions are both orders from the Premier and an assurance from the Attorney General that such orders are lawful. As I will return to below, aside from any regulatory consequences for the lawyer, uncertainty over which role is being exercised can jeopardize the client's interests via the applicability of the legal protection of solicitor-client privilege.[55]

A related fifth professional duty is the duty to withdraw. A Premier and Attorney General is at heightened risk of violating the lawyer's duty to withdraw when "a client persists in instructing the lawyer to act contrary to professional ethics," which I discussed in chapter 1 and to which I will return in chapter 4.[56] Again, here the Premier is the person who provides instructions as the ultimate representative of the organizational client. The risks would be either that the Attorney General would not recognize that they as Premier were instructing themselves to violate their professional obligations or that they would be unwilling to act on that recognition. Theoretically, a Premier who was also Attorney General could resign as Attorney General while remaining Premier – but such an incredible scenario would unavoidably generate speculation about the reason for resignation and cast doubt on their actions and decisions as Premier.

As a more practical matter, the roles of Premier and of Attorney General are demanding ones. It is legitimate to question whether one person can adequately fulfil both roles simultaneously and, more specifically, maintain their competence as a lawyer. Indeed, while this may first appear to be a practical issue instead of an ethical issue, it is the substantial risk of diminished competence that is the inflection point at which the practical issue transforms into an ethical issue. On one level, this is an issue of whether two major portfolios can be adequately managed by one person. Although increased delegation may appear to make the dual role manageable, there are limits to which a lawyer can delegate their professional functions and responsibilities.[57] More particularly, an Attorney General who is also Premier may not be able to remain competent as a lawyer, and provide competent and adequate service to the client, given the other demands on their time. As I mentioned in chapter 1, the rules of professional conduct caution against such dual roles: "A lawyer who engages in another profession, business or occupation concurrently with the practice of law must not allow such outside interest to jeopardize the lawyer's professional integrity, independence or competence."[58] To the extent that such a Premier and Attorney General purports to fulfil their responsibilities as chief law officer of the Crown through delegation, such success is illusory and is, in reality, an abdication of their role.[59] The more any lawyer delegates, and the less time they personally dedicate to their practice, the more risk they incur. This is not to suggest that some Attorneys General who are *not* Premiers do not also function as figureheads or rubber stamps – merely that the likelihood of this happening increases exponentially when that Attorney General is also Premier, just as the risks increase and the likelihood of avoiding negative outcomes decreases.

For these reasons, a Premier who appoints themselves Attorney General is at a special risk of contravening not only their professional duties as a lawyer, but also their unique statutory duty as Attorney General.

I turn next to the potential role of discipline, given that several of these rules may have been violated on the facts of *Roncarelli*. In particular, I use the facts to demonstrate that where a Premier who is also Attorney General acts in a way that is clearly unlawful, they will either be committing professional misconduct (by violating their duties of competence or of candour in their capacity as Attorney General) or conduct unbecoming (by acting contrary to the legal advice given by themselves as Attorney General to themselves as Premier).

3. The Discipline Question

What was the appropriate role of the Barreau as regulator in the *Roncarelli* saga? While discipline is only one function of law societies, just as disciplinary proceedings are only one regulatory tool to fulfil their mandate, my focus here is to examine whether Duplessis could and should have been disciplined – both at the time and if similar facts occurred now. Before doing so, I emphasize that discipline is not the exhaustive purpose of the rules of professional conduct. Lawyers should fulfil their duties and comply with the rules in letter and in spirit,[60] and not solely to avoid investigation and discipline from their regulators. While the rules of professional conduct themselves acknowledge that some of their imperatives are "aspirational,"[61] that acknowledgment is not an excuse for non-compliance. The rules engaged where a Premier is also Attorney General are anything but aspirational.

I recognize at the outset that, given Duplessis's political power, it seems impossible that the Barreau would even have seriously considered pursuing disciplinary action against him.[62] If the situation were to occur today, I hope and expect that the result might be different. But, disregarding the "would" question, I will focus instead on the "could" and "should" questions.

The first "could" question is whether Duplessis's actions were in violation of his professional duties as a lawyer, constituting either professional misconduct or conduct unbecoming. I first consider professional misconduct, which requires "a marked departure from the conduct expected of lawyers."[63] Duplessis could potentially have violated any of the rules I discussed in the previous part, which I will not repeat here. However, given how he appeared to fuse his roles and powers as Premier and Attorney General,[64] the rules about outside interests and conflicts of interest would appear to be particularly relevant on the facts. Although the duty of candour seems most relevant in the general situation of a Premier who is also Attorney General, on the specific facts of *Roncarelli*, the duty of competence seems equally relevant – with the caveat above that competence may not have been an appropriate inquiry for the Barreau at the time.[65] To the extent that *Roncarelli* arguably changed the state of the law, or established new law, on arbitrariness and discretion, it would seem unwise and unfair to allege that Duplessis, insofar as he advised himself or the Commissioner that the revocation was lawful, failed to fulfil his duty of competence.

However, there are strong indications that Duplessis, as a lawyer, knew or should have known that the proposed course of action was unlawful. Rand J. made this assertion:

The office of Attorney-General traditionally and by statute carries duties that relate to advising the Executive, including here, administrative bodies, enforcing the public law and directing the administration of justice. In any decision of the statutory body in this case, he [Duplessis] had no part to play beyond giving advice on legal questions arising. In that role his action should have been limited to advice on the validity of a revocation for such a reason or purpose and *what that advice should have been does not seem to me to admit of any doubt.*[66]

Similarly, Abbott J. held that

I have no doubt ... that respondent *knew and was bound to know as Attorney-General* that neither as Premier of the province nor as Attorney-General was he authorized in law to interfere with the administration of the Quebec Liquor Commission or to give an order or an authorization to any officer of that body to exercise a discretionary authority entrusted to such officer by the statute.[67]

While Martland J. did not explicitly hold that Duplessis should have known that his actions were unlawful, he noted that Duplessis's purported power to intervene was "a very dangerous proposition and one which is *completely alien to the legal concepts applicable to the administration of public office in Quebec*, as well as in the other provinces of Canada," which suggests that a competent lawyer would and should have known that those actions were unlawful.[68]

The literature is equally emphatic in this respect. Duplessis biographer Leslie Roberts, writing in 1960 concerning Duplessis's prosecutions of Jehovah's Witnesses, observed that "he must have been fully aware that the ultimate judgment was bound to go against him. He was too good a lawyer, as were the Law Officers of the Crown who surrounded him in the Attorney-General's office, not to have known."[69] Likewise, legal historian William Kaplan echoes Roberts, at least in regard to the appeals, writing that "Duplessis was a good enough lawyer to know that he would lose this legal battle in the end."[70] Though admittedly in hindsight, Mark Aranson more recently writes that "even a cub lawyer should" have known Duplessis's conduct was unlawful.[71] On the other hand, the decision of the Supreme Court of Canada was not unanimous.

Assuming that *Roncarelli* was correctly decided[72] – and, more importantly, that the Barreau would accept that it was correctly decided or at least that the nature of Duplessis's conduct was *res judicata* and would inquire into competence – these assertions are ones that a disciplinary panel would no doubt examine closely and weigh heavily in its own determinations on professional misconduct. However, to the extent that these assertions are exaggerated or unfounded, Duplessis or a lawyer in a similar position would have a credible argument that there was no misconduct. Indeed, recall that Duplessis claimed that it was his *duty* to take the actions he did.[73] One would expect, and a court on judicial review would presumably demand, that the Barreau would consider qualified expert evidence about whether Duplessis truly should have known that the course of conduct was unlawful. If he should not have known, there would be no misconduct.

Assuming that Duplessis knew or should have known that the conduct was unlawful, it would seem that he, as Attorney General, necessarily violated either his duty of competence or his duty of candour. If he believed the course of action to be lawful, the violation would be of competence. In contrast, if he believed that the course of action was unlawful, the potential violation becomes candour. However, he could conceivably argue that, as Attorney General, he instructed himself as Premier that the course of action would be unlawful, and as Premier decided to follow that course despite that advice. Indeed, a prudent and clever lawyer in such a situation might even diarize this formalistic distinction by authoring two memos – one memo from themselves as Attorney General to themselves as Premier advising that the proposed course of action was unlawful, and another memo from themselves as Premier to themselves as Attorney General indicating that they were proceeding despite that legal advice. Such a claim could, however, merely transform his actions from potential professional misconduct into potential conduct unbecoming.

Aside from disciplinary liability for professional misconduct in his practising role as Attorney General, Duplessis potentially attracted disciplinary liability for conduct unbecoming in his role as Premier. As Gavin MacKenzie puts it, conduct unbecoming is conduct that "tend[s] to bring discredit upon the legal profession or the administration of justice."[74] For a lawyer in public office, even in a non-practising role such as Premier, to disregard advice that their proposed actions would be unlawful – especially when they as Attorney General have provided that advice to themselves as Premier – risks discrediting the legal profession. Indeed, serious unlawful acts by any lawyer, even outside practice, would appear to do so. For example, while "most conduct unbecoming complaints involve convictions for criminal offences" and, "historically, only convictions for criminal offences involving moral turpitude were considered to bring discredit upon the profession,"[75] there can be a finding of conduct unbecoming even where the lawyer was acquitted of criminal charges related to the same conduct.[76] Thus, the actions of Duplessis as Premier in *Roncarelli* could almost certainly qualify as conduct unbecoming.

Biographer Conrad Black nonetheless asserts that Duplessis was cognizant of his professional obligations, at least to the administration of justice: "Duplessis himself was very disappointed at the verdict but responded as a loyal member of the bar to the judgement of the Supreme Court.... [he] had responded unrancorously to the final judgment."[77] Thus, insofar as Black's characterization is correct – despite, for example, Cartier's characterization that Duplessis "disdai[ned] ... public institutions"[78] – and would be shared by the Barreau, Duplessis would not face additional disciplinary liability for his public reaction to the Court's decision.[79]

Insofar as "good faith is not a defence to a charge of conduct unbecoming,"[80] whether Duplessis was *truly*, as he claimed, acting in good faith would be a relevant factor for the determination of any disciplinary penalty imposed for professional misconduct or conduct unbecoming.[81] As Rand J. noted, Duplessis "felt that action [the licence revocation] to be his duty, something which his conscience demanded of him."[82] Recall also Duplessis'a testimony: "je considère que c'est mon devoir comme Procureur Général et comme Premier Ministre en conscience dans l'exercice de mes fonctions officielles et pour remplir le mandat que le peuple m'avait confié et qu'il m'a renouvelé avec une immense majorité." ["I consider that it is my duty as both the Premier and as the Attorney General in conscientiously carrying out my official functions and to fulfil the mandate given to me by the people, and which they renewed with a large majority."][83] Justice Rand nevertheless characterized the conduct as "malicious."[84] Similarly, in the 2004 case of *Finney*, LeBel J. for the Supreme Court of Canada referred to Duplessis's conduct as Attorney General as "a classic example" of "intentional fault."[85] While *Finney* was about the civil liability of the Barreau and was not a disciplinary matter, this characterization nonetheless suggests that, at least if the facts of *Roncarelli* were to occur now, a disciplinary panel would likely reject any claim of good faith as a mitigating factor.

The necessary second "could" question, however, is whether the Barreau had at the time, or would have today, jurisdiction over Duplessis. Not long after the *Roncarelli* saga, the Quebec Court of Appeal in 1967 held in *Barreau c Wagner* that the Attorney General cannot be disciplined for conduct in the exercise of their duties of office.[86] While I question that holding,[87] one would assume there is a decent chance that the same law would have been applied to Duplessis. The question would then become whether Duplessis's actions were beyond the scope of his duties, which was the position of the majority in *Roncarelli*,[88] a finding which would vitiate the immunity recognized in *Wagner*.

That brings me to the "should" question: should the Barreau have disciplined Duplessis? The starting point for answering this question is that, as Gavin MacKenzie puts it, "[t]he purposes of law society discipline proceedings are not to punish offenders and exact retribution, but rather to protect the public, maintain high professional standards, and preserve public confidence in the legal profession."[89] I recognize that the regulation of extraprofessional conduct is largely considered, at least in the literature, to be a distraction from the core protective functions of a law society.[90] However, to characterize Duplessis's conduct as extraprofessional would require disaggregating his role and actions as Premier from those as Attorney General, which, as described above, Duplessis and Rand J. seemed to fuse.[91] Regardless, the consequences of Duplessis's actions were so severe, the denunciation of the majority of the Supreme Court of Canada so emphatic, and the resultant media attention and public awareness so widespread (at least in Québec),[92] it is difficult to see how an effective legal regulator could disregard the matter.

4. Other Legal and Practical Consequences

The choice to serve both as Premier and Attorney General also has other important legal and practical consequences that are worth emphasizing.

An important legal consequence for the client of the dual role is that communications may lose the protection of solicitor-client privilege if it is unclear whether they were made in the role as Premier or the role as Attorney General.[93] This impact is less important as a practical matter insofar as many such communications would qualify as protected Cabinet confidences.[94]

Another important practical consequence involves the Deputy Attorney General. The Deputy plays a key role that is largely overlooked in the legal literature.[95] It seems likely, where a Premier nominally appoints themselves as Attorney General, they are more reliant on the Deputy Attorney General – and via the Deputy, the government lawyers of the bureaucracy – than they otherwise would be. Indeed, it may be that, in such a situation, the Deputy Attorney General essentially fulfils the role normally played by a separate Attorney General, though without sitting in the Cabinet – an acting Attorney General in all but title, political power, and democratic legitimacy. Moreover, where the roles of Premier and Attorney General are held by the same person, there would remain two separate bureaucratic departments advising that person, one (Cabinet Office or Privy Council Office) in their capacity as Premier and one (Justice or Attorney General) in their capacity as Attorney General. As always, a Minister is entitled to decline to follow the advice of the bureaucracy, but the advice will still be provided.

Nonetheless, even where the Deputy Attorney General is the Attorney General in all but title, an Attorney General in name only still holds themselves out as practising law and, thus, their conduct is doubtlessly within the appropriate jurisdiction of the law society. Put another way, it will be no defence against law society discipline for the Attorney General to claim that they had delegated all their functions to the Deputy Attorney General and, in so doing, delegated professional responsibility as well.[96]

An additional complication when the same person is both Premier and Attorney General is the virtual negation of the ability for the Attorney General to use resignation as a principled means of disassociating themself from unconstitutional or otherwise unlawful actions by the Premier, as discussed in chapter 2.[97] By convention, such resignation is obligatory when the Premier or Cabinet interferes with a criminal prosecution and arguably obligatory when the Premier chooses to disregard advice that a course of action would be unconstitutional.[98] Theoretically, an oddly principled lawyer could resign as Attorney General to disassociate themselves as a lawyer from their own decision as Premier and a politician – but that scenario seems so unlikely as to be imaginary and, thus, meaningless. As discussed above,[99] a Premier's decision to resign as Attorney General but continue as Premier would unavoidably generate speculation about the reason for resignation and cast doubt on their actions and decisions as Premier.

Indeed, a Premier who is also Attorney General could circumvent, if not render meaningless, the constitutional principle identified in *Krieger v. Law Society of Alberta* – "that the Attorneys General of this country must act independently of partisan concerns when exercising their delegated sovereign authority to initiate, continue or terminate prosecutions"[100] – by claiming that their interventions in matters of prosecutorial decision-making were in their capacity as Attorney General and not in their capacity as Premier.

These practical and legal problems would be compounded if the Premier and Attorney General was not a lawyer. While it is unusual and problematic for the Premier to be their own Attorney General, Duplessis was not unique in that respect. Also problematic, though also not unique, is an Attorney General who is not a lawyer.[101] What appears unique, however, was the situation of E.C. Manning of Alberta, a non-lawyer Premier who appointed himself Attorney General.[102] Manning appears to have avoided the infamy of Duplessis, but that might have been more luck than anything else – or perhaps he closely followed the legal advice of his Deputy Attorney General.

One can imagine a situation in which the Premier is the only lawyer in their party's caucus. In such a situation, would it be less problematic for the Premier to serve as Attorney General or for the Premier to appoint a non-lawyer as Attorney General? I will consider the challenges posed by a non-lawyer Attorney General in chapter 6. In my view, a non-lawyer Attorney General is preferable to an Attorney General who is also the Premier. As I have argued above, an Attorney General who is Premier cannot meet their professional obligations as a lawyer. The non-lawyer Attorney General has no such professional obligations. Many other problems accompany the non-lawyer Attorney General, but different solutions are available for those problems, as I will discuss in chapter 6. With respect to Manning, there is simply no situation in which it is appropriate, or least non-problematic, for a non-lawyer Premier to also serve as Attorney General.

Reflections and Conclusion

In this chapter, I have demonstrated the legal ethics problems that can arise, or existing problems that can be exacerbated, when a Premier also serves as Attorney General. These problems are strikingly illustrated in the actions of Maurice Duplessis of Québec, as detailed in *Roncarelli*. Did Duplessis competently and candidly advise himself on the scope of his powers as Premier and the lawfulness of his proposed course of action? Did he adequately prioritize the interests of the government over his personal and political interests as Premier? While the answers to these questions are unknowable, it seems unlikely. Even if he did so, if only in his own mind, it seems clear that he may have violated his statutory duty as Attorney General to see that public affairs were conducted lawfully. Moreover, there was no realistic possibility that Duplessis, as Attorney General, could disassociate himself from Duplessis as Premier, through resignation or otherwise.

While there was no realistic prospect of regulatory proceedings against Duplessis at the time, similar facts would hopefully lead to investigation and discipline if they took place today. Indeed, the brazenness of Duplessis's conduct, and the warranted public attention that ensued, would arguably require public and visible action by the corresponding law society as regulator to maintain public confidence in the legal profession and the administration of justice and to protect the public interest.

From an idealistic perspective, lawyers who serve as both Premier and Attorney General at the same time have presumably done so because they did not appreciate that the dual role violated their professional obligations, and so increased awareness of the inherent problem will discourage lawyers from doing the same in the future. I harbour no illusion that such considerations would have affected Duplessis's decision-making. At the same time, and perhaps more realistically, a Premier could nonetheless appoint themselves Attorney General, making a rational decision that the likelihood of professional or political consequences outweighed the benefits. I acknowledge here the disillusioning possibility that the violation of the rules of professional conduct, and all the more so the imposition of discipline for doing so, may be seen as a political badge of honour. But the unavoidable harm remains very real, regardless of whether it is overlooked or unappreciated. It is the public interest that is harmed, if not the personal, political, or professional interests of the lawyer in question, when the government's chief law officer cannot meet their professional obligations. The harm is worse when that lawyer knowingly and deliberately puts themselves in that impossible position.

My conclusion is that it is simply impossible for a lawyer to adequately fulfil their professional obligations while serving as both Premier and Attorney General. Even in the absence of a specific prohibition, any lawyer tempted to take on such a dual role should be acutely aware of the challenges and ramifications that choice poses for their professional obligations as a lawyer. The mere fact that professional discipline would be unlikely does not change this reality. A non-lawyer should avoid this situation all the more.

Similar issues, though less severe, will arise for an Attorney General who is not the Premier but who also holds an additional portfolio. However, the calculus will be different in such a situation. While it may be more challenging for such a dual Minister to meet their professional obligations as a lawyer, it will not be *impossible* as it is for a Premier who is also Attorney General. In particular, such an Attorney General could recuse themselves from legal advice to the Ministry to which they are cross-appointed. Indeed, it is helpful to set out a spectrum running from no additional portfolio at one end to the role of Premier at the other. For smaller additional portfolios, the issues could be quite manageable if, indeed, that recusal was genuine. The larger and more complex the additional portfolio, the more problematic such recusal would become, until – at the additional portfolio of Premier – it would become untenable.

While the issues facing a cross-appointed Attorney General are clearest in the situation of Premier Duplessis, they could arise to varying extents in any cross-appointment. Such issues often arise when the Attorney General is cross-appointed as Solicitor General or Minister of Public Safety and, thus, is responsible for policing. As mentioned in chapter 1, some Canadian jurisdictions have not spun off the traditional public safety functions of the Attorney General into a separate ministry or department.[103] In those jurisdictions, though the Attorney General is not technically cross-appointed, they hold what would, in other jurisdictions be two portfolios.[104] Even where the roles are separate, they may be held by a single cross-appointed Minister.[105] In these situations, that Attorney General unavoidably becomes entangled in the complex relationship between police and Crown attorneys, potentially at both a macro and micro level.[106] In jurisdictions where the Attorney General has statutory responsibility for police oversight, such a cross-appointment can negate the intended perception and reality of avoiding self-investigation. Moreover, not only should cross-appointment be avoided for reasons of legal ethics, but for the same legal ethics reasons these Public Safety functions should be spun off into a separate ministry and a separate Minister.

A cross-appointment may well increase the risk that the Attorney General may need to resign from their role. Insofar as the Attorney General is a lawyer or held to the standards of a lawyer, resignation raises complex issues that do not face other members of Cabinet. I turn to these issues in the next chapter.

4 Complexity: Resignation[1]

The Attorney General, like all members of Cabinet, may be removed from that role for any reason or, indeed, for no reason at all. Unlike other ministers, however, the Attorney General is, as a lawyer and chief law officer of the Crown, restricted in the reasons for which they can resign. Conversely, the Attorney General may sometimes be required to resign in circumstances that would not require the resignation of another member of Cabinet. Moreover, they may be restricted in the ways in which they can announce their reasons for resignation. All of these constraints may also interact – or interfere – with the duty of the Attorney General as a lawyer to encourage respect for the administration of justice. Thus, the law of lawyering makes the "when," "why," and "how" of resignation demonstrably complex for the Attorney General. In this chapter, I identify and analyse these legal ethics issues around resignation to further demonstrate the complexity of the law of lawyering for the Attorney General. I begin in part 1 by revisiting the rules around withdrawal that I introduced in chapter 1 and considering how these rules interact with possible reasons for resignation. Then, in part 2, I consider the issue of confidentiality around resignation. Finally, in part 3, I consider how resignation and confidentiality interact with the duty to encourage respect for the administration of justice, which duty was canvassed in detail in chapter 2.

At the outset, I certainly acknowledge that that there will be situations where the law of lawyering requires or permits something less than withdrawal and resignation, such as, for example, recusal where the Attorney General themselves has a conflict of interest. My focus in this chapter is about when resignation is available or necessary – or not – under the law of lawyering.

1. Potential Reasons for Resignation

The constellation of reasons for which the Attorney General might resign engages the law of lawyering on withdrawal in complex ways.

As a lawyer, the Attorney General is bound by the rules of professional conduct around withdrawal. While not every withdrawal will result in resignation, resignation comprises a complete withdrawal from all matters. Thus, as a matter of legal ethics, an Attorney General may only resign in circumstances in which withdrawal is permissible under the law of lawyering and *must* resign in some circumstances. Most importantly, withdrawal is mandatory where "a client *persists* in instructing the lawyer to act contrary to professional ethics,"[2] but also where "discharged by a client,"[3] where "the lawyer is not competent to continue to handle a matter,"[4] where there is an impermissible conflict of interest,[5] and where a client persists in acting "dishonestly, fraudulently, criminally, or illegally" despite the lawyer's cautions.[6] Withdrawal is discretionary where "there has been a serious loss of confidence between the lawyer and the client,"[7] including where "a lawyer is deceived by this client" or "the client refuses to accept and act upon the lawyer's advice on a significant point."[8] Any withdrawal, whether discretionary or mandatory, must be "for good cause and on reasonable notice to the client."[9]

While the Canadian legal literature on the Attorney General recognizes certain circumstances in which the Attorney General should (or even must) resign, it does not explicitly relate those circumstances to the law of lawyering. I begin my analysis here by identifying these circumstances.

At least as a matter of public law, the Canadian literature on the Attorney General is clear that the Attorney General should or must resign in two circumstances. The first is where Cabinet interferes, or attempts to interfere, in the conduct of a criminal trial or appeal and, thus, breaches the constitutional principle that the Attorney General must be independent in their criminal law functions.[10] The second is where the Attorney General advises Cabinet that a proposed bill or action would be unconstitutional and Cabinet rejects that advice.[11] The case for resignation is even stronger in the federal context, where the Attorney General is required by statute to inform the House of Commons if a bill is contrary to the *Canadian Charter of Rights and Freedoms* or the *Canadian Bill of Rights*, as resignation might be preferable to making such a report.[12] A similar argument for resignation would apply where Cabinet rejects legal advice that a proposal is otherwise unlawful.[13]

However, it would be unlikely for an Attorney General to give such absolute advice that a proposal is unconstitutional, as opposed to positioning a proposal on a spectrum between low risk and high risk.[14] Nonetheless, there is certainly some threshold level of risk that equates with unconstitutionality, above which resignation is necessary or appropriate and below which the Attorney General may pursue other options.[15] The federal Department of Justice reportedly uses a "no credible argument" or "manifestly unconstitutional"[16] threshold for determining whether a bill is "inconsistent with"[17] the *Charter*. Similarly, Grant Huscroft has argued that resignation is appropriate only when "a bill is not even arguably consistent with the *Charter* – if, in other words, the Attorney General considers that the government is repudiating its *Charter* obligations."[18] These are extremely high thresholds, and there can be reasonable disagreement over what threshold is appropriate.

These rare situations should be contrasted with the more likely – and less problematic – situation where Cabinet rejects the Attorney General's policy advice, or legal advice other than that of unconstitutionality or unlawfulness. For example, Cabinet may not support the Attorney General's proposed reforms to the court system or accept the Attorney General's advice on litigation strategy in a civil proceeding, such as pursuing a settlement. Resignation would not be necessary in such circumstances.[19] An Attorney General who feels strongly about such a matter may, nonetheless, decide that resignation is appropriate. I note, however, that Kent Roach has criticized the distinction between legal advice and policy advice as inconsistent with the role of policy considerations in the determination of *Charter* compliance.[20] Thus, to be more precise, the rejection of policy advice that goes to constitutionality would be akin to the rejection of legal advice of unconstitutionality.

Several other situations, though less common in the literature, could also prompt a principled resignation. The Attorney General might resign because they lost confidence in the Prime Minister. More specifically, this could involve the Attorney General losing confidence in the Prime Minister as a leader, as could happen to any minister, or in the Premier as the *de facto* decision-maker for the Crown as the client, which would be unique to the Attorney General. For example, the Attorney General may feel obliged to disassociate themselves from comments or actions by other ministers that genuinely threaten respect for the administration of justice. This could involve a minister publicly questioning the integrity of the judiciary, as discussed in chapter 2. A similar situation would arise where a minister attempted to contact or influence a judge regarding an ongoing proceeding. While it is clear that a minister who contacts a judge should certainly resign,[21] the Attorney General might feel obliged to resign if a minister made such a call and refused to resign themselves or made such a call despite the Attorney General's admonition not to do so.

The Attorney General, like other ministers, might also resign as penance for their own personal or professional misconduct, or as vicarious penance of ministerial responsibility, that is, for some failure or misconduct by their ministry or department. As discussed in chapter 1, legal ethics is unclear as to the responsibility of a lawyer for the conduct of lawyers they supervise, as opposed to their clear responsibility for their non-lawyer staff. Ministerial responsibility thus purportedly contemplates an even larger scope of situations where resignation is necessary than does legal ethics – although, conversely, ministerial responsibility appears even less likely to actually lead to the resignation of an Attorney General.

How, then, do these public law bases for the Attorney General to resign interact with the law of lawyering around withdrawal? Attempts to influence the decision-making of the Attorney General in a criminal proceeding or rejections of advice of unconstitutionality would each constitute a serious loss of confidence, such that withdrawal would be open to the Attorney General as a matter of legal ethics. Moreover, persistent attempts to influence the decision-making of the Attorney General in a criminal proceeding – that is, after the Attorney General has explained why those attempts are unconstitutional – would require resignation, whether because the client is persisting in instructing the lawyer to violate their professional ethics or because the client is pursuing a dishonest or illegal course of action and refuses to abandon that course of action.[22] In contrast, rejecting legal advice, even of unconstitutionality, is not necessarily illegal or dishonest. Thus, resignation would only be mandatory when Cabinet accepts or agrees with the advice and proceeds anyway, as opposed to a situation where Cabinet rejects the advice of unconstitutionality on some honest basis.[23]

In contrast, rejection of the Attorney General's other legal advice, or their policy advice, would make withdrawal available, so long as this rejection constitutes a serious loss of confidence.[24] Similarly, a loss of confidence in the client (i.e., the Crown but, in practical terms, the Premier or Prime Minister) would constitute a serious loss of confidence. What about a loss of confidence in the Premier or Prime Minister, not as the *de facto* decision-maker for the Crown as the client but as a politician or a leader? The rules of professional conduct do not explicitly identify the required nature of the serious loss of confidence, so a resignation for such a purpose would likely also be discretionary. Resignation as penance would suggest that, in the view of the Attorney General, the client has lost confidence (or should have lost confidence) in the Attorney General as a lawyer.

Thus, the public law accounts on when the Attorney General must, should, or may resign align closely with the law of lawyering on withdrawal.

2. Confidentiality on Resignation

In contrast, there is less – if any – alignment between the public law accounts and the law of lawyering around confidentiality on resignation, that is, whether the resigning Attorney General may or should publicly reveal their reasons for resignation. Whereas the public law accounts appear to recognize that the Attorney General may, or even should, publicly reveal their reasons for resignation, the law of lawyering around confidentiality would appear to preclude such a reveal under virtually all circumstances.

While it is generally accepted that one function of a minister's resignation is to free them from Cabinet solidarity and Cabinet confidentiality, so as to allow them to publicly disagree with a decision they did not support,[25] there has been little examination of whether resignation is sufficient to allow the Attorney General to do so. Some commentators suggest that the Attorney General may, or even should, reveal their reasons for resignation. In discussing the career of former Ontario Attorney General Ian Scott, Justice Ian Binnie implicitly raised the possibility: "Much will be said at today's symposium about the 'independence of the attorney general.' Does he have the obligation to speak out publicly if his colleagues fail to accept his advice? Should he resign?"[26] Similarly, Huscroft discusses a signalling function of resignation but is unclear about whether the Attorney General publicly stating the reason for the resignation is part of that signalling:

> If the Attorney General considers that a bill is not even arguably consistent with the *Charter* – if, in other words, the Attorney General considers that the government is repudiating its *Charter* obligations – the Attorney General should resign in order to signal that the government is not committed to respecting the constitution. ... Good faith disagreement between the Attorney General and the government about the interpretation and application of the *Charter* is possible, but even in these circumstances it is not tenable for the Attorney General to continue in office; there is no room for public disagreement between the Crown and its Chief Law Officer about the requirements of the constitution.[27]

Presumably, without a public disclosure there could be little effective signalling, and the Prime Minister/Premier or other members of Cabinet should not be expected to objectively characterize the reason for the resignation. Huscroft's last sentence in this passage can also be read as suggesting that resignation might allow public disagreement, that is, that there is room for public disagreement between the Crown and its *former* Chief Law Officer. Similarly, Roach characterizes Hogg's view as being that "the Attorney General is bound by the convention of 'collective responsibility' of Cabinet and would have to resign the office *if he or she wished to continue to oppose the policy.*"[28]

Justice Marc Rosenberg and John Ll. J. Edwards have both considered this issue in the context of Cabinet interference with prosecutions. Rosenberg writes, extrajudicially, that "[t]he resignation of the Attorney General would *expose any attempted interference by the premier or the cabinet both to the public and especially to the press,* and would further entrench the convention of institutional independence."[29] Rosenberg quotes Edwards to similar effect: "[i]t must be emphasised that to recognise the inevitability of dismissal or resignation in these circumstances in no sense represents a weakening of the Attorney General's constitutional position. What it entails is *the removal of the issue from the confidential environment of Cabinet deliberations and its exposure to the full glare of public attention.*"[30] Both of these statements strongly imply that solicitor-client privilege and the lawyer's professional duty of confidentiality do not preclude such publicity – although they can also be read as suggesting that resignation itself will attract sufficient media and public attention to reveal the reasons for resignation.

How do these accounts interact with the law of lawyering? As set out above in part 1, there are several principled reasons for which the Attorney General must or might resign. However, regardless of the reason(s) for resigning and, thus, for ending the solicitor-client relationship, there is virtually no allowance under the rules of professional conduct for the Attorney General to publicly state the specific reason for resignation. All but one of the recognized exceptions would not apply: authorization by the client;[31] requirement by law, the courts, or the law society;[32] future harm;[33] fee collection;[34] solicitation of legal or ethical advice;[35] or addressing conflicts of interest.[36] A more amorphous and intangible harm, such as harm to the office of the Attorney General, would not qualify. In particular, the exception for future harm is narrow and has a high threshold, applying only "when the lawyer believes *on reasonable grounds* that there is an *imminent* risk of *death or serious bodily harm,* and disclosure is *necessary* to prevent the death or harm."[37] In addition, the confidentiality exceptions generally require that the lawyer "must not disclose more information than is required."[38] Even if the resignation is for reasons unrelated to the role of the Attorney General as a lawyer, such as the rejection of pure policy advice or for non-confidence in the Prime Minister as leader (and not as *de facto* client), the Attorney General, by resigning, is still withdrawing from *all* of their roles, including legal representation. Thus, although the reason for resignation would not be covered by solicitor-client privilege, it would be covered by confidentiality.

The one relevant exception to the duty of confidentiality would be where it is necessary for the lawyer to defend themselves – or "their associates or employees" – against allegations of criminality or negligence involving a legal matter or allegations of malpractice or misconduct.[39] This exception, like all existing exceptions, applies even absent withdrawal. Thus, where the Attorney General resigns in the face of such allegations, they would be able to reveal confidential information as necessary to defend themselves.

There are two ways to reconcile this clash between the public law accounts and the law of lawyering as they relate to the resignation of the Attorney General. One is to recognize a new exception to confidentiality specific to the Attorney General. However, given that solicitor-client privilege covers much information that is confidential, a parallel exception to solicitor-client privilege would have to be recognized by courts to make this exception meaningful. The other way to reconcile this clash – and one that I now view as more principled – is for the Attorney General to reveal their reasons for resignation in the House or Assembly such that they would be protected from law society discipline or other legal consequences by parliamentary privilege but liable to accountability imposed by that House or Assembly. I will return to this question in chapter 5 and chapter 7.

A unique exception to confidentiality specific to the Attorney General would centre on their amorphous role as "guardian of the public interest."[40] The role has been defined with reference to the Attorney General in litigation on behalf of the government and in advising on the constitutionality of bills and regulations,[41] as well as the more longstanding roles of seeking injunctions in the public interest against nuisances and non-compliance with the law.[42] It is unclear what the phrase might mean in other contexts,[43] such as the regulation of the legal profession by the law society,[44] or pursuing complaints of judicial misconduct.[45] Huscroft has criticized the phrase "guardian and protector of the public interest" as "misleading," because "[t]here is no independent, value-neutral public interest to be protected," at least in the *Charter* context.[46] However, in doing so, he quoted with approval Gerard Carney's position that "it would be more accurate to describe the Attorney as guardian *of the administration of justice.*"[47] Dodek has argued that the "guardian of the public interest" role, alongside the concept of the Attorney General as the "defender of the rule of law,"[48] supports what he argues is a "higher duty of government lawyers as custodians of the rule of law."[49] However, Roach and Dodek largely identify these special responsibilities as inward-looking. Roach describes the Attorney General as "defender of the rule of law *within government*"[50] and identifies the publicly visible options of resignation and litigation as a last resort.[51] Similarly, Dodek states that "[g]overnment lawyers are involved in protecting the rule of law *from the inside.*"[52]

Revisiting the above constellation of reasons for an Attorney General to resign, the question is this: are there any actions that are so wrongful and harmful to the public interest, the rule of law, or public confidence in the administration of justice that the Attorney General should not only advise against them, refuse to follow associated instructions, and resign, but also publicly announce and denounce those actions? This would seem to be what Rosenberg and Edwards are implying where Cabinet attempts to interfere with prosecutorial decisions.[53]

Although any potential abrogation of confidentiality has a serious impact on the client, the solicitor-client relationship, and the quality of legal advice provided,[54] the recognized exceptions discussed above demonstrate that such an impact is acceptable in some circumstances. Given the various exceptions to confidentiality, including public safety, one could compellingly argue that making public the reason for the resignation of the Attorney General serves the public interest in defending the rule of law. The fact that the situation has almost never arisen suggests that the absence of such an exception within the rules of professional conduct should not be determinative. As stated in the preface to the *Model Code of Professional Conduct* of the Federation of Law Societies of Canada, "[s]ome circumstances that raise ethical considerations may be sufficiently unique that the guidance in a rule or commentary may not answer the issue or provide the required direction."[55] Nonetheless, presumably the Attorney General would, as with other exceptions to confidentiality, be required to disclose only as much information as necessary.[56] A corresponding exception could be recognized to solicitor-client privilege.[57] The assertion and assessment of such a novel exception could, in itself and regardless of the outcome, serve the public interest.[58]

The difficulty with characterizing this previously unrecognized exception to confidentiality, however, is determining how it would apply in less extreme situations. Given the narrowness of the exceptions, especially that for future harm or public safety,[59] a similarly high threshold and narrow scope would seem appropriate and necessary for any new exception. Such an exception should apply to the most serious reasons for resignation – that is, interference with criminal proceedings and perhaps the rejection of advice of certain unconstitutionality – but should not apply to other reasons for resignation – that is, rejection of legal advice other than unconstitutionality or a loss of confidence in the Premier or Prime Minister as the apex representative of the Crown client or as a leader.

In summary, the law of lawyering, as it currently exists, appears to preclude the Attorney General from disclosing their reasons for resignation, except where the Attorney General is resigning under a cloud of allegations of criminality or negligence involving a legal matter or allegations of malpractice or misconduct. As I will return to in chapter 5 and chapter 7, the best solution to this disjoint between public law accounts of the Attorney General and the law of lawyering would be for the Attorney General to announce their reasons for resignation in the House or Assembly. Such an announcement would be protected from law society discipline due to parliamentary privilege, while leaving it open to the House or Assembly to impose accountability for that violation of confidentiality. If the courts were to recognize a special exception to solicitor-client privilege unique to the Attorney General, which seems unlikely, law societies could follow that lead by adopting a corresponding exception to confidentiality.

Any Attorney General announcing their reasons for resignation would also have to determine how that announcement would affect public respect for the administration of justice.

3. Resignation, the Duty to Encourage Respect for the Administration of Justice, and Self-respect

Against this backdrop on resignation and the Attorney General, I now return to the duty to encourage respect for the administration of justice that I discussed in chapter 2. I consider the professional obligation of the Attorney General to encourage respect for, and improve, their own role, given the importance of that role to the administration of justice. I focus particularly on the ideal of a principled resignation. I do so primarily by comparing and contrasting two key case studies: the resignation of Attorney General Brian Smith of British Columbia in 1988 and the refusal of federal Attorney General Jody Wilson-Raybould to resign in 2018–19. Despite my analysis of confidentiality in part 2 above,

I suggest that, in at least some circumstances unique to the Attorney General, compliance with the duty of confidentiality does not necessarily encourage respect for the administration of justice.

As discussed above in part 1, the consensus in the literature appears to be that principled resignations – that is, resignations that are required by or are consistent with the law of lawyering and the special role of the Attorney General as chief law officer of the Crown, particularly where there has been objectionable conduct by Cabinet or some of its members – are desirable because they help protect the office of the Attorney General from inappropriate pressure or interference. It is less clear whether the Attorney General themselves must publicly announce their reasons for resignation or if the mere act of resignation itself will promote sufficient political and media scrutiny.

I argue that principled resignations are also desirable because they fulfil the professional duty of the Attorney General as a lawyer to encourage respect for the administration of justice. Given the integral role of the Attorney General in the administration of justice – particularly, though not solely, in the administration of criminal justice – increasing public respect for, and understanding of, the office and role of the Attorney General necessarily tends to increase respect for the administration of justice more generally. But I also consider two converse possibilities: that a principled resignation discourages respect for the administration of justice and that a principled refusal to resign may also advance this professional duty.

While my focus is on the duty to encourage respect for the administration of justice, part of self-respect for the role of the Attorney General is the imperative to protect constitutional principles, particularly the principle from *Krieger v. Law Society of Alberta* ("that the Attorneys General of this country must act independently of partisan concerns when exercising their delegated sovereign authority to initiate, continue or terminate prosecutions").[60] Any attempt to weaken this principle clearly disrespects the role of the Attorney General. Moreover, any attempt to weaken the independence of the Attorney General also weakens, at least indirectly, the broader principle of the independence of the bar.[61]

Before proceeding, I emphasize that there is a public education element to the duty to encourage public respect for the administration of justice. In the context of the Attorney General, the more the public understands and appreciates the importance and rationale for the independence of the Attorney General as part of the administration of justice, the more they will respect the administration of justice when the Attorney General takes steps to protect that independence – such as a principled resignation. Indeed, John Ll. J. Edwards passionately decried ignorance around the role of the Attorney General – not only among the general public but among the legal profession.[62]

At the outset, I readily recognize the difficulty in disentangling self-aggrandizement of the Attorney General themselves, whether in service of ego, higher political ambitions, or otherwise, from the protection of the Office of the Attorney General. Nonetheless, I acknowledge the reality that, all else equal, the stronger and more independent the individual Attorney General, the stronger and more independent will be future Attorneys General.

3A: Resignation and Independence: Brian Smith of British Columbia

Resignation is perhaps the most powerful of the many ways in which an Attorney General can privately or publicly assert their independence and promote respect for that independence. For example, former Attorney General for Ontario Michael Bryant recounts in his memoir that, although the Premier's Office would review Bryant's speeches in advance, "it was an operating practice in my office to file the comments from the Premier's Office in the shredder. I took enormous pride in it."[63] But the most final, and the most striking, assertion of independence among these is a principled resignation. The only more striking assertion would be to litigate against their government in court – but while that has been suggested as a hypothetical option,[64] it seems even less likely to occur than a principled resignation. Less obvious in its importance and impact is a principled refusal to resign.

The archetypical principled resignation was that of Brian Smith as Attorney General of British Columbia in 1988. Indeed, Roach cites that resignation as evidence that "although considerable skepticism has been expressed about the resignation option [of the Attorney General], it is not totally illusory."[65] Here, I emphasize the references to the office of the Attorney General, to its special role in the administration of justice, and to honour and integrity:

> Mr. Speaker, for over five years I have had **the honour** to hold the post of Attorney-General. This is **an office of great sensitivity and neutrality in the administration of justice**. I now find that I can no longer carry out my duties, as I clearly do not have the support of the Premier and his office, who do not appreciate **the unique independence that is the cornerstone of the Attorney-General's responsibilities in a free parliamentary democracy**. ...

In removing myself from this office now it is my hope that I may protect its **unique independence**. I believe that there is a strong danger that the Premier wishes to bring the conduct of the office of the Attorney-General under closer control by his office and so **weaken the independence of the Attorney-General**. ...

Only by stepping down, only by speaking out now, can I hope to prevent a course which will **weaken the independence and erode the tradition of the office of the Attorney-General**. ... [D]uring the past week, amid speculation of cabinet reorganization, I have had a chance to review some of the comments that have been made by the Premier and others concerning who might occupy the office of Attorney-General. Any fair-minded observer would find these comments an implied lack of confidence in myself, but even more so **a diminished concept of the office of Attorney-General**. ...

I also know that during my term of office I have tried to give sound advice. I have always striven **to protect the honesty and integrity of the administration**. ...

[T]he reasons why the Premier wishes to remove me from my post and weaken my ministry.... instead has to do with **a fundamental misunderstanding as to why my office must remain independent and neutral**. ...

For me to have acted differently and to have done what I was requested to do would not only have **dishonoured my office** but also would have placed in peril the office of the Premier. I explained my position on several occasions to the Premier when those events occurred. I fervently hoped that I had established and explained **the importance of the neutrality and independence of my office** to the Premier. I now believe that I have failed to make that impression.

I can only conclude that it is because of **the way that I independently carried out my duties that I am slated to be removed from those duties**. ... But by speaking out now, and stepping down now, I may still deter these plans and save **the integrity of the office of the Attorney-General**.

I am resigning as **an act of honour**.[66]

Smith referred to two specific incidents that endangered the independence of his office. Smith had announced, before consulting the Premier, that the government would not appeal a controversial decision on abortion funding.[67] Smith had also refused the Premier's request to publicly deny that the RCMP was investigating a friend of the Premier.[68] In his speech, Smith also criticized the Premier's intention to appoint a non-lawyer to succeed Smith.[69]

The Premier denied these claims as "preposterous" and said "the reasons have no basis in fact,"[70] openly disputing that the resignation was a principled one.[71] Indeed, the next morning the Premier's office stated that "Mr. Smith's independence was at no time questioned or challenged, and to say otherwise is false."[72] Ironically, both the independence emphasized by Smith and the importance of that independence were reflected in revealing and tone-deaf criticism by the Minister of Municipal Affairs, who said that Smith in his speech, with its "negative-type comments," "didn't seem to be a team player."[73]

While Smith stated that the resignation was meant to protect the independence of the Attorney General, he later suggested that he, nonetheless, delayed resigning as long as he did so that he could protect the office of the Attorney General from the inside.[74]

I acknowledge that Smith may have had additional motivations for both his resignation and his public announcement of the reasons for that resignation. For example, Rosenberg suggests that "in fairness, the reasons for Smith's resignation continue to be somewhat obscure and there exists a body of opinion that his resignation was driven as much by politics as by concern for the Premier's interference in the Attorney General's office."[75] Despite that possibility, Smith's choices, at least on their face, demonstrate a purported commitment to the independence and role of the Attorney General. Indeed, noteworthy for my purposes is the suggestion that Smith resigned when he did because he knew that his removal as Attorney General by the Premier was imminent.[76]

Not surprisingly, the opposition party, in its response to Smith's speech, commended him for his courage ("it was a courageous move. ... We admire this startling, sudden but courageous decision").[77] More importantly, for my purposes, the opposition in doing so emphasized the independence and integrity of the Office of the Attorney General:

> The reasons that the Attorney-General has given for resigning from the cabinet are indeed substantial and important to the integrity of our parliamentary democracy. ... [T]he Attorney-General ... has outlined the unique status of the Attorney-General in our parliamentary system: an independent adviser, not just to the cabinet but to the Lieutenant-Governor, on behalf of Her Majesty and of the institutions of our great democracy. That integrity cannot be sullied, decentralized, decimated, cut up and pushed into the Premier's office for greater control to carry out the Premier's wishes. That integrity is absolutely inviolate, and the Attorney-General was right to make that the essence of his remarks to this Legislature today.[78]

The principled resignation also earned Smith a laurel from the editorial board of the *Toronto Star*, which recognized that he resigned because of alleged interference with the office of the Attorney General.[79] An editorial in the *Globe and Mail* characterized Smith's remarks as "accus[ing] [the Premier] of fundamental ignorance about the attorney-general's role in a democracy."[80] Smith's resignation was, thus, an opportunity to spur others to recognize the importance of the independence of the Attorney General.

While Smith, in his speech, referred to his likely successors as reflecting "a diminished concept of the office of Attorney-General,"[81] he made it clear that he saw his publicly announced resignation as deterrence from the appointment of such successors. I will show in the next case study – that of Jody Wilson-Raybould – that a refusal to resign may be aimed at a similar outcome. But, given the power of the Premier to easily remove or reassign the Attorney General like any other member of Cabinet and, indeed, in Smith's circumstances, the rumours of such pending removal, a refusal to resign would typically have little impact unless that refusal, and the reasons for it, were made public – most likely by the Attorney General. In contrast, in Wilson-Raybould's specific circumstances, the Prime Minister evidently sought to avoid, or at least delay, the fallout and public reaction to shuffling her into another portfolio.

*3B. Independence and the Refusal to Resign: Jody
    Wilson-Raybould of Canada*

The counterfactual to the principled resignation is the principled refusal to resign. The archetype here is Jody Wilson-Raybould as Minister of Justice and Attorney General for Canada from 2018 to 2019. In her own words from her Parliamentary testimony:

> For a period of approximately four months, between September and December of 2018, I experienced a consistent and sustained effort by many people within the government to seek to politically interfere in the exercise of prosecutorial discretion in my role as the Attorney General of Canada in an inappropriate effort to secure a deferred prosecution agreement with SNC-Lavalin. …
>
> Within these conversations, there were express statements regarding the necessity of interference in the SNC-Lavalin matter, the potential for consequences and veiled threats if a DPA [deferred prosecution agreement] was not made available to SNC.[82]

Wilson-Raybould explained that she refused to resign under these circumstances because remaining Attorney General was the only way to prevent these steps from being taken.[83]

While Wilson-Raybould did not explicitly articulate her situation in terms of encouraging respect for the administration of justice, she did emphasize the rule of law and prosecutorial independence: "We either have a system that is based on the rule of law, the independence of prosecutorial functions and respect for those charged to use their discretion and powers in a particular way, or we do not."[84] She also emphasized the importance of public confidence in the justice system, saying:

> I do not want members of this committee or Canadians to think that the integrity of our institutions has somehow evaporated. The integrity of our justice system, the integrity of the director of public prosecutions and prosecutors, is intact. So I don't want to create fear that this is not the case. It is incumbent upon all of us to uphold our institutions and to uphold the rule of law. That's why I'm here.[85]

In substance, this language is equivalent to public respect for the administration of justice and the actors in that administration.

Like Smith, Wilson-Raybould, in her public explanation of her decisions, emphasized integrity and the importance of the independence of the Attorney General:

> I have seen first-hand the negative impacts for freedom, equality and a just society that this can have, so when I pledged to serve Canadians as your Minister of Justice and Attorney General, I came to do so with a deeply ingrained commitment to the rule of law and the importance of acting independently of partisan, political and narrow interests in all matters. When we do not do that, I firmly believe, and know, that we do worse as a society. ...
>
> I was taught to always hold true to your core values and principles, and to act with integrity.[86]

In her memoirs, Wilson-Raybould was more emphatic: "This is about the rule of law and the norms and core principles of our democratic system. ... I was the attorney general, for fuck's sake."[87] As with Brian Smith and, again, not surprisingly, opposition legislators commended Wilson-Raybould for her integrity.[88]

Unlike Smith, Wilson-Raybould adamantly adhered to confidentiality and privilege, as well as Cabinet confidentiality, and refused to speak publicly about the matter until Cabinet waived those protections.[89]

3C. *Resignation, Refusal, and the Duty to Encourage*
Respect for the Administration of Justice

How then do these actions – a principled resignation or a principled refusal to resign – engage the duty to encourage respect for the administration of justice? And can a mere threat to resign, or a threat to announce the reasons for the refusal to resign, encourage that respect?

Here, again, the Attorney General is special – even unique – among lawyers.[90] I acknowledge that every lawyer's conduct engages the reputation of the legal profession and respect for the administration of justice. However, absent exceptional circumstances, a single lawyer's choice to resign or not to resign would typically engage the duty to encourage respect for the administration of justice in only a small way. In contrast, when a lawyer is not only high profile but is also, themselves, a key actor in the administration of justice – like the Attorney General – the impact of a principled resignation or refusal to resign on the basis of self-respect will have a much greater potential impact on public respect for the administration of justice.

By refusing to resign, an Attorney General in circumstances like those faced by Wilson-Raybould is not only preventing a successor from conduct that would discourage respect for the administration of justice by diminishing the role and independence of the Attorney General, but they are also creating the potential for important public education about that role. Indeed, without considering a Wilson-Raybould-type situation, Rosenberg does note that perhaps "a person of lesser worth would simply cave in to the cabinet directive or the demands of the premier," although he maintains that such cowardice would eventually become public.[91]

While the public announcement of a principled resignation or of a principled refusal to resign may both encourage and discourage respect for the administration of justice, the net effect is likely to encourage that respect. On one hand, the major breach of confidentiality and privilege inherent in the public announcement may be understood by the public (and perhaps also emphasized by opposing politicians and the media) and unavoidably tarnish public trust in lawyers. This reality could remain even if the Attorney General themselves, the profession, and the regulator were to determine that the breach was justified in nuanced circumstances. On the other hand, the Attorney General is uniquely positioned to alert the public to government actions that diminish the role of the Attorney General and to explain why that matters. As Rosenberg puts it, in the context of political interference in prosecutorial decision-making, "[t]he resignation of the Attorney General would expose any attempted interference by the premier or the cabinet both to the public and especially to the press, and would further entrench the convention of institutional independence."[92] Perhaps counter-intuitively, the Attorney General, by breaching confidentiality and privilege to reveal the reasons for the resignation or refusal, is telegraphing the importance of those reasons.

While the classic concept of the principled resignation – that of Smith – assumes that the Attorney General will make their reasons for resignation public, that does not seem to be a prerequisite for the public impact of that principled resignation. As I discussed above, the Canadian legal literature on the Attorney General seems to presume that a principled resignation has value and impact because that Attorney General will make the reasons for their resignation public. However, even where the Attorney General remains silent on the principled reasons for the resignation or refusal to resign, those principled reasons may well become public sooner or later. As Roach puts it, "[t]he AG's resignation or dismissal would of course result in much public interest and demands for explanations and accountability."[93] Indeed, the mere fact that an Attorney General declines to identify their reasons for resignation, particularly in response to direct questions, will raise red flags. Politicians – especially opposition politicians – or the bureaucracy, or the staff, colleagues, or friends of the Attorney General may well leak the reason. When the reasons for the principled resignation or refusal do become public, they would tend to encourage respect for the office of the Attorney General. Nonetheless, there is no guarantee that this revelation will happen and, indeed, there is a visceral impact that comes from the Attorney General announcing the reasons themselves at the time.

Likewise, while the consensus in the literature is that a principled resignation is the necessary choice where the independence of the Attorney General is at issue, the Wilson-Raybould situation suggests that a principled refusal to resign may also be a credible and impactful option. Indeed, the duty of the Attorney General to encourage respect for the administration of justice – including the office of the Attorney General itself – potentially resolves the conundrum that, purely as a matter of legal ethics, Wilson-Raybould may have been required to resign. Recall from part 1 that persistent attempts to influence the decision-making of the Attorney General in a criminal proceeding – that is, after the Attorney General has explained why those attempts are unconstitutional – would require resignation, whether because the client is persisting in instructing the lawyer to violate their professional ethics or because the client is pursuing a dishonest or illegal course of action and refuses to abandon that course of action.[94] In this respect and many others, "the rules of professional conduct – perhaps naively – do not take into account the possibility that the next lawyer will act unethically."[95] Where an Attorney General reasonably believes that a successor Attorney General will acquiesce in the face of government actions that damage the independent role of the Attorney General, their duty to encourage respect for the administration of justice arguably allows, or even requires, them to refuse to resign. While they may well be removed by the Premier or Prime Minister, the mere act of that removal may attract public and media attention. Indeed, from Smith's example, the most impactful choice an Attorney General may make is to resign just before they can be removed.

Short of announcement or resignation or both, the mere threat of any of these courses of action may encourage respect for the administration of justice because of the possibility of that threat and the reasons for it becoming public. Again, even if the government believes that the Attorney General would not dare to announce the reasons for their decision, there is the real risk that those reasons may nonetheless be made public by someone else. The threat itself may indeed become public. In such circumstances, this threat by the lawyer would seem to be not just acceptable but even honourable.[96]

The Attorney General may have many reasons to protect the independence and public reputation of their office. Among these is their professional obligation as a lawyer to encourage respect for the administration of justice – because they, themselves, are a key actor in the administration of justice. In other words, they have a duty of self-respect. As Commissioner McRuer wrote, "The office [of the Attorney General] should be restored to its traditional authority, responsibility and dignity. Its occupant should rank in precedence next to the Prime Minister."[97] Despite the passage of time, this imperative remains unachieved. There are many ways to fulfil this duty. A principled resignation is the most powerful way, if not necessarily the most effective. As the Wilson-Raybould situation illustrates, in some circumstances, a principled refusal to resign may also be a powerful way to do so.

With respect to Wilson-Raybould, in my view she would have been better advised to follow Smith's example of resigning at the last possible moment. Most importantly, there was no guarantee that the situation she faced, and her principled actions in that situation, would ever become public – and if they had not become public, it would have been a missed opportunity to encourage respect for the administration of justice by educating the public about the proper role and independence of the Attorney General. In addition, for better or worse, the law of lawyering does not adequately account for the situation Wilson-Raybould faced and the rational actions she took. It is an open question whether the duty to encourage respect for the administration of justice can justify a failure to follow the rules on obligatory withdrawal. But what about the rules on confidentiality?

While Wilson-Raybould's respect for confidentiality and privilege is commendable, Smith's approach better honoured his duty to encourage respect for the administration of justice. While I will discuss parliamentary privilege further in chapter 5 and chapter 7, I emphasize here that while Smith's breach of confidentiality was protected from law society discipline by parliamentary privilege,[98] parliamentary privilege itself has a substantive and principled basis and is by no means a mere technicality.[99] As the Supreme Court of Canada held in *House of Commons v. Vaid*, "[p]arliamentary privilege ... is one of the ways in which the fundamental constitutional separation of powers is respected. ... Parliamentary privilege does not create a gap in the general public law of Canada but is an important part of it, inherited from the Parliament at Westminster."[100] Given the fundamental role of the legislature in empowering the executive and holding it accountable, the ability of the Attorney General to disclose actions or intended actions by the Premier that would diminish the office of the Attorney General and, thus, discourage respect for the administration of justice falls squarely within the necessary functions protected by parliamentary privilege.[101] Therefore, if legal ethics does not allow for such an announcement even in the most extreme circumstances, the supervisory and disciplinary role of the law societies for that breach is rightly displaced. It is for the legislature to decide whether that breach of confidentiality was justifiable and, if not, what the appropriate accountability should be. Likewise, parliamentary privilege means that it is for Parliament to determine the consequences for any breach of solicitor-client privilege within the Chamber. Thus, parliamentary privilege does not trump confidentiality or solicitor-client privilege. Instead, it leaves the consequences, if any, for their breach up to Parliament, as opposed to the law society or the courts.

Indeed, announcing the reasons for resignation is the best way to ensure that, whether the independence of the Attorney General is not respected by the Premier or around the Cabinet table, the public's respect for the office of the Attorney General and appreciation of its role will increase. Again, while the reasons may eventually become public, it is better that the Attorney General announce them at the time of their resignation in order to ensure that the public is fully aware of those reasons.

This is not to say that the Attorney General should use the potential threat of resignation to pressure the government into following their policy priorities or every one of their legal recommendations.[102] Indeed, a resignation under those circumstances would discourage respect for the administration of justice. But where the government is clearly and persistently diminishing the role and independence of the office of the Attorney General, the threat and action of resignation is warranted precisely because such a resignation encourages respect for the administration of justice by promoting public awareness and understanding of that role.

Thus, while the Attorney General may well have a constitutional imperative to protect their independence and a statutory imperative to ensure that the constitutional principle of that independence is upheld, they also have a professional duty as a lawyer to protect that independence in order to encourage public respect for the administration of justice. Perhaps the most powerful tool to fulfil that professional duty is a principled resignation.

4. Conclusion

In this chapter, I have demonstrated how resignation by the Attorney General engages the law of lawyering in several complex ways. First, the public law accounts of when the Attorney General must or should resign do align closely with the law of lawyering around withdrawal. Secondly, however, the apparent expectation that the Attorney General should reveal their reasons for principled resignation does not align closely with the law of lawyering around confidentiality. Thirdly, resignation – and the disclosure of the reasons for that resignation – may further the duty to encourage respect for the administration of justice by encouraging public understanding of the unique role of the Attorney General. The principled refusal to resign, while honourable in its own way, is less clear in its importance and impact – and potentially violates the law of lawyering on mandatory withdrawal. Thus, in short, resignation is no simple matter for the Attorney General. Indeed, this is perhaps one of the ways in which the Attorney General is most unlike other members of Cabinet.

This chapter completes my examination of the theme of complexity in legal ethics for the Attorney General. I next consider the theme of accountability, beginning with the immunity of the Attorney General to law society discipline.

PART II

Accountability

5 Accountability: Immunity to Law Society Discipline[1]

In this chapter, I assess the disciplinary jurisdiction of the law societies over Attorneys General. As canvassed in chapter 1, the situation of the Attorney General is unique and complicated. They are the only lawyer in elected public office who necessarily practises law in the exercise of official functions.[2] Moreover, the provincial Attorney General has a complex relationship with the law society. As Minister of Justice, they are responsible to the legislature for the oversight of the law society's regulation of the legal profession.[3] They are also often an *ex officio* bencher of the law society.[4] However, as a lawyer, they are also a *member* of the law society. These factors raise two important questions. First, does the law society have disciplinary jurisdiction over the Attorney General? And second, should it? It is these questions I address in this chapter. While I focus my analysis on the peculiar situation of provincial and territorial Attorneys General, some of the same considerations apply to the federal Attorney General.[5]

I proceed in three parts. First, I review the various functions of the Attorney General to separate out three categories of conduct, given that the actual and appropriate scope of law society jurisdiction may vary across those categories. I also consider historical examples of attempted discipline of the Attorney General. Second, I consider whether the Attorney General is, as a matter of current law, within the disciplinary jurisdiction of the law societies. I begin by considering the law in territories and provinces other than Ontario. I argue that the Attorney General is generally not immune for their exercise of public functions, with some exceptions. I then consider the special case of Ontario under a provision unique to that province. Finally, I consider whether the Attorney General should be subject to discipline. I argue that the current law outside Ontario is appropriate and that the Ontario provision should not be adopted elsewhere. In particular, the importance of the rule of law and the protection of the public interest both suggest that the Attorney General should be subject to the same rules as all other lawyers. This consideration outweighs countervailing considerations, particularly the concern that the prospect of professional discipline would deter the Attorney General from the proper exercise of their functions of office. If I am wrong, and such deterrence is a primary concern, I argue that good-faith immunity is a better solution than absolute immunity.

But, first, why does accountability matter, particularly accountability that is for breaches of legal ethics and that is imposed by the law society? It is helpful here to distinguish between the basis or grounds for accountability and the form or mechanism of that accountability. As mentioned above and discussed in chapter 1, the Attorney General has many different roles. Their role as a lawyer is not their only role, but it is one of the primary ones and, in my view, the defining one. It follows that accountability for legal ethics breaches is one important basis for, or ground of, accountability. While the law society is not the *only* body that imposes accountability for legal ethics breaches, it must be one of them. Among other things, there are important roles for courts, particularly given lawyers' capacity as officers of the court, and for civil liability. There are also important roles for the media, political parties, the Canadian Bar Association and its branches, other lawyers' organizations, and the legal academy. The law society remains a primary and important body that imposes accountability for legal ethics breaches in fulfilling its statutory mandate. As I alluded to in chapter 1, the Attorney General is one of the most highly visible and possibly most powerful lawyers in the country. It is simply impossible for the law society to fulfil its statutory mandate if it does not regulate – or at least have the ability to regulate – that lawyer. For example, the role and visibility of the Attorney General gives them the ability and temptation to discourage respect for the administration of justice far more than most lawyers. While the complexity of the roles of the Attorney General might well make that regulation more difficult and complicated, that complexity does not make such regulation either unnecessary or avoidable. To whatever extent the law society lacks expertise in the roles and context of the Attorney General, it nonetheless has expertise in the practice of law by the Attorney General and in the other duties of lawyers under the law of lawyering. If nothing else, only the law society can disbar the Attorney General so as to prevent their further practice of law after leaving the role of Attorney General.[6] From a more principled perspective, and as I will return to below, the immunity of the Attorney General to law society regulation is inherently contrary to the principle of the rule of law.

To the extent that law society regulation is ineffective or unlikely, I address alternative mechanisms of accountability in chapter 7.

1. The Roles of the Attorney General: Three Categories of Conduct

The Attorney General's official conduct can be separated into three categories based on the major roles of the office that I described in chapter 1. The Attorney General is "chief law officer of the Crown" and, as such, provides legal advice to Cabinet and is responsible for all litigation involving the government.[7] These functions constitute the practice of law. As part of these legal functions, the Attorney General also has ultimate responsibility for all prosecutorial decisions – indeed, "[i]t is a constitutional principle that the Attorneys General ... must act independently of partisan concerns when exercising their delegated sovereign authority to initiate, continue, or terminate prosecutions,"[8] generally referred to as "prosecutorial discretion."[9] These functions are largely delegated to Crown prosecutors,[10] but a few such decisions must be made by the Attorney General personally.[11] The Attorney General is also the Minister of Justice and provides policy advice, not only in the areas of government for which they are responsible, but also more generally.[12] In this respect, they are like many lawyers who, in addition to legal advice, provide clients with policy advice.[13] Unlike other lawyers, however, they are squarely a partisan politician and a minister of the Crown and so their policy advice is appropriately and undeniably political.[14] Thus, the conduct of the Attorney General can be divided into three categories: (1) prosecutorial discretion, (2) the practice of law other than prosecutorial discretion, and (3) policy advice or ministerial decisions or political functions. The last category would include all conduct in office that does not constitute the practice of law. To the extent that the Attorney General has special duties to the courts and the administration of justice, as well as with respect to access to justice, these special duties would also fit in this third and residual category. While the Attorney General could also conceivably face discipline for conduct in their personal life,[15] my focus in this chapter is their conduct in office.

These three categories open up different spaces for professional misconduct or conduct unbecoming and, thus, give rise to different potential for disciplinary action. As discussed in chapter 1, to the extent that the Attorney General engages in the practice of law, they could conceivably violate many of the rules applicable to lawyers generally.[16] For example, in providing legal advice to Cabinet, they could violate rules such as those concerning loyalty, that is, honesty and candour, confidentiality, conflicts, and commitment to the client's cause.[17] They could also violate the rules on mandatory withdrawal.[18] While it is rare that a Canadian Attorney General would appear in court, it is not impossible.[19] Any Attorney General who did so could also conceivably violate rules such as those regarding the lawyer as advocate.[20] In the exercise of prosecutorial discretion, the rule on prosecutors would be relevant: "When acting as a prosecutor, a lawyer must act for the public and the administration of justice resolutely and honourably within the limits of the law while treating the tribunal with candour, fairness, courtesy and respect."[21] In policy and political functions, as in personal life, the applicable rules are those that apply to all lawyers, whether inside or outside practice. These rules include those on encouraging respect for the administration of justice, on courtesy and good faith, and on non-interference with fair trial rights.[22] Moreover, some policy decisions or policy advice to Cabinet could be inconsistent with the broad spirit of specific rules. For example, an Attorney General who recommends a significant cut in legal aid funding is arguably acting contrary to the duty to make legal services available and to the goal of access to justice.[23] Similarly, an Attorney General who gives Cabinet the legal advice that unilaterally reducing provincial judges' salaries would be high risk, but gives the policy advice to do so anyways, would seem to be threatening judicial independence.[24]

As I discussed in chapter 2, the two reported cases in which Attorneys General in Canada faced law society discipline both involved out-of-court criticism of the judiciary that allegedly violated the duty to encourage public respect for the administration of justice.[25] In *Barreau (Montréal) c Wagner*, a judge complained that Quebec Attorney General Claude Wagner had, during a speech to a bar organization, made "une attaque injustifiée de sa conduite comme juge" ("an unjustified attack on his conduct as a judge").[26] In *Law Society of Yukon v. Kimmerly*, Yukon Attorney General Roger Kimmerly gave an interview in which he criticized a judge of the Yukon Supreme Court for covering a territorial coat of arms that had been installed on a courtroom wall, saying that "[i]t brings the repute of the courts and the judiciary into disrespect in the Yukon, and I'm extremely saddened by the whole thing."[27] It may not be clear in the circumstances whether such public criticism of the judiciary is made as the government's lawyer or as a Cabinet member, that is, in the practice of law or in a policy or political function. However, the duty to encourage respect for the administration of justice would apply to conduct in either category.

While there are no reported Canadian cases of a law society seeking to discipline the Attorney General for conduct in the practice of law, such instances have occurred in the United Kingdom. Consider, for example, UK Attorney General Sir John Hobson, who was accused of submitting an affidavit that he "knew to be inaccurate and misleading" while appearing in an extradition hearing.[28] More recently, UK Attorney General Lord Peter Goldsmith was accused of manipulating his advice to Cabinet on the legality of the Iraq war due to political pressure.[29] These two examples are not *exactly* analogous to Canada, as, unlike Canadian Attorneys General, the UK Attorney General is not a member of Cabinet and is not the Minister of Justice.[30] However, the Goldsmith situation could certainly occur in Canada – although I do acknowledge that it is unlikely that a Cabinet member would make such a complaint or that the legal advice would become public so that other persons would know to complain, absent unusual circumstances.

As I will return to below, potential violations by the Attorney General would vary in severity and, thus, the appropriateness of law society discipline would likewise vary. My focus in this part is on the legal question, not the policy question, that is, the kinds of conduct for which law societies *could* discipline Attorneys General, as opposed to the kinds of conduct for which they *should* do so.

2. Is the Attorney General Immune?

As a matter of current law, Attorneys General outside Ontario are subject to law society discipline in official functions, with at least some exceptions. While the commonly cited 1967 decision of the Quebec Court of Appeal in *Barreau c Wagner* holds that the Attorney General is immune to discipline for all functions of office,[31] the Court's reasoning is formal and narrow. Moreover, that reasoning is no longer correct after the Supreme Court of Canada's 2002 decision in *Krieger v. Law Society of Alberta*.[32] *Krieger* suggests that the Attorney General is generally subject to law society discipline but immune for prosecutorial discretion absent bad faith. Beyond *Krieger*, the Attorney General will also be immune under parliamentary privilege for any statements made within the legislature and may, arguably, be immune for core policy functions absent bad faith. Ontario is a special case because of a unique provision in the province's *Law Society Act*, first adopted in 1970, that grants the provincial Attorney General immunity in all official functions.[33]

2A. Outside Ontario: In General

The case of *Barreau c Wagner*[34] is sometimes cited for the holding that the Attorney General, in the exercise of their official functions, is immune from professional discipline.[35] While this was indeed the holding of the Quebec Court of Appeal, the sources which mention this position do not look at the reasoning behind the holding – reasoning that was very narrow:

> Quand le ministre de la Justice exerce les pouvoirs qui lui sont conférés par la loi, il exerce le pouvoir exécutif de la Couronne et il agit pour la Couronne. Or, "nul acte de la Législature n'affecte les droits ou prérogatives de la Couronne, à moins qu'ils n'y soient compris par une disposition expresse" (art. 9 C.C.). *La Loi du Barreau* ne tombe pas sous l'exception et je suis d'avis que le dispositif du jugement du premier juge est bien fondé.[36]

> When the Minister of Justice exercises the powers conferred on him by the law, he exercises the executive power of the Crown and acts for the Crown. However, "[n]o act of the Legislature affects the rights or prerogatives of the crown, unless they are included therein by special enactment" (art. 9 C.C.). *La Loi du Barreau* does not fall under the exception, and I am of the opinion that the operative part of the judgment of the first judge is well founded.[37]

That is, the Minister of Justice, in exercising thier official powers, is part of the Crown; the *Civil Code* provides that "No act of the legislature affects the rights and prerogatives of the Crown, unless they are included therein by special enactment";[38] the act establishing the powers of the Barreau does not include such a provision;[39] and so the Minister is immune. The Court provides no further explanation or justification for the immunity.

The relevant provision, which was then article 9 of the *Civil Code*, is standard in Canadian interpretation acts.[40] It is a codification of a common law rule.[41] The common law rule has an exception for "necessary implication" – that is, the Crown may be bound in the absence of explicit language if necessary to the purpose of the legislation – and the codifications have been interpreted in the same way.[42] These rules have been criticized, for example, as being "inconsistent with the principles of a modern legal system and difficult to apply, creating uncertainty in the law."[43] Peter Hogg has suggested that the presumption be reversed, that is, that the Crown be liable unless a statute provides otherwise.[44] Two provinces have done so,[45] as has the Uniform Law Conference of

Canada in its 2015 *Model Interpretation Act*.[46] In contrast, the Law Reform Commission of Saskatchewan argued that "the consequences of reversal are unknown and unpredictable,"[47] recommending instead that the *Interpretation Act* be amended to require all new statutes to explicitly specify whether the Crown is bound or not.[48]

It is worth emphasizing that *Barreau c Wagner*, as a decision of the Quebec Court of Appeal, may be, at most, persuasive in the other provinces and territories. Moreover, it is not entirely obvious that some conduct, like giving a speech to lawyers or an interview to a reporter, is a function of office. Thus, for example, the Yukon Supreme Court refused to quash disciplinary proceedings against Attorney General Kimmerly for criticizing the Court in a media interview, not only because "the principle of ministerial immunity from a disciplinary inquiry by the Law Society ... has not been established," but also because the judge was not "persuaded that Mr. Kimmerly's conduct and statements at the time in question were made solely in the proper discharge of his ministerial responsibilities and totally divorced from his status as a member of the Law Society of Yukon."[49] For my purposes, I adopt a broad interpretation under which *all* policy and political functions, including speeches, are within the functions of office.

Furthermore, *Barreau c Wagner* must be read in light of the decision of the Supreme Court of Canada in *Krieger*. *Krieger* supports three separate, but related, propositions. First, *Barreau c Wagner* is no longer correct, as law society acts necessarily bind the Crown. Second, the Attorney General is generally subject to law society discipline, as are Crown prosecutors. Third, like Crown prosecutors, the Attorney General is immune to law society discipline in exercising prosecutorial discretion absent bad faith.

The decision of the Supreme Court of Canada in *Krieger* indicates that the holding in *Barreau c Wagner* is no longer correct and that law society acts bind the Crown even without a specific provision to that effect.[50] The Court in *Krieger* held that Crown prosecutors were generally subject to law society discipline, but immune for prosecutorial discretion absent bad faith.[51] The reasoning was as follows: the law society act prohibits the practice of law by non-members and gives the law society the power to discipline any member; Crown prosecutors practise law and so must be members; therefore, as members, Crown prosecutors are subject to discipline.[52] That is, the Law Society (of Alberta, in that case) "has the jurisdiction to regulate the conduct of all Alberta lawyers," and "[a]ll Alberta lawyers are subject to the rules of the Law Society – Crown prosecutors are no exception."[53] Among the contrary arguments, the Court noted the argument – rejected by the application judge – "that because the Act does not specifically state that it is binding on agents of the Crown, … it is of no force and effect as regards Crown prosecutors."[54] While the Supreme Court did not explicitly consider this argument, it did hold that the jurisdiction of the Law Society comes from the province's legislation on the legal profession and the practice of law (in Alberta, the *Legal Profession Act*), and that such jurisdiction includes Crown prosecutors.[55] If the Act did not bind the Crown, this would not be true. *Krieger*, thus, certainly overrides *Barreau c Wagner*.

Barreau c Wagner, therefore, is not only narrow and formal, but is now no longer correct. The Quebec Court of Appeal does not discuss why disciplinary immunity for the Attorney General is desirable, necessary, or consistent with legal principles other than those of statutory interpretation. Neither did the Court consider whether the Crown was bound by necessary implication. Moreover, this narrow reasoning is inconsistent with *Krieger*.

The reasoning in *Krieger* can, and should, be understood as meaning that the Attorney General is generally subject to law society discipline. While the Supreme Court did not specifically decide this point, it follows from logic of the reasons. If the law society has jurisdiction over all lawyers in the province, including Crown prosecutors,[56] and the Attorney General is a lawyer,[57] then the law society should have jurisdiction over the Attorney General. More specifically, Iacobucci and Major JJ. for the Court in *Krieger* were explicit that prosecutorial functions were functions of the Attorney General that were delegated to Crown prosecutors as agents.[58] If Crown prosecutors necessarily practise law when exercising functions delegated by the Attorney General, then those functions must also involve the practice of law to the extent that they are exercised personally by the Attorney General. Similarly, to the extent that Crown prosecutors are subject to discipline for the exercise of delegated powers, it follows that those powers are subject to discipline to the same extent when exercised by the person who delegates them. Moreover, if the Attorney General is to supervise, and ultimately be responsible for, the exercise of delegated powers, it would seem that they must be subject to law society discipline in the same way as are Crown prosecutors.[59]

While *Krieger* specifically deals with prosecutorial discretion and the rest of the practice of law, the reasons do suggest that the law society would also have jurisdiction over any policy advice (and private conduct) of Crown prosecutors and, thus, by extension, over the policy and political functions of the Attorney General. For example, the reasons state in broad language that "[a]ll conduct that is not protected by the doctrine of prosecutorial discretion is subject to the conduct review process."[60] Indeed, they explicitly recognize that law societies have jurisdiction over conduct outside of practice and use that recognition to strengthen the position that prosecutorial discretion, absent bad faith, is within that jurisdiction too:

> The conduct over which the Law Society has jurisdiction by virtue of [the *Legal Profession Act*] … is very broad, encompassing conduct which may be unrelated to one's legal practice. It would be an absurd interpretation of the statute to include such profession-unrelated conduct but exclude decisions of a prosecutor in a criminal matter.[61]

Thus, based on *Krieger*, the law society has jurisdiction over the Attorney General's conduct, not only in the practice of law, but also in policy and political functions.

John Ll. J. Edwards, writing in 1995, took a position similar to the one that the Supreme Court would later adopt in *Krieger* in 2002 – although, he explicitly considered the disciplinary liability of the Attorney General as well as that of Crown prosecutors.[62] Specifically, he argued that the Attorney General and Crown prosecutors should be subject to discipline as other lawyers are for conduct in the practice of law, except for prosecutorial discretion.[63] While Edwards did not specifically discuss the policy and political functions of the Attorney General, he did acknowledge that such conduct might be different, observing that "an additional complication, regrettably not addressed by the Quebec Court of Appeal in the *Wagner* case, arises if the attorney general also happens to occupy the portfolio of minister of justice or its equivalent."[64]

Much of what is necessarily implicit in *Krieger* is explicit in the subsequent decision of the Ontario Superior Court of Justice in *Law Society of Upper Canada v. Ontario Public Service Employees Union*.[65] There, the judge held that government employees who provide legal services are required to be paralegal licensees of the Law Society because the *Law Society Act* binds the Crown by necessary implication.[66] In doing so, the judge emphasized that otherwise "the purpose of the Act, namely, protection of the public with respect to the practice of law and the provision of legal services would, in my view, be totally frustrated. Such an interpretation would result in an anomaly and absurdity, and cannot have been intended."[67]

2B. Outside Ontario: Exceptions

Thus, following *Krieger*, the Attorney General is subject to law society discipline as a general rule. However, there are at least two exceptions. One exception, prosecutorial discretion, comes from *Krieger* itself. The other exception, parliamentary privilege, is external to *Krieger*. A potential third exception would cover core policy advice and decisions.

The Court in *Krieger* held that Crown prosecutors are immune from law society discipline in the exercise of prosecutorial discretion, absent bad faith, and it is clear that the rationale applies equally to the Attorney General themselves. The Court relied on the "constitutional principle in this country that the Attorney General must act independently of partisan concerns when supervising prosecutorial decisions."[68] Just as "the fundamental principle of the rule of law under our Constitution" protects prosecutorial discretion from both "political interference" by Cabinet and "judicial supervision,"[69] it also requires such "deference" from "statutory bodies like provincial law societies."[70] But similarly, just as judicial review is appropriate where there is an abuse of process,[71] law society discipline is appropriate where there is "bad faith or improper purpose."[72] These exceptions are justified because such conduct is beyond the legitimate scope of prosecutorial discretion: "an official action which is undertaken in bad faith or for improper motives is not within the scope of the powers of the Attorney General."[73] Here, the Court in *Krieger* adopted the general statement from the concurring reasons of McIntyre J. in *Nelles v. Ontario* that "public officers are entitled to no special immunities or privileges when they act beyond the powers which are accorded to them by law in their official capacities."[74] The Court in *Krieger* gave an example: "[a] prosecutor who laid charges as a result of bribery or racism or revenge."[75]

Like the Court in *Krieger*, Edwards's rationale for disciplinary immunity of the Attorney General and Crown prosecutors in prosecutorial discretion is constitutional principle.[76] He also seems to recognize that such immunity should not be absolute, insofar as he refers approvingly to the decision of the Supreme Court of Canada in *Nelles*, rejecting civil immunity for malicious prosecution.[77]

The second exception to disciplinary jurisdiction is absolute immunity for anything the Attorney General says in the legislature because of parliamentary privilege.[78] Thus, for example, the Attorney General could freely impugn the integrity of a judge or a lawyer or a party to a proceeding, or jeopardize fair trial rights by commenting on an ongoing proceeding, in blatant contravention of the rules of professional conduct, without the possibility of any disciplinary ramifications, as long as they did so in the legislature and nowhere else. They could even violate the law with impunity, for example, by disclosing the name of a young person under the *Youth Criminal Justice Act*.[79] While the Attorney General saying any of these things could face consequences within the legislature or be forced to resign,[80] those consequences cannot include law society discipline. Like immunity for prosecutorial discretion, this immunity for parliamentary privilege has a constitutional basis: "Parliamentary privilege ... is one of the ways in which the fundamental constitutional separation of powers is respected."[81] "The purpose of [parliamentary] privilege is to recognize Parliament's *exclusive* jurisdiction to deal with complaints within its privileged sphere of activity."[82] However, unlike the immunity for prosecutorial discretion, this immunity for parliamentary privilege seemingly has no exception for bad faith.[83]

A potential third exception to disciplinary jurisdiction is the Attorney General's exercise of policy functions. For example, the Attorney General in their role as Minister of Justice makes policy decisions and gives policy advice to Cabinet.[84] Given the protection of policy decisions in tort law, a credible argument could be made that such policy decisions – as well as policy advice – should also be beyond law society discipline. The Supreme Court of Canada has recognized civil immunity for "core policy" decisions, that is, "decisions as to a course or principle of action that are based on public policy considerations, such as economic, social and political factors, provided they are neither irrational nor taken in bad faith."[85] For example, the federal Attorney General's decision on a mercy application was such a policy decision.[86] Just as courts are a questionable forum to review multifaceted discretionary decisions about societal needs and priorities,[87] so too would be a law society disciplinary tribunal. Moreover, policy advice given and decisions made by the Attorney General may be controversial among the bench and bar.[88] For example, while a law society may have views about the appropriate design and funding of the legal aid system, such views would not be determinative and would certainly not be any more legitimate than those of the Attorney General or their ministry. The Attorney General's policy decisions about the law society including amendments to its enabling legislation, should even more so be protected from law society supervision. There is no apparent reason to treat policy advice differently than policy decisions.

Such immunity for core policy advice and decisions, however, would not cover *everything* done in the Attorney General's policy and political capacity. The Supreme Court of Canada has been explicit that core policy decisions are "a narrow subset of discretionary decisions, covering only those decisions that are based on public policy considerations, like economic, social, and political considerations."[89] For example, unfounded or unsupported criticism of the judiciary, even where nominally made in the execution of official duties and arguably in good faith, would not be a core policy decision.[90]

Thus, the law society generally has jurisdiction over the Attorney General, but with some exceptions. In legal functions, they would be immune only for exercises of prosecutorial discretion, absent bad faith. In policy and political functions, they would likely be immune for "core" policy decisions, absent bad faith. They would also be absolutely immune for anything they said in the legislature. Aside from these exceptions, they would be subject to professional discipline in the same way as all lawyers.

2C. Ontario: Subsection 13(3) of the Law Society Act

In Ontario, the immunity of the Attorney General to law society discipline is extended by statute to *all* conduct in official duties. Specifically, the Ontario Attorney General is immune not only for prosecutorial discretion and core policy decisions made in the absence of bad faith, but also for all other legal and policy or political functions. This additional immunity would likely apply only absent bad faith.

Subsection 13(3) of the Ontario *Law Society Act* grants the provincial Attorney General, in the exercise of duties of office, seemingly absolute immunity from law society discipline: "No person who is or has been the Attorney General for Ontario is subject to any proceedings of the Society or to any penalty imposed under this Act for anything done by him or her while exercising the functions of such office."[91] This provision is unique among Canadian law society acts[92] and may well be unique in the Commonwealth.[93] Edwards has suggested it be repealed.[94] With the exception of Edwards, this provision is rarely mentioned in any of the standard Canadian legal literature on the role of the Attorney General. As I will explain, this provision has a curious history.

The immunity provision originated in the 1970 *Law Society Act*[95] and has had no substantive amendments since its enactment.[96] It was accompanied by two other subsections, subsections that are unusual – but not unique – in Canada, and that have also not had any substantive amendments since then. Subsection 13(1) provides, "The Attorney General for Ontario shall serve as the guardian of the public interest in all matters within the scope of this Act or having to do in any way with the practice of law in Ontario or the provision of legal services in Ontario." The provision also grants them a corresponding power to "require the production of any document or thing pertaining to the affairs of the Society."[97] There was disagreement among legislators concerning whether this role as guardian of the public interest was part of the inherent role of the Attorney General,[98] although there was eventual agreement that it was related to the inherent role of the Attorney General and not to their status as an *ex officio* bencher.[99] Subsection 13(2) provides that any document or thing required under that power is admissible only in proceedings under the *Law Society Act*.[100] Subsections similar to 13(1) and 13(2), but not to subsection 13(3) on disciplinary immunity, were adopted in the Yukon in 1984.[101]

While the 1970 *Law Society Act*, including subsection 13(3), was adopted only a few years after the *Wagner* decision, there is no indication that legislators had considered that decision or intended to codify it. Instead, the 1970 *Act* was primarily a response to the McRuer Report on civil rights.[102] However, none of section 13 was specifically suggested by McRuer, either in his analysis of the role of the Attorney General or of the self-governing professions.[103] Indeed, only once did McRuer refer to the Attorney General using language close to "guardian of the public interest."[104] Further, while McRuer noted that the Attorney General was a bencher, he did not discuss whether the Attorney General *should* be a bencher.[105]

With respect to the self-governing professions, the major point of the McRuer Report was that "the granting of self-government is a delegation of legislative and judicial functions and can only be justified as a safeguard to the public interest."[106] However, the 1970 *Act* did not implement, for the Law Society, McRuer's recommendation that lay members be added to the "governing bodies" of professional regulators.[107] The 1970 *Act* did establish a new body – the Law Society Council – that included lay members.[108] Like the Council with its lay members,[109] section 13 seems to have been added as a substitute for lay benchers.[110] Indeed, the explanatory note for the bill suggests this purpose. The note provides a list that matches the recommendation numbers to the sections of the bill. For the recommendation on lay members of governing bodies, the note reads "Not adopted – but see ss. 14 and 27."[111] These were the sections of the bill that would become sections 13 and 26, on the Attorney General as "guardian of the public interest" and on the Law Society Council.[112]

Nothing in the record specifically mentions the intentions behind the immunity provision in subsection 13(3). It is not mentioned in the debates in the legislature or at the legislative committee of the whole.[113] The subsection did undergo amendment at the Legal and Municipal Committee. Whereas the provision initially provided that current and past Attorneys General were immune to disciplinary proceedings or penalties "for anything done by him while in such office," the committee narrowed it to cover only "anything done by him while <u>exercising the functions of such</u> office."[114] This amendment, which clarifies that the immunity is only for acts done in an official capacity, suggests that the provision was discussed at committee. However, no proceedings from those committee meetings are available.[115]

Bill 7 – which would become the 1970 *Act* – was, as first introduced, based on a draft bill composed by the Law Society and approved by Convocation.[116] However, this draft bill did not include section 13 or any of its three component subsections.[117] Thus, the Law Society's preferences for the bill cannot illuminate the purpose of subsection 13(3).[118]

Nonetheless, some reasonable inferences can be drawn from the inclusion of subsection 13(3) within the 1970 *Act* and, more specifically, within section 13. Recall that subsection 13(1) sets out the Attorney General's role as "guardian of the public interest" and grants a specific power to require production. Thus, it would seem that the disciplinary immunity granted in subsection 13(3) was considered necessary or advisable to facilitate the exercise of that role and that power, which included oversight of the Law Society. That is, disciplinary liability would impact the ability of the Attorney General to serve as "guardian of the public interest." However, recall that subsection 13(3) granted immunity "for anything done by him [the Attorney General] while exercising the functions of such office."[119] This scope is narrower than it was on first reading, which was "for anything done by him while in such office."[120] However, it could have been even narrower, that is, for anything done by him in the role as guardian of public interest under subsection 13(1).

Thus, subsection 13(3) seems to presume that the disciplinary powers of the Law Society could be used or perceived as being used – either by the Law Society itself or by a third party complaining to the Law Society – to retaliate against the Attorney General for their actions as "guardian of the public interest" or to pressure them against acting as such in the first place. It also seems to presume that actions taken by the Attorney General in the functions of office, but outside the role of "guardian of the public interest," could be used as grounds for discipline in order to restrain the exercise of the guardian role.

One possible explanation for this concern was that the Law Society had recently exceeded its apparent jurisdiction by conducting its own investigation into, and making its own denunciation of, the conduct of Justice Leo Landreville of the Supreme Court of Ontario.[121] The Treasurer of the Law Society, however, asserted that the while the Law Society did not have jurisdiction over judges, it nonetheless had "a right and a duty, as representing the Bar of Ontario, to make known its views upon matters relating to the administration of justice, and to communicate those views to the appropriate official or tribunal having jurisdiction over the particular matter in question."[122] These actions were clearly on the mind of legislators as they debated the 1970 *Act*. Commented one legislator:

> I say unhesitatingly that I was against the law society initiating the investigation into Landreville and I think that marred, to a large extent, the activities of the law society. It is no function of the law society to review the conduct of judges. ... I think the law society besmirched all of us by its activities there, and I hope they will not launch into the expression of initiatives in that way again.[123]

He emphasized the importance of establishing the boundaries of Law Society jurisdiction: "the central purpose of this bill is to bring home to the law society that they are only concerned with the regulation of the profession. ... We must make sure that they get the message from us."[124] In this context, it is understandable that legislators, and the public more generally, may have been concerned that the Law Society could abuse its disciplinary authority over the Attorney General.[125]

At the same time, another legislator suggested that the Attorney General was perceived by the public as being too cozy with the Law Society and the profession generally:

> It is all well and good, in section 14 [later renumbered as section 13], to support the principle that the Attorney General is representing the public. But to the public, Mr. Speaker, the Attorney General is one of the boys. We may feel and believe in our own minds that the Attorney General will do everything he can to represent the public, because that is his duty, his responsibility as a politician. But the general public does not necessarily think so. After all, he is a lawyer; he is one of them.[126]

Under this view, disciplinary retaliation against the Attorney General would seem unlikely. Indeed, clear disciplinary jurisdiction over the Attorney General would arguably be even more important. It is possible, however, that two contrasting views were prevalent among the public.

If there were concerns that the Law Society could abuse its disciplinary authority over the Attorney General, then it is curious that the absolute immunity in the original version of subsection 13(3) was amended to cover only the exercise of official duties. If the prospect of professional discipline for acts in the functions of office could be used to punish or restrain the Attorney General from acting as "guardian of the public interest," then presumably the prospect of professional discipline for acts outside the functions of office could be used in the same way.

While the scope of the immunity in subsection 13(3) appears absolute, it would likely be interpreted as only applying absent bad faith. There are no reported discipline decisions applying subsection 13(3). While there is one reported court decision interpreting the subsection, it merely rejected the argument that the subsection means that the *Law Society Act* does not bind the Crown or its employees.[127] However, while the disciplinary immunity in subsection 13(3) – "for anything done by him or her while exercising the functions of such office" – appears absolute, consistent with *Krieger*, it would likely be interpreted as not covering any bad faith conduct. Recall that such actions are not within the powers of office,[128] as "public officers are entitled to no special immunities or privileges when they act beyond the powers which are accorded to them by law in their official capacities."[129] Thus, any conduct in purported official functions, whether in prosecutorial discretion or otherwise within the practice of law or in policy or political functions, would be subject to discipline if taken in bad faith.

3. Should the Attorney General Be Immune?

Having considered the extent to which the Attorney General is immune to law society discipline, I now turn to the deeper question: *should* they be immune? While the arguments both for and against immunity can be expressed concisely, that brevity should not suggest that their weighing is simple. I ultimately conclude that the Attorney General should be subject to law society discipline and that, if they are to be made immune, that immunity should be limited to actions taken in good faith in the execution of official functions.

As in my discussion of subsection 13(3) above, I recognize that there are two purposes for which immunity may be necessary: for the actual ability of the Attorney General to function properly and for the public's *perception* of their ability to function properly. That is, even if disciplinary immunity is not actually necessary for the Attorney General to function, it may still be necessary for public confidence in that functioning.

3A. *Policy Arguments for Disciplinary Immunity*

In the civil context, the typical argument for immunity is that liability will have a "chilling effect," that is, that the potential for liability will cause a person – such as the Attorney General – to refrain from exercising their powers as they otherwise would.[130] Related to the chilling effect is the "floodgates" argument, that is, that the sheer volume of allegations and proceedings would interfere with the person's functioning.[131]

The chilling effect is also sometimes asserted in the context of law society discipline. For example, one argument against law society jurisdiction over courtroom conduct is that it will impede the duty of zealous advocacy.[132]

In the context of civil liability, these kinds of considerations are often dismissed as "speculative."[133] However, such concerns may be lessened by difficulties in proving the elements of the cause of action. Thus, in *Nelles*, Lamer J. (as he then was) held that the tort of malicious prosecution entails "a formidable burden of proof" and that the "plaintiff ... has no easy task."[134] It is unclear, and debatable, whether disciplinary proceedings against the Attorney General would, similarly, be rare and unlikely to prevail. To some extent, that depends on the law society's ability and willingness to dismiss frivolous complaints – and public perception of that ability. As the Attorney General is a politician, there may be particular concern that complaints may be used, or perceived as being used, as a political weapon.[135]

I note that a common solution to this chilling effect is to provide that public servants, as well as other persons exercising functions granted or imposed by law, are immune in tort, so long as they acted in good faith.[136] Such provisions for public servants typically preserve the liability of the Crown.[137] I have argued that good faith is too low a standard for professionals in the context of civil liability and they should, instead, be held to the standard of professional competence.[138] Similar considerations would apply in the disciplinary context. Malice or bad faith are not necessary elements for a finding of misconduct; a lawyer acting in good faith can still do significant harm to clients or others. Competence – the standard applicable for professional discipline[139] – is much lower than perfection.[140] Nonetheless, good-faith immunity remains a common compromise.

As discussed above, the history of subsection 13(3) suggests that disciplinary immunity was provided to protect the Attorney General's function as "guardian of the public interest." However, disciplinary immunity could arguably be necessary to protect the Attorney General's other functions, that is, as chief law officer of the Crown or as Minister of Justice. Even without the "guardian of the public interest" function, the Attorney General – if a lawyer – is still in the complex situation of being the minister responsible for the law society while simultaneously being a member of the law society and, thus, subject to professional discipline. While a credible argument could be made that the Attorney General's core policy advice and decisions are beyond law society jurisdiction, such an argument might be unsuccessful. If there is a public perception that the law society might use disciplinary proceedings to retaliate for policy functions, then broader immunity would be necessary to protect against such retaliation. Similarly, the Attorney General's function as law officer of the Crown might – like the role of Crown prosecutors[141] but outside the protected scope of prosecutorial discretion – entail unpopular or controversial positions and actions that make them a target for complaints. Immunity would be justified if necessary to protect the Attorney General's exercise of one (or more) of these functions, either in reality or in the perception of the public.

3B. Policy Arguments against Disciplinary Immunity

The primary consideration against disciplinary immunity is that it is contrary to the rule of law. It is often noted, in contexts such as civil liability, that in principle the same law should apply to governments (and those exercising government functions) that applies to anyone else.[142] That is, if there must be some immunity for government, that immunity should not be absolute, as "exempting all government actions from liability would result in intolerable outcomes."[143] Justice Lamer specifically made this point in *Nelles*, although in the context of civil – not disciplinary – immunity:

> It is said by those in favour of absolute immunity that the rule encourages public trust and confidence in the impartiality of prosecutors. However, it seems to me that public confidence in the office of a public prosecutor suffers greatly when the person who is in a position of knowledge in respect of the constitutional and legal impact of his conduct is shielded from civil liability when he abuses the process through a malicious prosecution. The existence of an absolute immunity strikes at the very principle of equality under the law and is especially alarming when the wrong has been committed by a person who should be held to the highest standards of conduct in exercising a public trust.[144]

The role of disciplinary liability in maintaining public confidence is presumably as significant as, if not more significant than, the role of civil liability. Thus, although the rule of law requires the Attorney General to be independent in the exercise of prosecutorial discretion,[145] it would also seem to require that the Attorney General otherwise be subject to discipline, at least where there is bad faith. Immunity, even good-faith immunity, protects both the competent Attorney General from frivolous disciplinary proceedings and the negligent or incompetent Attorney General from warranted ones.

Disciplinary immunity also compromises the law society's protection of the public interest. Thus, the Supreme Court in *Krieger* held that the law society has jurisdiction over Crown prosecutors partly because the law society has the unique power to restrict or bar that lawyer from future practice.[146] Any employment discipline of the Crown prosecutor could not be an adequate substitute for professional discipline by the law society. In the same way, the Attorney General may face political consequences for their conduct, such as being fired or forced to resign, but those consequences are not a substitute for professional discipline. A suspension or disbarment might be necessary in the public interest, and "[o]nly the Law Society can protect the public in this way."[147] Indeed, by disempowering the law society from doing so, this immunity arguably detracts from the independence of the bar. Conversely, as mentioned in chapter 1, the inability of the Premier to disbar the Attorney General makes the independence of the bar meaningful for the Attorney General.

3C. Recommendation and Alternative

Whether or not immunity for the Attorney General is appropriate depends on how one weighs the policy arguments. Is protection against the prospect of frivolous or retaliatory disciplinary proceedings more important than the rule of law and the ability of the law society to protect the public against a malicious or negligent lawyer? Disciplinary immunity is exceptional and, absent clear evidence or overwhelming concern, seems unjustified. I, therefore, recommend that section 13(3) be repealed in Ontario and not be adopted in the other provinces and territories. The Attorney General would remain immune, as in other provinces and territories, for prosecutorial and policy functions absent bad faith, and for anything said in the legislature.

While I conclude that the policy considerations against immunity outweigh those for it, I acknowledge that reasonable people can disagree on which set of considerations prevails. In the alternative to the repeal of subsection 13(3), the provision should be amended to explicitly provide that its immunity does not apply where there is bad faith. As mentioned above, this subsection would likely be interpreted in this way. However, explicit language would remove any uncertainty and promote public confidence in the Attorney General and the rule of law. Extending good-faith immunity to all official functions would provide a single standard across all categories of conduct, with the only remaining exception being absolute immunity under parliamentary privilege.

I have focused on the peculiar situation of provincial and territorial Attorneys General. While the federal Attorney General is similarly likely to be a lawyer, they are not the minister with policy responsibility for the law society of which they are a member. (They may, however, be an *ex officio* bencher under provincial law society acts.)[148] And yet, if the prospect of law society discipline were serious enough to negatively impact the execution of their other duties, statutory immunity from law society discipline would also be appropriate.[149]

4. Conclusion

The law society has disciplinary jurisdiction over the Attorney General, with some exceptions. More specifically, the Attorney General is immune, absent bad faith, in the exercise of prosecutorial discretion, likely immune (again, absent bad faith) in "core" policy advice and decisions, and absolutely immune for anything said in the legislature. In the practice of law other than prosecutorial discretion, the law society has the same jurisdiction as it does over other practising lawyers. In policy and political functions other than "core" policy decisions, the law society has the same jurisdiction as it does over all lawyers. In Ontario, immunity is extended to *all* public functions, including the practice of law other than prosecutorial discretion and policy and political functions other than "core" policy decisions. This statutory immunity, while absolute in its language, would likely be interpreted as applying only absent bad faith. Immunity, even good-faith immunity, is contrary to the rule of law and to public confidence. If any immunity is necessary, it should be limited to good faith.

It should be emphasized that while the law society has some disciplinary jurisdiction over the Attorney General, it may exercise that jurisdiction as it sees fit. That is, it may choose not to exercise it at all, or to apply its rules differently to the Attorney General than to other lawyers. For example, the law society may choose to pursue discipline only for the Attorney General's legal functions, not for policy functions, or only for egregious conduct. Such a choice would be consistent with the rule on lawyers in public office. While the rule states that "[a] lawyer who holds public office must, in the discharge of official duties, adhere to standards of conduct as high as those required of a lawyer engaged in the practice of law," the commentary provides that discipline will typically be limited to "conduct in office that reflects adversely upon the lawyer's integrity or professional competence."[150] It is for the law society – subject, of course, to judicial review – to decide how best to use its jurisdiction and resources in order to protect the public interest.

However, the question of policy is separate from the question of law. In other words, the disciplinary jurisdiction of the law society over the Attorney General is critical to the rule of law and to the ability of the law society to protect the public interest, regardless of whether the law society determines it is appropriate to exercise that jurisdiction in any specific instance.

6 Accountability: The Non-Lawyer Attorney General[1]

In the previous chapter, I canvassed the scope of the immunity of the Attorney General to law society discipline and the implications of that immunity for accountability. As I have mentioned in previous chapters, there is no requirement that the Attorney General be a lawyer. In this chapter, I explore this legal quirk, assess its implications for accountability, and propose some solutions. While the appointment of a non-lawyer as Attorney General is an issue of public law more broadly, it is also squarely an issue with huge legal ethics impact and implications.

As explained in chapter 1, some of the official duties of the Attorney General unquestionably constitute the practice of law. The Attorney General is the chief law officer of the Crown.[2] Among other things, they are "the official legal adviser of the Lieutenant Governor, and the legal member of the Executive Council"; "shall advise the heads of the several departments upon all matters of law"; and "ha[ve] the regulation and conduct of all litigation for or against the Crown."[3]

With some exceptions, the unlicensed practice of law is an offence.[4] The purpose of licensing, along with the rest of the self-regulation of the legal profession, is to protect the public interest.[5] Nonetheless, some Attorneys General are not licensed as lawyers, which is to say that they are not members of the corresponding law society in their province or territory. As Graham Steele asks, "Does it matter?"[6] More specifically, does this leave unprotected the interests of the government as client – or, more importantly, the public interest? Yes, indeed it does.

The long-running assumption and assertion in the case law and literature has been that the Attorney General is not required to be a lawyer. In 2013, the British Columbia Court of Appeal squarely confirmed this assumption in *Askin v. Law Society of British Columbia*.[7] This holding, despite its important consequences for the public interest, has been the subject of little analysis in the subsequent case law or literature.[8]

These consequences thus remain not only unaddressed, but also largely unacknowledged.

In this chapter, I provide a legal and policy analysis of the non-lawyer Attorney General and recommendations for legislative change. I begin, in part 1, by setting out and assessing *Askin* and its uptake in the case law and literature. I demonstrate that while the decision in *Askin* has two major weaknesses, the reasoning is presumably applicable across the country.[9] In part 2, I examine the legal consequences of *Askin* and its policy and/or practical consequences. I argue that it threatens the government's solicitor-client privilege and that it leaves the non-lawyer Attorney General unconstrained by the law of lawyering more broadly. Against this context, in part 3, I consider options for legislative reform and propose a path forward that will address the legal consequences of *Askin*. I recommend legislative amendments that would deem the non-lawyer Attorney General to be a member of the corresponding law society so long as they hold that role. I conclude by reflecting on the implications of my analysis. If nothing else, such statutory deeming would clearly identify the reasonable expectations of the legislature and the public, as well as signal to the law societies that the regulation of the legal profession must unavoidably include regulation of the Attorney General. I also recommend the recognition of a constitutional convention that only lawyers be appointed as Attorney General.

To foreshadow my discussion in this chapter, the most serious problem of a non-lawyer Attorney General is not lack of wisdom or knowledge. A legal education or a call to the Bar does not, in itself, guarantee wisdom. A non-lawyer Attorney General may be wise and effective, and a non-lawyer who has attended law school shares much of the knowledge of a licensed lawyer (although that knowledge may be outdated). Instead, the most serious problem is that a non-lawyer Attorney General is not subject to the law and norms of legal ethics or to the regulatory jurisdiction of the law society.

1. *Askin v. Law Society of British Columbia* and Its Uptake

The petitioner in *Askin* unsuccessfully argued that the appointment of a non-lawyer as Attorney General was invalid and that the non-lawyer Attorney General was violating the prohibition against the unlicensed practice of law under the *Legal Profession Act*.[10] She also argued that other provincial legislation, including legislation on the office of the Attorney General, similarly required that the Attorney General be a lawyer.[11]

The petitioner also argued, likewise unsuccessfully, that the Law Society had erred in its decision that it lacked "jurisdiction" to investigate her complaint against the non-lawyer Attorney General for unlicensed practice.[12] The reaction of the Law Society to the decision of the Court of Appeal was that "[t]he law society is content to have the matter once again resolved and to have confirmation of our interpretation of the *Legal Profession Act* and other statutes."[13]

The core holding in *Askin* can be broken down into two linked propositions. The first is a matter of constitutional law: the unconstrained ability to appoint members of Cabinet, including the Attorney General, is a prerogative power.[14] The second proposition, which is a question of statutory interpretation, is that BC legislation – including the *Legal Profession Act* – had not displaced that prerogative power.[15] In particular, the *Interpretation Act* deems that a statutory assignment of duties includes the necessary powers to fulfil those duties.[16]

In arriving at this decision, each level of court made a notable observation. Justice Stromberg-Stein of the Supreme Court of British Columbia held that, as a matter of statutory interpretation, "statutes imposing duties on a minister of the Crown cannot be read as requiring that in order to perform their duties, the minister must obtain additional authority under a statute of general application, such as the *Legal Profession Act*."[17] The Court of Appeal, considering a statutory interpretation argument applying the concept of necessary implication, adopted the position of the Attorney General that "[i]t is not necessary for the purpose of protecting the general public, the purpose of the *Legal Profession Act*, that the person appointed to the office of Attorney General be a member of the Law Society, or even that the person be legally trained."[18]

Neither level of court otherwise engaged with the petitioner's submissions that the public interest required the Attorney General to be a lawyer, that is, that "[p]rinciples of the public interest in the administration of justice also militate against a non-lawyer holding office as Attorney General" and that "[s]erious harm to the rights of individual citizens of the province is a very real risk where an unqualified person is appointed to the office of the Attorney General."[19]

Although not mentioned in *Askin*, a similar question was superficially answered in the 1919 decision of the Manitoba Court of Appeal in *Rex v. Nyczyk*.[20] The appellant in *Nyczyk* argued that the indictment was invalid because it was preferred under the authority of the acting Attorney General, who was not a lawyer.[21] However, the Court held that "[t]here is nothing in the statutes that I can find requiring the Attorney-General to be a barrister or a solicitor, although the holder of that office usually is a barrister."[22] Unfortunately, the Court did not elaborate or otherwise support this statement with any legal analysis. Moreover, Purdue C.J.M. applied the proposition that "[i]t is a general presumption of law that a person acting in a public capacity is duly authorized so to do."[23] This proposition appears to parallel the interpretive argument in *Askin* that statutory duties include the power to carry out those duties.

Similarly, MacKenzie J. in *Krieger v. Law Society of Alberta* asserted, without giving any support, that "an Attorney General does not have to be a lawyer."[24] Moreover, presaging the interpretation of the BC *Legal Profession Act* in *Askin*, she also asserted that "the intent and purpose of that Act [the Alberta *Legal Profession Act*] is to control the standards of lawyers. It is not in any way concerned with the functions of the Attorney General as such."[25] While the Supreme Court of Canada affirmed the result in *Krieger*, it made no comment on these parts of the reasons of MacKenzie J.

The assumption in almost all of the literature prior to *Askin* was that the Attorney General was not required to be a lawyer. For example, David Kilgour wrote in 1979 that "[t]he Attornies General of both our federal and provincial governments need not be lawyers but invariably have been since one's mind runneth not to the contrary."[26] Similarly, in 1995, Grant Huscroft noted that "[i]n Canada, … it is clear not only that the Attorney General might not be the best lawyer; the Attorney General might not be a lawyer at all."[27] However, neither Kilgour nor Huscroft cited any legal support for their assertions, instead merely observing the fact that non-lawyers had occasionally been appointed as Attorneys General.[28] As noted by Michael B. Murphy, former Attorney General for New Brunswick, this fact is "irrelevant. … The appointments simply have not been challenged."[29]

A more nuanced position was taken on behalf of the New Brunswick Branch of the Canadian Bar Association in 1987: "Given the nature of these duties and functions [of the Attorney General] it will be seen that only in exceptional circumstances could the office be discharged by one who is not a lawyer."[30] Unfortunately, this assertion was not explained. In particular, there was no indication of what might qualify as such "exceptional circumstances."[31] Neither was it clear whether the assertion was squarely one of law or one of policy, or both.

Many decades before any of this literature, however, W. Kent Power, in a 1939 note in the *Canadian Bar Review*, squarely considered the arguments that the Attorney General must be a lawyer as a matter of law and policy.[32] Power's motivation was the appointment of a non-lawyer Attorney General for Alberta in 1937, which Power identifies as likely the first such non-lawyer Attorney General in Canadian history.[33] Intriguingly, Power's legal analysis largely foreshadowed *Askin*. Like the applicant in *Askin*, Power recognized a legal argument based on the legislation governing the practice of law and the office of the Attorney General – but, like the courts in *Askin*, he recognized the impact of the prerogative power (the scope of which power he described as being "very nebulous" at the time).[34] Also, like Askin, Power suggested that as a matter of policy, a non-lawyer Attorney General would not be capable of effectively performing the duties of office and would, thus, endanger the public interest or, in Power's words, "the public welfare."[35]

The uptake of *Askin* in the subsequent legal literature and the case law has been minimal. Only two cases have applied it, and they have only done so for fairly narrow propositions that are far from unique to *Askin*. The Alberta Court of Queen's Bench (as it then was) relied on *Askin* for the proposition that "[i]n order to amend Crown Prerogative, the Legislature must express its intent in a clear and unambiguous manner."[36] Similarly, *Askin* was cited by a party before the Supreme Court of British Columbia for the proposition that prerogative powers are beyond judicial review.[37] The British Columbia Supreme Court has cited *Askin*, among other decisions, in holding that "[t]he object of the *Legal Profession Act* is the protection of the public."[38] It was also cited by the same court in its discussion of the statutory displacement of prerogative powers.[39]

The few commentators that have cited *Askin* have at most critiqued its result but not its reasoning. Adam Dodek described *Askin* as "surprising" and "strange."[40] However, he went no further. Indeed, he wrote soon after that "[p]remiers have the power and the right to appoint non-lawyers as their chief legal advisers."[41] Similarly, while Graham Steele observed that "[w]hen the Attorney General is not a lawyer, one may wonder in what meaningful sense he or she can offer legal advice to the government,"[42] he did not argue that *Askin* was problematic or wrong. Likewise, in analysing the application of solicitor-client privilege to the non-lawyer Attorney General, I myself have applied *Askin* without any critique.[43] Another author, Jennifer A. Klinck, cited *Askin* in a discussion of prerogative powers, but offered no critique as to its result or its reasoning.[44]

Notably, the commentators who have more fully critiqued *Askin* have all come out of the government of New Brunswick: government lawyer Eric Boucher, former Deputy Attorney General Judith Keating, and former Attorney General Michael B. Murphy.[45] In his analysis of the role of the Attorney General as "lore master" of the rule of law, Boucher expressed, in passing, "grave concern" with *Askin*.[46] In an unpublished speech that drew on an article by Murphy, Keating similarly characterized *Askin* as "a most unfortunate case."[47] Murphy went further, writing that the holding in *Askin* "defies all logic."[48] Like Murphy, Keating argued that "[t]he powers of the Executive Council Office to appoint a minister and assign responsibility, and the constitutional imperative for appointing the chief legal advisor are not mutually exclusive, and to accept such a proposition is to negate the fundamental role of the Attorney General and along with it the proper application of the rule of law."[49] Indeed, Keating ranks non-lawyer Attorneys General as "[the] most flagrant erosion of the role of the Attorney General"[50] and ultimately characterizes the appointment of non-lawyer Attorneys General as a failure of the responsibility, and even the legal duty, of the Premiers who appoint them.[51] She called on lawyers, the Canadian Bar Association, and the law societies to engage on this issue.[52] Boucher, likewise, called on law societies to do so:

> My hope is also that law societies will be compelled to deal with the problem of non-lawyer Attorneys General. By stressing the importance of appointing only practicing lawyers to the top legal job of the jurisdiction, hopefully law societies will be in a better position to impress upon government the importance of its role as guardian of the rule of law and of the Attorney General's role as its Lore Master.[53]

There is no indication, at least publicly, that law societies have fulfilled Keating's plea or Boucher's hope. In my view, this is not surprising, as law societies – in contrast to, for example, the Canadian Bar Association and its branches – seem reticent to engage with such issues. Moreover, the court in *Askin* held that the Law Society was correct that it had no jurisdiction over the appointment of a non-lawyer Attorney General.[54] This holding would provide a defensible justification for the law societies to avoid addressing this problem. It is less obvious why the Canadian Bar Association appears not to have addressed it, at least publicly.

Dodek has suggested that the existence of non-lawyer Attorneys General is largely ignored by the profession because it is a threat to "some of the most fundamental assertions of the Canadian legal system," particularly the self-regulation and the professional monopoly of the legal profession.[55] This would be a compelling rationale to ignore *Askin*, albeit a self-serving one – although, following this reasoning, one might expect lawyers to argue that *Askin* was wrongly decided and that Attorneys General *must* be lawyers.

As for the reasoning in *Askin*, it has two major weaknesses. With respect, I would argue that the least supported and most vulnerable conclusion by the Court of Appeal was that the public interest mandate of the Law Society does not, by necessary implication, grant the Law Society jurisdiction over the Attorney General.[56] If the public interest requires the Law Society to regulate government lawyers, as the Supreme Court of Canada established in *Krieger*,[57] then it is unclear as to why it would not require the regulation of the Attorney General as the chief government lawyer.[58] I do acknowledge that, on a narrow reading, *Krieger* holds that the law society has this authority "[b]ecause Crown prosecutors must be members of the Law Society" – suggesting that *Krieger* itself does not assist in determining whether Attorneys General must likewise be members.[59] More detailed reasoning would have been helpful from the courts in *Askin* on this point.

The second major weakness in *Askin* is the assumed scope of the prerogative power to appoint the Attorney General. Keating and Murphy both make an important argument that the power to appoint the Cabinet must be interpreted alongside the duty of the Attorney General as chief law officer, and that the former does not trump the latter.[60] Indeed, insofar as the Attorney General has a duty to promote and protect the rule of law, and the rule of law is a constitutional principle,[61] the prerogative power is arguably constrained by that principle.[62] Moreover, the Supreme Court of Canada in *Krieger* recognized that "the office of the Attorney General is one with constitutional dimensions recognized in the *Constitution Act, 1867*."[63] That is, there are constitutional reasons to require the Attorney General to be a lawyer, which legitimately constrain the otherwise absolute discretion to appoint the Cabinet. This argument is about the scope of the prerogative power and not its displacement by statute – and thus, if accepted, renders moot the statutory interpretation issue about displacement, which was the focus of the Court of Appeal in *Askin*. Nonetheless, explicit legal support for this argument about the scope of the prerogative power appears to be lacking. In contrast, courts have zealously protected undisplaced prerogative powers,[64] which suggests that they may be unlikely to recognize an apparently novel constraint on the prerogative power to appoint the Attorney General. Unfortunately, this argument was not raised before the chambers judge or on appeal in *Askin*.[65]

While *Askin* is not binding on courts outside British Columbia, its reasoning would appear to be applicable elsewhere. While the first proposition – that the unconstrained ability to appoint members of Cabinet, including the Attorney General, is a prerogative power – applies across Canada, the question of whether that prerogative power has been displaced by statute is a matter of statutory interpretation that could conceivably vary from province to province. Steele, for example, writes that

"[t]he BC Court of Appeal decision relies on some very careful interpretation of several BC statutes, so it is not clear that the case puts the
issue to rest for the rest of Canada."[66] Nonetheless, the key provision
in the BC *Interpretation Act* – that the imposition of a duty includes the
powers necessary to execute that duty – is a fairly typical one.[67] At the
same time, any courts outside BC purporting to rely on or follow *Askin*
as persuasive would be wise to address the two weaknesses in its reasoning discussed above.

In her unsuccessful application for leave to appeal to the Supreme
Court of Canada, Askin made the novel, but intriguing and compelling, argument that there is a Canadian constitutional convention that
only lawyers be appointed Attorney General.[68] Under this argument,
the few past appointments of non-lawyer Attorneys General become
rare exceptions to a convention instead of evidence that such appointments are lawful. Whether this argument is correct depends on the
three-part test from the *Patriation Reference*, as re-stated in *Conacher v.
Canada (Prime Minister)*: "first, what are the precedents; second, did the
actors in the precedents believe that they were bound by a rule; and
third, is there a reason for the rule?"[69] The first part of the test is clearly
met, as there are numerous precedents. The third part, the reason for
the rule, will become clear in part 2 – in short, that the Attorney General
can adequately uphold the rule of law and fulfil their other duties only
if they are a lawyer. The second part of the test, whether the appointing
Premiers felt they were required to appoint only lawyers as Attorneys
General, does not seem to be in serious doubt. In particular, why else
would Premiers almost always appoint lawyers as Attorneys General?[70]
The few exceptions would appear to prove the rule.

While *Askin* was perhaps correct, and its underlying reasoning is presumably applicable across Canada, it nonetheless has undesirable legal
and policy consequences. Before turning to these consequences, I note
that, insofar as the power of appointment at issue in *Askin* is indeed a
prerogative power, it can be constrained or removed by the legislature.

2. The Legal and Policy Consequences of *Askin*

The legal and policy consequences of *Askin* are, on balance, negative
for the government, as well as for the public. While, at first glance, it
may appear that the most important consequence is that the non-lawyer
Attorney General lacks adequate legal training and experience, it is the
discrete legal consequences that I argue are more problematic.

Perhaps the most important legal consequence of *Askin*, at least for
governments, is uncertainty over whether solicitor-client privilege

applies to communications involving a non-lawyer Attorney General. While this point has never been decided by a court or tribunal, there is disagreement in the literature. Dodek has argued that solicitor-client privilege would not apply, because a non-lawyer Attorney General is not a "professional legal advisor" following Wigmore's test.[71] In contrast, John Gregory has argued that the conduit exception applies to the non-lawyer Attorney General conveying advice from their Ministry to the Cabinet.[72] Similarly to Gregory, Tom D. McKinlay argues that "Attorneys General rely almost exclusively on the legal advice prepared by the expert counsel employed in the Department of Justice. The communication of such advice would clearly be covered by solicitor-client privilege, even if conveyed by an Attorney General who is not personally a lawyer ... [because] [s]olicitor-client privilege is not lost when it is communicated among non-lawyers within the government."[73] McKinlay, nonetheless, acknowledges that "in those rare cases that a non-lawyer Attorney General communicates their personal advice, divorced from the advice of his or her officials, ... any question of privilege would arise."[74] In contrast, I have argued elsewhere that the Attorney General alone is a lawyer – that is, a professional legal adviser – without being a member of the bar.[75] Under my approach, their legal advice would be privileged, whether or not they were conveying it from their departmental lawyers or providing it personally. This disagreement has yet to be resolved in the case law and, with respect to McKinlay, I am unconvinced that the issue "is largely academic."[76]

While advice from the Attorney General to Cabinet would be covered by Cabinet secrecy,[77] that secrecy has some weaknesses compared to solicitor-client privilege. In particular, Cabinet secrecy has an outer time limit and, in some circumstances, can end before that time has elapsed.[78] Particularly important for my analysis is that Cabinet secrecy does not preclude a minister from explaining their reasons for resignation or including issues in their memoirs.[79]

The most important legal consequence of *Askin*, in terms of the public interest, is that the non-lawyer Attorney General is not bound by the law of lawyering more generally, including, but not limited to, duties under the rules of professional conduct. Indeed, the law society has no regulatory authority over the non-lawyer Attorney General and, thus, its rules have no application to them.[80] Admittedly, many of these professional duties are owed to the client, and the government as client is unlikely to complain to the law society about the Attorney General regardless – indeed, the Premier has the immediate and ever-present option of simply removing the individual acting as Attorney General from Cabinet or shuffling them into another portfolio.

Client complaints are, however, not a formal prerequisite for law society investigation or discipline. Lawyers have other overarching duties than simply those owed to the client, including civility and the duty to encourage respect for the administration of justice.[81] Sadly, not all Attorneys General have fulfilled these duties.[82] Moreover, the Supreme Court of Canada held, in *Krieger*, that law society authority over Crown prosecutors is necessary to protect the public interest.[83] As I mentioned above, similar considerations would apply to the Attorney General.[84] While even a lawyer Attorney General enjoys some statutory and constitutional immunities to law society discipline, those immunities are – and should be – narrow.[85]

It is for this reason that, as I mentioned above, I respectfully question the conclusion of the Court of Appeal that "[i]t is not necessary for the purpose of protecting the general public, the purpose of the *Legal Profession Act*, that the person appointed to the office of Attorney General be a member of the Law Society."[86] At the same time, I acknowledge the argument that law society jurisdiction over the Attorney General has an undesirable chilling effect over the execution of their duties.[87] On balance, my view is that law society jurisdiction over the Attorney General, whether a lawyer or not, is an unavoidable element of the regulation of the legal profession in the public interest. Moreover, any negative impact of a chilling effect is outweighed by the positive impact of law society jurisdiction.

An interesting consequence of *Askin* is that the non-lawyer Attorney General has no professional duty of competence.[88] If I am correct that the non-lawyer Attorney General practices law, despite not being a member of the law society,[89] they may nonetheless be liable in negligence.[90] However, the duty of care would likely be owed solely to the client, and not to third parties or the public at large. The government would be unlikely to pursue an action in negligence against its own Attorney General and, even if it did so, it would likely be for political reasons. In contrast to the duty of care in negligence, the professional duty of competence is enforceable by the law society *regardless* of the wishes of the client. Following *Askin*, law societies would have no ability to discipline non-lawyer Attorneys General for breaches of the lawyer's duty of competence, among other things.

The practical consequence of *Askin* is that it permits the appointment of an Attorney General who, at least as a matter of training and experience, is unqualified for the role. Power, in 1939, argued that it is inappropriate and anemic for a non-lawyer Attorney General to merely convey the advice of lawyers in their department:

> The attorney-general should not be a mere conduit of the opinions of others, and it is not possible for him to be anything but that if he is not learned in the law. In order to come to any conclusion really worth while he must have that instinct for the spirit of the law which can be acquired only from professional learning and experience, and, in order to weigh the opinions of his assistants and be qualified to discuss them and to convey the result which to his own mind follows from them he must be able to think in legal terms and to formulate his conclusions in accordance with those terms.[91]

Brian Smith, on his resignation in 1988 as Attorney General for British Columbia, made a similar observation about non-lawyer Attorneys General: "I know from my experience that the Attorney-General requires considerable legal and constitutional sensibility in giving advice to government, or else the Attorney-General will simply be repeating, without understanding, the legal advice of others."[92] Recall also that the courts in *Askin* did not squarely address the petitioner's submissions that a non-lawyer Attorney General endangers both the public interest and the rights of individuals.[93] Moreover, the non-lawyer Attorney General has not been screened for character and integrity as have lawyers, although, admittedly, the utility of that screening is contested.[94]

At the same time, any requirement that the Attorney General be a lawyer, even a lawyer in good standing, would be a meagre floor on competence and integrity, and certainly on experience – but a floor nonetheless. One might dream of a world-class constitutional litigator like Ian Scott but end up with an undistinguished recent call.[95] Power, though somewhat poetically, ended his analysis with the assertion that at least a lawyer can "envisage the ideal at which he should aim."[96]

In the abstract, all else equal, a lawyer Attorney General is arguably more effective than a non-lawyer Attorney General. In reality, however, a mediocre lawyer may be a failure, while an otherwise exceptionally qualified non-lawyer may make a highly effective Attorney General. For example, former Minister of Justice and Attorney General for Canada, the Honourable Anne McLellan, argued in 2018 that "thoughtful[ness]" and "good judgment" are more important for an Attorney General than being a lawyer.[97] McLellan would, however, go on to state in a 2019 report for the Prime Minister's Office that "the federal [Attorney General and Minister of Justice] has always had legal training, and I believe that it is important to continue this tradition."[98]

Indeed, some commentators argue that a non-lawyer Attorney General may be *more* effective than a lawyer – depending on how one defines effectiveness. For example, Omar Ha-Redeye writes that "[s]ometimes lengthy experience in a profession is the biggest obstacle to reforming that profession."[99] Similarly, former Ontario premier Bob Rae described his non-lawyer Attorney General, Marion Boyd, as "an advocate for change."[100] Boyd herself said of her appointment that "I think what we are saying – and what the clear message from the government is – is that the justice system is not the prerogative of the legal profession only."[101] Shirley Bond, whose appointment triggered *Askin*, suggested that "as a non-lawyer serving as Attorney General, I bring a common-sense approach that most British Columbians can appreciate."[102] More dramatically, Vic Toews argued that the adoption of administrative measures against impaired driving in Manitoba was easier because the non-lawyer Attorney General was not fixated on the requirements of the *Canadian Charter of Rights and Freedoms*:[103]

> From the onset the greatest impediment to the development of this administrative program was the objection by the legal community, including my colleagues in the Manitoba Department of Justice, that this initiative should not be pursued because it violated the *Charter of Rights and Freedoms*. ... The advantage that we had in developing this program for the Province of Manitoba was that our Attorney General was not a lawyer; rather, he could have been a model for the archetypal reasonable man we used to read about in law school. His focus was not so much on the *Charter* objections to the program that the legal community was intent on providing but on finding a mechanism to protect the lives and property of the people of Manitoba.[104]

With respect to Toews, a fixation on the *Charter* – even an undue one – might not be considered a disadvantage by some. Contrast here Boyd, the non-lawyer Attorney General for Ontario, who wanted her lawyers to confirm the constitutionality of such impaired-driving measures before she recommended them.[105] A more fundamental concern than that of Toews is that the Attorney General cannot properly oversee the profession, including the law society and its enabling legislation, unless they are independent from that profession and immune to regulation by that law society.[106]

Particularly concerning is a non-lawyer Premier who appoints themselves as Attorney General, as did E.C. Manning of Alberta in 1955.[107] Puzzlingly, Manning would later observe that "I felt that if anybody was going to serve as Attorney General who was not a lawyer, there would be more public acceptance of it if I did it myself as premier."[108] Such a dual portfolio can be disastrous for the rule of law, even where the Premier and Attorney General is a lawyer, as demonstrated by the conduct of Quebec's Maurice Duplessis in the classic case of *Roncarelli v. Duplessis*.[109] While Attorney General for Ontario, Ian Scott wrote in 1989 that "[i]t is understood in our province that the attorney general is first and foremost the chief law officer of the Crown, and that the powers and duties of that office take precedence over any others that may derive from his additional role as minister of justice and member of Cabinet."[110] This understanding is all the more important when the Attorney General holds other portfolios.

In sum, while the Attorney General should arguably be a lawyer as a matter of policy, at least as a general rule, that argument is contested. Moreover, even if that argument is correct, it does not follow that the Attorney General must be a lawyer as a matter of law. Indeed, *Askin* holds the opposite. Nonetheless, there are significant adverse legal consequences to the appointment of a non-lawyer Attorney General. Most concerning for governments is that solicitor-client privilege may not apply. In contrast, what should be most concerning for the public, and most concerning for legislatures and governments insofar as their role is to protect the public interest, is that the law of lawyering does not fully apply, if it applies at all.

3. Options for Reform

As I explained in parts 1 and 2, *Askin* – even if correctly decided – has undesirable legal and policy consequences. What then are the options for reform? Insofar as the holding in *Askin* is an application of the Crown prerogative, there is no legal impediment to legislatures changing the law through legislation. Thus, the adverse legal consequences of *Askin* can be fixed. Further, the recognition of a constitutional convention that only lawyers be appointed as Attorney General would address the adverse policy consequences.

One option, as always, is to do nothing. As described above,[111] the most serious legal consequence of a non-lawyer Attorney General for the government is Dodek's argument that solicitor-client privilege does not apply. However, there is, as of yet, no case in which this argument has been accepted. Moreover, counterarguments are available. The other legal consequences of *Askin* may be unimportant or not pressing, at least to legislators. This do-nothing option is the easiest but is certainly not recommended.

A second and superficially simple option is to require, by statute, that the Attorney General be a lawyer in good standing with their provincial or territorial law society. Indeed, Power explains that such amendments were proposed, but rejected, in Alberta in the late 1930s.[112] As I mentioned in chapter 1, Commissioner James McRuer (as he then was) in his *Inquiry into Civil Rights*, recommended a statutory requirement that the Attorney General be a lawyer.[113]

This option would fix the legal consequences of *Askin*. However, this option leaves no recourse in situations where there are no lawyers in the caucus of the governing party. Moreover, this option would compromise the freedom of the Premier to select their Cabinet, which is desirable in itself and, regardless, is central to the Canadian system of responsible government. The Premier may have good – or, admittedly, bad – reasons to choose a non-lawyer Attorney General. While Keating suggests that if no lawyer-legislator is available, a lawyer who is not an elected legislator can be appointed Attorney General,[114] I disagree that such an appointment could be reconciled with responsible government.[115] Such an appointment would be less problematic if the Attorney General were removed from Cabinet, but such a reform is beyond the scope of this chapter.[116]

A third option, and one that would fix the legal consequences of *Askin* without impeding the freedom of the Premier to select their Cabinet, is both to require the Attorney General to be a lawyer in good standing with the provincial law society *and* to require the law society to admit any person appointed as Attorney General. One model here is the Ontario *Barristers Act*, which provides that the federal or provincial Attorney General (or a previous holder of one of those portfolios) may join the Ontario bar without meeting the admission requirements,[117] but does not *require* the federal Attorney General or provincial Attorney General to do so. If the goal, post-*Askin*, is to ensure that the non-lawyer Attorney General is bound by the law of lawyering, it is not enough to *allow* the Attorney General to become a lawyer; instead, the Attorney General must be *required* to become a lawyer.[118]

I recognize that a requirement to admit the non-lawyer Attorney General is, at least at first glance, an imposition on the independence of the law society. However, recall that the non-lawyer Attorney General practises law.[119] From this perspective, imposing this requirement on the law society merely completes, or fills a gap in, its statutory mandate to regulate the practice of law in the public interest and, further, ensures it can meet that mandate. Indeed, without such a requirement, the law society is prevented from meeting – or, more cynically, permitted to abdicate – its statutory mandate. In terms of the regulation of the profession and the law of lawyering, it is better that the Attorney General be a completely unqualified lawyer than a non-lawyer.

I argue that the best option is a fourth one: to amend provincial legislation to *deem* that the Attorney General is a member of the corresponding law society so long as they remain Attorney General. This option would fix the legal consequences of *Askin* without in any way impeding the freedom of the Premier to select their Cabinet, while impairing little, if at all, the independence of the law society or compromising the qualifications required to become a lawyer.

An important consequence of making or deeming the non-lawyer Attorney General a lawyer is that they would have an identifiable duty to encourage respect for the administration of justice, a duty which I discussed in chapter 2.[120] For my purposes, it is worth re-emphasizing that this duty does not prohibit criticism of lawyers, judges, or courts – indeed, it may often *require* such criticism.[121] Instead, this duty mandates only that such criticism be fair "bona fide and reasoned," not "petty, intemperate or unsupported."[122] While a naïve romantic might hope that all politicians would do so, this expectation seems appropriate of at least the Attorney General. The professional duty of civility would likewise apply to such criticism, at least nominally.[123] Post-*Groia*, however, litigation is not a "tea party"[124] to which a robust expectation of civility applies – and if anything, politics is less likely to attract a robust expectation of civility than litigation. There is thus little reason to suspect that a non-lawyer, under my proposals, will enthusiastically embrace their newfound duty of civility. However, the existence of a duty to encourage respect for the administration of justice has normative force in itself – even if that duty remains unenforced.

One seemingly problematic consequence is that, if made or deemed a lawyer, the non-lawyer Attorney General would have a professional duty of competence – a duty that they would seem to have no chance of fulfilling themselves.[125] However, the non-lawyer Attorney General, like all lawyers and all Attorneys General, can fulfil their duty of competence by "obtain[ing] the client's instructions to retain, consult or collaborate with a lawyer who is competent for that task."[126] Thus, their lawyers can assist them in fulfilling that duty of competence. Importantly, fulfilling this duty *requires* the non-lawyer Attorney General to consider the advice of their lawyers and, apparently, to adopt that advice unless they have a good basis for rejecting it.

Perhaps the most undesirable consequence of deeming or making the non-lawyer Attorney General a member of the law society is that they would have the right to appear as counsel in court. They should resist that temptation. Indeed, even a lawyer appointed Attorney General must be thoughtful and deliberate in their court appearances.[127] Any such appearance by a non-lawyer Attorney General would suggest at least hubris, if not, as Justice Rosenberg (writing extrajudicially about lawyer Attorneys General) warned, that they are "[u]sing the court process to push a personal or political agenda."[128]

If the chilling effect of law society jurisdiction over the Attorney General is considered a legitimate concern, then one of these options could be combined with an immunity provision like that on the Attorney General under the Ontario *Law Society Act*.[129] This combination would solve the problem of solicitor-client privilege without subjecting the Attorney General to the part of the law of lawyering enforced by the law society.

What about federally? The implications of *Askin* are less of a concern federally because, as a matter of federalism, provincial law cannot require the Attorney General for Canada – or, indeed, any person providing legal services to the federal government – to be a lawyer.[130] While Parliament could displace the prerogative and require the federal Attorney General to be a lawyer, that is, to be a member of a provincial bar, Parliament would have no power to concomitantly require any provincial bar to admit them as one. Nonetheless, section 1 of the Ontario *Barristers Act* guarantees the admission of the federal Attorney General to the Ontario Bar. Parliament could deem or require the Attorney General to be a lawyer, at least for the purposes of matters within federal jurisdiction, which, under section 91(8) of the *Constitution Act, 1867* (federal power over officers and employees of the federal government), would likely prevail over provincial legislation via paramountcy.[131] Indeed, as at the provincial level, my recommendation is that Parliament adopt legislation deeming the Attorney General for Canada to be a member of at least one provincial or territorial bar. Given that the seat of government is Ottawa, and that the Ontario *Barristers Act* allows the federal Attorney General to become a member of the Ontario bar, it might appear to make the most sense for Parliament to choose the Ontario bar. However, to ensure the law of lawyering applied to the Attorney General evenly across the country, the best approach would be for Parliament to deem the Attorney General to be a member of *every* provincial and territorial bar.

The modified *Barristers Act* approach – in which the law society is required to admit the Attorney General *and* they are required to join it – has both advantages and disadvantages insofar as the Attorney General remains a member of the law society after they cease to be Attorney General, at least until they apply for permission to surrender their licence. An advantage is that the law society has regulatory and disciplinary authority over them while they are Attorney General and retains that authority after they leave the portfolio.[132] In contrast, under the deeming approach, they would be removed from law society jurisdiction by ceasing to be Attorney General. This difference, admittedly, may be an insignificant or largely hypothetical one, given the reality that law societies seem unlikely to discipline Attorneys General regardless.[133] A slightly more complex legislative solution would be to specify that the law society retains permanent disciplinary jurisdiction over conduct while serving as Attorney General. Under either approach, however, courts would maintain authority over any breaches of law by the non-lawyer Attorney General, such as a breach of their lawyerly fiduciary duty to the client, even after they cease to be Attorney General.

On the other hand, a disadvantage to this modified *Barristers Act* approach is that, after leaving office, the former Attorney General has the lifetime ability to practise law, despite having no legal training, thereby posing a substantial risk to potential clients. This lifetime ability to practise law could also be seen as a gratuitous, arbitrary, and undeserved "perk,"[134] which is the antithesis of my purpose. Indeed, if this granting of a "perk" to non-lawyer Attorneys General was the intended purpose of this amendment to the *Barristers Act*, as suggested during the legislative debates,[135] then, with respect, the government and the Attorney General either overlooked or did not appropriately appreciate the important legal issues and law society independence considerations involved, as well as the importance of the public understanding and perception of the motivation and rationale for this change.

Another option would be to split the roles of the Minister of Justice and Attorney General[136] and to only require or deem the latter to be a member of the law society. As Dodek argues, "[w]e need to have a minister of justice who is responsible for justice policy in the same way that the minister of health is responsible for health policy. But it is not apparent that we need a lawyer in this role any more than we need a doctor as minister of health, a farmer as minister of agriculture or a teacher as minister of education."[137] While this splitting at the federal level was not endorsed in the recent *Review of the Roles of the Minister of Justice and Attorney General of Canada*,[138] it warrants careful consideration both federally and provincially. Under this approach, the Attorney General could be subject to law society authority, for the necessary reasons explained above, while the Minister of Justice could be free from that authority, avoiding the accompanying constraints.

As for the policy consequences of *Askin*, here Askin's constitutional convention argument is intriguing and potentially effective. A constitutional convention that only lawyers be appointed as Attorney General would recognize the applicable policy considerations without making them legally enforceable, while serving as a strong signal to Premiers that there may be political fallout for appointing a non-lawyer. Any Premier who concluded that the appointment of a non-lawyer was the best option, despite this disincentive, would be free to choose that option. The prerogative power would, thus, be constrained as a matter of politics but not as a matter of law. Alongside my other recommendations, legislatures should consider adopting legislation or passing motions purporting to recognize a constitutional convention that only lawyers be appointed as Attorney General. While the formal recognition of a constitutional convention is a matter for the courts,[139] such a declaration by the legislatures would be meaningful evidence in itself.

4. Reflections and Conclusion

As demonstrated in this chapter, *Askin* has received little attention in the case law and the literature. I argue that it warrants more. Aside from the weaknesses in its reasoning, *Askin* has problematic legal implications. Chief among these implications is the non-application of solicitor-client privilege and of the law of lawyering. The best way to overcome the legal implications of *Askin*, without affecting the freedom of the Premier to choose their Cabinet, is to amend provincial legislation to deem the Attorney General a member of the provincial law society so long as they hold that portfolio. At the federal level, Parliament should likewise legislatively deem the Attorney General for Canada to be a member of *all* provincial and territorial bars. This approach is preferable to the guaranteed, but voluntary, call in the Ontario *Barristers Act*, which, among other things, does not require the non-lawyer Attorney General to join the law society, detracts from the independence of the law society to control admission to the bar in the public interest, and can be seen as granting an arbitrary and gratuitous lifetime perk.[140] The intention of my recommendations is not to benefit the non-lawyer Attorney General but to protect the interests of the government as client, the public interest, and the ability of the law society to fulfil its statutory mandate.

Indeed, to leave the law societies unable to regulate non-lawyer Attorneys General is to hinder their ability to protect the public interest and public confidence in the administration of justice. To insert the law societies, at least in theory, into politics in this way is admittedly inconvenient, if not dangerous, for the independence and self-regulation of the legal profession – law societies may, indeed, be "content" with the status quo.[141] Nonetheless, the ability to regulate all Attorneys General is ultimately unavoidable to properly fulfil law societies' statutory mandate. Under any approach, law societies seem, in reality, unlikely to investigate or discipline the non-lawyer Attorney General – or for that matter, *any* Attorney General. While that reality is disillusioning, I leave that disillusionment for another day.[142]

The importance of the changes I have recommended is, nonetheless, much more than symbolic. The largely theoretical potential for discipline is not the only driver for compliance with legal obligations; there is a normative and political force to those obligations. As John Ll. J. Edwards observed, albeit in a slightly different context, the ultimate backstop for any Attorney General to act properly is their character and integrity.[143] This reality is, if anything, even more true for a non-lawyer Attorney General. To subject the non-lawyer Attorney General to the professional and legal obligations of all lawyers is, one would hope, to impress those obligations upon their integrity. If nothing else, there could potentially be political ramifications if a non-lawyer Attorney General did not meet these obligations. Such ramifications would be reinforced by recognizing a constitutional convention that only lawyers be appointed as Attorney General.

In any case, legislative clarity that these obligations apply to the non-lawyer Attorney General, via a clear statement of the legislature on behalf of the public, is a first step in actualizing them and raising public expectations. Such legislation would emphasize that the legislature will (or can or should) hold even the non-lawyer Attorney General to a higher standard than it does other members of Cabinet. It would provide a clear and articulable basis, although some might characterize this as a fig-leaf, for calls for the non-lawyer Attorney General to resign.

An analogy can be drawn here to the recent recommendation by McLellan to create a special oath of office for the Minister of Justice and Attorney General of Canada, one that would, among other things, explicitly acknowledge a duty to the rule of law.[144] McLellan argued that such an oath would "clarify" the role for the Attorney General, both for themselves and for others.[145] The legislative amendments I recommend would serve a similar function. I also echo McLellan's position that such changes are "not a purely symbolic gesture" and could, if nothing else, support the Attorney General's resignation after a breach.[146]

There is a clear role for the profession, if not the public, to push for clarification and change. As suggested by Keating, the Canadian Bar Association and its branches should encourage the Federation of Law Societies of Canada and its member law societies to adopt and make public a clear position on their actual and preferable jurisdiction over the non-lawyer Attorney General – and encourage Parliament and the legislatures to act on the recommendations proposed above.

While the implications of *Askin* are problematic, my view is that an absolute rule that only lawyers can be appointed as Attorney General would be problematic in a different way. At minimum, *Askin* is problematic in that it allows the appointment of an Attorney General who is unqualified as a matter of education, training, and experience. While a bare requirement to be a lawyer does not guarantee much, it does provide a minimum measure of preparation for the role. A deeper question is whether the non-lawyer Attorney General can genuinely appreciate, understand, and fulfil their duties to the rule of law – as its "protector" or "lore master."[147] The non-lawyer Attorney General is unduly reliant on the judgment of the lawyers who advise them – unless they reject that judgment, as espoused by Toews, which is not much better. As Murphy notes, "the Attorney General is not merely a figurehead."[148] On the other hand, I acknowledge the argument that a lawyer Attorney General is beholden to the legal profession, if not to the law society itself, and cannot effectively oversee that profession and that law society while simultaneously being a member of that profession and a licensee of that law society. On balance, the freedom of the Premier or Prime Minister to choose their Attorney General outweighs the benefits of requiring them to choose a lawyer. Thus, while I agree that the Attorney General should generally be a lawyer before their appointment, I disagree that there should be a legal *requirement* to that effect – although I do advocate the recognition of a corresponding constitutional convention.

While there is no way to overcome the negative policy consequences of a non-lawyer Attorney General – that is, that they are unavoidably untrained and unqualified in a technical sense, and their integrity has not been assessed by the corresponding law society, and they lack a lawyer's understanding and appreciation of the rule of law – my proposals do overcome the *legal* consequences. In doing so, they also provide a clear and objective and rigorous standard for the non-lawyer Attorney General to meet. Premiers are free to appoint non-lawyers as Attorneys General and eliminating that freedom would be problematic. At the same time, both appointer and appointee should bear the consequences of that choice, be they positive or negative. The public should expect more of the Attorney General, be they lawyers or non-lawyers, and – if nothing else – my proposal is a reasonable way to set and affirm those expectations. It is also a clear direction to law societies that regulating the legal profession in the public interest must mean regulating the Attorney General. I emphasize that to leave the chief legal officer of the Crown beyond law society authority, in law or in reality, is to require or allow law societies to abdicate their responsibility.

7 Accountability: Alternatives to Law Society Discipline

While Attorneys General are often among the highest-profile lawyers in the country – with the potential to greatly improve or damage public confidence in the legal profession through their conduct – they rarely attract law society discipline. As discussed in chapter 5, law societies have disciplinary jurisdiction over Attorneys General, with exceptions for the legal barriers of parliamentary privilege and prosecutorial discretion, as well as unique legislated immunity in Ontario. However, policy reasons and scarce allocation of regulatory resources make it unlikely that law societies will exercise that jurisdiction. How, then, might Attorneys General be held accountable for violating their obligations as lawyers? Further, should they be? There is a pressing need for a new approach.

In this chapter, I argue that parliamentary accountability provides a viable and appropriate alternative or adjunct to law society discipline of the Attorney General. I focus on four imperatives that apply to both lawyers and legislators, though embodied in different ways with different terminologies: (1) the duty to encourage respect for the administration of justice, (2) non-interference with judicial or administrative proceedings, (3) protection of fair trial rights, and (4) civility. I argue that Attorneys General are, rightly, held to higher standards than other legislators and that enforcement of those standards is necessary for public confidence in both the legal profession and the legislative branch of government. In particular, given that lawyers are held to higher standards and face greater restrictions in their conduct than the general public, it is consistent to hold Attorneys General to higher standards than legislators generally.[1]

By parliamentary accountability, I refer to consequences imposed on the Attorney General by, or in, the legislative assembly (or House of Commons) as a legislator or as a member of Cabinet. I distinguish this from the accountability of the Attorney General, as a member of Cabinet, to answer in the House for their decisions and actions, as well as those of their ministry or department, including those relating to criminal proceedings even where there is an independent Public Prosecution Service.[2]

I emphasize at the outset something I noted in chapter 4: parliamentary privilege itself has a substantive and principled basis and is by no means a mere technicality. As the Supreme Court of Canada held in *House of Commons v. Vaid*, "[p]arliamentary privilege ... is one of the ways in which the fundamental constitutional separation of powers is respected. ... Parliamentary privilege does not create a gap in the general public law of Canada but is an important part of it, inherited from the Parliament at Westminster."[3]

While my focus in this chapter is on Attorneys General, I would note that much of my analysis would apply equally, if perhaps not as urgently, to lawyer-legislators other than Attorneys General.

1. Attorneys General and the Rules of Professional Conduct

With few exceptions, Attorneys General are ostensibly subject to law society regulation.[4] According to the codes of conduct of Canadian law societies, lawyer-politicians are purportedly held to the same standards as practising lawyers.[5] The only explicit qualification to this standard is that law societies "[g]enerally ... [are] not concerned with the way in which a lawyer holding public office carries out official responsibilities, but conduct in office that reflects adversely upon the lawyer's integrity or professional competence may be the subject of disciplinary action."[6] As a matter of law, perhaps the most important exception to this jurisdiction is parliamentary privilege.[7]

In reality, law societies rarely seek to discipline Attorneys General.[8] These rare attempts have ultimately been unsuccessful.[9] Moreover, the academic near-consensus is that such proceedings – at least against non-practising lawyers – are a poor use of limited regulatory resources,[10] as is discipline for extra-professional conduct more generally.[11] Furthermore, such attempts to discipline lawyer-politicians may promote the actual or perceived politicization of law society regulation.[12] Following Harry Arthurs's "ethical economy" model, this reticence of law societies to exercise their disciplinary powers over lawyer-politicians is presumably the rational result of a careful and perceptive cost-benefit analysis of "public goodwill" and "professional solidarity."[13] A slightly more cynical perspective would be that law societies fear legislative retribution against their delegated powers of self-regulation, or a more narrow removal of their disciplinary powers over Attorneys General[14] – although that too can be expressed as the result of a rational and defensible cost-benefit analysis.

Nonetheless, as discussed in chapter 1, law society codes of conduct consider at least four imperatives that are relevant to the expectations, pressures, and temptations applicable to Attorneys General.[15] The most important three have to do with the functioning of the justice system. One of these imperatives is the duty to encourage respect for the administration of justice.[16] This duty includes not only refraining from inappropriate criticism of judges but also defending them against criticism.[17] What is unusual about this particular duty is that it explicitly applies to lawyers' extra-professional conduct.[18] A second, and related, imperative is non-interference with judicial or administrative proceedings.[19] A third imperative is to refrain from public or media statements that would endanger the fairness of ongoing judicial or administrative proceedings.[20] Thus, an Attorney General who groundlessly impugns the integrity of a judge, contacts a judge to influence the outcome of a proceeding involving a colleague or a constituent, or asserts the guilt of a person undergoing a trial violates their duties as a lawyer in addition to any duties they might have as a legislator. A fourth imperative, though one of contested importance, is civility.[21] I have elsewhere described civility as "[t]he elephant in the room" when it comes to legal ethics and lawyer-politicians,[22] and this, sadly, would appear just as true for Attorneys General specifically.

Thus, the crux is this: Attorneys General face pressure to violate their duties as lawyers; law societies seem reticent to use their disciplinary jurisdiction over Attorneys General; and legal considerations, such as parliamentary privilege, constrain such jurisdiction. If these violations are to have consequences, such consequences must come from elsewhere – sometimes as a practical matter and sometimes as a legal one.

While I acknowledge the important – but not unbounded – responsibility of legislators to advocate and problem-solve on behalf of their constituents,[23] this responsibility cannot and should not allow interference by legislators with tribunal or court proceedings or with fair trial rights – especially by Attorneys General.

What about competence? Recall that "professional competence" is one of the respects in which the law society will purportedly consider discipline of lawyers in public office.[24] Where an Attorney General expresses a legal opinion, the law society should be attentive to the competence of that opinion. Given the assertion supporting self-regulation that only lawyers can properly regulate lawyer competence, this would be an area where, presumably, the legislative assembly is not well-placed to evaluate the conduct of Attorneys General and impose discipline. Such a characterization would render in-chamber statements of legal opinion by Attorneys General immune to legal consequences, given parliamentary privilege, but this result seems unavoidable as a matter of principle. For this reason, I have purposefully *not* identified competence as a key imperative for Attorneys General – though I would hope that Attorneys General would refrain from expressing legal opinions that they are not competent to make. The Attorney General comprises a special case among lawyer-legislators: a lawyer who practises law in the course of their official duties. Here I hope and trust that, insofar as an Attorney General practises law, they would properly and actually be subject to law society discipline for significant defects in that practice, like any other practising lawyer – and potentially all the more so than other practising lawyers, given their public trust and visibility. Again, legislative assemblies would not be well-qualified to impose discipline in such matters, and so again, parliamentary privilege would preclude any legal consequences for legal opinions expressed in the chamber.

Before turning to potential alternative sources and mechanisms for consequences for Attorneys General who violate their professional obligations as lawyers, I must first address whether such consequences unlawfully infringe the jurisdiction of law societies. If they do, there is little point in continuing further. The leading case on this matter is the decision of the Court of Appeal for Ontario in *Wilder v. Ontario Securities Commission*.[25] Wilder, a lawyer who had been reprimanded by the provincial securities commission, argued that the Commission was intruding on the exclusive power of the provincial law society to regulate lawyers. Justice Sharpe, writing for the panel, adopted the reasons of the Divisional Court on judicial review, holding that the Law Society and the Commission had different statutory mandates, that there was no statutory indication that the Commission's powers did not apply to lawyers, and that any regulatory power held by the Commission over lawyers did not offend the independence of the bar or the rule of law.[26] Justice Sharpe did, however, caution that the Commission – and "any other public body exercising statutory authority" – must ensure that it did not encourage lawyers to breach solicitor-client privilege to defend against the exercise of such powers.[27]

While *Wilder* remains binding on lower courts, the Ontario Divisional Court subsequently purported to clarify and narrow *Wilder*, interpreting its holding as being that "not every requirement of an entity with which a registered professional interacts impinges on the exclusive authority of the professional regulator. Such entities are entitled to protect the integrity of proceedings before them."[28] More specifically, the Court held that, as a matter of statutory interpretation, a provincial authority (the director under the provincial Building Code) could penalize a licensee of a provincial regulator (the Association of Professional Engineers of Ontario) for matters of honesty and professionalism but not "character" or "competency."[29] With respect, the reasoning on the narrow point was not only conclusory but also specific to the statutes at issue.[30] Nonetheless, this post-*Wilder* decision both recognizes constraints on other provincial authorities and emphasizes the importance of statutory interpretation.

Whereas *Wilder* concerned the interaction between the overlapping jurisdictions of a provincial law society and another provincial authority, federalism considerations would further protect the jurisdiction of a federal authority over lawyers. Just as paramountcy means that a federal statute can prevail over provincial law society legislation to authorize the unlicensed practice of law,[31] it would also mean that a federal statute could authorize discipline of lawyers by a federal entity. Any post-*Wilder* constraints would not apply.

I emphasize here that a legislative assembly has inherent constitutional powers, not those delegated by statute as contemplated in *Wilder*. For this reason, the implications of *Wilder* for the overlapping jurisdiction of law societies and legislative assemblies are less clear.[32] Indeed, of all the alternatives to law society discipline of the Attorney General, parliamentary accountability is preferable and powerful precisely because it is *not* limited by *Wilder*.

Despite any alternative mechanisms for accountability of the Attorney General, and despite the reluctance of law societies to discipline Attorneys General, such disciplinary jurisdiction remains critically important because of the unique remedy available under law society proceedings. The law society has the sole power to disbar a lawyer, thereby prohibiting them from practising in the future.[33]

2. Possibilities for Parliamentary Accountability for Attorneys General

Given the reticence of law societies to discipline Attorneys General for their conduct, any accountability must come from elsewhere. As Adam Dodek has noted, lawyers face several forms of accountability beyond law society regulation.[34] For Attorneys General, one additional (and obvious) option is parliamentary accountability.

At the outset, I emphasize the distinction between conduct *within* the chamber and conduct *outside* the chamber. Only the former is protected by parliamentary privilege, which pre-empts law society discipline.

The question of law society discipline for conduct outside the chamber is one of regulatory discretion, as opposed to legal impossibility.

While I recognize a modest harnessing of parliamentary accountability for Attorneys General, I consider here a more vigorous, yet potentially more controversial, position. A modest proposal would be that Attorneys General should face parliamentary accountability for breaches of legislators' ethics or codes that are also breaches of lawyers' ethics or codes. A related question is whether Attorneys General should be held to a higher threshold standard than non-lawyer legislators under the same rules. The more important question, however, is whether Attorneys General can and should face parliamentary accountability for breaches of lawyers' ethics or codes that are *not* breaches of legislators' ethics or codes.

Consider, for example, a lawyer who alleges widespread corruption or political partiality among the Canadian judiciary without providing any specific allegations or any support for this generalization.[35] If such a lawyer is in private practice, they may face law society discipline for breaching their duty to encourage respect for the administration of justice. What if the lawyer is the Attorney General? If an Attorney General made these comments inside the chamber, they would be protected by parliamentary privilege and, thus, that Attorney General would be immune to law society discipline. If an Attorney General, instead, made these comments outside the chamber, that Attorney General would potentially – but not necessarily – face law society discipline. Whether or not they can or should (or do) face law society discipline, can and should an Attorney General face parliamentary accountability? In my view, the answer is yes.

I emphasize here that there are two complementary mechanisms for parliamentary accountability: the Speaker, acting on behalf of the chamber under the standing orders, and the Integrity Commissioner (or corresponding figure) under the code of conduct (legislated or otherwise) applicable to members.

2A. *Purposes and Powers*

From both a principled and practical perspective, a useful starting point is to compare and contrast the purposes of law society discipline and parliamentary accountability. The Canadian consensus is that "[t]he purposes of law society discipline proceedings are not to punish offenders and exact retribution, but rather to protect the public, maintain high professional standards, and preserve public confidence in the legal profession."[36] However, the purpose of parliamentary accountability is less clear. For example, Marc Bosc and Andre Gagnon observe that "[t]he Speaker's disciplinary powers are intended to ensure that debate remains focused."[37] Andrew Heard, in his discussion of the power of legislative assemblies to expel their members, argues that expulsion "is necessary to both the discipline and integrity of any legislature."[38] Heard is clear that "integrity" is intricately connected with public confidence: "[n]o legislature can be venerated as an institution of governance if it is populated with such unsavoury characters."[39]

In addition to differing purposes of accountability, there is also an important distinction between the powers of law societies and the powers of the assembly. Whereas law society disciplinary powers are subject to freedom of expression as protected under the *Canadian Charter of Rights and Freedoms*, parliamentary powers over members are absolute.[40]

2B. *The Speaker and the Standing Orders*

Insofar as misconduct by Attorneys General occurs in the chamber, much of that misconduct can be penalized, and effectively stopped, by the Speaker under standing orders and precedent. Of the four imperatives I have selected from law society codes of conduct, three or four could be imposed, at least in part, in this manner: prohibitions against criticizing specific judges and against incivility, through standards of "unparliamentary" language,[41] and prohibitions against interference with fair trial rights, through the *sub judice* convention.[42] Improper pressure on judges might also be regulated via the *sub judice* convention.[43] I recognize here that the *sub judice* convention is distinct and separate from the ethical duties of lawyers.[44] Instead, my point is that it happens to encompass comment by Attorneys General that would also breach their obligations as lawyers. The convention and the rule of conduct for lawyers do, however, share the purpose of, as Steele puts it, "prevention of prejudice to a judicial proceeding."[45] Given that, as Steele notes, the Speaker should intervene only in "exceptional cases,"[46] it may be that parliamentary accountability tolerates a higher degree of comment on a case before the courts than would a law society. However, the prohibition nonetheless exists and covers similar conduct as the rule of professional conduct for lawyers.

Indeed, given that this conduct is immunized from law society jurisdiction by parliamentary privilege, parliamentary accountability is the only route for consequences. Despite *Wilder*, it seems likely that the Speaker can discipline members, including Attorneys General, for breaches of legal ethics *per se* given the meaning and purpose of parliamentary privilege – as opposed to merely regulating by its own standards the conduct of Attorneys General that just so happens to also breach the requirements of legal ethics as otherwise enforceable by law societies. As held by the Supreme Court of Canada, parliamentary privilege allows "legislative activities to proceed unimpeded by any external body or institution, including the courts" by protecting exclusive self-jurisdiction over matters impacting "the dignity and efficiency of the House."[47]

Thus, the House of Commons or a provincial legislative assembly could presumably discipline an Attorney General for violating the obligations of lawyers – whether or not that conduct also violated the obligations of legislators. With respect, here, I disagree with the argument that parliamentary privilege is necessarily contrary to the rule of law.[48] Oversight and consequences merely lie with another authority, that is, the assembly itself, rather than the judiciary. The fact that such oversight is rarely exercised and that such consequences rarely occur does not mean that they are not *possible*.

Nonetheless, even if Attorneys General are subjected to the same rules as all other legislators, they could be held to a higher standard under some or all of those rules. For example, a level of incivility tolerated in a non-lawyer legislator might not be tolerated in a lawyer-legislator, especially an Attorney General. This, too, would seem to be up to the assembly to determine its own standards, including different standards for different legislators.

The more complicated issue is whether there can be parliamentary accountability for breaches of legal ethics that occur outside the chamber or are otherwise beyond the purview of the Speaker. Thus, I turn to codes of conduct for legislators, which cover (or can cover) conduct both inside *and* outside the chamber.

2C. *Legislators' Codes of Conduct and Conflict of Interest Codes for Cabinet Members*

With few exceptions, Canadian codes of conduct for legislators tend not to contain a basket or catch-all clause.[49] However, such codes – legislated or otherwise – do not limit the inherent power of a legislative assembly to discipline its members as a matter of parliamentary privilege.[50] This inherent power, unlike the powers of the Speaker, extends to conduct outside the Chamber, such as criminal offences.[51] Moreover, statements outside the Chamber have been held to violate the *sub judice* convention.[52] Thus, there is no apparent barrier to legislative assemblies disciplining Attorneys General for violations of their duties as lawyers, including – but not limited to – the four kinds of duties I have identified as priorities. Typically, such discipline is on the recommendation of the Integrity Commissioner or a parallel figure.[53]

While additional obligations may apply to Cabinet members, these codes are largely silent on the imperatives I have chosen as the focus of this chapter. Nonetheless, a key expectation, whether codified or not, is that Ministers will not attempt to influence judicial or quasi-judicial decision-making.[54] Indeed, Heard asserts that this expectation constitutes a constitutional convention.[55] Such attempts by Attorneys General would intuitively be more egregious.

2D. Pressure for Resignation

Aside from formal discipline up to and including expulsion, there is also the possibility of pressure for an Attorney General to resign as a member of Cabinet or even to resign as a legislator. As Ned Franks puts it, albeit perhaps romantically, "[t]here is no more fearsome voice in Canadian politics than the opposition baying for ministerial blood on the floor of the House of Commons."[56] (While John Ll. J. Edwards was adamant that accountability in Parliament was the most important and appropriate kind of accountability, he was focusing on ministerial responsibility for prosecutorial decision-making and was contrasting accountability in Parliament to supervision or accountability imposed by the courts.)[57] For the purposes of my analysis, the most important ministerial misconduct that might prompt resignation by the Attorney General is attempting to influence, or even to contact, a judge regarding a matter before them.[58] An Attorney General who resists calls for their resignation may well be removed from Cabinet. The media plays a critical role, though not the sole role, in promoting political accountability of this nature. For the Attorney General specifically, the Canadian Bar Association and its branches, and other lawyers' organizations, may also play a role.

3. Reflections and Conclusions

To the extent that law societies and assemblies have concurrent jurisdiction over the conduct of Attorneys General outside the chamber, those two sources are independent from each other. In other words, the law society may discipline an Attorney General whether or not they have been disciplined by the assembly. Likewise, the assembly may discipline an Attorney General whether or not they have been disciplined by their law society. Attorneys General may be disciplined by one authority, both, or neither. An analogy can be drawn here to in-courtroom conduct by lawyers, which may be addressed by the judge or the law society or both, because the judge and the law society have different mandates and powers.[59] The mere fact that a law society determines not to pursue professional discipline against an Attorney General, whether for principled or practical reasons, does not – and should not – mean that such an Attorney General cannot face other consequences for that same conduct. Neither should the fact that any attempted law society discipline was unsuccessful.

Parliamentary accountability for Attorneys General is a matter of both "can" and "should." Most of my focus in this chapter has been on the "can" question, that is, whether legislative assemblies *can* discipline Attorneys General for violations of the ethics and codes of conduct of lawyers. The "should" question is equally important but perhaps more straightforward to answer. Public confidence in both the legal profession and the legislative branch of government requires accountability for the Attorney General as a practising lawyer. To the extent that law societies cannot (or will not) impose such accountability, legislative assemblies should employ their inherent powers to do so, especially where parliamentary privilege precludes law society discipline as a matter of constitutional law. This double standard, far from being problematic or unfair, accurately reflects the dual identity and dual responsibilities of Attorneys General. The unavoidable prospect of politicization or political weaponization of such accountability does not make it any less necessary. While I acknowledge the idea that political consequences for Attorneys General, as for all lawyer-politicians, are primarily a matter for the ballot box, such a view is not only simplistic and ahistorical but reflects a thin conception of democracy.[60] Parliamentary accountability is not a complete substitute for law society discipline, but it has an important role to play in upholding public confidence in Attorneys General.

For greater certainty, codes of conduct for legislators and members of Cabinet should be amended to explicitly incorporate the law of lawyering as applying to the Attorney General and clarify that any legal ethics contraventions by the Attorney General constitute a breach of those legislated codes of conduct. Parallel changes to the Standing Orders, which would confirm the ability of the Speaker to disallow unethical conduct by the Attorney General, would also be advisable.

In closing this chapter, I do recognize that parliamentary consequences and political consequences both seem unlikely. Parliamentary consequences will be unlikely, especially in the context of a majority government. Political consequences, such as being shuffled into another portfolio, being forced to resign from Cabinet, or being removed from

Cabinet, may be more likely than parliamentary consequences, but not to a great extent. However, the *potential* for parliamentary or political consequences, like the potential for law society disciplinary consequences, encourages – or should encourage – the Attorney General to respect the law of lawyering.

8 Conclusion: Accountability, Integrity, and Self-Respect

In this concluding chapter, I draw together the ideas from the previous chapters to offer my reflections and recommendations.

The Attorney General, as an elected politician who practises law as part of their duties of office, faces a unique mix of tensions that increase the complexity of their duties as lawyers. Their apolitical role as chief law officer of the Crown is vastly different from their political role as Minister of Justice. This complexity is most visible around the professional duty of the Attorney General as a lawyer to encourage respect for the administration of justice. The only two public instances in which a Canadian law society has sought to discipline an Attorney General both involved breaches of this duty in the form of inappropriate criticism of judges. Both sets of proceedings were ultimately unsuccessful. Even an Attorney General who keeps their own public comments about judges measured may find themselves in a difficult position when Cabinet colleagues, including the Premier or Prime Minister, engage in such inappropriate criticism.

These tensions and this complexity are heightened where the Attorney General portfolio includes policing or where the Attorney General is cross-appointed to another portfolio, especially as Premier or Prime Minister. It can be difficult to separate a lawyer role from a non-lawyer role, all the more so when a single person is essentially attempting to provide legal advice to themselves as the representative of the Crown as the organizational client. In this context, it seems unlikely that even the most honest and conscientious lawyer could maintain their professional independence from themselves. In particular, it seems unlikely that a cross-appointed Attorney General can fulfil their duty of candour by providing frank, yet unwelcome, advice to themselves. Circling back to the duty to encourage respect for the administration of justice, the cross-appointed Attorney General may face even more political pressure – some self-imposed – to inappropriately criticize courts or judges. As I mentioned in chapter 2, in my view, the problems posed by an Attorney General who is also the Premier or Prime Minister are greater than the problems posed by the non-lawyer Attorney General – although both sets of problems are serious ones. Ideally, the Attorney General would be a lawyer who was not cross-appointed to another portfolio, particularly Public Safety. For the same legal ethics reasons, Public Safety functions should be spun off into a separate ministry in those jurisdictions where those functions currently remain within the ministry of the Attorney General.

Resignation poses complex and unique challenges for the Attorney General. The law of lawyering requires that they resign when other members of Cabinet would not be *required* to do so and that they cannot resign when other members of Cabinet *would* be able to do so. The overlay of lawyer-client confidentiality further complicates the issue of resignation. Indeed, the duty to encourage respect for the administration of justice arguably justifies, or even requires, the Attorney General to breach confidentiality to announce their reasons for a principled resignation – although they should do so in the House or Assembly for both practical and principled reasons around accountability.

This unique mix of tensions, in combination with the high visibility of the Attorney General, makes accountability particularly important. As a matter of law, ministerial immunity does not – and should not – preclude law society discipline of the Attorney General. In particular, *Krieger v. Law Society of Alberta* demonstrates that legislation on the legal profession does bind the Crown.[1] Law societies would be unable to fulfil their statutory mandate to protect the public interest without at least *some* regulatory and disciplinary jurisdiction over the Attorney General. Some immunity is necessary and appropriate as a matter of constitutional law, including the protection of both parliamentary privilege and prosecutorial discretion. Further immunity is unwise.

Accountability becomes even more complex when a non-lawyer is appointed as Attorney General. The law society has no jurisdiction over such a person even though they practise law. The ability to appoint a non-lawyer as Attorney General is a matter of the undisplaced Crown prerogative of the Governor in Council or Lieutenant Governor in Council to select their Cabinet on the recommendation of the Prime Minister or Premier. While this prerogative could be displaced by legislation, in my view, a preferable solution is to amend provincial and territorial legislation on the legal profession so that any non-lawyer Attorney General is deemed to be a member of the law society, at least during their time in that portfolio. This solution imposes the professional duties of all lawyers on the non-lawyer Attorney General, while ensuring that the Crown as a client enjoys solicitor-client privilege.

Parliamentary or political consequences, or both, are alternative sources of accountability for the Attorney General. In particular, many of the professional duties of the Attorney General as a lawyer have parallels in parliamentary law, including the duty to encourage respect for the administration of justice and to refrain from commenting on matters before a court. Both the professional duties of the Attorney General as a lawyer and the expectations of the Attorney General as a legislator and member of Cabinet have normative force that may anchor political pressure by the public, the media, and opposition legislators.

There is nothing romantic or idealistic about the accountability of the Attorney General for violations of the law of lawyering. However, for many reasons, such accountability remains unlikely in practice, whether in the form of law society discipline or parliamentary or political consequences. Given Cabinet confidences, solicitor-client privilege, and the professional duty of confidentiality applicable to the Attorney General and all public lawyers, much of the conduct of the Attorney General is unlikely to become public. Insofar as law society disciplinary matters begin as client complaints, the Crown as the client seems unlikely to make a complaint to the law society regarding its own Attorney General. Even where questionable conduct becomes known to the law society, and such conduct is not protected as prosecutorial discretion or parliamentary privilege, disciplinary proceedings remain unlikely. Even if a law society were to attempt to discipline the Attorney General, that law society (or the courts on judicial review) may apply some form of ministerial immunity or engage in some form of balancing of the role of the Attorney General as a politician with the role of the Attorney General as a lawyer, despite my analysis in chapter 5. And even if such disciplinary proceedings were successful, the legislature in that province – and in other provinces – might well respond by adopting the immunity provision from the Ontario *Law Society Act* so as to preclude such discipline in the future. Meaningful parliamentary consequences seem unlikely, at least in the context of a majority government. Meaningful political consequences also seem unlikely, based on the past experience canvassed in chapter 2. Thus, despite the doctrinal *potential* for accountability, actual accountability may be rare.

Options for Change

In this context, what potential legislative changes or other changes would assist the Attorney General in meeting their obligations under the law of lawyering? I begin with assessing proposals made by others before synthesizing the proposals I have considered in previous chapters.

As I mentioned in passing in chapter 1, one recurring proposal is to separate the roles of Attorney General and Minister of Justice, that is, to split the "two hats" so that they are held by two different people.[2] The Minister of Justice would be a legislator and member of Cabinet but not necessarily a lawyer, and the Attorney General would be a lawyer but not necessarily a member of Cabinet or even necessarily a legislator.[3] Proponents of this option, such as Adam Dodek, argue that the "two hats" model poses "an intolerable conflict ... a clash of loyalties and a conflict of interest" and emphasize that a combination of historical idiosyncrasy and inertia are an insufficient rationale to maintain the "two hats" model.[4] In contrast, the Honourable Anne McLellan, in her 2019 *Review of the Roles of the Minister of Justice and Attorney General of Canada* commissioned by the Prime Minister's Office, concluded that "such a structural change would diminish the credibility of the Attorney General's legal advice and lead to the loss of the broad perspective the joined roles provide to the person holding them."[5] This position is more a matter of public law than of legal ethics.

From a legal ethics perspective, separation of the "two hats" would reduce – if not eliminate – the risk that political factors would pose a conflict of interest for the Attorney General, in which that person's personal and political interests could influence the legal advice given to the Crown as the client. Removing the separate Attorney General from Cabinet, or even assigning that role to a bureaucrat instead of an elected legislator, would further reduce this risk.

However, with great respect to Dodek, in my own view, he is overly optimistic in his assertion that the Prime Minister's attempts to influence prosecutorial decision-making by Jody Wilson-Raybould (as discussed in chapter 4) "never would have happened at all if Canada had done the hard work already," that is, split the roles of Attorney General and Minister of Justice. I expect that the Prime Minister simply would have attempted to influence the Attorney General in the same way as he attempted to influence Wilson-Raybould as the Attorney General and Minister of Justice. However, I do acknowledge that the Prime Minister would have had fewer levers to improperly influence a separate Attorney General who was not in Cabinet. Similarly, I respectfully take issue with the view canvassed by McLellan that "[t]he fact that the two roles are held by one person can cause confusion on what issues it is permissible to discuss with that person."[6] Any such "confusion" stems from unacceptable ignorance, and such ignorance is a poor reason for change. I thus heartily agree with McLellan's recommendation of training for members of Cabinet and their staffers and for legislators, concerning as it is that such training is necessary.[7]

While separation of the "two hats" would be beneficial from a legal ethics perspective, and while I do not necessarily agree with McLellan's reasoning against such a separation, that separation might not be beneficial from a public law, public policy, or political science perspective. Canadian politicians and policy makers, as well as the Canadian public, would benefit from a more thorough articulation of the reasons for leaving the "two hats" model intact. Thus, I recommend further study of the proposal to separate the roles of Attorney General and Minister of Justice. Although I would not recommend that change at this time, it remains an option for the future.

I fully agree with Ian Scott's view that, as between the "two hats," the role of Attorney General is the more important: "[T]he attorney general is first and foremost the chief law officer of the Crown, and ... the powers and duties of that office take precedence over any others that may derive from his additional role as minister of justice and member of Cabinet."[8] Thus, I also endorse McLellan's recommendation to add some version of this language to federal legislation on the Department of Justice.[9]

Symbols and signals matter and, for that reason, I commend the steps taken by the Privy Council Office to follow McLellan's recommendation to amend the oath of office taken by each new Minister of Justice and Attorney General for Canada.[10] I recommend not only that the provinces and territories make their own parallel changes but that these oaths be codified in legislation. Likewise, I commend McLellan's recommendation that the official title of the Department of Justice be changed to "the Department of Justice and Office of the Attorney General of Canada."[11] As I set out in chapter 1, some provinces already use parallel naming. Indeed, I would go further than McLellan and recommend that the federal government and all provinces and territories adopt the Ontario model, in which the name of the ministry refers *only* to the Attorney General.[12]

In preceding chapters, I have considered several other legislative changes to the role of Attorney General. As discussed in chapter 5, I recommend that the Attorney General's near-absolute statutory immunity from Law Society discipline in the Ontario *Law Society Act* be abolished in that jurisdiction and not be adopted in other jurisdictions. This rejection of the Ontario approach is fundamentally a matter of the rule of law and of empowering – and trusting – the law society to fulfil its statutory mandate to protect the public interest. In my view, no narrower statutory immunity is advisable. However, if narrower immunity is advisable, such as immunity for core policy decisions, that immunity should be codified to reduce legal uncertainty.

As discussed in chapter 6, the non-lawyer Attorney General poses serious problems of legal ethics – both in uncertainty over the Crown's ability to claim solicitor-client privilege but also for the accountability of the Attorney General according to the law of lawyering. Possible legislative solutions would include requiring the Attorney General to be a member in good standing of the corresponding law society (or for the federal Attorney General, any law society); requiring the Attorney General to be a lawyer in good standing with the provincial law society *and* requiring the law society to admit any person appointed as Attorney General; or deeming that the Attorney General is a member of the corresponding law society so long as they remain Attorney General. The first option is legally viable because it would merely be a legislative displacement of the prerogative power to select the Cabinet. From a legal ethics perspective, the second option would appear to be the most effective. However, the third (deeming) option is more respectful of the independence of the law society while remaining almost as effective as the second option from a legal ethics perspective.

As discussed in chapter 7, legislated codes of conduct for legislators and members of Cabinet should be amended to explicitly incorporate the law of lawyering as applying to the Attorney General and clarify that any legal ethics contraventions by the Attorney General constitute a breach of those legislated codes of conduct. Parallel changes to the Standing Orders, which would confirm the ability of the Speaker to disallow unethical conduct by the Attorney General in the Chamber, would also be advisable.

Legislative changes do not seem particularly likely. However, law societies can also address some of these issues by amending their rules of professional conduct. One change would be to add a commentary to the rule on lawyers in public office and to the rule on the duty to encourage respect for the administration of justice.[13] These commentaries would explicitly identify the standard to which the Attorney General will be held. They could also articulate a balancing or moderated approach that would provide some defined leeway to the Attorney General given their multiple roles, particularly their political responsibilities.

The Attorney General should explicitly be held to the same standards of accountability as all other lawyers, as the current rule on lawyers in public office provides: "A lawyer who holds public office must, in the discharge of official duties, adhere to standards of conduct as high as those required of a lawyer engaged in the practice of law."[14] However, the commentary that follows tends to weaken this rule: "Generally, the Society is not concerned with the way in which a lawyer holding public office carries out official responsibilities, but conduct in office that reflects adversely upon the lawyer's integrity or professional competence may be the subject of disciplinary action."[15] This commentary would ideally be omitted. Any balancing should be within the duty to encourage respect for the administration of justice. If law societies do determine that it is appropriate and necessary to balance the duties of the Attorney General as a lawyer against the duties of the Attorney General as a politician, that balancing approach should be explicitly articulated in the commentary to the rule on lawyers in public office.

Regardless of any amendments to relevant legislation or rules of professional conduct, stakeholders should dramatically – and consciously – increase their expectations of the Attorney General and their willingness to impose consequences for shortcomings. As a matter of regulatory and disciplinary priorities, law societies treat the Attorney General as any other lawyer, with the caveat that their high public profile makes any misconduct, particularly a breach of the duty to encourage respect for the administration of justice, more serious and, thus, more important to address in order to maintain public confidence in the legal profession and in the administration of justice. Legislators and the media should, likewise, hold the Attorney General to the standard of a practising lawyer and play their vital roles in encouraging accountability. They should also critically evaluate – if not discourage – the appointment of a non-lawyer Attorney General and the cross-appointment of the Attorney General, particularly as Premier or Prime Minister.

Attorneys General should expect more of themselves and embrace their professional responsibilities as a lawyer. While it would be hubris for any Attorney General to compare themselves to Ian Scott or Roy McMurtry – whether in skill, honour, or integrity – aspirations are worthwhile and important.

At the End of the Day...

These twin realities of complexity and (non)-accountability mean that adherence to the professional duties of lawyers, the law of lawyering, and legal ethics more broadly will ultimately depend on the characteristics of the person in the role and those around them – both their advisors and the representatives of the Crown as the client. This theme is quite explicit and consistent in the work of John Ll. J. Edwards, particularly his later work in the 1980s. McLellan, in her *Report*, quoted approvingly Edwards's statement that "in the final analysis it is the strength of character, personal integrity and depth of commitment to the principles of independence and the impartial representation of the public interest, on the part of the holders of the office of Attorney General, which is of supreme importance."[16] Likewise, Brent Cotter quoted the same passage in his discussion of the achievements of former Attorney General for Ontario Ian Scott, recognizing the importance of "the personal values [Scott] espoused."[17] Although Edwards was focusing on criminal prosecutions, the concept readily applies to *all* aspects of the role of the Attorney General.

In the unique Canadian context of the "two hats" model, Edwards's emphasis on integrity and a commitment to independence is entirely consistent with Ian Scott's imperative, which McLellan recommended be codified in federal legislation,[18] that "the attorney general is first and foremost the chief law officer of the Crown, and that the powers and duties of that office take precedence over any others that may derive from his additional role as minister of justice and member of Cabinet."[19] Dodek may be right that the "two hats" create an unavoidable conflict of interest,[20] albeit one that is tolerated (whether by ignorance or by deliberate and conscious acceptance). Even if the two hats do not necessarily conflict, there will be tensions. Given that inevitability, it is critical that the Attorney General actively decides which role takes priority. It is clear from a legal ethics perspective that the lawyer role as chief law officer of the Crown should be that priority. Given the importance of that lawyer role to the rule of law, Scott's approach is consistent with, and perhaps even required by, a public law perspective.

I would also emphasize self-respect, which underlies the work of both Scott and Edwards. If the Attorney General and their own staff do not personally embrace the special role of the Attorney General, they cannot articulate that role to the public or to other members of Cabinet. To return to the lawyer's duty to encourage respect for the administration of justice, the Attorney General's essential role in the administration of justice means that they must develop and exhibit self-respect.

While different Attorneys General may articulate and express this self-respect in different ways, resignation is perhaps the most powerful of the many ways in which an Attorney General can privately or publicly assert their independence and promote respect for that independence. Self-respect may require resignation or at least the live and continuing prospect of resignation. A principled resignation should be the active and pre-emptive choice of the Attorney General themselves, well before resignation is imposed by outside forces. As Edwards puts it, "[t]he option of resignation is always open to an Attorney General ...

who, on grounds of principle or in the actual circumstances of a particular situation, feels sufficiently strong that he must take a public stand in opposition to the rest of his political colleagues."[21] Where controversy develops, the resigning Attorney General may demonstrate self-respect for their role by asserting confidentiality and privilege – not just because the rules require it but because it is the right thing to do.[22] Conversely, the resigning Attorney General may also demonstrate self-respect by publicly revealing the reasons for resignation, particularly where the actions of the Premier or Cabinet challenge the rule of law and require denunciation and public scrutiny. Regardless of their chosen course of action, such an Attorney General should be able to articulate how that choice is informed by, and reinforces awareness of and respect for, the unique role of the Attorney General.

The Attorney General should hold themselves to a higher standard even where any form of imposed accountability is incredibly unlikely. They should ensure that their political staff fully embrace that higher standard, not only in the spirit of ministerial accountability but also pursuant to the professional duty to supervise non-lawyer staff.[23] In this context, self-imposed accountability, in the form of resignation as penance for their own shortcomings or the shortcomings of their political staff, may be the only realistic form of accountability. It is likewise a deep expression of integrity and honour, at least when it is truly self-imposed and not a result of political pressure or a face-saving gesture to avert a likely or inevitable removal from the role by the Premier.

The Attorney General should also ensure that others, particularly other politicians and those other politicians' own political staffers, are aware of that higher standard and what it requires. Here, I circle back to the rule of professional conduct on mandatory withdrawal, which requires withdrawal only if a client "*persists* in instructing the lawyer to act contrary to professional ethics."[24] While it seems bizarre that, with all their power and all the governmental and political resources available to them, members of Cabinet and their staffers could be ignorant or contemptuous of the role of the Attorney General, that bizarre reality will only change through client and stakeholder education,[25] as well as accountability for members of Cabinet and their staffers. That accountability, however, is beyond the scope of this book.

Ultimately, a legal ethics approach challenges stakeholders – including voters, media, law societies, and the Attorney General themselves – to recalibrate their expectations of the Attorney General. The Attorney General is a unique politician. Being an effective politician is sometimes, but by no means always, antithetical to being an ethical Attorney

General. Being an ethical Attorney General is necessary, but not sufficient, to being a good Attorney General.

What, then, are the most important attributes of an ethical Attorney General? I circle back to the political temptations I identified in chapter 1 and returned to in chapter 7. As a lawyer, the Attorney General must meet the core duties of loyalty (including confidentiality, candour, conflicts, and "commitment to the client's cause"),[26] integrity,[27] and competence. Despite any political pressures, the Attorney General must give firm and unwelcome advice,[28] not interfere with fair trial rights,[29] encourage respect for the administration of justice,[30] and exhibit civility.[31] The Attorney General, more than other politicians, must closely supervise their non-lawyer political staffers and take complete professional responsibility for their shortcomings.[32] They must understand why their role is unique so that they can educate those around them about that uniqueness and its importance – particularly, but not only, around their independence in criminal law proceedings – even those who should not need to be educated. Ideally, the Attorney General would wholeheartedly embrace their duties as a lawyer and consider meeting those duties to be merely a floor and not a ceiling. All of these imperatives require integrity and honour. They may also sometimes require forgoing political advantage or tempering political ambition, at least temporarily.

I emphasize, one final time, that there is – and should be – nothing inherently romantic or idealistic about the accountability of the Attorney General for violations of the law of lawyering and the deliberate desire to avoid such violations, whether for noble or selfish reasons. Nonetheless, if these views are idealistic or romantic to the point of being unrealistic, then, with much respect to McLellan and despite my own misgivings, it may be necessary to split the "two hats."

Legal ethics for the Attorney General is a captivating and compelling area of scholarship with real-world impact. This book provides guidance for Attorneys General, their staff, their fellow members of Cabinet, legislators, the media, and the public. At the same time, this book also provides a doctrinal foundation not only for further doctrinal work but also for other approaches to legal ethics scholarship, including empirical, critical, historical, and comparative approaches – as well as approaches grounded in economics and in literature. However, the professional obligation of confidentiality may impede empirical work involving past or current Attorneys General and their staffs. For example, it would be instructive to survey past and present Attorneys General to gauge their agreement with Ian Scott's position that, under the "two hats" model, the Attorney General role takes precedence over the

Minister of Justice role. My work in chapters 2–5 suggests that legal history offers potential for a range of different projects on legal ethics and the Attorney General.

I end with my own *cri de coeur*, both as a lawyer who has practised in government and as an academic who has written in this area for about a decade. The role of Attorney General is not a stepping stone or a box to check on the way to the party leadership and Premiership. Among the roles in Cabinet, it is not like the others. It is a unique role that, like the practice of law itself, brings with it serious responsibilities and obligations as well as stringent, yet unavoidable and important, constraints. Consistent with Michael Bryant's reflections on his time as Attorney General for Ontario, the duties of the role *should* – in many ways – be both "daunting and inspiring."[33] The true weight of the role is likewise well-captured in observations by Roy McMurtry while serving as Attorney General for Ontario:

> The office of Attorney General is steeped in history and tradition. That history, those traditions, are not merely of academic or scholarly interest. The traditions of the office of Attorney General boil down in their essence to a set of very clear and very high standards of objectivity, against which every holder of the office … must daily measure his conduct. … Far from representing the dead hand of historical precedent, the traditions of the office of Attorney General represent a living standard of conduct which constantly and urgently commands the attention of everyone who is privileged to fill that office.[34]

As Commissioner James McRuer wrote, "[t]he office [of the Attorney General] should be restored to its traditional authority, responsibility and dignity. Its occupant should rank in precedence next to the Prime Minister."[35] Sadly, in the more than fifty years since, that restoration by many if not all indications remains unachieved.

For the Attorney General who does not aspire to the greatness of Ian Scott or Roy McMurtry, or for the Attorney General who sees the portfolio merely as another stepping stone towards greater political ambitions, my hope is that the prospect of accountability, in whatever potential form, will be an adequately effective driver of behaviour. That hope, however, seems unrealistic. Despite power if not prestige, conversely and regrettably the role of Attorney General brings little, if any, realistic prospect of meaningful accountability.[36] Essentially, in other words, any accountability must be self-imposed. This reality makes integrity and honour indispensable. In this context, a principled resignation is an act of character, whether or not the reasons for that principled resignation are made public. A principled resignation as self-imposed penance for failure is perhaps even more meaningful. Perhaps the greatest act of character – and one that may never become known to the public – would be for a prospective Attorney General to decline the appointment in the knowledge that they lack the necessary combination of virtues.

Notes

Foreword by Allan Rock

1 Allan Rock practised as a trial lawyer for two decades with a national law firm in Toronto, serving as a Bencher and then Treasurer of the Law Society of Ontario. He spent a decade as a senior minister in the federal government, including four years as Minister of Justice and Attorney General of Canada. He subsequently served as Canadian Ambassador to the United Nations in New York. He is President Emeritus of the University of Ottawa, where he also taught constitutional and international law.

Foreword by Michael Bryant

1 35th Attorney General of Ontario, 2003–7; LLM (Harvard), JD (Osgoode), MA, BA (UBC). Bryant taught constitutional law at King's College, London, and published on the subject during and after serving as Attorney. See e.g., Michael J. Bryant and Lorne Sossin, *Public Law: An Overview of Aboriginal, Administrative, Constitutional and International Law in Canada* (Toronto, ON: Carswell, 2002). Bryant was a Member of Provincial Parliament from 1999 to 2009, serving in the Ontario Liberal Party caucus, and Government House Leader (2007–9).

2 Remarks by Hon. R. Roy McMurtry, Dedication ceremony for the McMurtry-Scott Building at 720 Bay Street, (29 May 2005), online: <https://news.ontario.ca/en/release/89795/media-advisory-dedication-ceremony-for-the-mcmurtry-scott-building-at-720-bay-street> [https://perma.cc/23EM-JG3A]. Hon. Roy McMurtry repeated that story to me and used it at informal public occasions I attended, when I was Attorney and he was the Chief Justice of Ontario. The story was that Premier Davis used to jokingly refer to "that alternative government run out of King Street"

[where the Ministry building resided, until it transferred to 720 Bay Street, Toronto, now called the McMurtry Scott Building], because Davis would often learn of new Justice policies and decisions through the media before anything came to Cabinet.

3 F. Scott Fitzgerald (Francis Scott), *1896–1940. The Great Gatsby* (New York, NY: C. Scribner's Sons, 1925).

4 Oscar Wilde, *De Profundis* (New York, NY: Modern Library, 2010).

5 That is, idealism versus pragmatism. Robert Bork, serving at the time as Solicitor General, was the final player in the (1973) Saturday Night Massacre, when President Richard Nixon ordered a succession of people serving or acting as Attorney General, to fire a Special Prosecutor. Bork carried out the order, as Acting Attorney General, then reversed his intention to immediately resign after firing Archibald Cox, remaining as Acting Attorney General for two months, until Senator William Bart Saxbe was appointed Attorney General by President Nixon. For Bork's version, see Robert H. Bork, *Saving Justice: Watergate, the Saturday Night Massacre and Other Adventures of a Solicitor General* (New York, NY: Encounter Books, 2013). For competing scholarly critiques, see Antonin Scalia et al, "In Memoriam: Robert H. Bork" *Harv J L Public Policy* 36, no. 3 (2013): 1231.

6 Bork, *ibid*.

7 Walter Bagehot, *The English Constitution*, vol 28 (Ithaca, NY: Cornell University Press, 1966).

8 The answer to this rhetorical flourish is not zero. People and regulators have held Attorneys to account, but they are historical exceptions, as this book proves.

9 But note that this story is hardly flattering, to me, since I would have staked my career on the obscure jurisprudential subject of judicial salaries – a burning issue only for judges themselves, and constitutional scholars like Martin – and 'almost' resigning wrongly presumes that the condition precedent was unambiguous. Martin's point is, I believe, that Attorneys should at least be seriously thinking about it when their will is being bent to that of their political appointors.

1 Introduction: The Attorney General and the Practice of Law

1 *House of Commons Debates*, 41–2, no. 80 (5 May 2014): 4919 (Hon. Peter MacKay); Canadian Press, "MacKay Offers Few New Details on Supreme Court Spat" *The News (New Glasgow)* (3 May 2014), 15. For more detail, see chapter 2.

2 See, e.g., Cristin Schmitz, "MacKay Fell Short as AG, Lawyers Say" *The Lawyers Weekly* (30 May 2014), 1.

3 Tonda MacCharles and Bruce Campion-Smith, "Talks with Ex-minister 'Troubling,' MPs Told" *The Toronto Star* (26 February 2019), A1 [MacCharles & Campion-Smith].

4 PC 2019-0105 (25 February 2019), online: <https://orders-in-council .canada.ca/attachment.php?attach=37424&lang=en> [https://perma .cc/8XM4-RKDQ].

5 See, e.g., Jamie Strashin, "Wilson-Raybould May Not Have Broken the Law, But Her Wernick Tape Crossed Ethical Lines, Lawyers Say" *CBC News* (3 April 2019), online: <https://www.cbc.ca/news/politics/wilson -raybould-tape-1.5082119> [https://perma.cc/XK9F-WVFZ].

6 Steve Bruce, "Court to Hear Bid to End Strike" *The Chronicle Herald [Halifax]* (25 October 2019), A3.

7 *Ibid*. See also Francis Campbell, "Liberal Legislation Renders Injunction Moot" *The Chronicle Herald [Halifax]* (26 October 2019), A3.

8 See, e.g., Steven Chaplin, "The Attorney General Is Not the Legislature's Legal Advisor" *JPPL* 14 (2020): 189 at 190 [Chaplin]: "To a great extent, the conclusions [Martin] reaches are based on a romantic, misplaced and outdated understanding of the role of Attorney General in the United Kingdom, and a failure to appreciate the significantly different history and role of the Attorney General in Canada."

9 For reflections on Scott see, e.g., the Honourable Justice Ian Binnie, "Mr. Attorney Ian Scott and the Ghost of Sir Oliver Mowat" *Advocates' Soc J* 22, no. 4 (2004): 4; David J. Mullan and the Honourable Gary Trotter, "Retrospective: Ian Gilmour Scott, O.C., (1934–2006)" *Queen's LJ* 34 (2009): 769; W. Brent Cotter, "Ian Scott: Renaissance Man, Consummate Advocate, Attorney General Extraordinaire" in *In Search of the Ethical Lawyer*, ed. Adam Dodek and Alice Woolley (Vancouver: University of British Columbia Press, 2015), 202. (Now Justice Woolley of the Court of Appeal of Alberta.) For similar reflections on Roy McMurtry, see, e.g., Adam Dodek, "Remembering Attorney General Roy McMurtry" (19 April 2024), online (blog): *Slaw* <https://www.slaw.ca/2024/04/19/remembering-attorney -general-roy-mcmurtry/> [https://perma.cc/99TG-9XHP].

10 John Ll. J. Edwards, *The Law Officers of the Crown* (London: Sweet & Maxwell, 1964), 277 [Edwards, *Law Officers*]: "As a member of the Bar, however, the Attorney-General is in no way distinguishable from his professional brethren in being accountable to the Benchers of his Inn of Court regarding his own professional behaviour." See also John Ll. J. Edwards, "The Office of Attorney General: New Levels of Public Expectations and Accountability," in *Accountability for Criminal Justice: Selected Essays*, ed. Philip C. Stenning (Toronto: University of Toronto Press, 1995), 294 at 303: "I disapprove strongly of any legislative immunity that is designed to insulate the holder of the office

of attorney general from all forms of professional accountability." On the carve-out for prosecutorial decision-making see, e.g., 302–3.

11 Edwards more often referred to accountability in Parliament as being the most important and appropriate kind of accountability for the Attorney General, although in that context he was focusing on accountability for prosecutorial decision-making (via ministerial responsibility) and the interplay between Parliamentary accountability and accountability imposed by the courts. See, e.g., J. Ll. J. Edwards, "The Attorney General and the Charter of Rights," in *Charter Litigation*, ed. Robert J. Sharpe (Toronto: Butterworths, 1987), 45 [Edwards in Sharpe] at 46: "the accountability of the Attorney General, within his sphere of authority, is to be discharged on the floor of the legislature or in the Parliament of Canada, as the case may be." Edwards was keenly aware of the limitations of this accountability (at 47): "Looked at in realistic terms, there is no denying the fact that the practical exigencies of a crowded legislative timetable, and even more so the ineffectual questioning of the principal Law Officers of the Crown, have contributed to diminishing confidence in the argument that the proper place to subject the Attorney General to a full accounting for departmental activities is the legislative assembly."

12 Adam M. Dodek, "Canadian Legal Ethics: Ready for the Twenty-First Century at Last" *Osgoode Hall LJ* 46, no. 1 (2008): 6 [Dodek, "Ready"]. See also Andrew Flavelle Martin, "Where Are We Going? The Past and Future of Canadian Scholarship on Legal Ethics for Government Lawyers" *Can Bar Rev* 99, no. 2 (2021): 322 [Martin, "Where Are We Going?"].

13 See, e.g., Connie Sun, "The Discretionary Power to Stay Criminal Proceedings" *Dal LJ* 1, no. 3 (1974): 482; Peter Burns, "Private Prosecutions in Canada, the Law and a Proposal for Change" *McGill LJ* 21 (1975): 269; Frank Armstrong and Kenneth L. Chasse, "The Right to an Independent Prosecutor" *CR (NS)* 28 (1975): 160; Hon. L.K. Graburn, "The Relationship of the Crown Attorney to the Attorney General" *CR (NS)* (1976): 259; R. Camille Cameron, "Prosecutorial Control in Canada: The Definition of Attorney General in Section 2 of the *Criminal Code*" *UNB LJ* 30 (1981): 43; Law Reform Commission of Canada, *Controlling Criminal Prosecutions: The Attorney General and the Crown Prosecutor*, Working Paper 62 (Ottawa: The Commission, 1990); Bruce P. Archibald, "The Politics of Prosecutorial Discretion: Institutional Structures and the Tensions between Punitive and Restorative Paradigms of Justice" *Can Crim L Rev* 3 (1998): 69; Lori Sterling and Heather MacKay, "Constitutional Recognition of the Role of the Attorney General in Criminal Prosecutions: *Krieger v. Law Society of Alberta*" *SCLR (2d)* 20 (2003): 169 [Sterling & MacKay].

14 See, e.g., Kate Bezanson, "Constitutional or Political Crises? Prosecutorial Independence, the Public Interest, and Gender in the SNC-Lavalin

Affair" *UBC L Rev* 52 (2019): 761; Michael Murphy, "The Attorney General, Politics, and the Public Interest: Contributions to an Evolving Constitutional Convention" *CJLS* 37, no. 2 (2022): 209.

15 *Canadian Charter of Rights and Freedoms*, Part I of the *Constitution Act 1982*, being Schedule B to the *Canada Act 1982* (UK), 1982, c 11 [*Charter*]. See, e.g., Ian G. Scott, "The Role of the Attorney General and the Charter of Rights" *Crim LQ* 29 (1986–7): 187 [Scott, "Role and *Charter*"]; Hon. Ian Scott, "Law, Policy, and the Role of the Attorney General: Constancy and Change in the 1980s" *UTLJ* 39 (1989): 109 [Scott, "Constancy and Change"]; Grant Huscroft, "The Attorney General and Charter Challenges to Legislation: Advocate or Adjudicator?" *NJCL* 5 (1995): 125 [Huscroft, "Advocate or Adjudicator"] (now Justice Huscroft of the Court of Appeal for Ontario); Edwards in Sharpe, *supra* note 11; Kent Roach, "The Attorney General and the *Charter* Revisited" *UTLJ* 50, no. 1 (2000): 1; Mark J. Freiman, "Convergence of Law and Policy and the Role of the Attorney General" *SCLR (2d)* 16 (2002): 335; Grant Huscroft, "Reconciling Duty and Discretion: The Attorney General in the *Charter* Era" *Queen's LJ* 34 (2009): 773 [Huscroft, "Duty and Discretion"]; Kent Roach, "Not Just the Government's Lawyer: The Attorney General as Defender of the Rule of Law" *Queen's LJ* 31, no. 2 (2006): 598 [Roach, "Not Just"].

16 See, e.g., Adam M. Dodek, "Canadian Legal Ethics: A Subject in Search of Scholarship" *UTLJ* 50 (2000): 115 [Dodek, "Search"].

17 See, e.g., Jody Wilson-Raybould, *"Indian" in the Cabinet: Speaking Truth to Power* (Toronto: HarperCollins, 2021); Ian Scott with Neil McCormick, *To Make a Difference: A Memoir* (Toronto: Stoddart, 2001) [Scott, *To Make a Difference*]; Roy McMurtry, *Memoirs and Reflections* (Toronto: University of Toronto Press for the Osgoode Society for Canadian Legal History, 2013) [McMurtry, *Memoirs*]; Michael Bryant, *28 Seconds: A True Story of Addiction, Tragedy, and Hope* (Toronto: Viking, 2012) [Bryant, *True Story*]; Scott, "Role and *Charter*," *supra* note 15; Scott, "Constancy and Change," *supra* note 15. But for historical accounts, see Paul Romney, *Mr Attorney: The Attorney General for Ontario in Court, Cabinet, and Legislature, 1791–1899* (Toronto: The Osgoode Society, 1986). (See also J. Murray Beck, "Rise and Fall of Nova Scotia's Attorney General: 1749–1983" *Dal LJ* 8, no. 3 (1984): 125).

18 But see especially Brent Cotter, "The Prime Minister v the Chief Justice of Canada: The Attorney General's Failure of Responsibility" *Leg Ethics* 18 (2015): 73.

19 See, e.g., Adam Dodek, "The Impossible Position: Canada's Attorney-General Cannot Be Our Justice Minister" *The Globe and Mail* (22 February 2019) O1, 2019 WLNR 5866240, online: *The Globe and Mail* <https://www .theglobeandmail.com/opinion/article-the-impossible-position-canadas

-attorney-general-cannot-be-our/> [https://perma.cc/U3TK-263K] [Dodek, "Impossible"].

20 I nonetheless note that former Attorney General for Ontario Roy McMurtry has criticized the province's move to the single title. See McMurtry, *Memoirs, supra* note 17 at 188: "This dual title has been the tradition in most, if not all, of the Canadian provinces, but in Ontario the justice title was dropped during a temporary reorganization of government and, regrettably, never restored."

21 See, e.g., Alice Woolley, "Introduction to Legal Ethics" in *Lawyers' Ethics and Professional Regulation*, ed. Alice Woolley, Richard Devlin, and Brent Cotter (Toronto: Lexis Nexis Canada, 2021), 1 at 8: "The definition of "legal ethics" has engaged and troubled academic commentators for many years."

22 While the origins of this phrase are unclear, see, e.g., Geoffrey C. Hazard Jr. and W. William Hodes, *The Law of Lawyering* (New York: Harcourt Brace Jovanovich, 1985). See, e.g., Dodek, "Ready," *supra* note 12 at 6 [citations omitted]: "[L]egal ethics consists of much more than 'the law governing lawyers.' Legal ethics is concerned not only with the positivist inquiry of what is, but very much with the normative inquiry of what ought to be." On the relationship between legal ethics and philosophy, and specifically political philosophy and moral philosophy, see, e.g., Alice Woolley, "Legal Education Reform and the Good Lawyer" *Alta L Rev* 51, no. 4 (2014): 801, 809.

23 Alice Woolley and Amy Salyzyn, *Understanding Lawyers' Ethics in Canada*, 3rd ed. (Toronto: LexisNexis, 2023), 2–3. See also Frederick C. DeCoste, "From Formalism to Feminism: Seventy-Five Years of Theory in the Legal Academy" *Alta L Rev* 35, no. 1 (1996): 189 at 198–9, dismissing a formalist approach to legal ethics: "Sucked dry of politics and morality, and abstracted from normative standards, legal ethics becomes reduced to technology and instead of standing for something, lawyers merely are those expert in the manipulation of law's autarkic currency."

24 Dodek, "Search," *supra* note 16.

25 Dodek, "Ready," *supra* note 12 at 7 [emphasis in original].

26 But see, e.g., in the US context Diana N. Viggiano, "Aiming the Canons at the General: How Should Traditional Canons of Legal Ethics Guide and Constrain an Attorney General" *Geo J Leg Ethics* 22, no. 3 (2009): 1193, focusing on the investigative and prosecutorial roles.

27 *Ministry of the Attorney General Act*, RSO 1990, c M.17, s 5 [Ontario *MAG Act*]. See also, e.g., *Department of Justice Act*, RSC 1985, c J-2, s 5 [Federal *DOJ Act*]; *An Act Respecting the Role of the Attorney General*, RSNB 2011, c 116, s 2 [NB *AG Act*]; *The Department of Justice Act*, CCSM c J35, s 2.1 [MB *DOJ Act*]; *Attorney General Act*, RSBC 1996, c 22, s 2 [BC *AG Act*];

Department of Justice Act, RSY 2002, c 55, s 7 [YK *DOJ Act*]. See Bryant, *True Story*, *supra* note 17 at 287: "Consider my A.-G. duties, helpfully set forth in a statute. The breadth of these duties was daunting and inspiring for me when I first read them."

28 Ontario, *Royal Commission: Inquiry into Civil Rights: Report One* (Toronto: Queen's Printer for Ontario, 1968) (Hon. James Chalmers McRuer, Commissioner), vol. 2 at 954 [McRuer]. See also 956, Recommendation 11: "Statutory provision should be made that the Attorney General must be a member of the Bar of Ontario." Patrick Boyer, in his biography of McRuer, wrote that this recommendation was made "[i]n a drive to consolidate responsibility": J. Patrick Boyer, *A Passion for Justice: The Legacy of James Chalmers McRuer* (Toronto: University of Toronto Press for the Osgoode Society for Canadian Legal History, 1994), 311.

29 See, e.g., *Ontario v. Criminal Lawyers' Association of Ontario*, 2013 SCC 43 at para. 35; *R v. Thompson* (1913), 7 Alta LR 40 at 49, 14 DLR 175 (CA).

30 *Legal Profession Act*, SNS 2004, c 28, s 16(1) [*Legal Profession Act*]. See in parallel *Law Society Act*, RSO 1990, c L.8 [*Law Society Act*], which does not define the practice of law but does define the provision of legal services at s 1(5): "a person provides legal services if the person engages in conduct that involves the application of legal principles and legal judgment with regard to the circumstances or objectives of a person."

31 That other government positions with administration-of-justice mandates may involve specific aspects of the practice of law does not mean that those positions also practise law. Indeed, those positions are often exempted in statute from the practice of law or from the prohibition on the unlicensed practice of law. See, e.g., *Legal Profession Act*, *supra* note 30, ss 16(j)(k) (federal or provincial legislators or municipal councillors assisting constituents).

32 Ontario *MAG Act*, *supra* note 27, s 5(h).

33 Hon. Brian R.D. Smith, QC, "The Role of the Attorney General – Or Walking the Tightrope" *Advocate (Vancouver)* 46, no. 2 (1988): 255 at 260.

34 The Honourable Marc Rosenberg, "The Attorney General and the Administration of Criminal Justice" *Queen's LJ* 34, no. 2 (2009): 813 at 847. Ian Scott himself recognized this concern. See Scott, *To Make a Difference*, *supra* note 17 at 150, discussing *Reference re Bill 30, An Act to Amend the Education Act (Ont.)*, [1987] 1 SCR 1148, 40 DLR (4th) 18: "It was the only case I argued as attorney general, and I had to think long and hard before I did so. I did not want to be seen as grandstanding on a hot political issue."

35 Rosenberg, *supra* note 34 at 847–8.

36 Smith, *supra* note 33 at 260; Rosenberg, *supra* note 34 at 848.

37 Edwards in Sharpe, *supra* note 11 at 47.

38 See, e.g., Andrew Flavelle Martin, "Does the Attorney General Have a Duty to Defend Her Legislature's Statutes? A Comment on the *Reference Re Genetic Non-Discrimination Act*" *Manitoba LJ* 43, no. 2 (2021): 220.

39 See, e.g., Huscroft, "Advocate or Adjudicator," *supra* note 15; Huscroft, "Duty and Discretion," *supra* note 15; Scott, "Role and *Charter*," *supra* note 15.

40 *Askin v. Law Society of British Columbia*, 2013 BCCA 233, leave to appeal to SCC refused, 35463 (7 November 2013). See chapter 6.

41 See in parallel Adam M. Dodek, "Lawyering at the Intersection of Public Law and Legal Ethics: Government Lawyers as Custodians of the Rule of Law" *Dal LJ* 33, no. 1 (2010): 1 at 11 [Dodek, "Intersection"] on government lawyers [citation omitted]: "whole chapters in the applicable codes of conduct are absolutely irrelevant to government lawyers."

42 See above notes 32–6 and accompanying text.

43 See, e.g., Federation of Law Societies of Canada, *Model Code of Professional Conduct* (Ottawa: FLSC, 2009, last amended October 2022), r 5.1, online: <flsc.ca> [*FLSC Model Code*]. See also *Code of Professional Conduct of Lawyers*, RLRQ c B-1, r 3.1, arts. 20, 23 [*Quebec Code*].

44 See, e.g., *R v. Neil*, 2002 SCC 70 at para. 19.

45 See, e.g., *FLSC Model Code*, *supra* note 43, r 2.1: "A lawyer has a duty to carry on the practice of law and discharge all responsibilities to clients, tribunals, the public and other members of the profession honourably and with integrity." See also *Quebec Code*, *supra* note 43, arts. 4, 13, 20.

46 *FLSC Model Code*, *supra* note 43, r 3.1-2: "A lawyer must perform all legal services undertaken on a client's behalf to the standard of a competent lawyer." See also *Quebec Code*, *supra* note 43, arts. 20 ("A lawyer owes his client duties of integrity, competence, loyalty, confidentiality, independence, impartiality, diligence and prudence"), 21 ("A lawyer must engage in his professional activities with competence").

47 *FLSC Model Code*, *supra* note 43, r 3.2-2, commentary 3. "Occasionally, a lawyer must be firm with a client. Firmness, without rudeness, is not a violation of the rule. In communicating with the client, the lawyer may disagree with the client's perspective, or may have concerns about the client's position on a matter, and may give advice that will not please the client. This may legitimately require firm and animated discussion with the client."

48 *Ibid.*, r 3.1-2, commentary 6(b).

49 See, e.g., *ibid.*, r 5.1. See also *Quebec Code*, *supra* note 43, arts. 20, 23.

50 *FLSC Model Code*, *supra* note 43, r 3.7-7(b).

51 *Ibid.*, r 3.7-2 and r 3.7-2, commentary 1. See also *Quebec Code*, *supra* note 43, art. 48(1).

52 See, e.g., *FLSC Model Code*, *supra* note 43, r 3.7-1. See also *Quebec Code*, *supra* note 43, art. 51.

53 On the exception to confidentiality, see *FLSC Model Code, supra* note 43, r 3.3-3. See also *Quebec Code, supra* note 43, art. 65(6). On the corresponding exception to privilege, see also *Smith v. Jones,* [1999] 1 SCR 455, 169 DLR (4th) 385. On the interaction between exceptions to privilege and exceptions to confidentiality, see Adam M. Dodek, *Solicitor-Client Privilege* (Toronto: LexisNexis Canada, 2014) at paras. 2.15–17.

54 See chapter 5 and chapter 7.

55 See, e.g., *FLSC Model Code, supra* note 43, r 7.5-2: "A lawyer must not communicate information to the media or make public statements about a matter before a tribunal if the lawyer knows or ought to know that the information or statement will have a substantial likelihood of materially prejudicing a party's right to a fair trial or hearing." See also r 7.5-2, commentary 1: "Fair trials and hearings are fundamental to a free and democratic society. It is important that the public, including the media, be informed about cases before courts and tribunals. The administration of justice benefits from public scrutiny. It is also important that a person's, particularly an accused person's, right to a fair trial or hearing not be impaired by inappropriate public statements made before the case has concluded." See also *Quebec Code, supra* note 43, art 18: "A lawyer must not make public statements or communicate information to the media about a matter pending before a tribunal if the lawyer knows or should know that the information or statements could adversely affect a tribunal's authority or prejudice a party's right to a fair trial or hearing."

56 See, e.g., *FLSC Model Code, supra* note 43, r 5.6-1: "A lawyer must encourage public respect for and try to improve the administration of justice." See also r 5.6-1, commentary 3. See also *Quebec Code, supra* note 43, art. 12: "A lawyer must support respect for the rule of law. However, he may, for good reason and by legitimate means, criticize a legal provision, contest the interpretation or application thereof, or seek to have it repealed, amended or replaced."

57 See, e.g., *FLSC Model Code, supra* note 43, r 7.2-1: "A lawyer must be courteous and civil and act in good faith with all persons with whom the lawyer has dealings in the course of his or her practice." See also *Quebec Code, supra* note 43, arts. 4, 112.

58 See, e.g., *FLSC Model Code, supra* note 43, r 5.6-1, commentary 3. See also *Quebec Code, supra* note 43, art. 12.

59 See, e.g., *FLSC Model Code, supra* note 43, r 5.6-1.

60 Craig E. Jones, "On the Attorney General, the Courts and the New Ministry of Justice" *Advocate (Vancouver)* 71, no. 2 (2013): 189 at 192.

61 See, e.g., *FLSC Model Code, supra* note 43, r 5.1-3: "When acting as a prosecutor, a lawyer must act for the public and the administration of justice resolutely and honourably within the limits of the law while

treating the tribunal with candour, fairness, courtesy and respect."
See also r 5.1-3, commentary 1: "When engaged as a prosecutor, the
lawyer's primary duty is not to seek to convict but to see that justice is
done through a fair trial on the merits. The prosecutor exercises a public
function involving much discretion and power and must act fairly and
dispassionately." See also *Quebec Code, supra* note 43, art. 112: "When acting
as prosecutor in a criminal or penal matter, the lawyer must act in the
public interest and in the interest of the administration of justice and the
fairness of the judicial process."

62 *Krieger v. Law Society of Alberta*, 2002 SCC 65 at para. 3. As discussed by
Sterling and MacKay, *supra* note 13 at 170, Ian Scott asserted this principle
before its explicit recognition in *Krieger*: Scott, "Role and *Charter*," *supra*
note 15 at 191: "The absolute independence of the Attorney General on
questions of prosecution policy is accepted as an important constitutional
principle."

63 See, e.g., *FLSC Model Code, supra* note 43, r 7.2-3: "A lawyer must not use
any device to record a conversation between the lawyer and a client or
another lawyer, even if lawful, without first informing the other person of
the intention to do so."

64 See, e.g., above note 5 and accompanying text on Jody Wilson-Raybould.

65 See, e.g., *FLSC Model Code, supra* note 43, r 6.1-1: "A lawyer has complete
professional responsibility for all business entrusted to him or her and
must directly supervise staff and assistants to whom the lawyer delegates
particular tasks and functions." See also *Quebec Code, supra* note 43, art. 35:
"A lawyer … is responsible for the mandate and must adequately
supervise work performed by others who are collaborating with him in the
performance of the mandate."

66 See note 101 below and accompanying text.

67 See, e.g., *FLSC Model Code, supra* note 43, r 7.4-1. See also *Quebec Code, supra*
note 43, art. 78.

68 See, e.g., Andrew Flavelle Martin, "Legal Ethics versus Political Practices:
The Application of the Rules of Professional Conduct to Lawyer-
Politicians" *Can Bar Rev* 91, no. 1 (2013): 1 at 11–16.

69 *FLSC Model Code, supra* note 43, rr 7.3-1, 7.3-2.

70 See, e.g., *Members' Integrity Act, 1994*, SO 1994, c 38, s 10(a): "A member of
the Executive Council shall not … engage in employment or the practice
of a profession." While there is an exception where the minister receives
approval from the Integrity Commissioner (s 13.1), the criteria for such
an exception are strict and it is difficult to imagine a situation where the
Attorney General could meet those criteria.

71 *FLSC Model Code, supra* note 43, r 3.3-2. See also r 3.4-1, commentary 7:
"The lawyer's duty of confidentiality is owed to both current and former

clients, with the related duty not to attack the legal work done during a retainer or to undermine the former client's position on a matter that was central to the retainer." See also *Quebec Code*, *supra* note 43, arts. 60 ("A lawyer must ensure the confidentiality of all information concerning the affairs and activities of a client of which the lawyer becomes aware in the course of the professional relationship"), 63 ("A lawyer must not use confidential information with a view to obtaining a benefit for himself or for another person"), 65(1).

72 Andrew Flavelle Martin, "From Attorney General to Backbencher or Opposition Legislator: The Lawyer's Continuing Duty of Confidentiality to the Former Client" *Manitoba LJ* 43, no. 2 (2021): 247 [Martin, "Continuing Duty"].

73 See, e.g., MacCharles & Campion-Smith, *supra* note 3; Andrew Flavelle Martin, "The Legal Ethics Implications of the SNC-Lavalin Affair for the Attorney General of Canada" *Crim LQ* 67, no. 3 (2019): 161 at 172–5.

74 See, e.g., Martin, "Continuing Duty," *supra* note 72 at 254–6.

75 See generally Elizabeth Sanderson, *Government Lawyering: Duties and Ethical Challenges of Government Lawyers* (Toronto: LexisNexis Canada, 2018), 101–7 [Sanderson].

76 See, e.g., *FLSC Model Code*, *supra* note 43, r 3.2-3: "Although a lawyer may receive instructions from an officer, employee, agent or representative, when a lawyer is employed or retained by an organization, including a corporation, the lawyer must act for the organization in exercising his or her duties and in providing professional services." See also *Quebec Code*, *supra* note 43, art. 36: "Although a lawyer may receive instructions from a representative of the client with respect to the performance of the mandate, the lawyer must act for the client and serve and protect the client's interests."

77 See, e.g., *Memorandum of Understanding between the Attorney General of Ontario and the Chief Justice of the Ontario Court of Justice* (16 August 2016) [*AG-CJOCJ MOU*], cl 2.3(j), online: <https://www.ontariocourts.ca/ocj/memorandum-of-understanding/> [https://perma.cc/E56T-PQ3V]: "The Ministry of the Attorney General is responsible for: … [p]roviding legal representation to all judicial officers, where appropriate, on matters that arise as a result of the performance of the official's judicial functions. Where there is an apparent conflict of interest (as identified by the ministry, the affected judiciary or the Office of the Chief Justice), the Office of the Chief Justice will retain private sector legal counsel, in accordance with ministry policy." See also, e.g., *Baryluk (Wyrd Sisters) v. Campbell*, 2008 CanLII 55134 (ON SC); *Baryluk (Wyrd Sisters) v. Campbell*, 2009 CanLII 34041 (ON SC) at para. 11. See also 2009 CanLII 34042 (costs order against counsel personally). The Attorney General may also fund outside counsel in these circumstances.

78 Ontario *MAG Act*, *supra* note 27, s 5(d). The equivalent federal provision is discussed in Andrew Flavelle Martin, "The Attorney General's Forgotten Role as Legal Advisor to the Legislature: A Comment on *Schmidt v. Canada (Attorney General)*" *UBC L Rev* 52, no. 1 (2019): 201 [Martin, "Forgotten Role"] at 216–18.

79 John Ll. J. Edwards, *The Attorney General, Politics and the Public Interest* (London: Sweet & Maxwell, 1984), 207–35 [Edwards, *Public Interest*], as discussed, e.g., in Martin, "Forgotten Role," *supra* note 78 at 216–18.

80 *Krieger*, *supra* note 62 at para. 27, as discussed, e.g., in Martin, "Forgotten Role," *supra* note 78 at 215.

81 Huscroft, "Advocate or Adjudicator," *supra* note 15 at 160–1, quoting from Stephen Bindman, "Appointment of Amicus Curiae Believed to Be Unprecedented" *Law Times [Aurora]* (15–21 November 1993) at 18, as quoted, e.g., in Andrew Flavelle Martin, "The Attorney General *Is* the Legislature's Legal Advisor (Though Not Its *Only* Legal Advisor), Although That Role Is Admittedly Problematic and Should Probably Be Abolished: A Response to Steven Chaplin" *JPPL* 14, no. 3 (2020): 625 at 628 [Martin, "Response to Chaplin"]; *Miron v. Trudel*, [1995] 2 SCR 418, 124 DLR (4th) 693.

82 Huscroft, "Advocate or Adjudicator," *supra* note 15 at 128, discussed, e.g., in Martin, "Forgotten Role," *supra* note 78 at 216; The Honourable R. Roy McMurtry, "The Office of the Attorney General," in *The Cambridge Lectures: Selected Papers Based upon Lectures Delivered at the Cambridge Conference of the Canadian Institute for Advanced Legal Studies, 1979*, ed. Derek Mendes da Costa (Toronto: Butterworths, 1981), 1 at 1, discussed, e.g., in Martin, "Forgotten Role," *supra* note 78 at 216. See also W. Kent Power, "The Office of Attorney General" *Can Bar Rev* 17, no. 6 (1939): 416 at 429: "His [the Attorney General's] right and duty to advise the Legislature is also of very great importance."

83 Dodek, "Impossible," *supra* note 19: "Justice ministers are expected to advise Parliament." Dodek does, however, advocate change: "[W]e need a House of Commons and Senate who have independent legal advisers who are completely loyal to them. … The justice minister of the government of the day, representing the executive branch of government, simply should not be giving advice to the legislative branch."

84 Chaplin, *supra* note 8 at 190.

85 Martin, "Forgotten Role," *supra* note 78.

86 Chaplin, *supra* note 8 at 190.

87 Martin, "Response to Chaplin," *supra* note 81.

88 *Ibid.*, 631.

89 Andrew Flavelle Martin, "The Attorney General as Lawyer (?): Confidentiality upon Resignation from Cabinet" *Dal LJ* 38, no. 1 (2015): 147 at 162 [Martin, "Resignation"].

90 See, e.g., *FLSC Model Code, supra* note 43, r 3.4-5, as discussed in Martin, "Resignation," *supra* note 89 at 162. See also *Quebec Code, supra* note 43, art. 84.

91 See, e.g., Sanderson, *supra* note 75 at xxiii: "public servants practicing law in the service of the Crown within the federal Department of Justice or within its provincial or territorial counterparts or within client departments."

92 See, e.g., McRuer, *supra* note 28, vol. 2 at 942, 948–9. See also 957, Recommendation 8: "The legal services of the government should be reorganized so that all legal services come under the direction of the Attorney General."

93 Dodek, "Intersection," *supra* note 41 at 20–1; Sanderson, *supra* note 75 at 2, 48.

94 See, e.g., Andrew Flavelle Martin, "Loyalty, Conscience, and Withdrawal: Are Government Lawyers Different?" *Manitoba LJ* 46, no. 3 (2023): 1; Andrew Flavelle Martin, "Legal Ethics for Government Lawyers: Confronting Doctrinal Gaps" *Alta L Rev* 60, no. 1 (2022): 169; Martin, "Where Are We Going?" *supra* note 12 at 322; Andrew Flavelle Martin, "Legal Ethics and the Political Activity of Government Lawyers" *Ottawa L Rev* 49, no. 2 (2018): 263 [Martin, "Political Activity"]; Andrew Flavelle Martin, "The Government Lawyer as Activist: A Legal Ethics Analysis" *Windsor Rev Leg Soc Issues* 41 (2020): 28.

95 See, e.g., Sanderson, *supra* note 75 at 211–26 (chapter 5), esp. at 214–15. In Nunavut, the separation of the civil service from the political level, in which the role of the Deputy Attorney General is critical, is recognized in the context of the lawyer's duty to report up within the organizational client. See Law Society of Nunavut, *Code of Professional Conduct* (Nunavut: LSN, 2016, last amended 2022), online: <https://www.lawsociety .nu.ca/sites/default/files/public/NU%20Code%20of%20Conduct_%20 Adopted%20June%2016%202022%20FINAL.pdf>, r 3.2-8, commentary 5.1 "A lawyer in government service or acting for a government or public body should be aware of and respect the separation of the public service from the political level. While such a lawyer must advise progressively the next highest person within the public service and use any other mechanisms lawfully available to them, the lawyer should not violate the separation of the public service from the political level unless authorized to do so."

96 See, e.g., Sanderson, *supra* note 75 at 213, citing *Osborne v. Canada (Treasury Board)*, [1991] 2 SCR 69, 82 DLR (4th) 321.

97 See, e.g., Ontario *MAG Act, supra* note 27, s 3; Sanderson, *supra* note 75 at 214.

98 See, e.g., *Public Service of Ontario Act, 2006* [*PSOA*], s 2, being Schedule A to the *Public Service of Ontario Statute Law Amendment Act, 2006*, SO 2006, c 35.

99 See, e.g. *PSOA*, *supra* note 98, s 85(2). See also Sanderson, *supra* note 75 at 215.

100 I by no means suggest that the Deputy Attorney General is not important or worthy of further study.

101 See, e.g., *FLSC Model Code*, *supra* note 43, r 6.1-1 ("A lawyer has complete professional responsibility for all business entrusted to him or her and must directly supervise staff and assistants to whom the lawyer delegates particular tasks and functions"; r 6.2-2, commentary 1 ("A principal or supervising lawyer is responsible for the actions of students acting under his or her direction") and *Law Society of Ontario v. Forte*, 2019 ONLSTH 9. Contrast, e.g., r 3.3, commentary 9: "[T]his implied authority to disclose [confidential information] places the lawyer under a duty to impress upon associates, employees, students and other lawyers engaged under contract with the lawyer or with the firm of the lawyer the importance of non disclosure (both during their employment and afterwards) and requires the lawyer to take reasonable care to prevent their disclosing or using any information that the lawyer is bound to keep in confidence."

102 *Quebec Code*, *supra* note 43, art. 5.

103 *Ibid.*, art. 6.

104 Sanderson, *supra* note 75 at 219.

105 See, e.g., *FLSC Model Code*, *supra* note 43, r 3.1-2, commentary 6.

106 See, e.g., Deborah MacNair, "Crown Prosecutors and Conflict of Interest: A Canadian Perspective" *Can Crim L Rev* 7 (2002): 257 at 278; Sanderson, *supra* note 75 at 27–30.

107 But see Sanderson, *supra* note 75 at 29, on the separation of the two roles in the federal context: "there is actually considerable overlap between the express legal advisory duties assigned to each hat under the [federal] *Department of Justice Act*, and only one Department of Justice to fulfill the entirety of the public law functions."

108 See *ibid.* at 29–30. See, e.g., Federal *DOJ Act*, *supra* note 27, s 2(2): "The Minister is *ex officio* Her Majesty's Attorney General of Canada, holds office during pleasure and has the management and direction of the Department."

109 See, e.g., Sanderson, *supra* note 75 at 39–40.

110 See, e.g., Peter W. Hogg and Wade Wright, *Constitutional Law of Canada*, vol. 2, 5th ed. supp. (Toronto: Thomson Reuters, 2023) at § 59:4 [Hogg and Wright].

111 Scott, "Constancy and Change," *supra* note 15 at 112.

112 See Scott, "Role and *Charter*," *supra* note 15 at 105: "no direct conflict would arise if, in selecting between two possible courses of action, both of which were considered constitutional by the Attorney General, the government chose to reject the Attorney General's policy preference."

113 See, e.g., Hogg and Wright, *supra* note 110, vol. 1 at § 9:7. See also Scott, "Constancy and Change," *supra* note 15 at 115; Smith, *supra* note 33 at 257; Edwards, *Law Officers, supra* note 10 at 11, 224–5, and especially at 390 regarding the responsibility of the Attorney General for decisions of the Director of Public Prosecutions.

114 See, e.g., Dodek, "Impossible," *supra* note 19.

115 See, e.g., Hogg and Wright, *supra* note 110, vol. 1 at § 36:11 [citations omitted]: "[T]he Attorney General advises the Prime Minister or Premier on the legality of whatever is proposed by the government. In fulfilling this role the Attorney General acts with a degree of independence from the other ministers in the cabinet. By long tradition, the Attorney General upholds the rule of law, which means that he or she is under a duty to provide objective legal advice in order to make sure that government action complies with the *Charter* (and other laws). Canadian politicians understand that government is bound by the rule of law, and the Attorney General's advice on legal issues, even if it is unwelcome from a policy standpoint, normally has to be accepted by cabinet." See also Mark Freiman, "Convergence of Law and Policy and the Role of the Attorney General" *SCLR (2d)* 16 (2002): 335 at 339 [Freiman]: "The legal analysis of the Chief Law Officer of the Crown may not necessarily always be welcomed by government, but it is uniformly accepted notwithstanding its potentially limiting effect on policy choices."

116 See, e.g., Hogg and Wright, *supra* note 110, vol. 1 at § 36:11; Freiman, *supra* note 115 at 338–9; Scott, "Constancy and Change," *supra* note 15 at 120–1; McMurtry, *supra* note 82 at 2.

117 *Krieger, supra* note 62 at para. 3.

118 See, e.g., *FLSC Model Code, supra* note 43, r 3.1-2, commentary 10: "In addition to opinions on legal questions, a lawyer may be asked for or may be expected to give advice on non-legal matters such as the business, economic, policy or social complications involved in the question or the course the client should choose. In many instances the lawyer's experience will be such that the lawyer's views on non-legal matters will be of real benefit to the client."

119 *FLSC Model Code, supra* note 43, r 3.1-2, commentary 10: "The lawyer who expresses views on such matters should, if necessary and to the extent necessary, point out any lack of experience or other qualification in the particular field and should clearly distinguish legal advice from other advice." See also Scott, "Role and *Charter," supra* note 15 at 105: "In cases where legal and social policy is closely intertwined, as will often be the case in situations involving the *Charter of Rights*, the Attorney General must take care, in giving advice, to distinguish between legal opinion and policy preference."

120 See, e.g., Dodek, "Impossible," *supra* note 19.

121 The Hon. A. Anne McLellan, *Review of the Roles of the Minister of Justice
and Attorney General of Canada* (28 June 2019) at 31, online: *Government of
Canada* <https://www.pm.gc.ca/en/news/backgrounders/2019/08/14
/review-roles-minister-justice-and-attorney-general-canada> [https://
perma.cc/KE4U-TN8W]. I participated in a round-table briefing for
McLellan's report.

122 See generally Eric Colvin, "The Executive and the Independence of the
Judiciary" *Sask L Rev* 51, no. 2 (1986): 229 at 242–8. See, e.g., McMurtry,
Memoirs, supra note 17 at 184: "Early on in my tenure as attorney
general, I became concerned about the apparent conflict of interest as I
administered the courts in which my ministry was also a major litigant."
See also, e.g., *R v. Bodner*, 2003 ABCA 102 (chambers judge holding that
they could not hear a stay application because their decision could reduce
courts funding on which they relied). Thanks to a reviewer for bringing
this case to my attention. While the case law on judicial independence
is clear that financial independence has an "institutional or collective
dimension," with respect (and for understandable reasons) the courts
have largely left untouched the inherent problem alluded to in *Bodner*,
that is, that the courts are reliant for their funding on the decisions of
the most common litigant appearing before them. (Note that the judge
in *Bodner* held that the Supreme Court of Canada would not face the
same conflict as it was not funded by the Alberta government, at para. 31
["Although the Supreme Court may also have an interest in the outcome,
the application does not directly threaten the Supreme Court's budget.
Thus, the public's perception of partiality would be reduced."]) This
issue, as opposed to its management, is beyond the scope of this book.

123 See, e.g., Dodek, "Impossible," *supra* note 19: "The answer for why the
two offices are combined is simple, if unsatisfying: That's the way it has
always been in Canada, and because the combined role is what the law
dictates, according to the Department of Justice Act."

124 See, e.g., *AG-CJOCJ MOU, supra* note 77; *Courts of Justice Act*, RSO 1990,
c C.43, ss 71, 72, 77; *R v. Turtle*, 2020 ONCJ 429 at paras. 128–9: "As late
as 1990, the Attorney General of Ontario was largely responsible for
the administration of courts in this province. The judiciary in Ontario
were effectively a branch of the Attorney General's office. At the same
time Judges sat in judgement on matters where the Attorney General's
actions were the subject of the dispute. In those circumstances, Judicial
independence, while valued as an important constitutional principle,
was always subject to the appearance of conflict, if not actual conflict.
To remedy this problem, in 1990, the Attorney General and the Chief
Justice of the Ontario Court of Justice, in the first agreement of its kind

in Canada, entered into a Memorandum of Understanding that clarified their respective roles and how to manage their relationship." See also Roslyn J. Levine, "Straddling the Middle: The Superior Court's Executive Legal Officer" *JPPL* 12 (2018): 165 at 171.

125 Scott, "Constancy and Change," *supra* note 15 at 122.

126 McLellan, *supra* note 121 at 43, note 107.

127 See above note 69 and accompanying text.

128 See Hogg and Wright, *supra* note 110, vol. 1 at § 9:7.

129 See, e.g., Edwards in Sharpe, *supra* note 11 at 56–7.

130 See, e.g., Hogg and Wright, *supra* note 11, vol. 1 at § 9:3.

131 See, e.g., Jonathan Malloy, *The Paradox of Parliament* (Toronto: University of Toronto Press, 2023) at 67, 79, 134, 226.

132 See, e.g., Ned Franks, "Parliamentarians and Codes of Ethics" *JPPL* 2 (2009): 283 at 291: "Ministers are not like ordinary members of parliament when they contact departments and other agencies of government. They, and especially the prime minister, speak with power to coerce, reward, and punish. Nor are their staff in the same position as the staff of ordinary MPs." See also, e.g., Ian MacKenzie, "Under the Influence: Ministers (and Others) Communicating with Tribunals" (14 March 2023), online (blog): *Slaw* <https://www.slaw.ca/2023/03/14/under -the-influence-ministers-and-others-communicating-with-tribunals/> [https://perma.cc/KW4K-6FQP]: "Members of Parliament are expected to advocate for their constituents. However, when that MP is a Minister of the Crown (or a Parliamentary Secretary) there are limits on how far that advocacy can go."

133 See, e.g., *Legal Profession Act*, SNS 2004, c 28, s 16(4)(j) [NS *Legal Profession Act*]: "this Act does not prohibit … a member of (i) the House of Commons of Canada, (ii) the House of Assembly, or (iii) a council of a municipality, from acting as an advocate or representative of a person in the member's capacity as an elected representative."

134 See, e.g., *ibid.*, s 7(1)(b); *Law Society Act*, *supra* note 30, ss 12(1), (2).

135 But see *A.G. Can. v. Law Society of B.C.*, [1982] 2 SCR 307 at 335–6, 137 DLR (3d) 1, where Estey J., writing for the Court, holds that the Attorney General's role as an *ex officio* bencher is one of several legitimate "protective restraints" on self-governance as a manifestation of the independence of the bar: "The independence of the Bar from the state in all its pervasive manifestations is one of the hallmarks of a free society. Consequently, regulation of these members of the law profession by the state must, so far as by human ingenuity it can be so designed, be free from state interference, in the political sense, with the delivery of services to the individual citizens in the state, particularly in fields of public and criminal law. The public interest in a free society knows no area more

sensitive than the independence, impartiality and availability to the general public of the members of the Bar and through those members, legal advice and services generally. ... Having said all that, it must be remembered that the assignment of administrative control to the field of self-administration by the profession is subject to such important protective restraints as ... the presence of the Attorney General as an *ex officio* member of the Benchers." (But see, e.g., Alice Woolley, "Lawyers and the Rule of Law: Independence of the Bar, the Canadian Constitution and the Law Governing Lawyers" *NJCL* 34 (2015): 49 at 54, note 27: "Self-government may be a useful means to accomplish independence; the point here is only that it is not an essential or necessary feature of lawyerly independence.")

136 *Constitution Act, 1867* (UK), 30 & 31 Vict, c 3, reprinted in RSC 1985, Appendix II, no. 5, ss 92(13), 92(14), as discussed, e.g., in *Law Society of BC v. Mangat*, 2001 SCC 67 at paras. 38–46.

137 *Law Society Act, supra* note 30, s 13(1). This provision is discussed in more detail in chapter 5. See also *Legal Profession Act*, RSY 2002, c 134, s 106(1) [Yukon *Legal Profession Act*]: "The Minister shall serve as a guardian of the public interest in all matters within the scope of this Act."

138 See generally Craig E. Jones, "The Attorney General's Standing to Seek Relief in the Public Interest: The Evolving Doctrine of *Parens Patriae*" *Can Bar Rev* 86, no. 1 (2007): 121; Scott, "Role and *Charter*," *supra* note 15 at 196–9. With respect to charities, see, e.g., Kathryn Chan, "The Role of the Attorney General in Charity Proceedings in Canada and in England and Wales" *Can Bar Rev* 89 (2011): 373 [Chan]. See, e.g., Hogg and Wright, *supra* note 110, vol. 1 at § 59:4.

139 See, e.g., Chan, *supra* note 138.

140 See, e.g., Roach, "Not Just," *supra* note 15.

141 See, e.g., Ontario *MAG Act, supra* note 27, s 5(b); Federal *DOJ Act, supra* note 27, s 4(a); NB *AG Act, supra* note 27, s 2(a); MB *DOJ Act, supra* note 27, s 2(b); BC *AG Act, supra* note 27, s 2(b); YK *DOJ Act, supra* note 27, s 6(a).

142 Sanderson, *supra* note 75 at 32–3.

143 See, e.g., *FLSC Model Code, supra* note 43, rr 3.2-7 ("A lawyer must never: a) knowingly assist in or encourage any dishonesty, fraud, crime, or illegal conduct. b) do or omit to do anything that the lawyer ought to know assists in or encourages any dishonesty, fraud, crime, or illegal conduct by a client or others, or c) instruct a client or others on how to violate the law and avoid punishment"), 3.2-8 (requirement of reporting up where "a lawyer who is employed or retained by an organization to act in a matter in which the lawyer knows that the organization has

acted, is acting or intends to act dishonestly, fraudulently, criminally, or illegally," culminating in withdrawal if the client persists).

144 Sanderson, *supra* note 75 at 32, 33.

145 Scott, "Role and *Charter*," *supra* note 15 at 189, 193.

146 See above note 107.

147 See, e.g., Alice Woolley, "Legal Ethics and Regulatory Legitimacy: Regulating Lawyers for Personal Misconduct," in *Alternative Perspectives on Lawyers and Legal Ethics: Reimagining The Profession*, ed. Francesca Bartlett, Reid Mortensen, and Kieran Tranter (Oxford: Routledge, 2011), 241; Duncan Webb, "Nefarious Conduct and the 'Fit and Proper Person' Test," in *Alternative Perspectives on Lawyers and Legal Ethics: Reimagining the Profession*, ed. Francesca Bartlett, Reid Mortensen, and Kieran Tranter (Oxford: Routledge, 2011), 218.

148 See, e.g., *FLSC Model Code*, *supra* note 43, r 7.4-1, commentary 1: "Because such a lawyer [in public office] is in the public eye, the legal profession can more readily be brought into disrepute by a failure to observe its ethical standards." See also *Quebec Code*, *supra* note 43, art. 78.

149 *FLSC Model Code*, *supra* note 43, r 7.4-1, commentary 2.

150 *Ibid.*, r 5.6-1, commentary 1. See also *Quebec Code*, *supra* note 43, art. 12.

151 Edwards, *Public Interest*, *supra* note 79 at 67, quoted, e.g., in McLellan, *supra* note 121 at 11 and in Sanderson, *supra* note 75 at 69. See similarly John Ll. J. Edwards, "The Charter, Government and the Machinery of Justice" *UNB LJ* 36 (1987): 41 at 50: "The experience of both the older and newer members of the Commonwealth confirms my deep-seated conviction that, no matter how entrenched constitutional safeguards may be, in the final analysis it is the strength of character, personal integrity and personal commitment by the holder to the independent character of the Offices of Attorney-General … and of the Director of Public Prosecutions which is of abiding importance." Sanderson, *supra* note 75 at 226 makes a similar point about the Deputy Attorney General: "Regardless how the role of the Justice Deputy Ministers and Deputy Attorney Generals is delineated in the law or literature, much of its success – or failure – comes down ultimately to the integrity of the individual in the job."

152 Scott, "Constancy and Change," *supra* note 15 at 122.

2 Complexity: The Duty to Encourage Respect for the Administration of Justice

1 This chapter is adapted from Andrew Flavelle Martin, "The Lawyer's Professional Duty to Encourage Respect for – and to Improve – the

Administration of Justice: Lessons from Failures by Attorneys General" *Ottawa L Rev* 54, no. 2 (2023): 247. In this chapter, French quotations are followed by unofficial English translations.

2 See, e.g., Federation of Law Societies of Canada, *Model Code of Professional Conduct* (Ottawa: FLSC, 2009) as amended October 2022, r 5.6-1 [*FLSC Model Code*]. See also *Code of Professional Conduct of Lawyers*, RLRQ c B-1, r 3.1, art 11 [*Quebec Code*]. While my focus is on the Attorney General, much of my analysis and my conclusions would apply to lawyers generally.

3 See, e.g., *FLSC Model Code, supra* note 2, r 7.4-1 ("[a] lawyer who holds public office must, in the discharge of official duties, adhere to standards of conduct as high as those required of a lawyer engaged in the practice of law.") Commentary 2 qualifies this statement, apparently as a matter of disciplinary priorities: "[g]enerally, the Society is not concerned with the way in which a lawyer holding public office carries out official responsibilities, but conduct in office that reflects adversely upon the lawyer's integrity or professional competence may be the subject of disciplinary action." (Thanks to a reviewer on this point.) On the inconsistent interpretation of r 7.4-1, see Andrew Flavelle Martin, "Legal Ethics versus Political Practices: The Application of the Rules of Professional Conduct to Lawyer-Politicians" *Can Bar Rev* 91, no. 1 (2013): 1 at 16, 35–6 [Martin, "Lawyer-Politicians"]. See also *Quebec Code, supra* note 2, art. 78.

4 Elizabeth Sanderson, *Government Lawyering: Duties and Ethical Challenges of Government Lawyers* (Toronto: LexisNexis Canada, 2018), 114–17. At 116–17, Sanderson uses the example of Peter MacKay to illustrate this duty. See also Craig E. Jones, "On the Attorney General, the Courts and the New Ministry of Justice" *Advocate* 71, no. 2 (2013): 189 at 192: "for 300 years it was the traditional and honourable role of the attorney general to speak in defence of the courts when they were criticized, because by constitutional convention judges do not speak except through their judgments."

5 Sanderson, *supra* note 4 at 117.

6 See, e.g., James Plunkett, "The Role of the Attorney General in Defending the Judiciary" *J Judicial Admin* 19, no. 3 (2010): 160; Hon. Darryl Williams, "The Role of the Attorney General" *Pub L Rev* 13, no. 4 (2002): 252 at 254–8, 261–2; Tony Abbott, "Reflections on the Role of the Attorney General" *Pub L Rev* 13, no. 4 (2002): 273 at 275–81; Ben Heraghty, "Defender of the Faith – The Role of the Attorney-General in Defending the High Court" *Monash UL Rev* 28, no. 2 (2002): 206; Robert McLelland, "In Defence of the Administration of Justice: Where Is the Attorney-General" *UTSL Rev* 1 (1999): 118; Michael Kirby, "Attacks on Judges – A Universal Phenomenon" *Judicature* 81, no. 6 (1998): 238 at 243; Gerard Carney, "Comment – The Role of the Attorney-General" *Bond L Rev* [i] 9, no. 1 (1997): 7–9; L.J.

King, "The Attorney-General, Politics and the Judiciary" *UW Austl L Rev* 29, no. 2 (2000): 155 at 171–5; Tatum Hands and Danielle Davies, "Defend Thyself!" *Alt LJ* 28, no. 2 (2003): 65; Hon. Daryl Williams, "Who Speaks for the Courts?" in *Courts in a Representative Democracy* (Canberra: Australian Institute of Judicial Administration, 1995), 183 at 190–2 [*CIRD*]; David Soloman, "Who Speaks for the Courts? Commentary," in *CIRD* 195 at 198. To contrast the context in the United Kingdom, see, e.g., Rt. Hon. S.C. Silkin, "The Functions and Position of the Attorney-General in the United Kingdom" *Bracton LJ* 12, no. 1 (1978): 29 at 33 (role in prosecuting contempt of court). (For the corresponding role in Canada, see, e.g., Sanderson, *supra* note 4 at 115–16). For a recent comparative United Kingdom–United States–Australia analysis, see Scott Stephenson, "Constitutional Conventions and the Judiciary" *Oxford J Leg Stud* 41, no. 3 (2021): 750 at 773 ("[i]t is arguable that, in Australia, the constitutional convention requiring the Attorney-General to defend the judiciary against public attack has either been wholly eradicated or significantly reduced in scope"), 768–9 ("[t]here is little evidence of a constitutional convention that the [US] executive, or even the Attorney General, is under a duty to defend the judiciary from public attack. Indeed, there is, if anything, evidence of a countervailing convention entitling the executive, including the Attorney General, to say whatever it wishes about the judiciary. ... Furthermore, there is an established history of the Attorney General taking the lead in criticizing the judiciary"), 766–7, quoting New Zealand Cabinet Office, *Cabinet Manual* (Wellington: Department of Prime Minister and Cabinet, 2017) at para. 4.8, online: <dpmc.govt.nz/sites/default/files/2017-06/cabinet-manual-2017.pdf> [https://perma.cc/D3F5-H6LE] ("[t]he [New Zealand] Attorney-General ... has an important role in defending the judiciary by answering improper or unfair public criticism, and discouraging ministerial colleagues from criticizing judges and their decisions").

7 See, e.g., Jones, *supra* note 4: "the attorney's relationship with the judiciary itself ... has been decaying for a generation. ... [I]n recent years one is as likely to read of a provincial attorney general either standing mute as judges and their decisions are impugned (often if not usually unfairly), or even (in rare but nevertheless unforgivable circumstances) joining in the chorus of criticism, apparently out of a misplaced sense of populist solidarity." See also Heraghty, *supra* note 6 at 221–2 (albeit in the Australian context): "[t]he legal basis for this latter principle as defender of the judiciary is still an open question."

8 Harry Arthurs, "Why Canadian Law Schools Do Not Teach Legal Ethics," in *Ethical Challenges to Legal Education and Conduct*, ed. Kim Economides (Oxford: Hart, 1998), 105 at 114.

9 H.W. Arthurs, "The Dead Parrot: Does Professional Self-Regulation Exhibit Vital Signs?" *Alta L Rev* 33, no. 4 (1995): 800 at 802.

10 See, e.g., *FLSC Model Code*, *supra* note 2, rr 5.1-5 ("[a] lawyer must be courteous and civil and act in good faith to the tribunal and all persons with whom the lawyer has dealings."), 7.2-1 ("[a] lawyer must be courteous and civil and act in good faith with all persons with whom the lawyer has dealings in the course of his or her practice"). See also *Quebec Code*, *supra* note 2, art. 112: "[a] lawyer must act for a client resolutely and honourably, in compliance with the law, while treating the tribunal and all other participants in the justice system with candour, courtesy and respect."

11 *FLSC Model Code*, *supra* note 2, r 7.5-1. See also *Quebec Code*, *supra* note 2, art. 17: "[p]rovided he complies with this code, a lawyer may communicate information to the media, make public appearances or make public communications, including on a website, blog or online social network, by means of statements, photographs, images or videos."

12 *FLSC Model Code*, *supra* note 2, r 7.5-1, commentary 1.

13 *FLSC Model Code*, *supra* note 2, r 5.6-1. See also *Quebec Code*, *supra* note 2, art. 12.

14 *Stewart v. Canadian Broadcasting Corp*, 1997 CanLII 12318 (ON SC) at para. 268: "[r]ule 11 contains two separate directions. The lawyer should encourage public respect for the administration of justice. In addition, the lawyer should try to improve the administration of justice."

15 See, e.g., *Courts of Justice Act*, RSO 1990, c C.43, ss 71, 72, 77.

16 *FLSC Model Code*, *supra* note 2, r 5.6-1, commentary 1. See also *Quebec Code*, *supra* note 2, art. 12.

17 *FLSC Model Code*, *supra* note 2, r 5.6-1, commentary 1.

18 *Ibid.*, r 5.6-1, commentaries 1, 3.

19 *Ibid.*, r 5.6-1, commentary 3.

20 *Quebec Code*, *supra* note 2, art. 111.

21 *Ibid.*

22 2013 ONLSHP 6 [*Ann Bruce*].

23 *Ibid.* at para. 157.

24 See similarly Noel Semple, "Comment on Brooke MacKenzie, 'Professional Conduct on Social Media for Lawyers' (22 November 2022)" (28 November 2022), online (blog): *Slaw* <www.slaw.ca/2022/11/22/professional-conduct-on-social-media-for-lawyers/> [https://perma.cc/7T8H-89YA]: "I have always struggled with Rule 5.6-1. … Very often the best thing one can do to improve the administration of justice is to point out its flaws. But pointing out its flaws tends to undermine public respect for it, especially when nothing changes. Overall, I think Canadian legal culture errs on the side of excessive respect, and insufficient efforts to improve."

25 *Canadian Charter of Rights and Freedoms*, Part I of the *Constitution Act 1982*, being Schedule B to the *Canada Act 1982* (UK), 1982, c 11.

26 See, e.g., Andrew Flavelle Martin, "Legal Ethics for Government Lawyers: Confronting Doctrinal Gaps" *Alta L Rev* 60, no. 1 (2022): 169 at 177, citing *Doré v. Barreau du Québec*, 2012 SCC 12 at paras. 63–6 [*Doré*]; *Histed v. Law Society of Manitoba*, 2007 MBCA 150 at para. 79 [*Histed*], aff'g 2006 MBLS 6, leave to appeal to SCC refused, 32478 (24 April 2008): "It is clear if not trite that, at least in the context of civility and advertising, lawyers accept restrictions on their freedom of expression that would not be acceptable for the general public."

27 See, e.g., Alice Woolley, "Did Joe Groia Kill the Civility Movement?" *Leg Ethics* 21, no. 2 (2018): 159 (now Justice Woolley of the Court of Appeal of Alberta); *Groia v. Law Society of Upper Canada*, 2018 SCC 27 [*Groia*].

28 John Ll. J. Edwards, "The Office of Attorney General: New Levels of Public Expectations and Accountability," in *Accountability for Criminal Justice: Selected Essays*, ed. Philip C. Stenning (Toronto: University of Toronto Press, 1995), 294 at 300.

29 *Wagner (Re)* (4 November 1966), (Barreau de Montréal) [*Wagner (Re)*], as published in "Texte intégral du jugement et de la sentence dans l'affaire Wagner-Bérubé" *La Presse* (5 November 1966), 11; "La condemnation de Claude Wagner" *Le Devoir* (5 November 1966), 1 ["La condemnation de Claude Wagner"]. The speech was published as Hon. Claude Wagner, "Causerie prononcée par l'honorable Claude Wagner, c.r., ministre de la Justice de la Province De Québec, le dimanche 10 octobre 1965: La légalité au service de la vérité" *RB* 25, no. 8 (1965): 502 (quoted excerpt at 505) [Wagner Speech].

30 See André Fortin, "Le juge Jean-Paul Bérubé réfute les 'accusations' portées par Me Wagner" *Le Soleil* (19 October 1965), 12; "Je n'ai rien à me reprocher et demanderai au Barreau de la Province d'examiner ma conduite (Me Antonio Dubé)" *Le Soleil* (19 October 1965), 12.

31 *Wagner (Re)*, *supra* note 29; "La condemnation de Claude Wagner," *supra* note 29.

32 Wagner Speech, *supra* note 29 at 505 [emphasis added].

33 But see Lorenzo Paré, "Que fait le Barreau?" *L'Action* (13 October 1965), 4.

34 Wagner, as quoted in "Le Barreau a besoin d'une réforme en profondeur" *Le Nouvelliste* (11 October 1965), 6. See also Martin Pronovost, "Messieurs du Barreau, qu'est-ce que vous attendez pour jeter dehors les vendeurs du temple? – Wagner" *La Presse* (12 October 1965), 1–2; "Le ministre: Une poignée d'indésirables soulève le mépris contre la profession" *Le Devoir* (11 October 1965), 1–2; Lewis Seele, "Wagner Presses for Clean-Up in Courts" *Montreal Gazette* (11 November 1965), 23.

35 See, e.g., Wagner, as quoted in "Le ministre: Une poignée d'indésirables
    soulève le mépris contre la profession" *Le Devoir* (11 October 1965),
    1–2: "[s]ouvent, par notre conduite collective, nous avons provoqué le
    mépris et le sarcasme" ("[o]ften, through our collective conduct, we have
    provoked sarcasm and contempt").
36 Editorial Cartoon, *L'Action* (15 November 1966), 4.
37 See "La déclaration de Me Wagner" *La Presse* (5 November 1966), 11: "Je
    suis en désaccord avec le résumé des faits rendus publics par le conseil du
    Barreau de Montréal" ("I disagree with the facts published by the council
    of the Barreau de Montréal").
38 *Wagner (Re), supra* note 29: "[d]e telles remarques, lorsqu'elles sont faites,
    et même si elles sont faites de bonne foi, ne devraient l'être qu'après que
    des précautions raisonnables ont été prises pour vérifier l'exactitude des
    faits, *spécialement dans le cas présent où l'avocat qui les a prononcées était le
    ministre de la Justice de la province de Québec et un membre ex-officio du Conseil
    général du Barreau de la province de Québec*" ("[t]hese types of remarks, when
    made, even if made in good faith, should only be made after reasonable
    care has been taken to ascertain the veracity of the facts, *especially in the
    present case where the lawyer who made these remarks was the Minister of Justice
    of Quebec and an ex-officio member of the General Council of the Barreau of the
    province of Quebec*") [emphasis added].
39 *Wagner (Re), supra* note 29; "La condemnation de Claude Wagner," *supra*
    note 29.
40 *Quebec Code, supra* note 2, arts. 66, 84–5.
41 See "Wagner demande à un tribunal de réviser la décision du barreau"
    La Presse (18 November 1966), 43. See, e.g., Éditorial, "M. Wagner et le
    Barreau" *L'Action* (15 November 1966), 4: "[i]l pourrait profiter du droit de
    toute député de présenter un projet de loi à la Législature pour protéger
    les ministres contre d'autres jugements que ceux de la Chambre et de
    l'électorat" ("[h]e could benefit from using the right to propose a bill to
    the Legislature to protect ministers from judgments other than those of the
    House and the electorate"). See Martin, "Lawyer-Politicians," *supra* note 3
    at 27: "[a] different policy concern is whether enforcement of ethical rules
    against lawyer-politicians could result in a backlash by legislators against
    law societies, and possibly against self-regulation itself. At the lowest level,
    this could consist of statutory amendments to remove the authority to
    discipline lawyers for all or certain conduct while in political office."
42 See Réginal Martel, "Wagner songe à faire affranchir du Barreau les
    avocats du gouvernement" *La Presse* (9 November 1966), 1–2. The Barreau
    opposed this proposal: see, e.g., François Trepannier, "Le Barreau entend
    garder juridiction sur les avocats haut placés au ministère de la Justice" *La
    Presse* (7 January 1967), 1–2.

43 "Éditoriale: L'affaire Wagner" *Le Soleil* (9 November 1966), 4.

44 See "Texte intégral de la requête" *La Presse* (18 November 1966), 43, specifically at paras. 8–9.

45 *Wagner c Barreau de Montréal* (28 November 1966), Montréal 723–178 (Qc SC), Pothier J. [*Wagner c Barreau* SC], as published in "Le jugement du juge Philippe Pothier dans la cause de M. Claude Wagner contre le Barreau de Montréal" *Le Clairon (Saint-Hyacinthe)* (1 December 1966), 12, aff'd *Barreau (Montréal) c Wagner* (1967), [1968] BR 235 (CA) [*Wagner c Barreau* CA].

46 *Wagner c Barreau* SC, *supra* note 45.

47 See, e.g., "Le Barreau a besoin d'une réforme en profondeur" *Le Nouvelliste* (11 October 1965), 6, quoting Wagner's speech: "[j]e me félicité d'avoir accepté votre invitation parce que, pour la première fois depuis que j'ai assumé mes fonctions de ministre de la Justice, je rencontre les membres du Barreau, et je m'adresse à eux. Non seulement en tant que ministre, mais surtout en confrère" ("I am also pleased to have accepted your invitation because, for the first time since I assumed my duties as Minister of Justice, I am meeting the members of the bar and addressing them, not only as minister, but above all as a colleague").

48 *Wagner c Barreau* CA, *supra* note 45 at 237.

49 *Ibid.*, 237.

50 *Wagner c Barreau* SC, *supra* note 45.

51 *Quebec Code, supra* note 2, art. 19: "[a] lawyer must not, directly or indirectly, publish, broadcast, communicate or send writings or comments which are false or which he should know are false or assist anyone in doing so." There is no equivalent provision in the *FLSC Model Code, supra* note 2.

52 *FLSC Model Code, supra* note 2, r 5.6-1, commentary 3. See also *Quebec Code, supra* note 2, art. 12: "A lawyer must support respect for the rule of law. However, he may, for good reason and by legitimate means, criticize a legal provision, contest the interpretation or application thereof, or seek to have it repealed, amended or replaced."

53 "Canons of Legal Ethics," at canon 2(2), in Canadian Bar Association, *Proceedings of the Fifth Annual Meeting of the Canadian Bar Association Held in Ottawa, Ontario, September 1st, 2nd and 3rd, 1920* (Winnipeg: Bulman Bros, 1920), 261–4, reprinted as Canadian Bar Association, *Canons of Legal Ethics (Adopted by the Canadian Bar Association, September 2nd, 1920)* (Ottawa: The Association, 1955) [*CBA Canons*]. The Canons were officially adopted by the Law Society of Upper Canada in the first of the rulings that comprised its original 1964 *Professional Conduct Handbook* (Toronto: Law Society of Upper Canada, 1964), 5, Ruling 1.

54 *Loi organique et règlements du Barreau de la province de Québec (Adoptés le 25 octobre 1917)* (Montreal: Eug Goblensky & Co, 1917), 66–7, by-law 62, para. 7:

"un rapport de procédures judiciaires *faux, ou injurieux* pour l'honneur ou pour la dignité de la magistrature" ("a report of judicial proceedings that are *false or offensive* to the honour or dignity of the judiciary").

55 See, e.g., *Histed, supra* note 26.

56 2011 LSBC 29 [*Laarakker*], penalty at 2012 LSBC 2.

57 *Laarakker, supra* note 208 at paras. 45–6.

58 *Groia, supra* note 27, Moldaver J. for the majority. On the duty of competence, see, e.g., *FLSC Model Code, supra* note 2, r 3.1-2; *Quebec Code, supra* note 2, art. 21.

59 *Law Society of Yukon v. Kimmerly*, [1988] LSDD no 1 (Yk LS) [*Law Society v. Kimmerly*].

60 Hon. Ronald Veale and Andrea Bailey, "The Crest Affair: Judicial Independence and Yukon's Supreme Court," *Northern Rev* 50 (2020): 219 [Veale and Bailey].

61 *Ibid.*, 231.

62 *Law Society v. Kimmerly, supra* note 59.

63 *Ibid.*; Veale and Bailey, *supra* note 60 at 223.

64 *Law Society v. Kimmerly, supra* note 59.

65 Veale and Bailey, *supra* note 60 at 223.

66 *Ibid.*, 226.

67 At the time, the duty was codified in r XII of the Canadian Bar Association, *CBA Code of Professional Conduct* (Ottawa: Canadian Bar Association, 1974) ch. XII [1974 *CBA Code*], which had been adopted in the Yukon statute on the legal profession: "[t]he lawyer should encourage public respect for and try to improve the administration of justice." This language is nearly identical to the current version of the rule. For the current rule on lawyers in public office, see *FLSC Model Code, supra* note 2, r 7.4-1. See also *Quebec Code, supra* note 2, art. 78. For an analysis of *Law Society v. Kimmerly* in the interpretation of this rule, see Martin, "Lawyer-Politicians," *supra* note 3 at 15–16.

68 Veale and Bailey, *supra* note 60 at 228.

69 *Law Society v. Kimmerly, supra* note 59. Veale and Bailey, *supra* note 60 at 230, cite conflicting evidence by expert witnesses, with one characterizing the remarks as "petulant pique of a politician" and one characterizing them as "sensible" and "understandable."

70 *Law Society v. Kimmerly, supra* note 59.

71 Martin, "Lawyer-Politicians," *supra* note 3 at 16, 35–6. See, e.g., *FLSC Model Code, supra* note 2, r 7.4-1 ("[a] lawyer who holds public office must, in the discharge of official duties, adhere to standards of conduct as high as those required of a lawyer engaged in the practice of law"). See also *Quebec Code, supra* note 2, art. 78.

72 *Charter, supra* note 25.

73 *Doré, supra* note 26; *Histed, supra* note 26.

74 *Histed, supra* note 26 at para. 1.

75 *Ibid.*, paras. 13, 44. The others were rules on integrity, civility, upholding the integrity of the legal profession, and "observ[ing] the rules of professional conduct set out in the Code in the spirit as well as in the letter."

76 See above note 45 and accompanying text.

77 *Doré, supra* note 26; *Histed, supra* note 26; *Groia, supra* note 27.

78 See, e.g., Brent Cotter, "The Prime Minister v the Chief Justice of Canada: The Attorney General's Failure of Responsibility" *Leg Ethics* 18 (2015): 73 at 73 (now Senator Cotter): "an unseemly, and unprecedented, attack on the integrity of the Chief Justice of the Supreme Court of Canada, Beverley McLachlin, by the Prime Minister of Canada and the Attorney General of Canada … the unprincipled performance of the Attorney General of Canada in this controversy was an exceptional and troubling occurrence and serves as a cautionary tale." See also Hugo Cyr, "The Bungling of Justice Nadon's Appointment to the Supreme Court of Canada" *SCLR (2d)* 67 (2014): 73 at 76, note 14. See also Sanderson, *supra* note 4 at 116–17, who gives a concise account of the saga with a similar focus to my own account (though without explicit reference to the duty to encourage respect for the administration of justice). See also Carissima Mathen and Michael Plaxton, *The Tenth Justice: Judicial Appointments, Marc Nadon, and the Supreme Court Act Reference* (Vancouver and Toronto: University of British Columbia Press, 2020) at 124–39. I have suggested that the authors gave insufficient attention to the role of MacKay: Andrew Flavelle Martin, "But Why Him? A Review of *The Tenth Justice: Judicial Appointments, Marc Nadon, and the* Supreme Court Act *Reference* by Carissima Mathen and Michael Plaxton" *Dal LJ* 44, no. 2 (2021): 677 at 5–6.

79 *Reference re Supreme Court Act, ss 5 and 6*, 2014 SCC 21 [*Reference*].

80 Cotter, *supra* note 78 at 74–5; Tonda MacCharles, "Harper Refuses to Take Call from Judge" *The Toronto Star* (2 May 2014), A6; Sanderson, *supra* note 4 at 116.

81 Office of the Chief Justice of Canada, "For Immediate Release" (2 May 2014), online: <decisions.scc-csc.ca/scc-csc/news/en/4602/1/document .do> [https://perma.cc/D23A-5G3Y].

82 Canadian Press, "MacKay Offers Few New Details on Supreme Court Spat" *The News (New Glasgow)* (3 May 2014), 15.

83 *House of Commons Debates*, 41-2, no. 80 (5 May 2014), 4919 (Hon. Thomas Mulcair), online: <www.ourcommons.ca/Content/House/412 /Debates/080/HAN080-E.PDF> [https://perma.cc/E5F2-RKDK] [Canada *Hansard*], as referenced in Sanderson, *supra* note 4 at 116.

84 Canada *Hansard, supra* note 83 at 4919 (Hon. Peter MacKay), as quoted in Cotter, *supra* note 78 at 75, quoted partially in Sanderson, *supra* note 4 at 116.

85 Canada *Hansard, supra* note 83 at 4919 (Hon. Peter MacKay), as quoted in Sanderson, *supra* note 4 at 117.

86 Sanderson, *supra* note 4 at 116.

87 Cotter, *supra* note 78 at 76–7.

88 *Ibid.*, 76–7.

89 *Ibid.*, 77; Adam Dodek, as quoted in Cristin Schmitz, "MacKay Fell Short as AG, Lawyers Say" *The Lawyers Weekly* (30 May 2014), 1 [Schmitz].

90 Cotter was surely correct insofar as he was referring to parliamentary privilege. See chapter 5.

91 Adam Dodek, as quoted in Schmitz, *supra* note 89.

92 Michael Bryant, "By Politicizing Judicial Appointments, Harper Risks Constitutional Crisis" *The Globe and Mail* (19 May 2014), online: <www.theglobeandmail.com/opinion/by-politicizing-judge-appointments-harper-risks-constitutional-crisis/article18722354/> [https://perma.cc/48KJ-TYGG]. In the same op-ed, Bryant also characterized MacKay as "politically impotent" and "feckless."

93 Canadian Judicial Council, *Ethical Principles for Judges* at 44, 5.B.4 (Ottawa: The Council, 2021), online: <https://cjc-ccm.ca/en/what-we-do/initiatives/ethical-principles-judges-0> [https://perma.cc/58MT-PJNF].

94 See, e.g., Schmitz, *supra* note 89.

95 See, e.g., Cotter, *supra* note 78 at 76.

96 Letter from Wilder Tayler, Secretary General of the International Commission of Jurists, to Dr. Gerald Heckman (23 July 2014), 7, online (pdf): <www.icj.org/wp-content/uploads/2014/07/Canada-JudicialIndependenceAndIntegrity-CIJL-OpenLetter-2014.pdf> [https://perma.cc/GYU5-3BBA], quoted in Cotter, *supra* note 78 at 76.

97 See, e.g., *Department of Justice Act*, RSC 1985, c J-2, s 4: "[t]he Minister [of Justice] is the official legal adviser of the Governor General"; *Ontario v. Criminal Lawyers' Association of Ontario*, 2013 SCC 43 at para. 5, referring to Attorneys General as "the Chief Law Officers of the Crown"; *FLSC Model Code, supra* note 2, r 3.2-3: "[a]lthough a lawyer may receive instructions from an officer, employee, agent or representative, when a lawyer is employed or retained by an organization, including a corporation, the lawyer must act for the organization in exercising his or her duties and in providing professional services." See also *FLSC Model Code*, r 3.2-3, commentary 1: "[a] lawyer acting for an organization should keep in mind that the organization, as such, is the client and that a corporate client has a legal personality distinct from its shareholders, officers, directors and employees. While the organization or corporation acts and gives instructions through its officers, directors, employees, members, agents or representatives, the lawyer should ensure that it is the interests of the organization that are served and protected."

98 Consider also *Quebec Code*, *supra* note 2, art. 115: "[a] lawyer must not encourage a client, witness or other person to do or say anything which he could not do or say himself in respect of a judge, tribunal, member of a tribunal or any other participant in the justice system."

99 *FLSC Model Code*, *supra* note 2, r 3.7-2 and commentary 1. See also *Quebec Code*, *supra* note 2, art. 48(1).

100 See, e.g., *FLSC Model Code*, *supra* note 2, r 3.7-7(b): "[a] lawyer must withdraw if: … a client persists in instructing the lawyer to act contrary to professional ethics"; *Quebec Code*, *supra* note 2, arts. 49(2), (4): "[a] lawyer must cease to act for a client, except where a tribunal orders otherwise: … if, notwithstanding the lawyer's advice, the client or a representative of the client persists in contravening a legal provision or in inciting the lawyer to do so; [or] … if the client persists in exercising a recourse or filing proceedings that the lawyer considers abusive."

101 *FLSC Model Code*, *supra* note 2, r 5.1-2(b): "[w]hen acting as an advocate, a lawyer must not: … knowingly assist or permit a client to do anything that the lawyer considers to be dishonest or dishonourable."

102 See above note 19 and accompanying text.

103 See, e.g., Bryant, *supra* note 92, as quoted by Sanderson, *supra* note 4 at 117: "[i]n another era, the justice minister would have resigned."

104 For an argument that the Attorney General has at least the discretion to announce their reasons for withdrawal, see chapter 4.

105 Cotter, *supra* note 78 at 76.

106 See, e.g., Michael Bryant, as quoted in Schmitz, *supra* note 89: "[i]t's the obligation of the attorney general to stand up for the chief justice, at least behind closed doors, and in another era, the attorney general would speak up publicly to the prime minister."

107 *FLSC Model Code*, *supra* note 2, r 5.6-1, commentary 3. See also *Quebec Code*, *supra* note 2, art. 12.

108 *FLSC Model Code*, *supra* note 2, r 3.7-7. See also *Quebec Code*, *supra* note 2, art. 49. For existing examples of mandatory withdrawal that are not listed in rule 3.7-7 but are otherwise required by the rules of professional conduct, see Alice Woolley and Amy Salyzyn, *Understanding Lawyers' Ethics in Canada*, 3rd ed. (Toronto: LexisNexis Canada, 2023) at 143–4; *FLSC Model Code*, *supra* note 2, rr 3.4-1 (conflicts of interest), 3.2-7 (among other things "[a] lawyer must never … knowingly assist in or encourage any dishonesty, fraud, crime, or illegal conduct"), 3.2-8 (conduct by organizational client).

109 *R v. Campbell* (1994), 25 Alta LR (3d) 158, [1995] 2 WWR 469 (QB) [*Campbell* cited to Alta LR], aff'd *Reference re Remuneration of Judges of the Provincial Court of Prince Edward Island; Reference re Independence and Impartiality of Judges of the Provincial Court of Prince Edward Island*, [1997] 3

SCR 3, 150 DLR (4th) 577 [*PEI Judges Reference* cited to SCR]; *Charter*, *supra* note 25, s 11(d).

110 See Diana Coulter, "Klein's Remarks Stir Legal Storm" *Edmonton Journal* (3 May 1994), A1, 1994 WLNR 3190690 [Coulter, "Klein's Remarks"].

111 Thanks to Adam Dodek on this point.

112 Coulter, "Klein's Remarks," *supra* note 110. See also Kathleen Engman, "Klein Must Retract, Law Society Says" *Edmonton Journal* (4 May 1994), A1, 1994 WLNR 3215241: "[i]n a speech to newspaper editors Tuesday [3 May] in Calgary, Klein reiterated that the judge's decision to absent himself from court was a 'labor problem' and said if he were chief provincial court Judge Ed Wachowich, 'I would fire the guy.'"

113 Alberta, Legislative Assembly, *Alberta Hansard*, 23–2 (2 May 1994), 1578 (Hon. Ralph Klein).

114 *Ibid.*, 1578 (Hon. Ken Rostad).

115 *Ibid.*, 1578 (Laurence Decore).

116 *Ibid.*, 1578 (Laurence Decore).

117 *Ibid.*, 1578 (Hon. Ralph Klein).

118 *Ibid.*, 1622 (Hon. Ken Rostad).

119 See, e.g., Diana Coulter, "No Apology to Court, Says Klein" *Edmonton Journal* (5 May 1994), A7, 1994 WLNR 3137648.

120 *Campbell*, *supra* note 109 at 274–5.

121 See Diana Coulter, "Judges Get Klein's Letter of Clarification" *Edmonton Journal* (7 May 1994), A1 [Coulter, "Letter"].

122 *PEI Judges Reference*, *supra* note 109 at para. 286. See, e.g., Larry Johnsrude, "Klein Censured by Chief Justice" *Edmonton Journal* (19 September 1997), A3, 1997 WLNR 4119638. With respect to both Johnsrude and Klein, "censured" seems perhaps an overstatement.

123 "Acquittal Angers Corporate Affairs Minister: Ouellet Renews Call for Appeal in Sugar Firms Ruling" *The Globe and Mail* (22 December 1975), 8 ["Acquittal"]; *Re Ouellet (Nos 1 and 2)*, 1976 CanLII1250 (QC CA) [*Ouellet*].

124 *House of Commons Debates*, 30–1, vol. 10 (20 December 1975), 10222 (Hon. André Ouellet) [Canada *Hansard* II]; "Acquittal," *supra* note 123.

125 Canada *Hansard* II, *supra* note 124 at 10223 (Hon. Ron Basford).

126 *Ibid.*, 10223 (Hon. Ron Basford). See also *ibid.* at 10234 (Hon. Ron Basford): "[o]n the point of order raised by the hon. member for St. John's East (Mr. McGrath), Beauchesne is quite clear in both citation 149(j) and 152(4) that the type of remarks that are deemed to be unparliamentary, as the hon. member for Fundy-Royal (Mr. Fairweather) has indicated, are those that cast reflections upon the conduct of judges, or a personal attack or censure. My colleague made it clear that that was not what he was engaged in. He indicated clearly that it was not the type of remark he was intending to make. … I indicated that I did not want to go any further, and I refused in the

question period to go any further with the questions of the hon. member for St. John's East because, as I indicated, in my view the judge in this particular case was acting in the course of his duties. It is a matter which may or may not be appealed upon the advice and decision of myself and departmental officials, and I do not think it would be proper for me to go further."

127 *Ouellet, supra* note 123.

128 Canada *Hansard* II, *supra* note 124 at 10234 (Hon. André Ouellet). Basford reinforced this weak apology: see above note 124.

129 *Ouellet, supra* note 123 at 103, Montgomery JA: "[i]t is appellant's subsequent conduct that I find impossible to condone. His half-apologies, attempting to place the blame upon the press, I regard as an aggravation rather than as an extenuation, and still more so his technical defences, such as his unwarranted attempts to take shelter behind his immunity as a Member of Parliament."

130 See *House of Commons Debates*, 30–1, vol. 11 (16 March 1976), 11822 (Hon. André Ouellet): "[b]oth during and after the trial, I refrained from any public statement on that case. Recently, as a result of a clearly calculated indiscretion, my case has given rise to a highly partisan political debate. It has become quite clear to me in the past few days that my most basic rights, not so much before the courts, but especially before the public at large, as a defendant appealing a decision, could be seriously jeopardized by that political debate, while even my own resolution to keep silent-which goes back to the beginning of my trial-is questioned and used against me by some people. I repeat, I strongly intend to keep that resolution."

131 *FLSC Model Code, supra* note 2, r 3.7-2, commentary 1. See also *Quebec Code, supra* note 2, art. 48(1).

132 Thanks to a reviewer on this point.

133 Hon. Jason Kenney, "Speaking Notes for the Honourable Jason Kenney, P.C., M.P. Minister of Citizenship, Immigration and Multiculturalism at an Event at the Faculty of Law, University of Western Ontario" (11 February 2011), online: *Government of Canada* <www.canada.ca/en /immigration-refugees-citizenship/news/archives/speeches-2011/jason -kenney-minister-event-faculty-law-university-western-ontario.html> [https://perma.cc/9GY8-A7HL].

134 *House of Commons Debates*, 40–3, vol. 145, no. 131 (15 February 2011), 8196–7 (Geoff Regan): "Mr. Speaker, while the Minister of Citizenship, Immigration and Multiculturalism is insulting and denigrating the Canadian courts and attacking the integrity of judges, the Minister of Justice sits and does nothing. He preaches about law and order but does not practise what he preaches. His oath of office is to preserve the integrity of our legal system. Has he forgotten his oath or does he share his colleague's opinion?"

135 *Ibid.*, 8197 (Hon. Jason Kenney).

136 See, e.g., Audrey Macklin and Lorne Waldman, "When Cabinet Ministers Attack Judges, they Attack Democracy" *The Globe and Mail* (18 February 2011), A17, 2011 WLNR 3232187 [no mention of Nicholson]. See also Richard Foot, "Supreme Court Chief Justice Takes on Kenney; Beverley McLachlin Answers Immigration Minister's Criticism of Federal Court Decisions" *Vancouver Sun* (15 August 2011), B1, 2011 WLNR 16122241 [no mention of Nicholson].

137 Mia Rabson, "Bar Association Spanks Kenney for Publicly Taking Judges to Task" *Winnipeg Free Press* (24 February 2011), A6 [again, no mention of Nicholson].

138 Richard Foot, "Supreme Court Chief Justice Takes on Kenney" *Vancouver Sun* (15 August 2011), B1, 2011 WLNR 16122241. I note in passing that this comment, like the speech itself, is a flagrant rejection of the principle of judicial independence.

139 Ontario, Legislative Assembly, *Official Report of Debates (Hansard)*, 43–1, no. 125 (26 February 2024) [Ontario *Hansard* 125], 7234 (Hon. Doug Ford): "I am going to make sure we have like-minded judges." See also Ontario, Legislative Assembly, *Official Report of Debates (Hansard)*, 43–1, no. 126 (27 February 2024), 7298: "I'm sick and tired of judges letting these people out on bail. We're going to hire tough judges, tough JPs. That's what we're doing." See, e.g., Jacques Gallant, "Ford Reiterates Call for 'Like-Minded Judges'" *The Toronto Star* (27 February 2024), A1.

140 Ontario *Hansard* 125, *supra* note 139 at 7298, 7337, 7338 (Hon. Doug Downey).

141 Craig McInnes, "A-G Raps Premier for Criticizing Judge: Letter from B.C. Supreme Court Chief Rebukes Campbell" *The Vancouver Sun* (24 October 2001), A1, 2001 WLNR 6659116, quoting Attorney General Geoff Plant.

142 *Ibid.*, also quoting Attorney General Geoff Plant. Contrast here more recent comments by the Attorney General for British Columbia criticizing a judge: Vaughn Palmer, "Lawyers Rap Sharma, but She Appears to Have Public Support; Even B.C. United Agrees When She Calls Out Victim-Shaming and Lenient Sentencing" *The Vancouver Sun* (12 December 2023), A3, 2023 WLNR 42044372.

143 *FLSC Model Code*, *supra* note 2, r 5.6-1, commentary 3. See also *Quebec Code*, *supra* note 2, art. 12.

144 On ministerial immunity, see chapter 3. On balancing, see above note 71 and accompanying text.

145 John Ll. J. Edwards, *The Attorney-General, Politics and the Public Interest* (London: Sweet & Maxwell, 1984), 69, quoted in the Hon. A. Anne McLellan, *Review of the Roles of the Minister of Justice and Attorney General of Canada* (June 28, 2019), 11, online: *Government of Canada* <https://www.pm.gc.ca/en/news/backgrounders/2019/08/14/review-roles-minister-justice-and-attorney-general-canada#:~:text=I%20recommend%20

that%20the%20oath,making%20decisions%20about%20prosecutions%20
independently> [https://perma.cc/G7DG-WMLE].
146 See above notes 94–5 and accompanying text.
147 See, e.g., Sanderson, *supra* note 4 at 117; Stephenson, *supra* note 6.
148 See chapter 5.

3 Complexity: The Cross-Appointed Attorney General

1 This chapter is adapted from Andrew Flavelle Martin, "The Premier
   Should Not Also Be the Attorney General: *Roncarelli v Duplessis* Revisited
   as a Cautionary Tale in Legal Ethics and Professionalism" *Man LJ* 44, no.
   3 (2021): 155. In this chapter, French quotations are followed by unofficial
   English translations.
2 I will refer to Premiers in this chapter, but the same considerations would
   apply to a Prime Minister who was also Minister of Justice and Attorney
   General, albeit subject to federalism considerations, assuming that
   person was a lawyer. See Andrew Flavelle Martin, "The Implications of
   Federalism for the Regulation of Federal Government Lawyers" *Dal LJ*
   43, no. 1 (2020): 363 especially at 383–6.
3 *Askin v. Law Society of British Columbia*, 2013 BCCA 233 [*Askin* BCCA], aff'g
   2012 BCSC 895 [*Askin* BCSC], leave to appeal to SCC refused, 35463 (7
   November 2013). See esp. *Askin* BCSC at paras. 29–30: "The prerogative
   power of the Lieutenant Governor to appoint ministers of cabinet is of
   constitutional significance, and cannot be removed, replaced, qualified,
   or extinguished without express legislative language or by necessary
   implication. … Further, as the royal prerogative is a branch of the common
   law, the legislature would need clear and unambiguous indication that it
   intended to change it." [Citations omitted.] See also *Askin* BCCA at para.
   31. I will discuss *Askin* and its implications further in chapter 6.
4 See, e.g., *Ontario v. Criminal Lawyers' Association of Ontario*, 2013 SCC 43 at
   para. 35.
5 I mentioned in chapter 1 the inherent challenges that arise in the Canadian
   context because the Attorney General is also the Minister of Justice. (See,
   e.g., The Hon. A. Anne McLellan, *Review of the Roles of the Minister of Justice
   and Attorney General of Canada* (28 June 2019), 23–4, online: <https://www
   .pm.gc.ca/en/news/backgrounders/2019/08/14/review-roles-minister
   -justice-and-attorney-general-canada> [https://perma.cc/65RB-J9WF];
   Adam Dodek, "The Impossible Position: Canada's Attorney-General
   Cannot Be Our Justice Minister" *The Globe and Mail* (22 February 2019), O1,
   2019 WLNR 5866240, online: <https://www.theglobeandmail.com
   /opinion/article-the-impossible-position-canadas-attorney-general-cannot
   -be-our/> [https://perma.cc/Y262-GQJP].) Instead, my focus is on an
   Attorney General and Minister of Justice who is also the Premier.

6 But see recently Northwest Territories, where as of December 2023 Premier
  R.J. Simpson was also Minister of Justice: Government of Northwest
  Territories, "Premier Simpson Announces Cabinet Portfolio Assignments"
  (12 December 2023), online: <https://www.gov.nt.ca/en/newsroom
  /premier-simpson-announces-cabinet-portfolio-assignments> [perma.cc
  /G73C-RXJ9].

7 See Paul Romney, *Mr Attorney: The Attorney General for Ontario in Court,
  Cabinet, and Legislature, 1791–1899* (Toronto: The Osgoode Society, 1986),
  159–60: "Often the party leaders were lawyers, and it became the practice
  for the leader of the government party in each section of the province
  [Canada West and Canada East] to take the office of attorney general
  for that section. In Upper Canada the tradition continued even after
  Confederation in 1867. Between 1841 and 1899 there were only about six
  years in which the leading government politician in Upper Canada and
  Ontario was not the attorney general. ... Though these developments were
  unexampled in the history of England and its empire, they were logical
  consequences of the province's political history and social structure." See
  also 169.

8 John Sandfield MacDonald: Bruce W. Hodgins, "Macdonald, John
  Sandfield" in *Dictionary of Canadian Biography*, vol. 10 (Toronto: University
  of Toronto/Université Laval, 2003) <http://www.biographi.ca/en/bio
  /macdonald_john_sandfield_10E.html> [https://perma.cc/R7AQ-JSA9]:
  "the provisional lieutenant governor of Ontario, Sir Henry William Stisted,
  asked Sandfield Macdonald to become the first premier of Ontario. His
  coalition government was sworn in on 15 and 20 July 1867; besides the
  premier, who became attorney general, the cabinet contained another
  Baldwinite, a coalition Grit, and two Conservatives." Sir Oliver Mowat:
  Paul Romney, "Mowat, Sir Oliver" in *Dictionary of Canadian Biography*, vol.
  13 <http://www.biographi.ca/en/bio/mowat_oliver_13E.html> [https://
  perma.cc/Z2F3-GJCN]: "On 25 Oct. 1872, at the Urging of [Edward] Blake,
  George Brown, and Alexander Mackenzie, Mowat Became Premier and
  Attorney General of Ontario." Arthur Sturgis Hardy: David G. Burley,
  "Hardy, Arthur Sturgis" in *Dictionary of Canadian Biography*, vol. 13 <http://
  www.biographi.ca/en/bio/hardy_arthur_sturgis_13E.html> [https://
  perma.cc/2PYS-K98X]: "When [Oliver] Mowat retired in 1896, [Arthur
  Sturgis] Hardy as the senior minister became the new premier and
  attorney general, on 21 July."

9 Romney, *supra* note 7 at 160.

10 See, e.g., Barry L. Strayer, *Canada's Constitutional Revolution* (Edmonton:
   University of Alberta Press, 2013), 8. Surprisingly, Premier and Attorney
   General E.C. Manning of Alberta was not a lawyer, a point to which I will
   return below. See below note 102 and accompanying text.

11 *Roncarelli v. Duplessis*, [1959] SCR 121, 16 DLR (2d) 689 [*Roncarelli* cited
to SCR]. That Duplessis was both Attorney General and Premier is
mentioned in passing in Grant Huscroft, "The Attorney General and
Charter Challenges to Legislation: Advocate or Adjudicator?" *NJCL* 5
(1995): 125 at 132, note 29. (Now Justice Huscroft of the Court of Appeal
for Ontario.)

12 And, likewise, in the tort of misfeasance in public office. See Harry
Wruck, "The Continuing Evolution of the Tort of Misfeasance in Public
Office" *UBC L Rev* 41, no. 1 (2008): 69 at 74: "This case was important in
defining misfeasance in public office with some degree of specificity. It also
demonstrated why the tort had fallen into disuse. In *Roncarelli*, Duplessis
expressly admitted at trial that he was biased against Jehovah's Witnesses.
In most cases it is extremely difficult to establish that a public official has
acted with malice or for an improper purpose or in bad faith."

13 *Roncarelli, supra* note 11 at 132–3. The direction and revocation occurred in
late November and early December of 1946: 132–3.

14 While the events in *Roncarelli* pre-date the more recent trend in which
the Attorney General's law enforcement responsibilities are spun off to
a separate Minister of Public Safety or Solicitor General, and Duplessis's
purported power to order the commission to revoke the licence is likely
one that would presently rest with the Solicitor General, my focus is on
the Attorney General's core function to advise on the legality of such an
action.

15 *Roncarelli, supra* note 11 at 133. See, e.g., Lorne Sossin, "The Rule of
Law and the Justiciability of Prerogative Powers: A Comment on *Black
v. Chretien*" *McGill LJ* 47, no. 2 (2002): 435 at 455: "It will be rare where
evidence can be proffered that demonstrates decisionmakers acted in
bad faith, or for ulterior or arbitrary motives. *Roncarelli*, where Premier
Duplessis testified as to his ulterior motives, was surely exceptional in this
regard." (Now Justice Sossin of the Court of Appeal for Ontario.)

16 Geneviève Cartier, "The Legacy of *Roncarelli v. Duplessis*: 1959–2009"
McGill LJ 55 (2010): 375 at 389 [citation omitted] [Cartier, "Legacy"].

17 Pierre Laporte, *The True Face of Duplessis* (Montreal: Harvest House,
1960), 67, originally published as Pierre Laporte, *Le vrai visage de Duplessis*
(Montreal: Les Editions de l'Homme, 1960), 65 ("Monsieur Duplessis
dominait complètement ses ministres. … Que tel député plutôt que tel
autre soit titulaire d'un ministère, cela importait assez peu, car monsieur
Duplessis était le commencement et la fin de tout. Sur certaines questions
relevant de leur compétence il ne les consultait même pas.") See similarly
Leslie Roberts, *The Chief: A Political Biography of Maurice Duplessis* (Toronto:
Irvin & Co, 1963), 4–5: "Cabinet Ministers quickly learned to hold their
tongues when confronted by decisions directly affecting their departments,

on which they had not been consulted, or even informed about prior to public announcement from [Duplessis'] office. ... He got away with it ... partly because he surrounded himself with men who (with rare exceptions ...) were more concerned with the spoils of office than with personal dignity."

18 See Roberts, *supra* note 17, 118: "after his early collisions with colleagues of character or strong conviction, he was at pains always to surround himself with pliant Ministers and to keep the instruments of power firmly in his own hands." See also Léon Dion, *Québec, 1945–2000, vol 2: Les intellectuels et le temps de Duplessis* (Québec: Presses de l'Université Laval, 1993), 97: "À son double titre de premier ministre et de procureur général, Duplessis bafoue sans retenue les droits de la personne." Consider here the failures of federal Minister of Justice and Attorney General Peter MacKay, as analysed in, e.g., Brent Cotter, "The Prime Minister v the Chief Justice of Canada: The Attorney General's Failure of Responsibility" *Leg Ethics* 18 (2015): 73 (now Senator Cotter) and discussed in chapter 2.

19 Marguerite Paulin, *Maurice Duplessis: Powerbroker, Politician*, translated by Nora Alleyn (Montréal: XYZ Pub, 2005), 168, 221, originally published in French as Marguerite Paulin, *Maurice Duplessis: le noblet, le petit roi* (Montréal: XYZ Pub, 2002), 184 ("Pour ce faire, Maurice Duplessis consolide son pouvoir : premier ministre du Québec, il assume avec poigne la fonction de procureur général en plus de diriger les relations intergouvernementales." [Alleyn translation: "To do this, Maurice Duplessis consolidates his power: Premier of Quebec, he assumes with a heavy fist the function of Attorney General in addition to directing intergovernmental relations."]) and 236 ("Le premier ministre Duplessis consolide son pouvoir en remplissant la fonction de procureur général et en dirigeant les relations intergouvernementales." [Alleyn translation: "Premier Duplessis consolidates his power by fulfilling the function of Attorney General and directing intergovernmental relations."]). As Paulin notes at 168 and 221, Duplessis also made himself minister for intergovernmental affairs. See also Dion, *supra* note 18 at 35: "Duplessis exerce lui-même le plus de pouvoirs possible. Quand il délègue, ce n'est que de façon conditionnelle. Premier ministre, il occupe en outre le poste de procureur général" [Alleyn translation: "Duplessis himself exercises as much power as possible. When he delegates, it is only conditionally. As Premier, he also holds the post of Attorney General"]. See also William Kaplan, *The World War Two Ban on Jehovah's Witnesses in Canada: A Study in the Development of Civil Rights* (Stanford, CA: SJD, Stanford University, 1998), 412: "Duplessis ran the province in an authoritarian manner, but it was in his dual role as premier and attorney general that he stamped his pattern on the government."

20 See above note 10 and accompanying text.

21 As I will discuss below, there is a legitimate concern that both portfolios cannot be adequately fulfilled. Indeed, it is quite possible, if not likely, that the "other" portfolio becomes neglected, an afterthought, or an empty gesture. See below note 58 and accompanying text.

22 See, e.g., Andrew Flavelle Martin, "Legal Ethics versus Political Practices: The Application of the Rules of Professional Conduct to Lawyer-Politicians" *Can Bar Rev* 91, no. 1 (2013): 1 at 37 [Martin, "Political Practices"].

23 Federation of Law Societies of Canada, *Model Code of Professional Conduct* (Ottawa: FLSC, 2009, last amended 2022), online: *Federation of Law Societies of Canada* <www.flsc.ca> [*FLSC Model Code*]; *Code of Professional Conduct of Lawyers*, CQLR c B-1, art 3.1 [*Quebec Code*].

24 Barreau de la Province de Québec, *Lois et règlements (en vigueur le 1 Septembre 1939)* (Montréal: Thérien Frères Limitée, 1939) [*1939 règlements*], made pursuant to *Loi du Barreau,* RSQ 1925, c 210, s 8. While the 1939 by-laws were published in English only, I will provide translations, where appropriate, from the bilingual 1955 by-laws: Barreau de la Province de Québec, *Lois et règlements annotes | Statute and By-Laws Annotated* (Montréal: Le Barreau, 1955) [*1955 règlements*], made pursuant to *Loi du Barreau,* 2–3 Eliz II, ch 59, s 22.

25 *1939 règlements, supra* note 24 at 83, by-law 54 [emphasis added]: "Sont dérogatoires à l'honneur et à l'exercice de la profession, *entre autre actes,* les suivants ..."

26 Canadian Bar Association, "Canons of Legal Ethics" in Canadian Bar Association, *Proceedings of the Fifth Annual Meeting of the Canadian Bar Association Held in Ottawa, Ontario, September 1st, 2nd and 3rd, 1920* (Winnipeg: Bulman Bros, 1920), 261–4 [*CBA Canons*], reprinted as Canadian Bar Association, *Canons of Legal Ethics (Adopted by the Canadian Bar Association, September 2nd, 1920)* (Ottawa: The Association, 1955). I note that the *CBA Canons* had no legal force in themselves, and that the original Discipline by-laws of the Barreau pre-dated the *CBA Canons* by approximately three years. See *Loi organique et règlements du Barreau de la province de Québec (Adoptés le 25 octobre 1917)* (Montreal: Eug Goblensky & Co, 1917), 66, by-law 62.

27 Amy Salyzyn, "From Colleague to Cop to Coach: Contemporary Regulation of Lawyer Competence" *Can Bar Rev* 95, no. 2 (2017): 489 at 496.

28 *Roncarelli, supra* note 11 at 134, 135.

29 *Ibid.,* 133.

30 *Ibid.,* 130.

31 *Nelles v. Ontario,* [1989] 2 SCR 170 at 210, 60 DLR (4th) 609.

32 *McCullock Finney c Barreau (Québec),* 2004 SCC 36 at para. 39 [*Finney*].

33 P.W. Hogg, "Judicial Review: How Much Do We Need?" *McGill LJ* 20, no. 2 (1974): 157 at 165. See similarly Geneviève Cartier, "Administrative Discretion and the Spirit of Legality: From Theory to Practice" *Can JL & Soc'y* 24, no. 3 (2009): 313 at 315–17.

34 Mary Liston, "Witnessing Arbitrariness: *Roncarelli v. Duplessis* Fifty Years On" *McGill LJ* 55 (2010): 689.

35 *Ibid.*, 696.

36 *Ibid.*, 695.

37 See, e.g., *R v. Neil*, 2002 SCC 70 at para. 19. See also, e.g., *FLSC Model Code, supra* note 23, rr 3.2-2 (candour), 3.4-1 (conflicts), 3.4-1 commentary 5 (commitment, etc.). See also *Quebec Code, supra* note 23, ss 20 (confidentiality), 37 (candour), 71 (conflicts). See also *CBA Canons, supra* note 26, 3.1 (candour), 3.2 (conflicts).

38 *FLSC Model Code, supra* note 23, r 3.1-2; *Quebec Code, supra* note 23, arts 20, 21. But see above note 27 and accompanying text.

39 *FLSC Model Code, supra* note 23, r 7.4-1. I say purportedly because the interpretation and application of this rule has been uneven. See Martin, "Political Practices," *supra* note 22 at 11–16. See also *Quebec Code, supra* note 23, art. 78, specifically on conflicts of interest for lawyers in public office.

40 See, e.g., *Act respecting the Ministère de la Justice*, CQLR c M-19, s 3: "The Minister ... sees that the administration of public affairs is in accordance with the law."

41 *An Act Respecting the Department of the Attorney General*, RSQ 1941, c 46, s 4: "The duties of the Attorney-General are the following: ... To see that the administration of public affairs is in accordance with the law." Note that, unlike the 1941 version of this statute, the modern version separates the duties of the Attorney General from those of the Minister of Justice and assigns this duty to the latter: CQLR c M-19, *supra* note 40, s 33.

42 *Roncarelli, supra* note 11 at 153.

43 See, e.g., Kent Roach, "Not Just the Government's Lawyer: The Attorney General as Defender of the Rule of Law" *Queen's LJ* 31, no. 2 (2006): 598.

44 See, e.g., *FLSC Model Code, supra* note 23, r 3.2-3: "Although a lawyer may receive instructions from an officer, employee, agent or representative, when a lawyer is employed or retained by an organization, including a corporation, the lawyer must act for the organization in exercising his or her duties and in providing professional services." See also *Quebec Code, supra* note 23, art. 36: "Although a lawyer may receive instructions from a representative of the client with respect to the performance of the mandate, the lawyer must act for the client and serve and protect the client's interests."

45 *FLSC Model Code, supra* note 23, r 3.2-2, commentary 3. See also *Quebec Code, supra* note 23, art. 37: "A lawyer is honest and candid when communicating with clients or advising them."

46 *FLSC Model Code, supra* note 23, r 3.2-2, commentary 3.

47 See, e.g., Bernard Saint-Aubin, *Duplessis et son époque* (Montréal: La Presse, 1979), 251: "il tombe sous le sens que sans les déclarations publiques de Duplessis, il n'aurait jamais été condamné à verser des dommages intérêts. Sur le plan juridique, il a commis une erreur grave. Par contre, sur le plan politique, il en a tiré des avantages immenses" ("It seems logical that without Duplessis's public statements, he would never have been ordered to pay damages. Legally, he made a serious mistake. On the other hand, on the political level, he derived immense advantages from it").

48 *FLSC Model Code*, *supra* note 23, r 7.3-1. This rule also mentions "competence."

49 See, e.g., *Goodman v. Rossi* (1994), 21 OR (3d) 112 at 132, 120 DLR (4th) 557 (Div Ct), rev'd on other grounds (1995), 24 OR (3d) 359, 125 DLR (4th) 613 (CA): "More and more we read and hear about the practice of law becoming the business of law; the diminution of the nobility of the profession; the surfacing of a new breed of lawyers who have cast aside the attributes of independence and responsibility to become little more than mouthpieces for their clients." See more recently, albeit in the criminal context, *R v. Samra* (1998), 41 OR (3d) 434 at 446, 129 CCC (3d) 144 (CA): "There is an erroneous premise underlying the appellant's submissions in this case – that defence counsel is but a mouthpiece for his client."

50 *FLSC Model Code*, *supra* note 23, r 3.2-3: "Although a lawyer may receive instructions from an officer, employee, agent or representative, when a lawyer is employed or retained by an organization, including a corporation, the lawyer must act for the organization in exercising his or her duties and in providing professional services." See also commentary 1.

51 *Ibid.*, r 7.3-1, commentary 1: "A lawyer must not carry on, manage or be involved in any outside interest in such a way that makes it difficult to distinguish in which capacity the lawyer is acting in a particular transaction, or that would give rise to a conflict of interest or duty to a client." See also commentary 2: "When acting or dealing in respect of a transaction involving an outside interest, the lawyer should be mindful of potential conflicts and the applicable standards referred to in the conflicts rule and disclose any personal interest."

52 *Ibid.*, r 3.4-2(a). The conditions in r 3.4-2(b) allowing implied consent would not apply, even though the client is a government.

53 See, e.g., *Askin* BCCA at para. 31, aff'g *Askin* BCSC at paras. 29–30, leave to appeal to SCC refused, 35463 (7 November 2013). See chapter 6.

54 *FLSC Model Code*, *supra* note 23, r 7.3-1, commentary 1. See also *Quebec Code*, *supra* note 23, art. 11(2): "When a lawyer engages in activities which do not relate to the profession of lawyer, in particular in connection with a job, a function, an office or the operation of an enterprise: … he must avoid creating or allowing any ambiguity to persist as to the capacity in which he is acting."

55 See below note 93 and accompanying text.

56 *FLSC Model Code, supra* note 23, r 3.7-7. See also *Quebec Code, supra* note 23, art. 49(2): "A lawyer must cease to act for a client, except where a tribunal orders otherwise: ... if, notwithstanding the lawyer's advice, the client or a representative of the client persists in contravening a legal provision or in inciting the lawyer to do so."

57 Recall *FLSC Model Code, supra* note 23, r 6.1-1: "A lawyer has complete professional responsibility for all business entrusted to him or her." See also *Quebec Code, supra* note 23, art. 35: "A lawyer ... is responsible for the mandate and must adequately supervise work performed by others who are collaborating with him in the performance of the mandate."

58 *Ibid.*, r 7.3-1. See also *Quebec Code, supra* note 23, art. 11(1): "When a lawyer engages in activities which do not relate to the profession of lawyer, in particular in connection with a job, a function, an office or the operation of an enterprise: ... he must ensure that those activities do not compromise his compliance with this code."

59 See below notes 95–6 and accompanying text.

60 See, e.g., *FLSC Model Code, supra* note 23, r 3.1-1, definition of "competent lawyer": "(g) complying in letter and spirit with all rules pertaining to the appropriate professional conduct of lawyers."

61 *Ibid.*, preface at 6: "Some sections of the Code are of more general application, and some sections, in addition to providing ethical guidance, may be read as aspirational."

62 I am aware of no indication that Roncarelli made, or considered making, a complaint to the Barreau.

63 *Strother v. Law Society of British Columbia*, 2018 BCCA 481 at para. 64 [citations omitted].

64 See above note 28 and accompanying text.

65 See above note 27 and accompanying text.

66 *Roncarelli, supra* note 11 at 142 [emphasis added].

67 *Ibid.*, 185 [emphasis added].

68 *Ibid.*, 155 [emphasis added].

69 Roberts, *supra* note 17 at 126.

70 Kaplan, *supra* note 19 at 444, citing Roberts, *supra* note 17 at 126–7.

71 Mark Aronson, "Some Australian Reflections on *Roncarelli v. Duplessis*" *McGill LJ* 55 (2010): 615 at 637–8 (quotation is from 637).

72 In contrast, Roderick MacDonald has argued that the decision of the Supreme Court of Canada could and might have been different: Roderick A. MacDonald, "Was Duplessis Right?" *McGill LJ* 55 (2010): 401.

73 See above note 28 and accompanying text.

74 Gavin MacKenzie, *Lawyers & Ethics: Professional Responsibility and Discipline* (Toronto: Thomson Reuters Canada, 1993) (loose-leaf updated 2023, release 5) at ch. 26, 26.8. While MacKenzie refers here to "lawyers' personal or private

conduct," there is clear precedent that conduct by lawyers in public office, outside the practice of law, can constitute conduct unbecoming. See *Nova Scotia Barristers' Society v. Morgan*, 2010 NSBS 1 [*Morgan*]: "Mr. Morgan made the comments which are the subject of this Complaint in his capacity as Mayor of Cape Breton Regional Municipality and at no time did he state or was he retained to act as a lawyer for and on behalf of the Municipality in the case giving rise to Mr. Justice Murphy's decision. Therefore Mr. Morgan made the comments described in the Complaint in his 'personal or private capacity' … rather than in a 'lawyer's professional capacity'." See also, e.g., *Law Society of Upper Canada v. Jackson*, 2017 ONLSTH 64 at para. 17 [*Jackson*]: "Conduct unbecoming a barrister or solicitor is conduct, including in a lawyer's personal or private capacity, that tends to bring discredit upon the legal profession."

75 MacKenzie, *supra* note 74 at ch. 26, 26.8.

76 See, e.g., *Jackson*, *supra* note 74 at paras. 15–17.

77 Conrad Black, *Duplessis* (Toronto: McClelland & Stewart, 1977) at 389–90. This mention of Duplessis as a lawyer is largely omitted in Black's subsequent revised version: Conrad Black, *Render unto Caesar: The Life and Legacy of Maurice Duplessis*, rev. ed. (Toronto: Key Porter, 1998) at 286–7. See also *CBA Canons*, *supra* note 26, 2.1: "His should maintain towards the Judges of the Courts a courteous and respectful attitude and insist on similar conduct on the part of his client."

78 Cartier, "Legacy," *supra* note 16 at 389 [citation omitted]; see also above note 16 and accompanying text.

79 *FLSC Model Code*, *supra* note 23, r 5.6-1: "A lawyer must encourage public respect for and try to improve the administration of justice." See also *CBA Canons*, *supra* note 26, 2.1: "He should maintain towards the Judges of the Courts a courteous and respectful attitude." See also *1939 règlements*, *supra* note 24 at 83, by-law 54: "Sont dérogatoires à l'honneur et à l'exercice de la profession, entre autre actes, les suivants : … 6. Manquer, dans sa conduite ou par ses paroles, au respect dû aux tribunaux et au Barreau" ("The following are derogations from the honor and exercise of the profession, among other acts: … 6. Fail, in his conduct or in his words, with respect due to the courts and to the Bar"). (See also *1955 règlements*, *supra* note 24 at 68, by-law 66: "33. Shows lack of proper respect for the Court or Bar by word, deed or appearance.") Contrast for example *Morgan*, *supra* note 74, as discussed, e.g., in Martin, "Political Practices," *supra* note 22 at 11–12, where Cape Breton mayor and Nova Scotia lawyer John Morgan reacted to an adverse court decision by publicly accusing the province's entire bench of political bias.

80 *Hesje v. Law Society of Saskatchewan*, 2015 SKCA 2 at paras. 93–4 (quotation is from para. 93), applying *Law Society of Saskatchewan v. Merchant*, 2009 SKCA 33, leave to appeal to SCC refused, 33156 (23 July 2009). Contrast *Law Society*

of Upper Canada v. Carey, 2017 ONLSTH 25 at para. 63, aff'd 2018 ONLSTA 4: good faith can be a defence to a charge of professional misconduct.

81 For the factors going to penalty, see, e.g., *Faminoff v. The Law Society of British Columbia*, 2017 BCCA 373 at para. 36. For absence of bad faith as a mitigating factor, see, e.g., *Law Society of Upper Canada v. Edward Emil Patrick Iglar*, 2004 ONLSAP 7 at para. 55; *Law Society of Upper Canada v. Richard Keith Watson*, 2008 ONLSHP 59 at para. 15.

82 *Roncarelli, supra* note 11 at 133.

83 *Ibid.*, 134.

84 *Ibid.*, 141. Aronson, *supra* note 71 at 637 argues that "the Attorney General's malice consisted only of honest yet egregious ingredients…. hubris or stupidity." See also 634: "His illegality may have been neither intentional nor subjectively reckless, but the illegality was both so obvious and so outrageous that it was inexcusable in a prime minister and Attorney General."

85 *Finney, supra* note 32 at para. 39.

86 *Barreau (Montréal) c Wagner* (1967), [1968] BR 235 at 235, 1967 CarswellQue 253 (CA) [*Wagner*], discussed in chapter 2.

87 In chapter 5.

88 See *Roncarelli, supra* note 11 at 141, Rand J.: "To deny or revoke a permit because a citizen exercises an unchallengeable right totally irrelevant to the sale of liquor in a restaurant is equally beyond the scope of the discretion conferred."

89 MacKenzie, *supra* note 74 at ch. 26, 26.1.

90 See, e.g., Andrew Flavelle Martin, "The Limits of Professional Regulation in Canada: Law Societies and Non-Practising Lawyers" *Leg Ethics* 19, no. 1 (2016): 169 at 172, quoting Adam Dodek.

91 See above notes 28–9 and accompanying text.

92 See Eric M. Adams, "Building a Law of Human Rights: *Roncarelli v. Duplessis* in Canadian Constitutional Culture" *McGill LJ* 55 (2010): 437 at 451–3.

93 See, e.g., Adam M. Dodek, *Solicitor-Client Privilege* (Toronto: LexisNexis Canada, 2014) at para. 4.114: "There are many lawyers who serve in elected and appointed positions. With the exceptions of Attorneys General, they are clearly not acting in their capacity as professional legal advisers and communications with them will not be privileged." See also *FLSC Model Code, supra* note 23, r 7.3-1, commentary 1: "A lawyer must not carry on, manage or be involved in any outside interest in such a way that makes it difficult to distinguish in which capacity the lawyer is acting in a particular transaction." See also *Quebec Code, supra* note 23, art. 11(2): "When a lawyer engages in activities which do not relate to the profession of lawyer, in particular in connection with a job, a function, an office or the operation of an enterprise … he must avoid creating or allowing any ambiguity to persist as to the capacity in which he is acting."

94 See, e.g., Yan Campagnolo, *Le secret ministériel: théorie et pratique* (Quebec: Presses de l'Université Laval, 2020); Yan Campagnolo, "Cabinet Secrecy in Canada" *JPPL* 12, no. 3 (2019): 583; Yan Campagnolo, "Rethinking Cabinet Secrecy" *JPPL* 13, no. 3 (2020): 497.

95 But see, e.g., Deborah MacNair, "The Role of the Federal Public Sector Lawyer: From Polyester to Silk" *UNB LJ* 50 (2001): 125 at 133–7 and, more recently, Elizabeth Sanderson, *Government Lawyering: Duties and Ethical Challenges of Government Lawyers* (Toronto: LexisNexis Canada, 2018), 211–26 (ch. 5).

96 Recall *FLSC Model Code, supra* note 23, r 6.1-1: "A lawyer has complete professional responsibility for all business entrusted to him or her." See also *Quebec Code, supra* note 23, art 35.

97 See chapter 4.

98 See chapter 4.

99 See above note 56 and corresponding text.

100 *Krieger v. Law Society of Alberta*, 2002 SCC 65 at para. 3.

101 See chapter 6.

102 See, e.g., Strayer, *supra* note 10 at 8; Brian Brennan, *The Good Steward: The Ernest C. Manning Story* (Calgary: Fifth House, 2008), 125–6.

103 See, e.g., John Ll. J. Edwards, "The Attorney General and the Charter of Rights," in *Charter Litigation*, ed. Robert J. Sharpe (Toronto: Butterworths, 1987), 45 at 56–7. On the issues around this separation, and then holding both portfolios, see, e.g., Roy McMurtry, *Memoirs and Reflections* (Toronto: University of Toronto Press for the Osgoode Society for Canadian Legal History, 2013), 268–9 [McMurtry, *Memoirs*].

104 In these jurisdictions, it is not uncommon for a non-lawyer, often a former police officer, to hold this dual role. Such an appointment raises issues that I will return to in chapter 6.

105 For example, Roy McMurtry of Ontario: McMurtry, *Memoirs, supra* note 103 at 269.

106 See, e.g., John Ll. J. Edwards, "The *Charter*, Government and the Machinery of Justice" *UNB LJ* 36 (1987): 41 at 46: "Where the one Department of Justice is responsible for supervising the entire administration of justice, the relationships between the police and the prosecutors can sometimes touch highly sensitive questions of authority." See also, e.g., Hon. David Clark and Mary E. Hatherly, "The Organizational Structure of the Department of Justice in Relation to the Office of Attorney-General in New Brunswick" *UNB LJ* 37 (1988): 198 at 229–31. But for a discussion of the benefits of keeping these functions in a single ministry and minister see Gordon F. Gregory, "The Attorney-General in Government" *UNB LJ* 36 (1987): 59 at 65–7.

4 Complexity: Resignation

 1 Parts 1 and 2 of this chapter are adapted from Andrew Flavelle Martin, "The Attorney General as Lawyer (?): Confidentiality upon Resignation from Cabinet" *Dal LJ* 38, no. 1 (2015): 147.

 2 Federation of Law Societies of Canada, *Model Code of Professional Conduct* (Ottawa: FLSC, 2009) as amended October 2022 [*FLSC Model Code*], r 3.7-7(b) [emphasis added]. See also *Code of Professional Conduct of Lawyers*, RLRQ c B-1, r 3.1, art. 49(2) [*Quebec Code*].

 3 *FLSC Model Code, supra* note 2, r 3.7-7(a); *Quebec Code, supra* note 2, art. 49(1).

 4 *FLSC Model Code, supra* note 2, r 3.7-7(c); *Quebec Code, supra* note 2, art. 49(3).

 5 *FLSC Model Code, supra* note 2, r 3.4-1; *Quebec Code, supra* note 2, art. 71.

 6 *FLSC Model Code, supra* note 2, r 3.2-8(c).

 7 *Ibid.*, r 3.7-2; *Quebec Code, supra* note 2, art. 48(1).

 8 *FLSC Model Code, supra* note 2, r 3.7-2, commentary 1.

 9 *Ibid.*, r 3.7-1.

10 See, e.g., The Hon. Marc Rosenberg, "The Attorney General and the Administration of Criminal Justice" *Queen's LJ* 34 (2009): 813 at 819–20 [emphasis added]: "The most important of these constitutional conventions is that although the Attorney General is a cabinet minister, he or she acts independently of the cabinet in the exercise of the prosecution function. *This convention is now so firmly entrenched in the Canadian political system that any deviation would likely lead to the resignation of the Attorney General or would, at the very least, spark a constitutional crisis.*" Note that the Supreme Court of Canada, in *Krieger v. Law Society of Alberta*, 2002 SCC 65 at para. 3 [*Krieger*], clarified that this is a constitutional principle, not merely a constitutional convention: "It is a constitutional principle that the Attorneys General of this country must act independently of partisan concerns when exercising their delegated sovereign authority to initiate, continue or terminate prosecutions."

11 See, e.g., John Ll. J. Edwards, "The Attorney General and the Charter of Rights," in *Charter Litigation*, ed. Robert J. Sharpe (Toronto: Butterworths, 1987), 45 at 53 [Edwards in Sharpe]; Grant Huscroft, "Reconciling Duty and Discretion: The Attorney General in the *Charter* Era" *Queen's LJ* 34 (2009): 773 at 794–5 [Huscroft, "Duty and Discretion"] (now Justice Huscroft of the Court of Appeal for Ontario); Grant Huscroft, "The Attorney General and *Charter* Challenges to Legislation: Advocate or Adjudicator?" *NJCL* 5 (1995): 125 at 138 [Huscroft, "Advocate or Adjudicator"]; and Lorne Sossin, "Speaking Truth to Power? The Search for Bureaucratic Independence in Canada" *UTLJ* 55 (2005): 1 at 45 (framing resignation as an "obligation") (now Justice Sossin of the Court of Appeal for Ontario).

12 See, e.g., Elmer A. Driedger, "The Meaning and Effect of the Canadian Bill
   of Rights: A Draftsman's Viewpoint" *Ottawa L Rev* 9, no. 2 (1977): 303 at 311:
   "The Government could not politically afford to put itself in a position
   in which the Minister of Justice would resign over the issue or make
   an adverse report against the Government in the House of Commons
   as required by section 3 of the Bill of Rights." Janet L. Hiebert has
   described this excerpt as Driedger "speculat[ing] that if cabinet insisted
   on approving a bill that violated rights, the Minister of Justice would
   likely feel compelled to resign rather than risk being put in the position
   of having to make a report to Parliament that the government knowingly
   was introducing legislation inconsistent with rights": "Parliamentary
   Engagement with the *Charter*: Rethinking the Idea of Legislative Rights
   Review" *SCLR (2d)* 58 (2012): 87 at 89. See also Edwards in Sharpe, *supra*
   note 11 at 53, as discussed in Kent Roach, "The Attorney General and
   the *Charter* Revisited" *UTLJ* 50, no. 1 (2000): 1 at 35 [Roach, "Revisited"]:
   "Professor Edwards's advocacy of resignation may also be too high
   an ideal in the practical world of politics and may only result in the
   appointment of a more compliant Attorney General."
13 See, e.g., Lori Sterling, "The *Charter's* Impact on the Legislative Process:
   Where the Real 'Dialogue' Takes Place" *NJCL* 23 (2007): 139 at 147
   [emphasis in original]: "*In extremis*, the Attorney General might resign
   if he or she believes that government action is being taken illegally or
   unconstitutionally."
14 See, e.g., Lori Sterling and Heather Mackay, "The Independence of the
   Attorney General in the Civil Law Sphere" *Queen's LJ* 34, no. 2 (2009):
   891 at 901: "it is rare for the Attorney General, or his or her constitutional
   lawyers, to opine that a particular piece of legislation is 'constitutional' or
   'unconstitutional.' Instead, they provide a risk analysis, based on existing
   case law, which assesses the likelihood that the law would not be upheld
   due to a contravention of the *Charter*."
15 See, e.g., Kent Roach, "Not Just the Government's Lawyer: The Attorney
   General as Defender of the Rule of Law" *Queen's LJ* 31, no. 2 (2006):
   598 at 634–42 [Roach, "Not Just"], where Roach discusses appropriate
   alternatives to resignation.
16 See Jennifer Bond, "Failure to Report: The Manifestly Unconstitutional
   Nature of the *Human Smugglers Act*" *Osgoode Hall LJ* 51, no. 2 (2014): 377
   at 384, 385, n. 29; Alice Woolley, "The Lawyer as Advisor and the Practice
   of the Rule of Law" *UBC L Rev* 47, no. 2 (2014): 743 at 743–4 (now Justice
   Woolley of the Court of Appeal for Alberta).
17 *Department of Justice Act*, RSC 1985, c J-2, s 4.1(1).
18 Huscroft, "Duty and Discretion," *supra* note 11 at 794–5; Huscroft,
   "Advocate or Adjudicator," *supra* note 11 at 138 [emphasis in original]: "In

my view, the Attorney General should resign only if the government has rejected his or her advice that its proposed legislation is *clearly* inconsistent with the *Charter* – if, in other words, the Attorney General considers that the proposed legislation is not even arguably constitutional." For a critique of Huscroft's position, see Bond, *supra* note 16 at 386–90.

19 See, e.g., Ian G. Scott, "The Role of the Attorney General and the Charter of Rights" *Crim LQ* 29, no. 2 (1987): 187 at 193–5 [Scott, "Role"].

20 See Roach, "Revisited" at 34–5 critiquing Scott, "Role," *supra* note 19 at 196 and The Honourable Ian Scott, "Law, Policy, and the Role of the Attorney General: Constancy and Change in the 1980s" *UTLJ* 39, no. 2 (1989): 109 at 126.

21 Consider, for example, the 1990 resignation of Sports Minister Jean Charest: see, e.g., "When a Minister Calls a Judge" Editorial, *The Globe and Mail* (25 January 1990), A6.

22 See Andrew Flavelle Martin, "The Legal Ethics Implications of the SNC-Lavalin Affair for the Attorney General of Canada" *Crim LQ* 67, no. 3 (2019): 161 at 171 [Martin, "SNC-Lavalin"].

23 See generally Huscroft, "Duty and Discretion," *supra* note 11, and Huscroft, "Advocate or Adjudicator," *supra* note 11.

24 See above notes 7–8 and accompanying text on *FLSC Model Code, supra* note 2, r 3.7-2 and commentary 1. See also *Quebec Code, supra* note 2, art. 48(1).

25 See, e.g., *Accountable Government: A Guide for Ministers and Ministers of State* (Ottawa: Privy Council Office, 2011) at para. I.2: "Ministers and Ministers of State cannot dissociate themselves from or repudiate the decisions of Cabinet or their Ministry colleagues unless they resign from the Ministry," online: Office of the Prime Minister <https://publications .gc.ca/collections/collection_2011/bcp-pco/CP1-3-2011-eng.pdf> [https:// perma.cc/X4VS-FZWM]. See also Peter W. Hogg and Wade Wright, *Constitutional Law of Canada*, 5th ed. supp., vol. 1 (Toronto: Carswell, 2007) (looseleaf 2023, release 1), section 9.7 [Hogg and Wright]: "All cabinet ministers collectively accept responsibility for cabinet decisions. This means that a cabinet minister is obliged to give public support to any decision reached by the cabinet, even if the minister personally opposed the decision within cabinet and still disagrees with it. If the minister does decide to express dissent in public, then the minister should resign." Hogg further asserts that the resignation itself does not free the minister to announce why he resigned: "Even after a Minister resigns or is dismissed, the obligations of [Cabinet] confidentiality and unanimity continue, but the Prime Minister will normally give permission to the minister to publish his or her reasons for resignation." (*Ibid.*, also at 9.4(d).) However, this assertion – for which Hogg and Wright provide no authority – is overly formalistic and appears to be contrary to actual practice.

26 The Honourable Justice Ian Binnie, "Mr. Attorney Ian Scott and the Ghost of Sir Oliver Mowat" *Advocates' Soc J* 22, no. 4 (2004): 4 at 9.

27 Huscroft, "Duty and Discretion," *supra* note 11 at 794–5.

28 Roach, "Not Just," *supra* note 15 at 606–7, citing Peter W. Hogg, *Constitutional Law of Canada*, 3rd ed. (Scarborough: Carswell, 1992), 1265 and note 16 [emphasis added]. The corresponding text in the current edition is Hogg and Wright, *supra* note 25, vol. 2, section 36.5(d). Although Hogg and Wright state that the Attorney General who did not resign would have to support the Cabinet decision, it does not necessarily follow, as Roach suggests, that this is the same as saying that the Attorney General could *oppose* the policy – in contrast to merely remaining silent – after resigning.

29 Rosenberg, *supra* note 10 at 819–20 [emphasis added].

30 John Ll. J. Edwards, *The Attorney General, Politics and the Public Interest* (London: Sweet & Maxwell, 1984), 379, as quoted by Rosenberg, *supra* note 10 at 820 [emphasis added].

31 *FLSC Model Code, supra* note 2, r 3.3-1(a). See also *Quebec Code, supra* note 2, arts. 60, 65(1).

32 *FLSC Model Code, supra* note 2, rr 3.3-1(b), (c). See also *Quebec Code, supra* note 2, arts. 60, 65(2), (4).

33 *FLSC Model Code, supra* note 2, r 3.3-3. There is a corresponding exception to solicitor-client privilege where "an identifiable individual or group is in imminent danger of death or serious bodily harm": *Smith v. Jones*, [1999] 1 SCR 455 at para. 85, 169 DLR (4th) 485. See also *Quebec Code, supra* note 2, art. 65(6).

34 *FLSC Model Code, supra* note 2, r 3.3-5. See also *Quebec Code, supra* note 2, art. 65(3).

35 *FLSC Model Code, supra* note 2, r 3.3-6.

36 *Ibid.*, r 3.3-7. See also *Quebec Code, supra* note 2, art. 65(5).

37 *FLSC Model Code, supra* note 2, rr 3.3-3 [emphasis added]. See also *Quebec Code, supra* note 2, art. 65(6).

38 See *FLSC Model Code, supra* note 2, rr 3.3-3, 3.3-4, 3.3-5.

39 *Ibid.*, r 3.3-4.

40 See, e.g., Debra M. McAllister, "The Attorney General's Role as Guardian of the Public Interest in *Charter* Litigation" *Windsor YB Access Just* 21 (2002): 47; Roach, "Not Just," *supra* note 15. See John Ll. J. Edwards, "The *Charter*, Government and the Machinery of Justice" *UNB LJ* 36 (1987): 41 [Edwards, "Machinery"], 43: "Reading the parliamentary debates, public journals and newspapers of the respective Commonwealth countries exhibits little of substance by way of public explanation of the Attorney-General's special responsibilities as the avowed guardian of the public interest"; Gordon F. Gregory, "The Attorney-General in Government" *UNB LJ* 36 (1987):

59 at 64: "The Attorney-General also has a role in civil issues before the courts, in which he acts not as counsel to government but fulfills his own independent role as what is sometimes referred to as 'guardian of the public interest'. In that capacity he may apply, and is ordinarily extended the right, to intervene *ex officio* in private litigation"; Mark J. Freiman, "Convergence of Law and Policy and the Role of the Attorney General" *Sup Ct L Rev (2d)* 16 (2002): 335 at 337: "the reality is that the Attorney General is *not* like any other lawyer, and it is the uniqueness of the role of the Attorney General as Chief Law Officer of the Crown that for me is the focus of the implications of any convergence of law and policy."

41 See especially Roach, "Not Just," *supra* note 15; McAllister, *supra* note 40.

42 See, e.g., Sterling and MacKay, *supra* note 14 at 914–22. See also John Ll. J. Edwards, *The Law Officers of the Crown* (London: Sweet & Maxwell, 1964) [Edwards, *Law Officers*], 286, as described by Huscroft, "Duty and Discretion," *supra* note 11 at 797.

43 See, e.g., Huscroft, "Duty and Discretion," *supra* note 11 at 797, identifying this as a "term popularized by John Edwards" and quoting Edwards's description of that term in *Law Officers, supra* note 42 at 286, as "wide-ranging and still somewhat undefined."

44 See *Law Society Act*, RSO 1990, c L.8, s 13(1): "The Attorney General for Ontario shall serve as the guardian of the public interest in all matters within the scope of this Act or having to do in any way with the practice of law in Ontario or the provision of legal services in Ontario." This provision may seem fairly explicit, but see *LaBelle v. Law Society of Upper Canada* (2001), 56 OR (3d) 413, 151 OAC 284 (CA), aff'g 52 OR (3d) 398, [2001] OJ No 60 (QL) (SC), leave to appeal to SCC refused, 29120 (5 December 2002). In *LaBelle*, at para. 4, the Court of Appeal expressed "reservations about [the motion judge's] interpretation" of the provision: "It is sufficient to dispose of this appeal to find, as we do, that the Attorney General is not charged by the Act with the responsibility to investigate complaints against lawyers in this province. That role has been given by the legislature to the Law Society of Upper Canada. The function assigned to the Attorney General by s. 13 of the Act – to serve as guardian of the public interest – does not obligate the Attorney General to direct such investigations or to cause them to be directed, nor does it confer upon the appellant, in the circumstances of the present case, a cause of action against the Attorney General for failing to direct or to compel the direction of such investigations." (Section 13(1), at that time read "or having to do with the legal profession in any way" instead of the current "having to do in any way with the practice of law in Ontario or the provision of legal services in Ontario").

45 See, e.g., *Mackin v. New Brunswick (Judicial Council)* (1987), 82 NBR (2d) 203, 44 DLR (4th) 730 (CA), Ryan J.A., dissenting: "The Attorney General is the

guardian of the public interest. He, above all ministers, is charged with responsibility for the administration of justice. It is his duty to concern himself with matters of a public nature because the people of this province have a continuing interest in seeing that laws are obeyed; and that all officers of the law, within the different levels of the justice system, do not abrogate their responsibilities or defy the tenets of their appointment or position. In matters related purely to the administration of justice, the Attorney General, because of the strength of his office, is an appropriate person to bring his concerns about the conduct of any provincial court judge, before the Judicial Council."

46 Huscroft, "Duty and Discretion," *supra* note 11 at 797 and 798.

47 Gerard Carney, "Comment – The Role of the Attorney General" *Bond L Rev* 9 (1007): 1 at 6, as quoted in Huscroft, "Duty and Discretion," *supra* note 11 at 797, note 63 [emphasis in original (Carney)].

48 See, e.g., Roach, "Not Just," *supra* note 15. See also Adam M. Dodek, "Lawyering at the Intersection of Public Law and Legal Ethics: Government Lawyers as Custodians of the Rule of Law" *Dal LJ* 33, no. 1 (2010): 1 [Dodek, "Intersection"] where Dodek mentions these two roles together at 18 and discusses them at 18–20. Dodek cites these phrases to, *inter alia*, Edwards and Roach. See also Michael H. Morris and Sandra Nishikawa, "The Orphans of Legal Ethics: Why Government Lawyers Are Different – and How We Protect and Promote that Difference in Service of the Rule of Law and the Public Interest" *Can J Admin L Prac* 26 (2013): 171 at 175, using the phrase "guardian of the rule of law."

49 Dodek, "Intersection," *supra* note 48 at 18, 25.

50 Roach, "Not Just," *supra* note 15 at 600 [emphasis added].

51 *Ibid.*, 633.

52 Dodek, "Intersection," *supra* note 48 at 23 [emphasis added].

53 *Supra* note 30 and accompanying text, where Rosenberg quotes Edwards.

54 See, e.g., *Smith v. Jones, supra* note 33 at para. 46, Cory J. discussing the parallel importance of solicitor-client privilege: "Clients seeking advice must be able to speak freely to their lawyers secure in the knowledge that what they say will not be divulged without their consent. ... The privilege is essential if sound legal advice is to be given in every field. ... Without this privilege clients could never be candid and furnish all the relevant information that must be provided to lawyers if they are to properly advise their clients." Consider also the principle of fundamental justice of "commitment to the client's cause": *Canada (AG) v. Federation of Law Societies of Canada*, 2015 SCC 7 at para. 8. Public disclosure of the reasons of the Attorney General for resignation would appear to be inconsistent with such commitment.

55 *FLSC Model Code, supra* note 2 at page 6, preface.

56 *Ibid.*, rr 3.3-3, 3.3-4, 3.3-5: "must not disclose more information than is required." See also *Quebec Code*, *supra* note 2, art. 69: "In all cases in which a lawyer communicates confidential information, he may only communicate such information as is necessary to achieve the purposes of the communication."

57 The Supreme Court has explicitly recognized that the categories of exceptions to privilege are not closed: *Solosky v. The Queen* (1979), [1980] 1 SCR 821 at 836, 105 DLR (3d) 745, per Dickson J. (as he then was).

58 Without encouraging illegality, I do note that such a test case would appear to be ethical: see *FLSC Model Code*, *supra* note 2, r 3.2-7 and commentary 4.

59 *Ibid.*, r 3.3-3. See also *Quebec Code*, *supra* note 2, art. 65(6).

60 *Krieger*, *supra* note 10 at para. 3.

61 See, e.g., Amy Salyzyn, "A False Start in Constitutionalizing Lawyer Loyalty in *Canada (Attorney General) v. Federation of Law Societies of Canada*" *SCLR (2d)* 76 (2016): 169, discussing Roy Millen, "The Independence of the Bar: An Unwritten Constitutional Principle" *Can Bar Rev* 84, no. 1 (2005): 107, and Alice Woolley, "Lawyers and the Rule of Law: Interdependence of the Bar, the Canadian Constitution and the Law Governing Lawyers" *NJCL* 34 (2015): 49.

62 See, e.g., Edwards, "Machinery," *supra* note 40 at 43: "Perhaps the biggest obstacle to providing satisfactory answers to these questions [about prosecutorial decision-making] – answers that would satisfy the uneasy conscience of society – is the degree of public ignorance that exists throughout every Commonwealth country (I make no exceptions) as to the essential role and functions of the Office of Attorney-General. To speak in the same breath of the Minister of Justice, a portfolio that is often combined with the position of Attorney-General, is apt to create added confusion in the public mind. Reading the parliamentary debates, public journals and newspapers of the respective Commonwealth countries exhibits little of substance by way of public explanation of the Attorney-General's special responsibilities as the avowed guardian of the public interest. Our law schools have no better record in this regard. There is a singular absence of any serious attention being given to this historic office in the teaching programme of the vast majority of law schools throughout the English speaking world. Little wonder then that the great mass of lawyers, to say nothing of the ordinary public, lack any perception of the delicate tightrope which the Attorney-General of every jurisdiction, national or provincial, must walk between the adjacent fields of mainstream politics and independent, non-partisan judgments."

63 Michael Bryant, *28 Seconds: A True Story of Addiction, Tragedy, and Hope* (Toronto: Viking, 2012), 65.

64 Roach, "Not Just," *supra* note 15 at 633–4, discussing Edwards in Sharpe, *supra* note 11 at 53.

65 Roach, "Revisited," *supra* note 12 at 21 note 94.

66 British Columbia, *Official Report of Debates of the Legislative Assembly (Hansard)*, 34–2, vol. 10, no. 18 (28 June 1988), 5498–9 [emphasis added] (Hon. B.R. Smith) [Smith, *Hansard*], online: <https://www.leg.bc.ca/hansard-content/Debates/34th2nd/34p_02s_880628p.htm> [https://perma.cc/BT3B-5SER]. See also Lynn Messerschmidt, "An Interview with Brian Smith" *The Whig-Standard* (1 October 1988), 1, quoting Brian Smith: "I resigned when I did because I simply could not do it anymore. ... I just could not carry on any longer."

67 Smith, *Hansard*, *supra* note 66 at 5498–9; Jane O'Hara with John Pifer, "A Rude Shock for Vander Zalm" *Maclean's* (11 July 1988), 18 [O'Hara with Pifer].

68 Smith, *Hansard*, *supra* note 66 at 5499; O'Hara with Pifer, *supra* note 67.

69 Smith, *Hansard*, *supra* note 66 at 5498.

70 Tim Harper, "Vander Zalm Rejects Accusations as Resignation Sparks Controversy" *The Toronto Star* (30 June 1988), A8. See also Gary Mason and Keith Baldrey, *Fantasyland: Inside the Reign of Bill Vander Zalm* (Toronto: McGraw-Hill Ryerson, 1989), 254, quoting Vander Zalm: "Mr. Smith's stated reasons for resigning have no basis in fact."

71 "B.C. Attorney-General Resigns from Cabinet, Cites Split with Premier" *The Globe and Mail* (29 June 1988), A1, 1988 WLNR 2401322: "I can assure you there was no interference with my office and I don't believe in any way that it was a matter of principle," quoted, e.g., in Stan Persky, *Fantasy Government: Bill Vander Zalm and the Future of Social Credit* (Vancouver: New Star Books, 1989), 196. See also Bill Vander Zalm, *For the People: Hindsight – Insight – Foresight* (Vancouver: The Author, 2008), 359: "[Smith] had complete free reign over his responsibilities. ... [N]either I nor my deputy had a clue of what he was talking about."

72 British Columbia, *Official Report of Debates of the Legislative Assembly (Hansard)*, 34–2, vol. 10, no. 19 (29 June 1988), 5530 (Mark Willson Rose) online: < https://www.leg.bc.ca/hansard-content/Debates/34th2nd/34p_02s_880629p.htm > [https://perma.cc/89DL-AJ73].

73 Persky, *supra* note 71 at 196.

74 Messerschmidt, *supra* note 66: "Smith said that he felt an obligation to remain in his job as long as possible so he could ensure that the neutrality of his office was respected."

75 Rosenberg, *supra* note 10 at 819, note 19 [citation omitted]. See also Vander Zalm, *supra* note 71 at 360 [alleging political motives]. Contrast Graham Leslie, *Breach of Promise: Socred Ethics under Vander Zalm*, rev. ed. (Madeira Park, BC: Harbour Publishing, 1991), 339: "[I]t is clear that Smith resigned

in protest over Premier Vander Zalm's totally inappropriate interference in the administration of the attorney general's ministry." While Rosenberg was writing in 2009, I am not aware of any subsequent materials further illuminating Smith's resignation. I note here, with respect, that while a 1990 working paper by the Law Reform Commission of Canada noted that "[h]is stated reason for doing so was attempted interference from the Cabinet in what should be an independent prosecutorial responsibility for determining whether charges should be laid," that reason is not clear from Smith's resignation speech: Law Reform Commission of Canada, *Controlling Criminal Prosecutions: The Attorney General and the Crown Prosecutor* (Ottawa: The Commission, 1990), Working Paper 62 at 2, note 4.

76 See, e.g., Mason and Baldrey, *supra* note 70 at 252: "[Smith] knew he was going to be fired in the cabinet shuffle that would happen any day. Smith wanted to quit rather than be fired; that way he could control the drama and the headlines." See also Messerschmidt, *supra* note 66, quoting Brian Smith: "I knew that there were rumors that in the Cabinet shakeup I wasn't going to be around. I felt that was because I was carrying out my duty."

77 British Columbia, *Official Report of Debates of the Legislative Assembly (Hansard)*, 34th Parl, 2d Sess (28 June 1988), 5499 (Michael F. Harcourt) [Harcourt *Hansard*], online: <https://www.leg.bc.ca/hansard-content /Debates/34th2nd/34p_02s_880628p.htm> [https://perma.cc/QG7F -C8NA]. See also Persky, *supra* note 71 at 196: "[T]he opposition NDP gave him [Smith] a thunderous ovation. Socred backbenchers also applauded, as did some cabinet ministers."

78 Harcourt *Hansard*, *supra* note 77.

79 "Darts and laurels" *The Toronto Star* (2 July 1988), SA2: "For resigning as a matter of principle from Premier Bill Vander Zalm's cabinet. In tendering his resignation, Smith accused the premier of interfering with the independence of the attorney-general's office. The premier has denied the allegations although his record in meddling in other departments is well known. While admittedly the two are political rivals, it is still reassuring to know some politicians will resign as a matter of principle."

80 "Full Speed Astray" *The Globe and Mail* (30 June 1988), A6, 1988 WLNR 2401680.

81 Smith, *Hansard*, *supra* note 66 at 5499.

82 Parliament of Canada, *Evidence, House of Commons*, 42–1 (27 February 2019), no. 135 at 2, online: <www.ourcommons.ca/DocumentViewer /en/42-1/JUST/meeting-135/evidence> [https://perma.cc/5XX2-9DMB] [*Wilson-Raybould Testimony*].

83 *Ibid.*, 8, 19, 25. See also 22: "As long as I was the Attorney General, I was going to ensure that the independence of the director of public

prosecutions in the exercise of their discretion was not interfered with."
See also Martin, "SNC-Lavalin," *supra* note 22 at 172, explaining that the
law of lawyering does not take this problem into account. See also Roach,
"Revisited," *supra* note 12 at 35 [emphasis added], discussing Edwards in
Sharpe, *supra* note 11 at 53: "Professor Edwards's advocacy of resignation
may also be too high an ideal in the practical world of politics *and may only
result in the appointment of a more compliant Attorney General.*"

84 *Wilson-Raybould Testimony, supra* note 82 at 5.

85 *Ibid.*, 23.

86 *Ibid.*, 7. See also 26: "I have always acted with integrity, with purpose and
with principle. I was doing that in my role as the Attorney General when it
came to SNC and the potential for a deferred prosecution agreement."

87 Jody Wilson-Raybould, *"Indian" in the Cabinet: Speaking Truth to Power*
(Toronto: HarperCollins, 2021), 214 [Wilson-Raybould]. See also 239: "Then,
of course, there is the rule of law. On SNC-Lavalin this was the heart of the
matter. The attempts to pressure were a violation of the principle of the rule
of law and the related principle of prosecutorial independence."

88 See, e.g., *Wilson-Raybould Testimony, supra* note 82 at 7 (Hon. Lisa Raitt): "I
appreciate your honour, and I appreciate your honesty, and I appreciate
your integrity and grit in coming forward in the way you have"; at 23
(Charlie Angus): "what I feel we've witnessed is not politics; we've
witnessed a lesson in integrity."

89 See, e.g., *ibid.*, 28: "I have received the order in council and the waiver
that's been provided to me to speak to this committee and to the Ethics
Commissioner about matters that would be covered by solicitor-client
privilege and cabinet confidences for the time that I was the Minister of
Justice and Attorney General of Canada." See also 11: "I am not at liberty
to discuss that as the meetings and discussions between the Prime Minister
and me, other than what's covered in the waiver with respect to SNC and
deferred prosecution agreements, are covered by cabinet confidence." See
also Wilson-Raybould, *supra* note 87 at 227: "I was certain I would need
to speak publicly at some point, but I knew I was constrained from doing
so by solicitor-client privilege and Cabinet confidentiality." PC 2019-0105
(25 February 2019), online: <orders-in-council.canada.ca/attachment.
php?attach=37424&lang=en> [https://perma.cc/9C6W-M6T6].

90 See, e.g., Roach, "Not Just," *supra* note 15 at 620: "On any view of the
matter, the government is not a regular client and the Attorney General
is not a regular lawyer. The idea that the government can simply instruct
the Attorney General, as an individual or a corporation would instruct
their lawyers, produces a danger of inadequate respect for the rule
of law that in Canada imposes special constitutional obligations on
governments."

91 Rosenberg, *supra* note 10 at 820.

92 *Ibid.*, 819–20.

93 Kent Roach, "Prosecutorial Independence and Accountability in Terrorism
Prosecutions" *Crim LQ* 55, no. 4 (2010): 486 at 502, citing Rosenberg, *supra*
note 10 at 819–20.

94 See Martin, "SNC-Lavalin," *supra* note 22.

95 *Ibid.*, 172. I note that I should have used the more respectful term
"idealistically" instead of "naively."

96 In particular, this threat would not breach *FLSC Model Code*, *supra*
note 2, r 3.7-2, commentary 1: "the lawyer should not use the threat of
withdrawal as a device to force a hasty decision by the client on a difficult
question."

97 Ontario, *Royal Commission: Inquiry into Civil Rights: Report One* (Toronto:
Queen's Printer for Ontario, 1968) (Hon. James Chalmers McRuer,
Commissioner), vol. 2 at 955.

98 See chapter 5.

99 See chapter 7.

100 *Canada (House of Commons) v. Vaid*, 2005 SCC 30 at paras. 21, 29, per Binnie
J. for the Court.

101 See, e.g., *ibid.*, para. 29: "The historical foundation of every privilege
of Parliament is necessity. If a sphere of the legislative body's activity
could be left to be dealt with under the ordinary law of the land without
interfering with the assembly's ability to fulfill its constitutional
functions, then immunity would be unnecessary and the claimed
privilege would not exist."

102 See, e.g., *FLSC Model Code*, *supra* note 2, r 3.7-2, commentary 1: "the
lawyer should not use the threat of withdrawal as a device to force a
hasty decision by the client on a difficult question." See also *Quebec Code*,
supra note 2, arts. 48(1) and (2).

5 Accountability: Immunity to Law Society Discipline

1 This chapter is adapted from Andrew Flavelle Martin, "The Immunity of the
Attorney General to Law Society Discipline" *Can Bar Rev* 94, no. 2 (2016): 413.

2 I will mention below the unusual, but by no means impossible, situation
where the Attorney General is not a lawyer. See *infra* note 57. See chapter 6.

3 See, e.g., *Ministry of the Attorney General Act*, RSO 1990, c M.17, s 5 [*MAG Act*].

4 See, e.g., *Law Society Act*, RSO 1990, c L.8, s 12(2).

5 In this chapter, I use the term "Canadian Attorneys General" to refer
to provincial, territorial, and federal Attorneys General. I use the term
"federal Attorney General" to refer specifically to the Attorney General
for Canada.

6 See by analogy *Krieger v. Law Society of Alberta*, 2002 SCC 65 at para. 58 [*Krieger*]: "A prosecutor whose conduct so contravenes professional ethical standards that the public would be best served by preventing him or her from practising law in any capacity in the province should not be immune from disbarment. Only the Law Society can protect the public in this way."

7 See chapter 1.

8 *Krieger, supra* note 6 at para. 3. See similarly Ian G. Scott, "The Role of the Attorney General and the Charter of Rights" *Crim LQ* 29, no. 2 (1987): 187 at 189–91 [Scott, "Attorney General and the Charter"]. See also *R v. Cawthorne*, 2016 SCC 32 at para. 24, McLachlin C.J. [*Cawthorne*] ("a prosecutor – whether it be an Attorney General, a Crown prosecutor, or some other public official exercising a prosecutorial function – has a constitutional obligation to act independently of partisan concerns and other improper motives"; and at para. 26, holding that "the principle that prosecutors must not act for improper purposes, such as purely partisan motives" is a principle of fundamental justice, at para. 26; and noting that "the law presumes that the Attorney General – also a member of Cabinet – can and does set aside partisan duties in exercising prosecutorial responsibilities" at para. 32).

9 *Krieger, supra* note 6 at paras. 46–7, on the scope of prosecutorial discretion: "Without being exhaustive, we believe the core elements of prosecutorial discretion encompass the following: (a) the discretion whether to bring the prosecution of a charge laid by police; (b) the discretion to enter a stay of proceedings in either a private or public prosecution ... (c) the discretion to accept a guilty plea to a lesser charge; (d) the discretion to withdraw from criminal proceedings altogether ... and (e) the discretion to take control of a private prosecution. ... Put differently, prosecutorial discretion refers to decisions regarding the nature and extent of the prosecution and the Attorney General's participation in it" [citations omitted]. *R v. Anderson*, 2014 SCC 41 at para. 44, Moldaver J. added to this list: "further examples to those in *Krieger* include: the decision to repudiate a plea agreement ...; the decision to pursue a dangerous offender application; the decision to prefer a direct indictment; the decision to charge multiple offences; the decision to negotiate a plea; the decision to proceed summarily or by indictment; and the decision to initiate an appeal" [citation omitted].

10 See, e.g., *Krieger, supra* note 6 at para. 42: "This [prosecutorial] discretion is generally exercised directly by agents, the Crown attorneys, as it is uncommon for a single prosecution to attract the Attorney General's personal attention." See also The Honourable Ian Scott, "Law, Policy, and the Role of the Attorney General: Constancy and Change in the 1980s" *UTLJ* 39, no. 2 (1989): 109 at 115 [Scott, "Constancy and Change"]: "Most of the decisions that are made about prosecutions and the conduct of civil

or criminal trials are made by my agents. ... I, of course, bear political responsibility for the decisions taken and must answer for them."

11 See, e.g., the offence of wilfully promoting hatred in the *Criminal Code*, RSC 1985, c C-46, s 319(2) [*Criminal Code*]. Subsection 319(6) provides that "[n]o proceeding for an offence under subsection (2) shall be instituted without the consent of the Attorney General." Note that some such duties may be delegable. See, e.g., Public Prosecution Service of Canada, Public Prosecution Service of Canada Deskbook (Ottawa: Her Majesty the Queen in Right of Canada, 2014), Guideline 3.5, "Delegated Decision-Making," online: <www.ppsc-sppc.gc.ca/eng/pub/fpsd-sfpg/index.html> [https://perma.cc/MF3Z-MCMN].

12 See, e.g., *MAG Act*, *supra* note 3, ss 5(c), (i): "The Attorney General ... (c) shall superintend all matters connected with the administration of justice in Ontario; ... (i) shall superintend all matters connected with judicial offices." See, e.g., *Krieger*, *supra* note 6 at para. 27: "the Attorney General is also the Minister of Justice." See, e.g., Scott, "Constancy and Change," *supra* note 10 at 111–15, see especially: "I believe that it is the function of an independent attorney general to bring the focus of justice to questions of politics," at 112; "I believe that an independent attorney general has a special role regardless of the policy field in which that issue is presented," at 114. Scott also argues that this policy and political role as Minister of Justice is secondary to the legal role: "It is understood in our province [Ontario] that the attorney general is first and foremost the chief law officer of the Crown, and the powers and duties of that office take precedence over any others that may derive from his additional role as minister of justice and member of Cabinet," at 122.

13 Federation of Law Societies of Canada, *Model Code of Professional Conduct* (Ottawa: FLSC, 2009) as amended October 2022 [*FLSC Model Code*], r 3.1-2, commentary [10]: "In addition to opinions on legal questions, a lawyer may be asked for or may be expected to give advice on non-legal matters such as the business, economic, policy or social complications involved in the question or the course the client should choose. In many instances the lawyer's experience will be such that the lawyer's views on non-legal matters will be of real benefit to the client. The lawyer who expresses views on such matters should, if necessary and to the extent necessary, point out any lack of experience or other qualification in the particular field and *should clearly distinguish legal advice from other advice*" [emphasis added]. See also Scott, "Attorney General and the Charter," *supra* note 8 at 195: "In cases where legal and social policy is closely intertwined, as will often be the case in situations involving the Charter of Rights, the Attorney General must take care, in giving advice, to distinguish between legal opinion and policy preference."

14 See, e.g., *Krieger*, *supra* note 6 at para. 29: "the Attorney General is not only a member of Cabinet but also Minister of Justice, and in that role holds a position with partisan political aspects."

15 See, e.g., *Law Society of Upper Canada v. David Bradfield Sloan*, 2012 ONLSHP 176 (the lawyer had been convicted of child pornography offences and was disbarred, at paras. 38–40); *The Nova Scotia Barristers' Society v. Anne Calder*, 2012 NSBS 2 (the lawyer had been convicted of narcotics trafficking offences and was permitted to resign, at para. 10).

16 There would be some rules that would be obviously inapplicable, such as those on fees and disbursements and preservation of client property. See, e.g., *FLSC Model Code*, *supra* note 13, rr 3.5, 3.6. See also, e.g., *Code of Professional Conduct of Lawyers*, RLRQ c B-1, r 3.1, arts. 94, 101 [*Quebec Code*].

17 *FLSC Model Code*, *supra* note 13, rr 3.2-2 (honesty and candour), 3.3 (confidentiality), 3.4 (conflicts), 3.7 (withdrawal). See also *Quebec Code*, *supra* note 16, arts. 37 (honesty and candour), 60 (confidentiality), 71–4 (conflicts), 48–9 (withdrawal).

18 *FLSC Model Code*, *supra* note 13, rr 3.7 (withdrawal), 3.2-8 (withdrawal, organizational client). See also *Quebec Code*, *supra* note 16, arts. 48–9 (withdrawal).

19 Consider especially Ontario Attorney General Ian Scott, as discussed, e.g., in The Honourable Marc Rosenberg, "The Attorney General and the Administration of Criminal Justice" *Queen's LJ* 34, no. 2 (2009): 813 at 847 [Rosenberg]. Rosenberg did suggest that such appearances are only appropriate in rare circumstances: "The Attorney General must be very careful that his or her appearance in court is not mistaken for partisan activity. When great counsel, such as Ian Scott, have been appointed to the position of Attorney General, the courts have benefited from their advocacy in their occasional court appearances. Their intervention in important constitutional cases is proper and welcomed. I would be concerned, however, if the Attorney General appeared in more mundane cases, and especially in any criminal case."

20 *FLSC Model Code*, *supra* note 13, r 5.1. See also *Quebec Code*, *supra* note 16, art. 112.

21 *FLSC Model Code*, *supra* note 13, r 5.1-3. See also commentary [1]: "When engaged as a prosecutor, the lawyer's primary duty is not to seek to convict but to see that justice is done through a fair trial on the merits. The prosecutor exercises a public function involving much discretion and power and must act fairly and dispassionately." See also *Quebec Code*, *supra* note 16, art. 112.

22 *FLSC Model Code*, *supra* note 13, rr 5.6-1 (encouraging respect for administration of justice), 7.2-1 (courtesy and good faith), 7.5-2 (fair trial

rights). See also r 7.5-1: "*Provided that there is no infringement of the lawyer's obligations to the client, the profession, the courts, or the administration of justice,* a lawyer may communicate information to the media and may make public appearances and statements" [emphasis added]. See also *Quebec Code, supra* note 16, arts, 12 ("support[ing] respect for the rule of law"), 17 (communication with the media), 18 (fair trial rights), 112 (courtesy).

23 *FLSC Model Code, supra* note 13, r 4.1-1: "A lawyer must make legal services available to the public efficiently and conveniently and, subject to rule 4.1-2, may offer legal services to a prospective client by any means." See, e.g., the 2002 censure of Attorney General Geoff Plant by the membership of the Law Society of British Columbia for a cut to legal aid funding.

24 Such a decision would seem to discourage public respect for the administration of justice. See, e.g., *Provincial Court Judges' Assn. of New Brunswick v. New Brunswick (Minister of Justice)*, 2005 SCC 44.

25 *FLSC Model Code, supra* note 13, r 5.6-1. See also *Quebec Code, supra* note 16, art. 12.

26 *Barreau (Montréal) c Wagner*, [1968] BR 235 at 235, 1967 CarswellQue 253 (CA) [*Barreau c Wagner*]. This is the phrasing of the Court.

27 *Law Society of Yukon v. Kimmerly*, [1988] LSDD No. 1 (YLS).

28 As described, e.g., in John Ll. J. Edwards, "The Office of Attorney General: New Levels of Public Expectations and Accountability," in *Accountability for Criminal Justice: Selected Essays*, ed. Philip C. Stenning (Toronto: University of Toronto Press, 1995), 294 at 300 [Edwards, "Public Expectations"]. See also, e.g., John Ll. J. Edwards, *The Law Officers of the Crown* (London: Sweet & Maxwell, 1964), 277–8 [Edwards, *Law Officers*]. As Edwards indicates, the Inner Temple dismissed the charges. No reasons are available. While the minutes of the Benchers of the Inner Temple contain a record of the complaint and the acquittal, they do not include reasons: Inner Temple, "Minutes of a Meeting of the Bench Table Held on the 21st October, 1963, and Adjourned to the 22nd October, 1963" *Bench Table Order Book*, BEN/1/42 (January 1963–December 1967), 208 at 208. This document is held at the Archives of the Inner Temple.

29 See, e.g., Clare Dyer, "Attorney General Spared Trial by Bar" *The Guardian* (14 July 2005), online: <www.theguardian.com/politics/2005/jul/14/uk.iraq> [https://perma.cc/8NH2-5W5H]. The Bar Council dismissed the complaints on the basis – as phrased by Dyer – that "it has no power to investigate the provision of legal opinions to ministers by the government's law officers." However, no reasons are available, and so I am unable to consider the Goldsmith rationale further. This matter is somewhat analogous to the case of John Yoo, who as a lawyer in the US Department of Justice, gave contrived advice on the legality of torture. The Office of Professional Responsibility's recommendation to refer him for

professional discipline was rejected by Associate Deputy Attorney General David Margolis. See, e.g., David D. Cole, "The Sacrificial Yoo: Accounting for Torture in the OPR Report" *J Nat'l Security L Pol'y* 4 (2010): 455.

30 See, e.g., Edwards, *Law Officers*, *supra* note 28 at 166–7. See also Edwards, "Public Expectations," *supra* note 28 at 301, noting that an "additional complication, regrettably not addressed by the Quebec Court of Appeal in the *Wagner* case, arises if the attorney general also happens to occupy the portfolio of minister of justice."

31 *Barreau c Wagner*, *supra* note 26 at 235.

32 *Krieger*, *supra* note 6.

33 *Law Society Act*, *supra* note 4, s 13(3); originally *The Law Society Act*, SO 1970, c 19, s 13(3) ["the 1970 *Act*"].

34 *Barreau c Wagner*, *supra* note 26.

35 See, e.g., Halsbury's Laws of Canada (online), *Legal Profession*, "Regulation of Practice: Outside Interests and the Practice of Law: Public Office" (III.5(3)) at HLP-108 "Holding Public Office" (Cum Supp Release 59); Adam Dodek, "Public Office and Standards of Conduct" *National Magazine* (April–May 2013), online: <https://web.archive.org/web/2023123 1190114/http://web.archive.org/web/20130730042805/http://www .nationalmagazine.ca/Articles/April_-_May_2013/Public_office_and _standards_of_conduct.aspx > [Dodek, "Public Office"]; Andrew Flavelle Martin, "Legal Ethics versus Political Practices: The Application of the Rules of Professional Conduct to Lawyer-Politicians" *Can Bar Rev* 91, no. 1 (2013): 1 at 18 [Martin, "Political Practices"]; Canadian Bar Association, *Code of Professional Conduct* (Ottawa: CBA, 2009), online: <http://web .archive.org/web/20090126223259/http://www.cba.org/CBA/activities /pdf/codeofconduct06.pdf> at 78 (ch X, commentary 8, footnote 10), as quoted in Martin, "Political Practices," supra note 35, 18, note 86; Andrew Flavelle Martin, "The Attorney General as Lawyer (?): Confidentiality upon Resignation from Cabinet" *Dal LJ* 38, no. 1 (2015): 147 at 160; Edwards, "Public Expectations," *supra* note 28 at 300–1. See also Cristin Schmitz, "MacKay Fell Short as AG, Lawyers Say" *The Lawyers Weekly* 34, no. 4 (30 May 2014): 1, where Schmitz describes Adam Dodek's suggestion that *Barreau c Wagner* may preclude disciplinary proceedings against federal Attorney General Peter MacKay.

36 *Barreau c Wagner*, *supra* note 26 at 237, quoting art. 9 CCLC (*Civil Code of Lower Canada*).

37 This translation, except for the quotation from the CCLC, *supra* note 36, is unofficial.

38 Art. 9 CCLC, *supra* note 36. This provision was unchanged since 1866: Paul-A. Crépeau and John E.C. Brierley, eds., *Civil Code 1866–1980: An Historical and Critical Edition* (Montréal: McGill University & Chambres des Notaires du Québec, 1981), 3.

39 Now *An Act Respecting the Barreau du Québec*, CQLR c B-1. The provincial
statutes on the self-regulation of the legal professions have various names.
Most are called the *Legal Profession Act* (see, e.g., SBC 1998, c 9); some are
called the *Law Society Act* (see, e.g., the Ontario *Act, supra* note 4). Indeed,
the term "law society" itself is not always used (see, e.g., the Nova Scotia
Barristers' Society). For consistency, I will use the phrases "law society
acts" and "law societies" to refer to all regulators of the legal profession
and their enabling statutes.

40 See, e.g., *Legislation Act, 2006,* SO 2006, c 21, Sched F, s 71: "No Act or
regulation binds Her Majesty or affects Her Majesty's rights or prerogatives
unless it expressly states an intention to do so." See also *Interpretation Act*, RSC
1985, c I-21, s 17; *Interpretation Act*, RSNS 1989, c 235, s 14; *The Interpretation and
Consequential Amendments Act*, SM 2000, c 26, s 49; *Interpretation Act*, RSA 2000,
c I-8, s 14; *The Legislation Act*, SS 2019, c L-10.2, s 2–20; *Interpretation Act*, RSNB
1973, c I-13, s 32; *Interpretation Act*, RSNL 1990, c I-19, s 12.

41 See, e.g., Peter W. Hogg, Patrick J. Monahan, and Wade K. Wright, *Liability
of the Crown*, 4th ed. (Toronto: Carswell, 2011), 397–406 (common law
rule), 406–10 (codification in statute) [Hogg, Monahan, and Wright]. See
also Ruth Sullivan, *The Construction of Statutes*, 7th ed. (Toronto, ON:
LexisNexis Canada, 2022), para. 27.01[1] [Sullivan]. See also Law Reform
Commission of Saskatchewan, *Crown Immunity: Final Report* (Saskatoon:
Law Reform Commission, of Saskatchewan, 2013), 2–3 (common law rule),
4–5 (codification), online (pdf): <lawreformcommission.sk.ca/Crown
_Immunity_Report.pdf> [https://perma.cc/2XCD-ZDZ7] [LRCS].

42 See, e.g., Hogg, Monahan, and Wright, *supra* note 41 at 411–17; Sullivan,
supra note 41 at paras. 27.01[6]; LRCS, *supra* note 41 at 3–4.

43 LRCS, *supra* note 41 at 1 [citation omitted]. See also, e.g., Hogg, Monahan,
and Wright, *supra* note 41 at 456–9, see especially 457 (uncertainty
and unpredictability) and 459 ("conflicts with the basic constitutional
assumption that the Crown should be under the law").

44 Hogg, Monahan, and Wright, *supra* note 41 at 456–60.

45 *Interpretation Act*, RSPEI 1988, c I-8, s 14; *Interpretation Act*, RSBC 1996,
c 238, s 14(1), as discussed, e.g., in Sullivan, *supra* note 41 at para. 27.01[1];
Hogg, Monahan, and Wright, *supra* note 41 at 409–10; LRCS, *supra* note 41
at 4. The BC Act provides an exception for land use and planning, which is
not relevant for my purposes.

46 Uniform Law Conference of Canada, *Model Interpretation Act*, s 20(1),
online: <https://www.ulcc-chlc.ca/ULCC/media/EN-Uniform-Acts
/Model-Interpretation-Act.pdf> [https://perma.cc/K22M-V6A2]. Section
20(2) provides for exceptions.

47 LRCS, *supra* note 41 at 19. I note, however, that the successor statute, *The
Legislation Act*, SS 2019, c L-10.2, did not implement this recommendation.

48 *Ibid.*, 20; *The Interpretation Act, 1995*, SS 1995, c I-11.2.

49 *Kimmerly v. Law Society of Yukon*, 3 YR 54 at para. 4, [1987] YJ No 39 (QL). It is unclear from the brief reported oral reasons whether counsel cited *Barreau c Wagner* in argument in front of the application judge.

50 *Krieger, supra* note 6.

51 *Ibid.*, para. 4; see also para. 56 (while the case concerned a provincial Crown prosecutor, the Court explicitly stated that the same analysis would apply to federal Crown prosecutors).

52 *Ibid.*, paras. 40–1. I acknowledge that, on a narrow reading of *Krieger*, Crown attorneys must be lawyers only because – and to the extent that – they appear in court. However, in my view there is no particular support for such a narrow reading given paras. 40–1.

53 *Ibid.*

54 *Ibid.*, para. 20, discussing the *Legal Profession Act*, SA 1990, c L-9.1 (now RSA 2000, c I-8). See *Krieger v. Law Society of Alberta* (1997), 149 DLR (4th) 92, 205 AR 243 (QB) at para. 75: "In enacting the *Legal Profession Act*, the Legislature must be taken to have known that prosecutors are all barristers who act in the courts of civil or criminal jurisdiction of this Province. The purpose of the Act was to ensure that barristers are people of integrity. Nothing in the Act suggests that only certain barristers and solicitors are subject to it. Clearly the Legislature intended that the Act would apply to all lawyers whether acting as prosecutors or not. It would be absurd to hold that a barrister who conducted himself or herself in a grossly dishonest way should not be subject to dismissal from the Society simply because the dishonesty occurred whilst the barrister was engaged in prosecutorial activities. That could not have been the intention of the Legislature when it passed the *Legal Profession Act*."

55 *Krieger, supra* note 6 at para. 4; Alberta *Legal Profession Act, supra* note 54.

56 *Krieger, supra* note 6 at paras. 40–1.

57 While the Attorney General is almost always a lawyer, they are not required to be a lawyer. See chapter 6. The Law Society would have no jurisdiction over a non-lawyer Attorney General.

58 *Krieger, supra* note 6 at para. 42: "In making independent decisions on prosecutions, the Attorney General and his agents exercise what is known as prosecutorial discretion. This discretion is generally exercised directly by agents, the Crown attorneys."

59 Thanks to Candice Telfer for this suggestion.

60 *Krieger, supra* note 6 at para. 4.

61 *Ibid.*, para. 53.

62 Edwards, "Public Expectations," *supra* note 28 at 298, describing "a relatively new development that concerns the extent to which an attorney general and his agents, be they the director of public prosecutions, Crown

Counsel, or state prosecutors, are amenable to the disciplinary processes of the professional body that is responsible for maintaining minimum standards of professional conduct." See also 299–300, where Edwards specifically considers two of the Attorneys General mentioned above, John Hobson of the United Kingdom and Claude Wagner of Quebec.

63 *Ibid.*, 302: "[t]here should be no serious question raised if what is at issue is the professional conduct of the prosecutor in the handling of a case as it proceeds through the criminal courts. If the alleged breach of ethical standards consists of, for example, misleading the court, pressuring Crown witnesses as to their forthcoming testimony, or failing to observe the essential requirements of pre-trial disclosure to the defence, no exemption based on the office should protect the prosecutor from his or her accountability to the disciplinary processes that extend to all members of the profession. … The boundary line is crossed if the body seeking to exercise the disciplinary review powers of the law society focuses its attention on the *decisions* made by the prosecutor in charge of the case [emphasis in original]." See also 300, discussing the Hobson case mentioned above: "The professional conduct of the attorney general, however, was concerned with his observance of the appropriate standards by which every lawyer is subject to the assessment of his peers. Hobson enjoyed no preferential status in this regard, simply because he was the incumbent attorney general."

64 *Ibid.*, 300–1.

65 *Law Society of Upper Canada v. Ontario Public Service Employees Union*, 2014 ONSC 270 [*LSUC v. OPSEU*].

66 *Ibid.*, para. 1; *Law Society Act, supra* note 4.

67 *LSUC v. OPSEU, supra* note 65 at para. 60.

68 *Krieger, supra* note 6 at para. 30.

69 *Ibid.*, para. 32.

70 *Ibid.*, paras. 45–6.

71 *Ibid.*, para. 32.

72 *Ibid.*, para. 51.

73 *Ibid.*, para. 51.

74 *Ibid.*, para. 51, quoting from *Nelles v. Ontario*, [1989] 2 SCR 170 at 211, 60 DLR (4th) 609 [*Nelles*].

75 *Kreiger, supra* note 6 at para. 52.

76 Edwards, "Public Expectations," *supra* note 28 at 298: "What cannot be ignored, however, are the serious constitutional issues that emerge from the shadows if the breadth of the professional body's disciplinary powers are expanded in a way that crosses the boundary line between (a) the prosecutor as an ordinary member of the legal profession who, like his colleagues in the defence bar, specializes in the practice of criminal law, and (b) the state or Crown prosecutor in his capacity as the

public embodiment of the attorney general's constitutional powers and prerogatives in the area of criminal law."

77 *Ibid.*, 304: "I welcome this additional form of public accountability encompassing the office of attorney general and its prosecutorial agents."

78 See, e.g., *Canada (House of Commons) v. Vaid*, 2005 SCC 30 [*Vaid*], as discussed, e.g., in Martin, "Political Practices," *supra* note 35 at 17.

79 *Youth Criminal Justice Act*, SC 2002, c 1, ss 110(1), 129, 138. Consider, e.g., two instances in Ontario where a minister, other than the Attorney General, resigned after the naming in the legislature of a young person contrary to corresponding provisions of the *Young Offenders Act*, RSC 1985, c Y-1: Solicitor General Bob Runciman, where the naming was in a throne speech, and Corrections Minister Rob Sampson, where the naming was by a legislator of the governing party. These are discussed, e.g., in Lorne Sossin and Valerie Crystal, "A Comment on 'No Comment': The *Sub Judice* Rule and the Accountability of Public Officials in the 21st Century" *Dal LJ* 36, no. 2 (2013): 535 at 539–40. (Now Justice Sossin of the Court of Appeal for Ontario.)

80 See chapter 7.

81 *Vaid, supra* note 78 at para. 21.

82 *Ibid.*, para. 4 [emphasis in original]; see, e.g., para. 20: "Quite apart from the potential interference by outsiders [courts or tribunals] in the direction of the House, such external intervention would inevitably create delays, disruption, uncertainties and costs which would hold up the nation's business and on that account would be unacceptable."

83 See, by analogy, *ibid.*, para. 4, rejecting the assertion that "an allegation of discrimination destroys any privilege that might otherwise immunize the Speaker's conduct from external review."

84 See, e.g., *Krieger, supra* note 6 at para. 27.

85 *R v. Imperial Tobacco Canada Ltd.*, 2011 SCC 42 at para. 90, McLachlin C.J. [*Imperial Tobacco*].

86 *Hinse v. Canada (AG)*, 2015 SCC 35 at para. 36, Wagner and Gascon JJ. (the Court is clear that the holding is restricted to mercy decisions prior to 2002 amendments to the *Criminal Code, supra* note 11, by the *Criminal Law Amendment Act, 2001*, SC 2002, c 13, s 71, at paras. 34, 36).

87 See, e.g., Hogg, Monahan, and Wright, *supra* note 41 at 226–7.

88 Consider, e.g., some of the many controversial decisions made by a single Attorney General, Ian Scott, as discussed in Ian Scott with Neil McCormack, *To Make a Difference: A Memoir* (Toronto: Stoddart, 2001): to abolish QCs, at 138; to change the appointment process for provincial judges, at 138–9; to restructure the structure of the province's courts, at 176; to allow contingency fees in class actions, at 182; and to support no-fault car insurance, at 183. See, e.g., W. Brent Cotter, "Ian Scott: Renaissance Man, Consummate Advocate, Attorney General Extraordinaire," in *In Search of the Ethical Lawyer*, ed. Adam

Dodek and Alice Woolley (Vancouver: University of British Columbia Press, 2015), 202 at 211–12. (Now Justice Woolley of the Court of Appeal for Alberta.)

89 *Imperial Tobacco, supra* note 85 at para. 88.

90 Where the Attorney General must know that such criticism is unfounded, bad faith may be apparent.

91 *Law Society Act, supra* note 4, s 13(3).

92 *Legal Profession Act*, RSY 2002, c 134, s 106 [Yukon *Act*] (originally SY 1984, c 17, s 108) has similar language to ss 13(1) and 13(2) (which subsections I discuss below) but no equivalent to s 13(3).

93 Edwards, "Public Expectations," *supra* note 28 at 303: "There may be other examples of this kind of extraordinary protection conferred on attorneys general in other parts of the Commonwealth, but I am unable to cite any other historical precedents for this kind of immunity."

94 *Ibid.*: "To say the least, it seems incongruous to confer upon every attorney general in Ontario the ex officio rank of a bencher of the governing body and simultaneously clothe the same person with total immunity from the disciplinary powers of the law society. In my opinion, the Ontario provision cited above, or any parallel enactments, should be totally removed from the statute book." (Edwards provides no further argument for repeal, although he does note at 304 that absolute disciplinary immunity is inconsistent with *Nelles*, and he is clear in the rest of the article that the Attorney General should generally be as liable as other lawyers.) But see also Edwards, *Law Officers, supra* note 28 at 277–8, writing in the UK context: "As a member of the Bar, however, the Attorney-General is in no way distinguishable from his professional brethren in being accountable to the Benchers of his Inn of Court regarding his own professional behaviour."

95 The 1970 *Act, supra* note 33.

96 *The Government Reorganization Act, 1972*, SO 1972, c 1, s 9(7), changed the reference to "the Minister of Justice and Attorney General" to simply "the Attorney General" [*The Government Reorganization Act*]. The *Law Society Amendment Act, 1998*, SO 1998, c 21, s 7(3) [*Law Society Amendment Act, 1998*] substituted "proceedings of the Society or to any penalty imposed under this Act" for "disciplinary proceedings of the Society or to any penalty imposed in Convocation or in a committee of benchers."

97 *Law Society Act, supra* note 4, s 13(1). The same change to the term "the Minister of Justice and Attorney General" was made by *The Government Reorganization Act, supra* note 96, s 9(7). The *Law Society Amendment Act, 1998, supra* note 96, s 7(1) replaced "document, paper, record or thing" with "document or thing." The *Access to Justice Act, 2006*, SO 2006, c 21, Sched C, s 13 was part of the amendments extending law society regulation to Ontario paralegals. It replaced "having to do with the legal profession in any way" with "having to do in any way with the practice of law in Ontario or the provision of legal services in Ontario."

98 There was a suggestion during debate that the Attorney General has always had this role: "And even if section 14 [later 13] were absent, the Attorney General as the person who is responsible for and commandeers this legislation through the House is the guardian of the public interest in our name." Ontario, Legislative Assembly, *Official Record of Debates (Hansard)*, 28th Leg, 3rd Sess [*Hansard*], no. 37 (14 April 1970), 1488 (Elmer Walter Sopha). In contrast, the Attorney General argued that this was new: "one finds here something new, something we have not had before": *Hansard*, no. 71 (19 May 1970), 2860 (Hon. Arthur Wishart).

99 *Ibid.*, no. 71 (19 May 1970), 2863 (James Edward Bullbrook): "Section 13 is not talking about you [the Attorney General] as a bencher. It is not; it is talking about you as the Attorney General of the province of Ontario. … The Attorney General of Ontario does not have to be an *ex officio* bencher to guard the public interest; that is inherent in his very office." Accordingly, subsection 13(1) was amended at the committee of the whole to remove a reference to Attorney General as an *ex officio* bencher. Whereas the bill as introduced read "The Minister of Justice and Attorney General for Ontario in his capacity as an *ex officio* bencher shall serve as the guardian of the public interest," it was amended to read "The Minister of Justice and Attorney General for Ontario shall serve as the guardian of the public interest": no. 71 (19 May 1970), 2864.

100 *Law Society Act, supra* note 4, s 13(2). The same change to the term "the Minister of Justice and Attorney General" was made by *The Government Reorganization Act, supra* note 96, s 9(7). The *Law Society Amendment Act, 1998, supra* note 96, s 7(2) made the same change to "document, paper, record or thing" and replaced "disciplinary proceedings of the Society or to any penalty imposed in Convocation or in a committee of benchers" with "proceedings of the Society or to any penalty imposed under this Act."

101 The Yukon *Act, supra* note 92, s 106(1) uses broader language than s 13(1) but requires a court application: "The Minister shall serve as a guardian of the public interest in all matters within the scope of this Act, and for this purpose may apply by originating application to the Supreme Court for an order requiring the society or any member to produce any document, record, or thing pertaining to the affairs of the society." Section 106(2) is similar to 13(2): "No admission of any person in any document, record, or thing produced under subsection (1) is admissible in evidence against that person in any proceedings other than disciplinary proceedings under this Act."

102 *Hansard, supra* note 98, no. 4 (27 Feb 1970), 96 (Hon. Arthur Wishart): "Mr. Speaker, this bill is just what the title says it is, an Act to revise and completely review The Law Society Act, … following generally the recommendations of the Hon. Mr. McRuer"; Ontario, *Royal Commission:*

Inquiry into Civil Rights (Toronto: Queen's Printer for Ontario, 1968, 1969, 1970) (Hon. James Chalmers McRuer, Commissioner) [*McRuer Report*]. The Commission issued three reports in five volumes. *Report Number One* had three volumes and was published in 1968. *Report Number Two*, the fourth volume, was published in 1969. *Report Number Three*, the fifth volume, was published in 1971.

103 *McRuer Report Number One, supra* note 102, vol. 2, Section 6, 929–56 ("The Role of the Attorney General in Government"); *Ibid.*, vol. 3, Section 4, 1159–228 ("Self-Governing Professions and Occupations").

104 *Ibid.*, vol. 2, Section 6, at 932: "guardian of the interests of the public."

105 *Ibid.*, vol. 3, Section 4, at 1165 (noting that the Attorney General is a bencher); *ibid.*, vol. 2, Section 6 and vol. 3, Section 4 (no mention of whether the Attorney General should be a bencher).

106 *Ibid.*, vol. 3, Section 4, at 1162.

107 *Ibid.*, vol. 3, Section 4, at 1166, 1209.

108 The 1970 *Act*, *supra* note 33, s 26.

109 See, e.g., *Hansard*, *supra* note 98 no. 32 (8 April 1970), 1285 (James Edward Bullbrook, reading from Harold Greer, "Law Society Dodges Public Interest" *Peterborough Examiner* [5 March 1970]): "And far from appointing laymen as benchers, the society proposes instead a 'law society council.'" See also, e.g., no. 32 (8 April 1970), 1289 (Patrick Daniel Lawlor): "As we come to the Law Society Act, that principle [lay benchers] in effect has been abandoned. What has been substituted for it is the concept of a council."

110 See also *LaBelle v. Law Society of Upper Canada*, 52 OR (3d) 398 at paras. 18–20, [2001] OJ No 60 (SC), aff'd 56 OR (3d) 413, [2001] OJ No 4263 (CA): "At the same time as s. 13 was passed, s. 26 was also enacted which established a body known as the Law Society Council 'to consider the manner in which the members of the Society are discharging their obligations to the public and generally matters affecting the legal profession as a whole'. ... Clearly, the 1970 legislation contemplated some form of public accountability on the part of the Law Society." See also Christopher Moore, *The Law Society of Upper Canada and Ontario's Lawyers, 1797–1997* (Toronto: University of Toronto Press, 1997), 284 [Moore]: "Some of the changes firmly established due process and public supervisory authority over the Law Society."

111 Bill 7, *An Act to Consolidate and Revise the Law Society Act*, 28th Leg., 3rd Sess., Ontario, 1970 [Bill 7]. I acknowledge that the explanatory note does not form part of the bill, but it does provide some context.

112 There was minor renumbering as a result of amendments to the bill. For consistency, outside of this instance I refer to the relevant provision as section 13.

113 First reading: *Hansard, supra* note 98, no. 4 (27 February 1970), 96. Second
  reading: Nos 32 (8 April 1970), 1281–96, 33 (9 April 1970), 1322–43, 37
  (14 April 1970), 1478–504. Committee of the whole: Nos 71 (19 May 1970),
  2849–77, 80 (26 May 1970), 3210–22, 81 (27 May 1970), 3237–49. Third
  reading: No 81 (28 May 1970), 3250–1. Royal Assent: No 114 (26 June
  1970), 4640–2.

114 Bill 7, *supra* note 111, as at first reading and as amended by the Legal and
  Municipal Committee [emphasis from annotation on amended bill].

115 Committee *Hansard* was not published at that time. Neither the Archives
  of Ontario nor the Legislative Library at Queen's Park hold any
  transcripts or other records from that committee at that time.

116 *Hansard, supra* note 98, no. 32 (8 April 1970), 1282–4 (James Edward
  Bullbrook, reading from a letter from Treasurer W.G.C. Howland to
  Leader of the Opposition Robert F. Nixon [5 June 1969]). As detailed in
  the letter as read, a draft was approved by Convocation on 16 November
  1968 and circulated to the profession on 17 December 1968 (at 1252);
  amendments were approved by Convocation on 26 February 1969 and
  circulated to the profession on 20 March 1969 (at 1283); and further
  amendments were approved by Convocation on 18 April 1969 (at 1284).
  The amended version of 18 April 1969 was "sent to the Attorney General
  with a request that it be enacted by the Legislature" (at 1283–4). This
  approach, with the law society drafting the bill, was criticized. See, e.g.,
  Hansard, ibid., no. 37 (14 April 1970), 1492 (Elmer Walter Sopha): "I am
  one of those who question the right of the society to even initiate this
  bill. I think the Attorney General was wrong in allowing the society to be
  the proponent of this bill. This bill should have been written indoors by
  legislative counsel." In this respect, the 1970 *Act* was the last of its kind.
  See, e.g., Moore, *supra* note 110 at 284: "No longer would the Law Society
  draft its own acts and expect to see them promptly passed into law"
  [citation omitted].

117 The draft bill was an enclosure to a letter from Treasurer W.G.C. Howland
  to the profession (undated but presumably 17 December 1968). The
  amendments of 26 February 1969 were an enclosure to a letter from
  Treasurer W.G.C. Howland to the profession (20 March 1969). Further
  amendments were contained in a minute from Convocation (18 April
  1969) at cxli. These three documents are held at the Archives of the Law
  Society of Upper Canada.

118 The Law Society may have commented on section 13, including
  subsection 13(3), at the Legal and Municipal Committee. However, as
  mentioned above, no records are available. See note 115.

119 The 1970 *Act, supra* note 33, s 13(3).

120 Bill 7, *supra* note 111.

121 See, e.g., William Kaplan, *Bad Judgment: The Case of Mr Justice Leo A. Landreville* (Toronto: University of Toronto Press, 1996), 99–108, and especially 104 on jurisdiction [Kaplan]; Moore, *supra* note 110 at 273: "And in 1965, in a rare instance of venturing into ethical questions that went beyond its statutory mandate, convocation voted to deplore the continuation in office of Mr. Justice Leo Landreville, who had recently been acquitted of criminal charges but whose fitness for legal or judicial rank remained hotly controversial." Thanks to the reviewer for suggesting that I consider the impact of the Landreville matter. Writing in 1996, Kaplan at 104 characterized the Landreville matter in harsh terms: "the Law Society already had some experience in character assassination. This was not the first time that it had, on its own initiative, solicited evidence against an individual and used that evidence in an effort to ruin that person's standing and reputation in the community. However, this was the first time that the Law Society had acted in such a way against a judge" [citation omitted].

122 John D. Arnup statement (13 December 1965) held by the LSUC Archives, as quoted in Kaplan, *supra* note 121 at 107 and at 214, n. 103.

123 *Hansard, supra* note 98, no. 37 (14 April 1970), 1490 (Elmer Walter Sopha).

124 *Ibid.*

125 On the other hand, another legislator noted that the Law Society had a reputation among lawyers for the fairness of its disciplinary process. See *ibid.*, no. 33 (9 April 1970), 1329 (James Renwick): "I think it is fair to say that if you were to ask the men that have been subjected to the rigours of the disciplinary procedures and had been disbarred, and struck from the rolls, that they would say that there had been a scrupulous care and attention paid to assessing the evidence and the quality of discipline and the way in which the investigations were carried on which led up to any disciplinary action being taken."

126 *Ibid.*, no. 32 (8 April 1970), 1295 (James Beecham Trotter).

127 *LSUC v. OPSEU, supra* note 65 at para. 61.

128 *Krieger, supra* note 6 at para. 51.

129 *Ibid.*, para. 51, quoting from *Nelles, supra* note 74 at 211.

130 See, e.g., *Nelles, supra* note 74 at 196–7, Lamer J. (as he then was). While Lamer J. wrote only for himself and two others – a plurality but not a majority of the six judges – La Forest J. (at 218–19) concurred in brief separate reasons (except for the *Charter* issues, which are not relevant to this discussion). Given that *Nelles* was an analysis of the civil liability of the Attorney General and Crown prosecutors, it is particularly relevant in this context. See also Hogg, Monahan, and Wright, *supra* note 41 at 280; Edwards, "Public Expectations," *supra* note 28 at 304.

131 See, e.g., *Nelles, supra* note 74 at 179.

132 See, e.g., *Groia v. The Law Society of Upper Canada*, 2016 ONCA 471 at para.
127, MacPherson J.A. (the court rejects this argument). Justice Brown,
dissenting, seemed to recognize a greater role for zealous advocacy: see,
e.g., paras. 353–4.

133 See, e.g., *Nelles, supra* note 74 at 197. See, e.g., *Hill v. Hamilton-Wentworth
Regional Police Services Board*, 2007 SCC 41 at paras. 56–7, 60–1, McLachlin
C.J. [*Hill*], aff'g (2005), 76 OR (3d) 481 at para. 63, 259 DLR (4th) 676
(CA), MacPherson J.A., both discussed in, e.g., Andrew Flavelle Martin,
"Statutory Good-Faith Immunity for Government Physicians: Cogent
Policy or a Denial of Justice?" *McGill JL Health* 4, no. 2 (2011): 75 [Martin,
"Statutory Good-Faith Immunity"].

134 *Nelles, supra* note 74 at 194. See also *Miazga v. Kvello Estate*, 2009 SCC
51 at para. 50. See also *Cawthorne, supra* note 8 at para. 32: "whatever
the circumstances of the particular case, the bar for finding that a
prosecutor's conduct was prompted by an improper motive is rightly
very high"; at para. 29, "The Minister, like the Attorney General or other
public officials with a prosecutorial function, is entitled to a strong
presumption that he exercises prosecutorial discretion independently of
partisan concerns."

135 See, e.g., Dodek, "Public Office," *supra* note 35; Martin, "Political
Practices," *supra* note 35 at 23–4.

136 See, e.g., Hogg, Monahan, and Wright, *supra* note 41 at 167.

137 See, e.g., *ibid*.

138 Martin, "Statutory Good-Faith Immunity," *supra* note 133 (specifically
discussing physicians).

139 *FLSC Model Code, supra* note 13, r 3.1-2: "A lawyer must perform all legal
services undertaken on a client's behalf to the standard of a competent
lawyer." See also *Quebec Code, supra* note 16, art. 21: "A lawyer must
engage in his professional activities with competence."

140 *FLSC Model Code, supra* note 13, r 3.1-2, commentary [15]: "This rule [on
competence] does not require a standard of perfection." In this respect,
the disciplinary standard of competence is similar to (although not the
same as) the reasonableness standard in negligence. See, e.g., *Hill, supra*
note 133 at para. 73, McLachlin C.J.: "The standard is not perfection, or
even the optimum, judged from the vantage of hindsight. It is that of a
reasonable officer, judged in the circumstances prevailing at the time the
decision was made. ... The law of negligence does not require perfection
of professionals; nor does it guarantee desired results. ... Rather, it accepts
that police officers, like other professionals, may make minor errors or
errors in judgment which cause unfortunate results, without breaching
the standard of care. The law distinguishes between unreasonable
mistakes breaching the standard of care and mere "errors in judgment""

which any reasonable professional might have made and therefore, which do not breach the standard of care" [citations omitted].

141 See, e.g., *Krieger v. Law Society of Alberta*, 2000 ABCA 255 at para. 32: "a prosecutor acts as agent of the Attorney General and in so doing, makes difficult and often unpopular decisions in the interest of justice and the public good."

142 See, e.g., Hogg, Monahan, and Wright, *supra* note 41 at 2–3.

143 *Imperial Tobacco*, *supra* note 85 at para. 76, McLachlin C.J.

144 *Nelles*, *supra* note 74 at 195. Edwards, "Public Expectations," *supra* note 28 at 304, notes with reference to subsection 13(3) that "This underlying philosophy [of apparently absolute immunity] is in stark contrast to the landmark decision of the Supreme Court of Canada in *Nelles*." See also, e.g., *Roncarelli v. Duplessis*, [1959] SCR 121 at 142, 16 DLR (2d) 689, Rand J.: "That, in the presence of expanding administrative regulation of economic activities, such a step and its consequences are to be suffered by the victim without recourse or remedy, that an administration according to law is to be superseded by action dictated by and according to the arbitrary likes, dislikes and irrelevant purposes of public officers acting beyond their duty, would signalize the beginning of disintegration of the rule of law as a fundamental postulate of our constitutional structure."

145 *Krieger*, *supra* note 6 at para. 32.

146 *Ibid.*, paras. 50, 58.

147 *Ibid.*, para. 58.

148 See, e.g., *Law Society Act*, *supra* note 4, s 12(1).

149 I assume that such a provision would properly belong in the provincial law society acts as opposed to a federal statute, but it could be argued that, in order to protect the proper federal jurisdiction over criminal law, Parliament could enact such a provision. It is unnecessary, for my purposes, to determine this issue. For a discussion, see, e.g., Hogg, Monahan, and Wright, *supra* note 41 at 450–6; Sullivan, *supra* note 41 at paras. 27.9–27.10; LRCS, *supra* note 41 at 7.

150 *FLSC Model Code*, *supra* note 13, r 7.4-1 and commentary [2]. See also *Quebec Code*, *supra* note 16, art. 11.

6 Accountability: The Non-Lawyer Attorney General

1 This chapter is adapted from Andrew Flavelle Martin, "The Non-Lawyer Attorney General: Problems and Solutions" *UNB LJ* 72 (2021): 257.

2 See, e.g., *Ontario v. Criminal Lawyers' Association of Ontario*, 2013 SCC 43 at para. 35: "As Chief Law Officer of the Crown, the Attorney General has special responsibilities to uphold the administration of justice."

3 *Public Service Act*, RSNS 1989, c 376, s 29(1) (a), (c), (e). The language is very similar across Canadian jurisdictions. See, e.g., *Department of Justice Act*, RSC 1985, c J-2, ss 4, 5; *Ministry of the Attorney General Act*, RSO 1990, c M.17, s 5; *Attorney General Act*, RSBC 1996, c 22, s 2; *An Act Respecting the Role of the Attorney General*, RSNB 2011, c 116, s 2.

4 See, e.g., *Legal Profession Act*, SNS 2004, c 28, s 17(1)(a).

5 See, e.g., *ibid.*, s 4(1): "The purpose of the Society is to uphold and protect the public interest in the practice of law." See also, e.g., Gavin MacKenzie, *Lawyers & Ethics: Professional Responsibility and Discipline* (Toronto: Thomson Reuters Canada, 1993) (loose-leaf updated 2023, release 5) at Ch. 26, 26.1: "[t]he purposes of law society discipline proceedings are not to punish offenders and exact retribution, but rather to protect the public, maintain high professional standards, and preserve public confidence in the legal profession." See also, e.g., *The Law Society of Manitoba v. Bueti*, 2018 MBLS 4 at para. 4: "the purpose of a discipline hearing is to protect the public interest."

6 Graham Steele, "Is There a Lawyer in the House? The Declining Role of Lawyers in Elected Office" *Can Parl Rev* 40, no. 4 (2017): 2 at 7, online: <http://www.revparl.ca/40/4/40n4e_17_steele.pdf> [https://perma .cc/5ADX-ESUH].

7 *Askin v. Law Society of British Columbia*, 2013 BCCA 233 [*Askin* BCCA], aff'g 2012 BCSC 895 [*Askin* BCSC], leave to appeal to SCC refused, 35463 (7 November 2013).

8 But see Steele, *supra* note 6.

9 While the reasoning is partly reliant on a provincial statute, the relevant statutory language is not unique to BC. See below note 67 and accompanying text.

10 *Askin* BCSC, *supra* note 7 at paras. 1, 7; *Askin* BCCA, *supra* note 7 at para. 11. Indeed, on appeal, she argued not only that the *Legal Profession Act*, SBC 1998, c 9 [*Legal Profession Act*], required the Attorney General to be a lawyer (*Askin* BCCA at para, 50), but, further, that the *Queen's Counsel Act*, RSBC 1996, c 393, required the Attorney General to have been a lawyer for five years (*Askin* BCCA at para. 47). It is unclear from the reasons in *Askin* BCSC whether she made this argument before the chambers judge.

11 *Askin* BCSC, *supra* note 7 at para. 22; *Askin* BCCA, *supra* note 7 at paras. 44–5, 50.

12 *Askin* BCSC, *supra* note 7 at paras. 12, 16, 26.

13 Charlotte Santry, "AG Doesn't Need to Be a Lawyer: B.C. Appeal Court" *Canadian Lawyer Magazine* (8 May 2013), (quoting Deborah Armour, the Society's chief legal officer), online: <https://www.canadianlawyermag .com/news/general/ag-doesnt-need-to-be-a-lawyer-b.c.-appeal-court /271985> [https://perma.cc/YJT2-ZSQE].

14 *Askin* BCSC, *supra* note 7 at paras. 29–30: "The prerogative power of the Lieutenant Governor to appoint ministers of cabinet is of constitutional significance, and cannot be removed, replaced, qualified, or extinguished without express legislative language or by necessary implication. ... Further, as the royal prerogative is a branch of the common law, the legislature would need clear and unambiguous indication that it intended to change it" [citations omitted]. See also *Askin* BCCA, *supra* note 7 at para. 31.

15 *Legal Profession Act*, *supra* note 10; *Askin* BCSC, *supra* note 7 at paras. 22–6; *Askin* BCCA, *supra* note 7, especially at para. 50.

16 *Askin* BCSC, *supra* note 7 at para. 23, quoting *Interpretation Act*, RSBC 1996, c 238, s 27(2) [BC *Interpretation Act*]: "If in an enactment power is given to a person to do or enforce the doing of an act or thing, all the powers that are necessary to enable the person to do or enforce the doing of the act or thing are also deemed to be given." See also *Askin* BCCA, *supra* note 7 at para. 45.

17 *Askin* BCSC, *supra* note 7 at para. 24.

18 *Askin* BCCA, *supra* note 7 at para. 50.

19 *Askin* BCSC, *supra* note 7 at paras. 2(f), 2(g).

20 *Rex v. Nyczyk* (1919), 30 Man R 17, 31 CCC 240 (CA) [*Nyczyk* cited to Man R].

21 *Ibid.*, 18–19.

22 *Ibid.*, 19, Perdue C.J.M. See also Cameron J.A. at 22: "That [the acting Attorney General] the Honourable T. C. Norris was not a lawyer is immaterial."

23 *Ibid.*, 19 [citation omitted].

24 *Krieger v. Law Society of Alberta* (1997), 149 DLR (4th) 92 at para. 72, 51 Alta LR (3d) 363 (QB) [*Krieger* QB], rev'd on other grounds 2000 ABCA 255 [*Krieger* ABCA], aff'd on other grounds 2002 SCC 65 [*Krieger* SCC].

25 *Krieger* QB, *supra* note 24 at para. 72; *Legal Profession Act*, SA 1990, c L-9.1.

26 David Kilgour, "Editorial Note to Lord Hailsham's 'Lecture on the Law Officers and the Lord Chancellor'" *Alta L Rev* 17, no. 2 (1979): 141 at 141.

27 Grant Huscroft, "The Attorney General and Charter Challenges to Legislation: Advocate or Adjudicator?" *NJCL* 5 (1995): 125 at 134. (Now Justice Huscroft of the Court of Appeal for Ontario.)

28 Kilgour, *supra* note 26 at 141 (E.C. Manning, Alberta, 1955); Huscroft, *supra* note 27 at 135, note 36 (James MacRae, Manitoba, 1988; Marion Boyd, Ontario, 1993).

29 Michael B. Murphy, QC, "The Case for an Unelected and Independent Attorney General" *Solicitors' J* (November 2013): 1 at 10.

30 Hon. Charles J.A. Hughes et al., "The Future of the Office of Attorney-General in New Brunswick" *UNB LJ* 37 (1988): 190 at 190 [Hughes et al.].

31 *Ibid.*, 190.

32 W. Kent Power, "The Office of Attorney General" *Can Bar Rev* 17, no. 6
    (1939): 416.

33 *Ibid.*, 416.

34 *Ibid.*, 418–22. See esp. 422: "that contention brings us again into that very
    nebulous realm of the scope of the royal prerogative."

35 *Ibid.*, 424–9.

36 *Engel v. Alberta (Executive Council)*, 2019 ABQB 490 at para. 32. But see
    below note 56 on displacement of a prerogative power by necessary
    implication.

37 *Da'naxda'xw/Awaetlala First Nation v. British Columbia Hydro
    and Power Authority*, 2015 BCSC 16 at para. 139, rev'd on other
    grounds 2016 BCCA 163, leave to appeal to SCC refused, 37074
    (10 November 2016).

38 *Gowling Lafleur Henderson LLP v. Cardero Resource Corp.*, 2014 BCSC 892 at
    para. 18.

39 *Democracy Watch v. British Columbia (Lieutenant Governor)*, 2022 BCSC 1037
    at paras. 44, 46, aff'd 2023 BCCA 404 at para. 14.

40 Adam Dodek, "The Curious Case of the Non-Lawyer Attorney General:
    White Tiger of the Legal System" (29 May 2013), online (blog): *Slaw*
    <http://www.slaw.ca/2013/05/29/the-curious-case-of-the-non-lawyer
    -attorney-general-white-tiger-of-the-legal-system/> [https://perma.cc
    /K2LW-M7TB] [Dodek, "White Tiger"]: "It seems strange that the occupant
    of the highest legal office of the province could be a non-lawyer. It seems
    strange further still that this person is charged by statute with many
    important legal responsibilities, including acting as the official legal
    adviser to the Lieutenant Governor and to the Cabinet." See also Omar Ha-
    Redeye, "Possibilities Under a Non-Lawyer AG in Ontario" (1 July 2018),
    online (blog): *Slaw* <http://www.slaw.ca/2018/07/01/possibilities
    -under-a-non-lawyer-ag-in-ontario/> [https://perma.cc/M7BZ-73YM]:
    "it may seem as an inconsistency."

41 Adam Dodek, "Does Solicitor-Client Privilege Apply to an Attorney-
    General Who Is Not a Lawyer?" (6 August 2013), online (blog): *Slaw*
    <www.slaw.ca/2013/08/06/does-solicitor-client-privilege-apply-to-an
    -attorney-general-who-is-not-a-lawyer/> [https://perma.cc/KKQ4-BT4E]
    [Dodek, "Solicitor-Client Privilege"].

42 Steele, *supra* note 6 at 7.

43 Andrew Flavelle Martin, "The Attorney General as Lawyer (?):
    Confidentiality upon Resignation from Cabinet" *Dal LJ* 38, no. 1 (2015): 147
    at 166–9 [Martin, "Confidentiality"].

44 Jennifer A. Klinck, "Modernizing Judicial Review of the Exercise of
    Prerogative Powers in Canada" *Alta L Rev* 54, no. 3 (2017): 997 at 1002, note
    40 and 1018, note 163.

45 Recall also here the earlier view of the New Brunswick Branch of the
Canadian Bar Association that the Attorney General should be a lawyer
absent undefined "exceptional circumstances": Hughes et al., *supra* note 30.

46 Eric Pierre Boucher, "Civil Crown Counsel: Lore Masters of the Rule
of Law" *JPPL* 12 (2018): 463 at 483. Here, Boucher echoed the "grave
concern" of Judith Keating, then a former Deputy Attorney General for
New Brunswick and later Senator Keating: Judith Keating, QC, "The Role
of the Attorney General: A Crisis of Conscience" (27 April 2017) Canadian
Bar Association, Teleconference, online [membership required]: <https://
www.cba.org/Sections/Public-Sector-Lawyers-Forum/Resources/MP3
/TeleconferenceOct-1916-(5)> [https://perma.cc/ABX6-GWDJ].

47 *Ibid.*, 50:05 to 50:07; Murphy, *supra* note 29 at 10.

48 Murphy, *supra* note 29 at 12.

49 Keating, *supra* note 46 at 50.43 to 51.09; Murphy, *supra* note 29 at 10.

50 Keating, *supra* note 46 at 48.13 to 48.25.

51 *Ibid.*, 44.06 to 45.04: "As fiduciaries and trustees of the constitutional
makeup of their respective jurisdictions, Premiers have an obligation to
ensure that the institutions as established serve to facilitate the provision of
independent legal advice and protect the exercise of the fundamental role
of the Attorney General. To do otherwise, in my view, by ... appointing
non-lawyers as Attorneys General and non-lawyers as Deputies Attorney
General ... is to allow for the rule of law to be overridden by political
imperatives."

52 *Ibid.*, 59.41 to 59.50.

53 Boucher, *supra* note 46 at 484.

54 *Askin* BCSC, *supra* note 7 at para. 26. *Askin* BCCA, *supra* note 7 notes this
argument at para. 23 but does not explicitly consider it.

55 Dodek, "White Tiger," *supra* note 40.

56 With respect to the chambers judge, she may have overstated her
holding at para. 30 that "as the royal prerogative is a branch of the
common law, the legislature would need clear and unambiguous
indication that it intended to change it." A prerogative power can be
displaced by necessary implication. See, e.g., *Ross River Dena Council
Band v. Canada*, 2002 SCC 54 at para. 54, as quoted, e.g., by *Askin* BCCA,
supra note 7 at para. 32 [citations omitted]: "this displacement [of a
prerogative power] occurs only to the extent that the statute does so
explicitly or by necessary implication." See also *Canadian Federation
of Students v. Ontario*, 2019 ONSC 6658 at para. 94 (Div Ct), aff'd 2021
ONCA 553: "The Crown cannot exercise its prerogative powers in a
manner contrary to legislation or in circumstances where legislation
has displaced the Crown's prerogative power explicitly or by necessary
implication."

57 *Krieger* SCC, *supra* note 24 at para. 58.

58 Thanks to Senator Keating for inspiring this point.

59 *Krieger* SCC, *supra* note 24 at para. 4.

60 Keating, *supra* note 46 at 50.43 to 51.09; Murphy, *supra* note 29 at 10–12.

61 *Reference re Secession of Quebec* [1998] 2 SCR 217 at paras. 70–1, 161 DLR (4th) 385.

62 Murphy, *supra* note 29 at 10, 12. Murphy roots his rule of law argument in the preamble to the *Constitution Act, 1982* and the *Canadian Charter of Rights and Freedoms*, Part I of the *Constitution Act 1982*, being Schedule B to the *Canada Act 1982* (UK), 1982, c 11 [*Charter*].

63 *Krieger* SCC, *supra* note 24 at para. 26; *Constitution Act, 1867* (UK), 30 & 31 Vict, c 3, reprinted in RSC 1985, Appendix II, no 5.

64 See, e.g., *Canada (Prime Minister) v. Khadr*, 2010 SCC 3 at paras. 34–7.

65 *Askin* BCCA, *supra* note 7 at para. 11: "Ms. Askin filed a factum raising numerous grounds of appeal and seeking a number of orders. Counsel appeared for Ms. Askin on the hearing of the appeal, and properly limited the grounds of appeal and the nature of the order sought." Even a generous reading of the appellate factum, however, does not reveal this particular constitutional argument. Moreover, no notice of constitutional question was given: *Askin* BCSC, *supra* note 7 at para. 31.

66 Steele, *supra* note 6 at 8.

67 See, e.g., *Interpretation Act*, RSNS 1989, c 235, s 19(b): "In an enactment, … where power is given to the Governor in Council or a public officer to do or enforce the doing of any act, all necessary powers are also given to enable him to do or enforce the doing of the act"; *Interpretation Act*, RSC 1985, c I-21, s 31(2): "Where power is given to a person, officer or functionary to do or enforce the doing of any act or thing, all such powers as are necessary to enable the person, officer or functionary to do or enforce the doing of the act or thing are deemed to be also given."; *Legislation Act, 2006*, SO 2006, c 21, s 78: "If power to do or to enforce the doing of a thing is conferred on a person, all necessary incidental powers are included."

68 *Askin*, *supra* note 7, *Application for Leave to Appeal* at 34–46, Memorandum of Argument (31 July 2013) (Supreme Court of Canada, 35463) at paras. 40–6 [*Askin* SCC leave application].

69 *Conacher v. Canada (Prime Minister)*, 2009 FC 920 at para. 37, aff'd 2010 FCA 131 at para. 12, citing *Re: Resolution to amend the Constitution* [1981] 1 SCR 753 at 888, 125 DLR (3d) 1 [*Patriation Reference*].

70 See above note 25 and accompanying text. See also *Askin* SCC leave application, *supra* note 68 at 65–70 (four non-lawyers appointed Attorney General in the history of British Columbia, including the Attorney General whose appointment was being challenged), 71–7 (one non-lawyer (Acting)

Attorney General in the history of Canada, including Upper Canada and Lower Canada).

71 Adam M. Dodek, *Solicitor-Client Privilege* (Markham: LexisNexis Canada, 2014) at paras. 4.28–4.34; Dodek, "Solicitor-Client Privilege," *supra* note 41.

72 Martin, "Confidentiality," *supra* note 43 at 166–9. But see below note 91 and accompanying text.

73 Halsbury's Laws of Canada (online), *Crown*, "Crown Privilege: Solicitor-Client Privilege: The Solicitor" (IX.1.(2)) at HCW-222 "Non-Lawyer Attorney General" (2021 Re-issue) [citations omitted] [McKinlay].

74 *Ibid.*

75 Martin, "Confidentiality," *supra* note 43 at 166–9.

76 McKinlay, *supra* note 73.

77 Thanks to a reviewer on this point.

78 See, e.g., Yan Campagnolo, "The Political Legitimacy of Cabinet Secrecy" *RJTUM* 51, no. 1 (2017): 51 at 84–91.

79 *Ibid.*, 85–6.

80 See chapter 5. See also *Krieger* QB, *supra* note 24 at para. 72: "Because of the fact that an Attorney General does not have to be a lawyer, that official may well escape the disciplinary scrutiny of the *Legal Profession Act*. That is of no concern because the intent and purpose of that Act is to control the standards of lawyers. It is not in any way concerned with the functions of the Attorney General as such. The Attorney General, although an Honourary Bencher, need not be a lawyer. An Attorney General, not a lawyer, would of course never be subject to any scrutiny by the Law Society. That situation is reasonable because the purpose of the *Legal Profession Act* is to govern the conduct of lawyers not that of Attorneys General."

81 Federation of Law Societies of Canada, *Model Code of Professional Conduct* (Ottawa: FLSC, 2009, last amended 2022), rr 5.6-1, 7.2-1, online: *Federation of Law Societies of Canada* <www.flsc.ca> [*FLSC Model Code*]. See also *Code of Professional Conduct of Lawyers*, RLRQ c B-1, r 3.1, arts 4, 12 [*Quebec Code*].

82 See, e.g., Brent Cotter, "The Prime Minister v the Chief Justice of Canada: The Attorney General's Failure of Responsibility" *Leg Ethics* 18 (2015): 73, discussing federal Minister of Justice and Attorney General Peter MacKay. See also chapter 2.

83 *Krieger* SCC, *supra* note 24 at para. 58.

84 See above note 57. See also chapter 5.

85 *Ibid.*, 422–39.

86 See above note 18.

87 See chapter 5.

88 *FLSC Model Code, supra* note 81, r 3.1-2. See also *Quebec Code, supra* note 81, art. 21.

89 See above note 75 and corresponding text.

90 I recognize that, as the *Model Code* emphasizes, the standard of competence
     is not identical to negligence. See *FLSC Model Code, supra* note 81, r 3.1-2,
     commentary 15: "This rule [competence] does not require a standard of
     perfection. An error or omission, even though it might be actionable for
     damages in negligence or contract, will not necessarily constitute a failure
     to maintain the standard of professional competence described by the rule."

91 Power, *supra* note 32 at 426.

92 British Columbia, *Official Report of Debates of the Legislative Assembly
     (Hansard)*, 34th Parl., 2nd Sess. (28 June 1988) at 5498 (Hon. B.R. Smith),
     online: <https://www.leg.bc.ca/hansard-content/Debates
     /34th2nd/34p_02s_880628p.htm> [https://perma.cc/UVD3-MGH2].
     Thanks to Adam Dodek for reminding me of this part of Smith's speech.

93 See above note 19. Contrast B. Schwartz and D. Rettie, "Interview with
     Rick Mantey: Exposing the Invisible" *Man LJ* 28, no. 2 (2001): 187 at 191:
     "Did the whole administration of justice fall down when Jim McCrae
     [a non-lawyer] was the Attorney General? I don't think so."

94 See, e.g., Alice Woolley, "Tending the Bar: The Good Character
     Requirement for Law Society Admission" *Dal LJ* 30 (2007): 27 (now Justice
     Woolley of the Court of Appeal for Alberta).

95 See, e.g., W. Brent Cotter, "Ian Scott: Renaissance Man, Consummate
     Advocate, Attorney General Extraordinaire," in *In Search of the Ethical
     Lawyer*, ed. Adam Dodek and Alice Woolley (Vancouver: University of
     British Columbia Press, 2015), 202.

96 Power, *supra* note 32 at 429.

97 Fatima Sayed, "Mulroney's Reputation 'on the Line', Say Critics, if She
     Won't Oppose Ford on Notwithstanding Clause" *National Observer* (18
     August 2018), online: <https://www.nationalobserver.com/2018/09/18
     /news/mulroneys-reputation-line-say-critics-if-she-wont-oppose-ford
     -notwithstanding-clause> [https://perma.cc/8ZQF-ULE6].

98 The Hon. A. Anne McLellan, *Review of the Roles of the Minister of Justice and
     Attorney General of Canada* (28 June 2019), 9 [McLellan], online: <https://
     www.pm.gc.ca/en/news/backgrounders/2019/08/14/review-roles
     -minister-justice-and-attorney-general-canada> [https://perma.cc/8JA4
     -FN5J]. With great respect to McLellan, in my view, membership in the
     provincial Bar (or, at the federal level, membership in *a* provincial bar) is
     necessary as opposed to merely legal training.

99 Ha-Redeye, *supra* note 40. See also comments by lawyer Clayton Ruby on
     the appointment of Marion Boyd as Attorney General for Ontario: "She
     brings a new perspective and I think that's hopeful. ... The only question
     is, can she understand the legal issues? If she's bright, she'll have no
     difficulty": Paul Moloney, "Minister's Lack of Legal Training May Be an
     Asset, Lawyers Say" *The Toronto Star* (4 February 1993), A11.

100 Bob Rae, *From Protest to Power: Personal Reflections on a Life in Politics* (Toronto: Viking, 1996), 251.

101 Tom Onyshko, "Ontario's New Attorney General Has Ambitious Plans for Reform" *The Lawyers Weekly* 12, no. 40 (26 February 1993) (QL). See also Monique Conrod, "'We Didn't Think There Would Be Any Problem. We Really Didn't.' Bill 167 Defeat Was Major Disappointment for Boyd" *The Lawyers Weekly* 15, no. 5 (2 June 1995) (QL): "I think the perspective that someone who's a layperson, a lay advocate, a feminist, and someone who has worked on social justice issues previous to being attorney general, is very important to focus attention on some parts of the job that may not have had as much attention in the past, and at a time when the general public is looking to the justice system from the perspective of: How does it serve the general public? Is it only focused on issues that the legal profession itself is interested in, or is it really focused on providing justice for the general population? So I think it was an ideal time for a new perspective to come to the job."

102 Jeremy Hainsworth, "B.C. Ministry Merger Assailed" *The Lawyers Weekly* 31, no. 48 (27 April 2012).

103 *Charter*, *supra* note 62.

104 Vic Toews, "The *Charter* in Canadian Society" *SCLR (2d)* 19 (2003): 345 at 347–8. (Now Toews J. of the Manitoba Court of King's Bench.)

105 See, e.g., Editorial, "Consulting Unlimited" *The Toronto Star* (22 February 1995), A20: "Last November, she pronounced herself in favor of a 90-day licence suspension for drivers accused of impaired driving. But Boyd – not a lawyer herself – said she just wanted to have her legal advisers double-check the constitutionality of the idea, even though Manitoba already has implemented it."

106 See chapter 5.

107 See, e.g., Kilgour, *supra* note 26 at 141 (mentioning Manning but not acknowledging any concern).

108 Brian Brennan, *The Good Steward: The Ernest C. Manning Story* (Calgary: Fifth House, 2008), 126. See also Barry L. Strayer, *Canada's Constitutional Revolution* (Edmonton: University of Alberta Press, 2013), 8: "It was said of Mr. Manning, who of course was not a lawyer, that he did not have enough faith in any lawyer to entrust him with the role of Attorney General."

109 *Roncarelli v. Duplessis*, [1959] SCR 121, 16 DLR (2d) 689, concerning Quebec Premier and Attorney General Maurice Duplessis, as noted, e.g., in Huscroft, *supra* note 27 at 132, n. 29. See also Keating, *supra* note 46 at 16:33 to 16:35. See chapter 5.

110 The Honourable Ian Scott, "Law, Policy, and the Role of the Attorney General: Constancy and Change in the 1980s" *UTLJ* 39, no. 2 (1989): 109 at 122 [Scott, "Constancy and Change"].

111 See above note 71 and accompanying text.

112 Power, *supra* note 32 at 417.

113 Ontario, *Royal Commission: Inquiry into Civil Rights: Report One* (Toronto: Queen's Printer for Ontario, 1968) (Hon. James Chalmers McRuer, Commissioner), vol. 2 at 954. See also 956, Recommendation 11: "Statutory provision should be made that the Attorney General must be a member of the Bar of Ontario."

114 Keating, *supra* note 46 at 52.12 to 52.29.

115 See, e.g., Steele, *supra* note 6 at 8: "It is constitutionally permissible to appoint non-MLAs to Cabinet, but that option creates a raft of other issues having to do with responsible government."

116 See chapter 8.

117 *Barristers Act*, RSO 1990, c B.3, s 1, as amended by *Accelerating Access to Justice Act, 2021*, SO 2021, c 4, Sched. 1, s 1. Note that prior to this amendment in April 2021, this provision oddly applied only to the federal Attorney General and not the provincial Attorney General. The addition of the provincial Attorney General to this provision, as well as the larger issue of non-lawyer Attorneys General, was largely ignored during the legislative debates, although one opposition legislator did ask "Why give the Attorney General that power? How does it serve the people of this province?" – though the question was left unanswered: Ontario, Legislative Assembly, *Official Report of Debates (Hansard)*, 42–1, no. 228 (1 March 2021), 11660 (Catherine Fife) [Fife], online: <https://www.ola.org/en/legislative-business/house-documents/parliament-42/session-1/2021-03-01/hansard> [https://perma.cc/HQ6P-CLVW]. (See also Fife's unanswered questions about how the provision was related to the purported topic of the bill, i.e., access to justice: 11657, 11660).

118 I note here that, based on the wording of the *Barristers Act, supra* note 117, I have suggested elsewhere that there is some residual uncertainty over whether an Attorney General admitted under that provision would be subject to the disciplinary jurisdiction of the Law Society: Andrew Flavelle Martin, "The Implications of Federalism for the Regulation of Federal Government Lawyers" *Dal LJ* 43, no. 1 (2020): 363 at 385–6 [Martin, "Federalism"]. While that uncertainty was raised in the context of the federal Attorney General, now that this provision has been extended to apply to provincial Attorneys General, the same uncertainty would apply to provincial Attorneys General called under that provision.

119 See, e.g., above note 75 and accompanying text.

120 *FLSC Model Code, supra* note 81, r 5.6-1. See also *Quebec Code, supra* note 81, art. 12.

121 *FLSC Model Code, supra* note 81, r 5.6-1, commentary 3. See also *Quebec Code, supra* note 81, art. 12.

122 *FLSC Model Code, supra* note 81, r 5.6-1, commentaries 3, 4. See also *Quebec Code, supra* note 81, art. 12.

123 *FLSC Model Code, supra* note 81, r 7.2-1; *Quebec Code, supra* note 81, art. 112. See also *FLSC Model Code*, r 7.2-4: "A lawyer must not, in the course of a professional practice, send correspondence or otherwise communicate to a client, another lawyer or any other person in a manner that is abusive, offensive, or otherwise inconsistent with the proper tone of a professional communication from a lawyer."

124 *Groia v. Law Society of Upper Canada*, 2018 SCC 27 at para. 3: "trials are not – nor are they meant to be – tea parties."

125 *FLSC Model Code, supra* note 81, r 3.1-2. See also *Quebec Code, supra* note 81, art. 21.

126 *FLSC Model Code, supra* note 81, r 3.1-2, commentary 6(b). See chapter 1.

127 The Honourable Marc Rosenberg, "The Attorney General and the Administration of Criminal Justice" *Queen's LJ* 34, no. 2 (2009); 813 at 846–9.

128 *Ibid.*, 848.

129 *Law Society Act*, RSO 1990, c L.8, s 13(3): "No person who is or has been the Attorney General for Ontario is subject to any proceedings of the Society or to any penalty imposed under this Act for anything done by him or her while exercising the functions of such office." See chapter 5.

130 Martin, "Federalism," *supra* note 118 at 374–83.

131 *Ibid.*, 386–9, especially 388 on 91(8); *Constitution Act, 1867* (UK), 30 & 31 Vict., c 3, reprinted in RSC 1985, Appendix II, no 5.

132 But see note 118 above.

133 Consider again here Peter MacKay, as discussed in chapter 2.

134 Fife, *supra* note 117 at 11656, 11660.

135 *Barristers Act, supra* note 117; Fife, *supra* note 117 at 11660: "Tell me why giving the Attorney General the right and the authorization for current and former Attorneys General to be called to the Ontario bar without having to meet law society licensing requirements – and he calls this a perk."

136 See, e.g., Adam Dodek, "The Impossible Position: Canada's Attorney-General Cannot Be Our Justice Minister" *The Globe and Mail* (22 February 2019) O1, 2019 WLNR 5866240, online: <https://www.theglobeandmail.com/opinion/article-the-impossible-position-canadas-attorney-general-cannot-be-our/> [https://perma.cc/26PE-F2KV] [Dodek, "Impossible Position"]. See also Murphy, *supra* note 29 at 14.

137 Dodek, "Impossible Position," *supra* note 136.

138 McLellan, *supra* note 98 at 31.

139 *Patriation Reference, supra* note 69 at 853. I note that Power, *supra* note 32 at 422–3, though not considering a constitutional convention, gives little weight to "tradition and custom" in itself.

140 Fife, *supra* note 117 at 11656, 11660. See above note 134 and accompanying text.

141 See above note 13. See also Murphy, *supra* note 29 at 11: the failure of the law society to take jurisdiction is "disconcerting."

142 For alternatives to law society discipline, see chapter 7.

143 John Ll. J. Edwards, *The Attorney-General, Politics and the Public Interest* (London: Sweet & Maxwell, 1984), 69 [Edwards, *The Attorney-General*], quoted, e.g., in McLellan, *supra* note 98 at 11: "In the final analysis it is the strength of character, personal integrity and depth of commitment to the principles of independence and the impartial representation of the public interest, on the part of the holders of the office of Attorney General, which is of supreme importance." See also Murphy, *supra* note 29 at 7: "The implementation of the Rule of Law which is so critical to the integrity of our democratic system of government depends entirely on the integrity of the person holding the position of Attorney General." Again, as a counterpoint, see Peter MacKay.

144 McLellan, *supra* note 98 at 42: "I propose we develop a Canadian oath which refers specifically to the Attorney General's unique role in upholding the rule of law, giving independent legal advice, and making decisions about prosecutions independently."

145 *Ibid.,* 42.

146 *Ibid.,* 43.

147 Kent Roach, "Not Just the Government's Lawyer: The Attorney General as Defender of the Rule of Law" *Queen's LJ* 31, no. 2 (2006): 598 at 600: "The Attorney General is not simply the government's lawyer, but *the protector of the rule of law* within government" [emphasis added]; Boucher, *supra* note 46 at 465 [citations omitted, emphasis in original]: "While it is correct and perhaps convenient to describe the Attorney General's role as that of custodian of the rule of law, guardian of the rule of law or guardian of the public interest, it is more practical to describe him or her as the *exclusive interpreter* of the rule of law, a role which, in a fit of whimsy, I have dubbed *Lore Master of the Rule of Law*."

148 Murphy, *supra* note 29 at 12–13.

7 Accountability: Alternatives to Law Society Discipline

1 See, e.g., *Histed v. Law Society of Manitoba*, 2007 MBCA 150 at paras. 79, 111, 287 DLR (4th) 577, leave to appeal to SCC refused, 32478 (24 April 2008).

2 See especially John Ll. J. Edwards, *The Law Officers of the Crown* (London: Sweet & Maxwell, 1964) [Edwards, *Law Officers*] at 11, 224–5, and especially at 390 regarding the responsibility of the Attorney General for decisions of the Director of Public Prosecutions; The Hon. A. Anne McLellan, *Review of the Roles of the Minister of Justice and Attorney General of Canada* (28 June 2019), 9 [McLellan], online: <https://www.pm.gc.ca/en/news/backgrounders/2019/08/14/review-roles-minister-justice-and-attorney-general-canada> [https://perma.cc/8JA4-FN5J] at 16, citing Edwards, *Law Officers* at 225; The Honourable Ian Scott, "Law, Policy, and the Role of the Attorney General: Constancy and Change in the 1980s" *UTLJ* 39, no. 2 (1989): 109 at 115.

3 *Canada (House of Commons) v. Vaid*, 2005 SCC 30 at paras. 21, 29, Binnie J. for the Court.

4 See chapter 5; Andrew Flavelle Martin, "Legal Ethics versus Political Practices: The Application of the Rules of Professional Conduct to Lawyer-Politicians" *Can Bar Rev* 91, no. 1 (2012): 1 [Martin, "Political Practices"].

5 Federation of Law Societies of Canada, *Model Code of Professional Conduct* (Ottawa: FLSC, 2009, last amended 2022), r 7.4-1, online: *Federation of Law Societies of Canada* <https://flsc.ca/what-we-do/model-code-of-professional-conduct/> [*FLSC Model Code*]: "A lawyer who holds public office must, in the discharge of official duties, adhere to standards of conduct as high as those required of a lawyer engaged in the practice of law." See also *Code of Professional Conduct of Lawyers*, RLRQ c B-1, r 3.1, art. 11 [*Quebec Code*].

6 *FLSC Model* Code, *supra* note 5, r 7.4-1, commentary 2. See also *Quebec Code, supra* note 5, art. 11.

7 See, e.g., Martin, "Political Practices," *supra* note 4 at 17–18; chapter 5.

8 See, e.g., *Law Society of Yukon v. Kimmerly*, [1988] LSDD No 1 (QL) (Yukon Minister of Justice), as discussed, e.g., in Martin, "Political Practices," *supra* note 4 at 15–16 and in chapter 2; *Barreau (Montréal) c Wagner* (1967), [1968] BR 235 (Que), as discussed in chapter 2 (Quebec Attorney General).

9 As discussed in chapter 2, the charges against Kimmerly were dismissed on the merits and those against Wagner were quashed on judicial review.

10 See, e.g., Andrew Flavelle Martin, "The Limits of Professional Regulation in Canada: Law Societies and Non-Practising Lawyers" *Leg Ethics* 19, no. 1 (2016): 169 at 172. See also, e.g., Martin, "Political Practices," *supra* note 4 at 25–6 (allocation of regulatory resources).

11 See, e.g., Alice Woolley, "Legal Ethics and Regulatory Legitimacy: Regulating Lawyers for Personal Misconduct" in *Alternative Perspectives on Lawyers and Legal Ethics: Reimagining the Profession*, ed. Francesca Bartlett, Reid Mortensen, and Kieran Trantor (London: Routledge, 2011), 241. (Now Justice Woolley of the Court of Appeal of Alberta.) In contrast, see recently

Dr Jha v. College of Physicians and Surgeons of Ontario, 2022 ONSC 769 at paras. 116–22 (Div. Ct.). Thanks to Amy Salyzyn for bringing this case to my attention.

12 See, e.g., Martin, "Political Practices," *supra* note 4 at 25.

13 See, e.g., Harry Arthurs, "Why Canadian Law Schools Do Not Teach Legal Ethics" in *Ethical Challenges to Legal Education and Conduct*, ed. Kim Economides (Oxford: Hart, 1998), 105 at 112 [Arthurs in Economides], as quoted and discussed, e.g., in Alice Woolley, "Regulation in Practice: The 'Ethical Economy' of Lawyer Regulation in Canada and a Case Study in Lawyer Deviance" *Legal Ethics* 15, no. 2 (2012): 243 at 243: "a tendency to allocate its scarce resources of staff time, public credibility and internal political consensus to those disciplinary problems whose resolution provides the highest returns to the profession with the least risk of adverse consequences."

14 See, e.g., Martin, "Political Practices," *supra* note 4 at 27–30.

15 See also Martin, "Political Practices," *supra* note 4 at 31–3, discussing other rules that could be relevant: undertakings, advertising, responsibility for conduct of staff, and surreptitious recording of conversations. On undertakings and lawyer-politicians, see Andrew Flavelle Martin, "Consequences for Broken Political Promises: Lawyer-Politicians and the Rules of Professional Conduct" *JPPL* 10, no. 2 (2016): 337.

16 See, e.g., *FLSC Model Code*, *supra* note 5, r 5.6-1: "A lawyer must encourage public respect for and try to improve the administration of justice." See also *Quebec Code*, *supra* note 5, art. 12. See also, e.g., Martin, "Political Practices," *supra* note 4 at 31–2.

17 *FLSC Model Code*, *supra* note 5, r 5.6-1, commentary 3.

18 *FLSC Model Code*, *supra* note 5, r 5.6-1, commentary 1. See also, e.g., Martin, "Political Practices," *supra* note 4 at 32.

19 *FLSC Model Code*, *supra* note 5, r 5.1-2 (d): "When acting as an advocate, a lawyer must not … endeavour or allow anyone else to endeavour, directly or indirectly, to influence the decision or action of a tribunal or any of its officials in any case or matter by any means other than open persuasion as an advocate." While this duty, by its wording, applies only to the lawyer as advocate, the spirit of this rule is clear. Moreover, the general duty of integrity would include such non-interference. See, e.g., rr 2.1-1 ("A lawyer has a duty to carry on the practice of law and discharge all responsibilities to clients, tribunals, the public and other members of the profession honourably and with integrity."), 7.3-1 ("A lawyer who engages in another profession, business or occupation concurrently with the practice of law must not allow such outside interest to jeopardize the lawyer's professional integrity, independence or competence."). See also, e.g., Martin, "Political Practices," *supra* note 4

at 31–2. See also *Quebec Code, supra* note 5, arts. 4 (honour and integrity), 11 (outside interests).

20 *FLSC Model Code, supra* note 5, r 5.7-2.

21 See, e.g., Martin, "Political Practices," *supra* note 4 at 34. For the debate over civility, see, e.g., Alice Woolley, "Does Civility Matter?" *Osgoode Hall LJ* 46, no. 1 (2008): 175; Michael Code, "Counsel's Duty of Civility: An Essential Component of Fair Trials and an Effective Justice System" *Can Crim L Rev* 11 (2007): 97. (Now Justice Woolley of the Court of Appeal for Alberta and Justice Code of the Superior Court of Justice in Ontario.)

22 Martin, "Political Practices," *supra* note 4 at 34.

23 See *Members' Integrity Act, 1994*, SO 1994, c 38, s 5: "This Act does not prohibit the activities in which members of the Assembly normally engage on behalf of constituents in accordance with Ontario parliamentary convention" [Ontario *Members' Integrity Act*]; *Integrity Act*, SNu 2001, c 7: "This Act does not prohibit the activities in which members properly engage on behalf of constituents in accordance with parliamentary convention." See also, e.g., Law Society of Ontario, By-Law 4, s 30, para. 6 (allowing an unlicensed MPP or their unlicensed staff to provide legal services on behalf of a constituent), online <https://lso.ca /about-lso/legislation-rules/by-laws/by-law-4> [https://perma.cc /3GBM-XUK2].

24 See above note 6 and accompanying text.

25 *Wilder v. Ontario Securities Commission* (2001), 53 OR (3d) 519 at paras. 8–11, 28–30, 197 DLR (4th) 193 (CA) [*Wilder* CA], aff'g 47 OR (3d) 361, 184 DLR (4th) 165 (Div. Ct.), Swinton J. for the panel. Followed by, *inter alia*, the BC Court of Appeal in *Walker v. British Columbia (Securities Commission)*, 2011 BCCA 415 and by the Ontario Financial Services Commission in *Al-Hajam v. Allstate Insurance Co of Canada*, [2005] OFSCD No. 17 at para. 38, note 4. Contrast *150960 Canada Inc Const*, [2002] OLRD No. 777 at para. 7: "In our opinion, the Board [Ontario Labour Relations Board] does not have that type of supervisory jurisdiction over lawyers."

26 *Wilder CA, supra* note 25 at paras. 8–11, 28–9.

27 *Ibid.*, paras. 30–4 (quotation is from para. 34).

28 *Assn of Professional Engineers of Ontario v. Ontario (Minister of Municipal Affairs and Housing)* (2007), 284 DLR (4th) 322 at para. 55, 225 OAC 287 (Div. Ct.).

29 *Ibid.*, para. 68.

30 *Ibid.*, paras. 61–76.

31 *Law Society of British Columbia v. Mangat*, 2001 SCC 67.

32 See below note 47 and accompanying text.

33 *Krieger v. Law Society of Alberta*, 2002 SCC 65 at para. 58: "Only the Law Society can protect the public in this way."

34 Adam M. Dodek, "Lawyering at the Intersection of Public Law and Legal Ethics: Government Lawyers as Custodians of the Rule of Law" *Dal LJ* 33, no. 1 (2010): 1 at 34–5 [citations omitted]: "Despite the existence of de jure self-regulation, in practice Canadian lawyers are subject to multiple overlapping forms of regulation. They are subject to regulation by their respective law societies, to internal regulation through their firm or organization if they practice in an organizational setting, the oversight of the courts, external regulation by other regulatory bodies such as securities commissions (domestic and foreign), government regulation, and tort and insurance."

35 See, e.g., *Nova Scotia Barristers' Society v. Morgan*, 2010 NSBS 1 (Mayor of Cape Breton, Nova Scotia), discussed, e.g., in Martin, "Political Practices," *supra* note 4 at 11–12.

36 Gavin MacKenzie, *Lawyers & Ethics: Professional Responsibility and Discipline*, looseleaf (Release No. 5, December 2023) (Toronto: Thomson Reuters Canada, 2023), § 26:1, quoted with approval in, e.g., *Guttman v. Law Society of Manitoba*, 2010 MBCA 66 at para. 75; *Howe v. Nova Scotia Barristers' Society*, 2019 NSCA 81 at para. 190; *Cusack v. The Lawyers' Professional Indemnity Co*, 2013 ONSC 5511 at para. 58.

37 Marc Bosc and Andre Gagnon, *House of Commons Procedure and Practice*, 3rd ed. (Ottawa: The House of Commons, 2017), online: <https://www.ourcommons.ca/procedure/procedure-and-practice-3/index-e.html> [https://perma.cc/8F7Z-C7DJ], at 13-3-4, 600.

38 Andrew Heard, "The Expulsion and Disqualification of Legislators: Parliamentary Privilege and the Charter of Rights" *Dal LJ* 18, no. 2 (1995): 380 at 393 [Heard, "Expulsion"].

39 *Ibid.*, 393.

40 See, e.g., *ibid.*, 393: "A legislative assembly is the sole judge of the broad grounds for expelling a member."

41 Bosc and Gagnon, *supra* note 37, "References to the Sovereign, Royal Family, Governor General and Members of the Judiciary" at 13-3-4, 621–2; "Unparliamentary Language" at 13-3-4, 623–5.

42 *Ibid.*, "The *Sub Judice* Convention" at 13-3-4, 632–6. See Graham Steele, "The *Sub Judice* Convention: What to Do When a Matter Is 'Before the Courts'" *Can Parl Rev* 30, no. 4 (2007): 5; Lorne Sossin and Valerie Crystal, "A Comment on 'No Comment': The *Sub Judice* Rule and the Accountability of Public Officials in the 21st Century" *Dal LJ* 36, no. 2 (2013): 535 at 551–3. *Sub Judice* is a convention but is not *only* a convention – see Sossin and Crystal at 538–57. (Now Justice Sossin of the Court of Appeal for Ontario.)

43 See, e.g., *ibid.*, 552–3 (role of *sub judice* rule as protecting judicial independence).

44 Steele, *supra* note 42 at 6.

45 *Ibid.*, 7. See also 8, characterizing the convention as "a principled parliamentary courtesy to the courts."

46 *Ibid.*, 7. Steele at 13–14 nonetheless admonishes that "almost all *sub judice* issues can be resolved if parliamentarians show some restraint in their approach to judicial proceedings … [p]arliamentarians need to show restraint."

47 *Vaid*, *supra* note 3 at paras. 20, 29, Binnie J. for the Court.

48 See, e.g., Evan Fox-Decent, "Parliamentary Privilege and the Rule of Law" *Can J Admin L & Prac* 20 (2007): 117. With respect, insofar as Fox-Decent equates the rule of law with the availability of judicial review, his position seems to become a tautological one.

49 But see the problematic concept of Ontario Parliamentary Convention in the *Members' Integrity Act, 1994*, SO 1994, c 38, ss 28(1), 30(1), 31(6), (7): Ian Stedman, *Understanding the Unwritten Rules: Examining the Use of Ontario Parliamentary Convention to Guide the Conduct of Elected Officials in Ontario* (University of Toronto, LLM Thesis, 2015) [unpublished].

50 See, e.g., *Harvey v. New Brunswick (Attorney General)* [1996] 2 SCR 876 at para. 64, 137 DLR (4th) 142, McLachlin J. (as she then was) concurring: "The history of the prerogative of Parliament and legislative assemblies to maintain the integrity of their processes by disciplining, purging and disqualifying those who abuse them is as old as Parliament itself." (see also para. 62: "When faced with behaviour that undermines their fundamental integrity, legislatures are required to act. That action may range from discipline for minor irregularities to expulsion and disqualification for more serious violations"), quoted with approval in *Duffy v. Canada (Senate)*, 2020 ONCA 536 at para. 39, Jamal J.A. (as he then was) for the panel, leave to appeal to SCC refused, 39361 (11 February 2021). See also *Vaid*, *supra* note 3 at para. 59, also quoted with approval in *Duffy* at para. 41. See also, e.g., Legislative Assembly of the Northwest Territories, *Guide to the Rules Relating to the Conduct of Members* (undated) at 1, online: <https://www.ntassembly.ca/sites/assembly/files/code_of_conduct_guide.pdf> [https://perma.cc/892D-GSCC]: "Responsibility for disciplining or censuring a Member of the Assembly lies with the Legislative Assembly itself, and is a fundamental aspect of the privileges enjoyed by the Legislative Assembly as a house of parliament. Neither the Code of Conduct nor this Guide impinges upon, restricts or narrows the Legislative Assembly's fundamental right to regulate its internal affairs. Any role assigned to the Integrity Commissioner is for the purpose of assisting the Legislative Assembly in exercising this authority."

51 See generally *Harvey*, *supra* note 50; Heard, "Expulsion," *supra* note 38.

52 See, e.g., Ontario, Office of the Integrity Commissioner, *Report of the Honourable Coulter A. Osborne, Integrity Commissioner Re: Robert Runciman, MPP, Member for Leeds-Grenville* (Toronto: Office of the Integrity Commissioner, 2006) at para. 21, as discussed, e.g., in Stedman, *supra* note 48 at 101–2.

53 See, e.g., Ontario *Members' Integrity Act, supra* note 23, s 34.

54 See, e.g., Ned Franks, "Parliamentarians and Codes of Ethics" (2009) 2 *JPPL* 283 at 289–90; Editorial, "When a Minister Calls a Judge" (25 January 1990) *The Globe and Mail*, A6, 1990 WLNR 4531541.

55 Andrew Heard, *Canadian Constitutional Conventions: The Marriage of Law and Politics*, 2nd ed. (Don Mills, ON: Oxford University Press, 2014), 189–90 [Heard, *Conventions*], quoted, e.g., in Stedman, *supra* note 48 at 56: "A fundamental convention prohibits Cabinet ministers from trying to interfere in a dispute and cajoling a nudge to decide in the interest of the government or its supporters. … Ministers should neither criticize a judge publicly nor make private representations to judges." With respect to Heard, I am unaware of case law recognizing this specific convention, either in its own right or as part of the more general constitutional principle of judicial independence (see, e.g., *Reference re Remuneration of Judges of the Provincial Court (P.E.I.)*, [1997] 3 SCR 3, 150 DLR (4th) 577). In fairness to Heard, he may be using the characterization in a looser sense. See, e.g., Heard, *Conventions* at 12–21, discussing "the orthodox view of conventions" (by which he refers to the definition and test in *Re: Resolution to amend the Constitution*, [1981] 1 SCR 753, 125 DLR (3d) 1) and contrasting it to two other "views." See also 214, Table 7.1, distinguishing among "fundamental conventions," "semi-rigid conventions," and "flexible conventions."

56 C.E.S. Franks, "Parliamentarians and the New Code of Ethics" *Can Parl Rev* 28, no. 1 (2005): 11 at 15.

57 See, e.g., John Ll. J. Edwards, "The Attorney General and the *Charter of Rights*" in *Charter Litigation*, ed. Robert J. Sharpe (Toronto: Butterworths, 1987), 45 at 46: "the accountability of the Attorney General, within his sphere of authority, is to be discharged on the floor of the legislature or in the Parliament of Canada, as the case may be." As discussed in chapter 5, Edwards was likewise adamant that the Attorney General was and should be liable to professional discipline in the same way as any other lawyer. See, e.g., Edwards, *Law Officers, supra* note 2 at 277: "As a member of the Bar, however, the Attorney-General is in no way distinguishable from his professional brethren in being accountable to the Benchers of his Inn of Court regarding his own professional behaviour."

58 See above notes 54–5 and accompanying text.

59 See *Groia v. The Law Society of Upper Canada*, 2016 ONCA 471 at para. 103, Cronk J.A. for the majority, rev'd on other grounds 2018 SCC 27:

"The Law Society's mandate to ensure that lawyers conduct themselves professionally in and out of the courtroom, does not in any way conflict with or erode a trial judge's trial management power or the independent authority of the courts. … [T]he trial judge's authority and that of the regulator exist in tandem but are focused on different inquiries and are exercised for different purposes." See also *FLSC Model Code*, *supra* note 5, r 5.1-5, commentary 1: "Legal contempt of court and the professional obligation outlined here [courtesy] are not identical, and a consistent pattern of rude, provocative or disruptive conduct by a lawyer, even though unpunished as contempt, may constitute professional misconduct." Likewise, see r 3.1-2, commentary 15, distinguishing between incompetence (a matter for law societies) and negligence (a matter for courts).

60 See, e.g., Heard, "Expulsion," *supra* note 38 at 393: "A legislative assembly is the sole judge of the broad grounds for expelling a member. … [T]he privileges of Canadian legislative assemblies include the power to expel their members."

8 Conclusion: Accountability, Integrity, and Self-Respect

1 *Krieger v. Law Society of Alberta*, 2002 SCC 65.
2 See, e.g., Adam Dodek, "The Impossible Position: Canada's Attorney-General Cannot Be Our Justice Minister" *The Globe and Mail* (22 February 2019), O1, 2019 WLNR 5866240, online: <https://www.theglobeandmail.com/opinion/article-the-impossible-position-canadas-attorney-general-cannot-be-our/> [https://perma.cc/LGP7-ZZAW].
3 See, e.g., *ibid.*; The Hon. A. Anne McLellan, *Review of the Roles of the Minister of Justice and Attorney General of Canada* (28 June 2019), 22–3, online: *Government of Canada* <https://www.pm.gc.ca/en/news/backgrounders/2019/08/14/review-roles-minister-justice-and-attorney-general-canada> [https://perma.cc/8JA4-FN5J].
4 See, e.g., Dodek, *supra* note 2.
5 McLellan, *supra* note 3 at 31.
6 *Ibid.*, 22, 23.
7 *Ibid.*, 40–1.
8 The Honourable Ian Scott, "Law, Policy, and the Role of the Attorney General: Constancy and Change in the 1980s" *UTLJ* 39, no. 2 (1989): 109 at 122, as quoted approvingly in McLellan, *supra* note 3 at 11.
9 McLellan, *supra* note 3 at 43, quoting Scott, *supra* note 8 at 122: "The legislation which governs the Attorney General and the Minister of Justice should reflect the Attorney General's role as 'first and foremost' the chief law officer of the Crown, whose duties in that office take precedence over their duties as minister of justice and member of Cabinet."

10 *Ibid.*, 42–3.

11 *Ibid.*, 43.

12 *Ministry of the Attorney General Act*, RSO 1990, c M.17.

13 Federation of Law Societies of Canada, *Model Code of Professional Conduct* (Ottawa: FLSC, 2009) as amended October 2022, online: <flsc.ca> [*FLSC Model Code*], rr 5.6-1 (public respect for the administration of justice), 7.4-1 (public office). See also *Code of Professional Conduct of Lawyers*, RLRQ c B-1, r 3.1, arts. 11 (outside interests), 12 (supporting the rule of law) [*Quebec Code*].

14 *FLSC Model Code*, *supra* note 13, r 7.4-1. See also *Quebec Code*, *supra* note 13, art. 11.

15 *FLSC Model Code*, *supra* note 13, r 7.4-1, commentary 2.

16 John Ll. J. Edwards, *The Attorney-General, Politics and the Public Interest* (London: Sweet & Maxwell, 1984), 67 [Edwards, *Public Interest*], quoted, e.g., in McLellan, *supra* note 3 at 11 and in Elizabeth Sanderson, *Government Lawyering: Duties and Ethical Challenges of Government Lawyers* (Toronto: LexisNexis Canada, 2018), 69. See similarly John Ll. J. Edwards, "The Charter, Government and the Machinery of Justice" *UNB LJ* 36 (1987): 41 at 50: "The experience of both the older and newer members of the Commonwealth confirms my deep-seated conviction that, no matter how entrenched constitutional safeguards may be, in the final analysis it is the strength of character, personal integrity and personal commitment by the holder to the independent character of the Offices of Attorney-General … and of the Director of Public Prosecutions which is of abiding importance." See similarly Gordon F. Gregory, "The Attorney-General in Government" *UNB LJ* 36 (1987): 59 at 62: "The Attorney-General must constantly realize that we depend upon the integrity of the individual who holds the Office of Attorney-General."

17 W. Brent Cotter, "Ian Scott: Renaissance Man, Consummate Advocate, Attorney General Extraordinaire," in *In Search of the Ethical Lawyer*, ed. Adam Dodek and Alice Woolley (Vancouver: University of British Columbia Press, 2015), 202 at 218–19.

18 McLellan, *supra* note 3 at 43, note 107.

19 Scott, *supra* note 8 at 122.

20 Dodek, *supra* note 2.

21 Edwards, *Public Interest*, *supra* note 16 at 353. (Such a disagreement would constitute a "serious loss of confidence" so as to make withdrawal available as a matter of legal ethics: *FLSC Model Code*, *supra* note 13, r 3.7-2. See chapter 4.)

22 See here, e.g., Jody Wilson-Raybould, as discussed in chapter 4.

23 *FLSC Model Code*, *supra* note 13, r 6.1-1. See also *Quebec Code*, *supra* note 13, art. 35.

24 *FLSC Model Code, supra* note 13, r 3.7-7(b) [emphasis added].

25 See, e.g., McLellan, *supra* note 3 at 40–1.

26 See, e.g., *R v. Neil*, 2002 SCC 70 at para. 19.

27 See, e.g., *FLSC Model Code, supra* note 13, r 2.1: "A lawyer has a duty to carry on the practice of law and discharge all responsibilities to clients, tribunals, the public and other members of the profession honourably and with integrity." See also *Quebec Code, supra* note 13, arts. 4, 13.

28 *FLSC Model Code, supra* note 13, r 3.2-2, commentary 3: "Occasionally, a lawyer must be firm with a client. Firmness, without rudeness, is not a violation of the rule. In communicating with the client, the lawyer may disagree with the client's perspective, or may have concerns about the client's position on a matter, and may give advice that will not please the client. This may legitimately require firm and animated discussion with the client."

29 See, e.g., *ibid.*, r 7.5-2: "A lawyer must not communicate information to the media or make public statements about a matter before a tribunal if the lawyer knows or ought to know that the information or statement will have a substantial likelihood of materially prejudicing a party's right to a fair trial or hearing." See also *Quebec Code, supra* note 13, art. 18 ("A lawyer must not make public statements or communicate information to the media about a matter pending before a tribunal if the lawyer knows or should know that the information or statements could adversely affect a tribunal's authority or prejudice a party's right to a fair trial or hearing."). See also *FLSC Model Code*, r 7.5-2, commentary 1: "Fair trials and hearings are fundamental to a free and democratic society. It is important that the public, including the media, be informed about cases before courts and tribunals. The administration of justice benefits from public scrutiny. It is also important that a person's, particularly an accused person's, right to a fair trial or hearing not be impaired by inappropriate public statements made before the case has concluded."

30 See, e.g., *FLSC Model Code, supra* note 13, r 5.6-1: "A lawyer must encourage public respect for and try to improve the administration of justice." See also *Quebec Code, supra* note 13, art. 12. See also *FLSC Model Code*, r 5.6-1, commentary 3.

31 See, e.g., *FLSC Model Code, supra* note 13, r 7.2-1: "A lawyer must be courteous and civil and act in good faith with all persons with whom the lawyer has dealings in the course of his or her practice." See also *Quebec Code, supra* note 13, art. 112.

32 See, e.g., *FLSC Model Code, supra* note 13, r 6.1-1: "A lawyer has complete professional responsibility for all business entrusted to him or her and must directly supervise staff and assistants to whom the lawyer delegates particular tasks and functions." See also *Quebec Code, supra* note 13, art. 35.

33 Michael Bryant, *28 Seconds: A True Story of Addiction, Tragedy, and Hope* (Toronto: Viking, 2012): "Consider my A.-G. duties, helpfully set forth in a statute. The breadth of these duties was daunting and inspiring for me when I first read them."

34 The Honourable R. Roy McMurtry, "The Office of the Attorney General," in *The Cambridge Lectures: Selected Papers Based upon Lectures Delivered at the Cambridge Conference of the Canadian Institute for Advanced Legal Studies, 1979*, ed. Derek Mendes da Costa (Toronto: Butterworths, 1981), 1 at 5–6.

35 Ontario, *Royal Commission: Inquiry into Civil Rights: Report One* (Toronto: Queen's Printer for Ontario, 1968) (Hon. James Chalmers McRuer, Commissioner), vol. 2 at 955. See also John Ll. J. Edwards, "The Office of Attorney General: New Levels of Public Expectations and Accountability," in *Accountability for Criminal Justice: Selected Essays*, ed. Philip C. Stenning (Toronto: University of Toronto Press, 1995), 294 at 324: "It requires a very strong attorney general, fully cognizant of the history of the office, and confident of his or her constitutional position, to withstand such pressures. There should never be any doubt, however, as to the single line of accountability that flows upwards to the desk of the attorney general, as the accountable minister of the Crown. Regrettably, there is evidence that many new incumbents come into the office of the attorney general without the requisite appreciation of these issues, and a greater commitment to the appropriate principles, and to educating all concerned about them, seems to be called for in many, if not most, jurisdictions."

36 With the greatest of respect to McMurtry, who wrote that "[t]he politically nonpartisan nature of the legal decision the Attorney General must make, and the strong tradition of legislative accountability of the office, constitute one of the most important bulwarks of the rule of law" (*ibid.*, 6), such accountability seems illusory if not merely hypothetical.

Index